Asians and Pacific Islanders in American Football

Sport, Identity, and Culture

Series Editor: Gerald R. Gems (North Central College)

The Sport, Identity, and Culture series addresses the important role sport plays in social, cultural, and political contexts throughout history. While the series is primarily historical in its focus, it welcomes interdisciplinary projects. It is intentionally broad in its conceptualization, as sport—its organization, practice, and meanings—exists both within and beyond the territorial, cultural, social, ethnic, racial, gender, psychological, and chronological borders that construct and define individual and group identity.

Editorial Board

Linda J. Borish, Western Michigan
Susanna Hedenborg, Malmö University
Malcolm MacLean, University of Gloucestershire
Patricia Anne Vertinsky, University of British Columbia
Gertrud Pfister, University of Copenhagen

Titles in the Series

Asians and Pacific Islanders in American Football

Historical and Contemporary Experiences

Joel S. Franks

LEXINGTON BOOKS
Lanham • Boulder • New York • London

Published by Lexington Books
An imprint of The Rowman & Littlefield Publishing Group, Inc.
4501 Forbes Boulevard, Suite 200, Lanham, Maryland 20706
www.rowman.com

Unit A, Whitacre Mews, 26-34 Stannary Street, London SE11 4AB

British Library Cataloguing in Publication Information Available

Library of Congress Cataloging-in-Publication Data Available

ISBN 978-1-4985-6097-9 (cloth : alk. paper)
ISBN 978-1-4985-6098-6 (electronic)
ISBN 978-1-4985-6099-3 (pbk. : alk. paper)

∞™ The paper used in this publication meets the minimum requirements of American National Standard for Information Sciences Permanence of Paper for Printed Library Materials, ANSI/NISO Z39.48-1992.

Printed in the United States of America

Contents

Preface

As a youth, I was too small to play organized American football beyond junior high, but I was brought up in a family culture in which sports such as football played a significant role. I can remember that as a child no event, including Christmas, excited me more than my first live San Francisco 49er game in 1957. Further, I avidly collected football cards and programs, hoping that I too could gallop for touchdowns like my football heroes.

Yet, I have long since left behind any unmixed love of the game, although I do think football was, in many respects, better when I first became acquainted with it than it is now. For example, in the coming pages, readers will run across skilled, quick, and well-under-200-pound linemen, as well as gridiron virtuosos lauded for their ability to run, pass, kick, block, and defend in the mid-twentieth century. I cannot say that Americans who played football back then were more talented than those who we see on twenty-first century gridirons. Perhaps lingering in nostalgia excessively, I can say that football was more fun to watch, more accessible to ordinary athletes with relatively ordinary bodies, if they were men, and I would guess the game was more fun to play.

Putting nostalgia aside, it seems clear that American football has never been able to shed its tenacious link to violence—a violence that many of us fear today cannot be restricted to the football field. It seems, however, that there is something uniquely disturbing about contemporary American football culture's embrace of violence. In the past, American football was undoubtedly brutal—so much so that early in the twentieth century the sport was banned on many college and high school campuses. However, the sport's viciousness was more of a dirty and not so well-kept secret. At the risk of overgeneralizing, brutality on the gridiron was something to deny or ignore by coaches, players, school administrators, and fans; not something to celebrate. Contemporary American football, conversely, has not shied away from glorifying violence, although considering recent coverage of the pervasiveness of gridiron-related head traumas, those responsible for American football's success have clearly found themselves in a state of denial and backtracking.[1]

Accordingly, as I explore historical and contemporary Asian American and Pacific Islander participation in American football, I want to warn readers that I am not in a mood to celebrate that participation. I think about tragic Samoan American football heroes such as Mark Tuinei and Junior Seau and wonder if their lives might not have been better without football. I know that if my son had ever wanted to play American football, my Japanese American wife and I would have been concerned and this was years before the topic of head traumas became a media hot-potato. And the fact that I did not worry about my daughter playing American football evokes the issue of gender. American football has been and remains defiantly male.

Misogyny has shadowed football, as well as other elite, commercialized sports in the United States and elsewhere, but perhaps more so. While, of course, many elite and weekend athletes respect women, recent reports of professional, college, and high school football players committing acts of violence against females exceed troubling. Perhaps football players are no more prone to physical battering and sexual abuse than other athletes or even the population at large. But it appears American society is more prepared to punish a teacher engaging in sexual abuse than a National Football League (NFL) star.

Football offers other problems embracing race, class, and sexual orientation. I will discuss these throughout the book. Nevertheless, I confess to a weakness when it comes to stereotype busting. Despite my concerns about the sport, I enjoy telling readers about Asian Americans doing well in American football because Asian Americans have not been expected to be gridiron heroes. Likewise, I enjoy telling readers about Pacific Islander quarterbacks because Pacific Islanders are supposed to be gigantic, physically intimidating offensive linemen or defenders.

Admittedly, by focusing on the breaking down of stereotypes, this narrative of Asian and Pacific Islander experiences with football occasions a certain amount of sanguinity. Indeed, American football has propelled people across social barriers, nurturing optimism about the interplay of sport and democracy. Yet we will find that football has reinforced the very same social barriers that make it easier for stereotypes to exist and harder for democracy to thrive.

Readers will note that I do not focus on elite college and professional athletes. They get attention, but they should share the stage with non-elite, often anonymous athletes who have paraded their skills for community, high school, and semi-pro teams. One of my prime concerns as a sport historian is to do populist history. While populist ideas and political movements have often been derailed into various forms of knuckle-headed nativism, racism, and economic panaceas, populism, at its best, has sustained democracy because it advances the notion that a society should value the lives of ordinary people as much, if not more than its economic and political elites.

On a much more trivial level, populist sport history takes seriously the ways in which sport has shaped and been shaped by athletes and non-athletes of ordinary means and possessing ordinary athletic skills, compared at least to those who have graced professional and top-level amateur sports. Thus, to be sure, people of Asian and Pacific Islander ancestry have reached the competitive heights of football but it is how such people have used the sport to solidify a sense of community and have found in American football the means to express passion and joy on a public park or high school gridiron that matters more to me.

Accordingly, readers will come across names of generally anonymous athletes competing for various community and high school teams in Hawai'i and the U.S. mainland. I fully realize that readers can move swiftly through these names and get the gist of things. However, if a populist sport history is anything, it should be about paying tribute to the strivings of ordinary people—not just Hall of Famers, All-Americans, and All-Pros. By naming names of a portion of those who took time away from their family obligations, work, and studies to play a game important to them and to Americans in general seems the least I can do.

OTHER MATTERS TO CONSIDER

A word or two about terminology is advisable. I must apologize to the global followers of various forms of football. Out of convenience as much as out of habit, I will use the term football in place of the more correct, American football. Moreover, since I will spend a great deal of time and energy on football on the Hawaiian Islands, I will try to adhere to the concerns of indigenous Hawaiians and Asian and Pacific Islander scholars and refer to "Hawaii" as Hawai'i.

Following the lead of scholars of Asian and Pacific Islander experiences, I have considered people who can trace their ancestry to Asian societies in Pakistan, India, Cambodia, Laos, Vietnam, Thailand, Mongolia, China, Korea, Japan, Indonesia, and the Philippines, as well as indigenous Oceana societies found in Guam, Tonga, Samoa, and Hawai'i proper subjects for this book. Finally, the fact that some of these people have possessed mixed racial and ethnic ancestry only complicates things in a more interesting way.

I have used a variety of sources for this book. I have relied a great deal on newspaper coverage, whether digitized or microfilmed. In part, this is because newspapers offer substantial information about elite and non-elite Asian and Pacific Islander football players but I have also found newspapers an interesting indicator of attitudes toward Asian and Pacific Islander ethnic groups historically. Keep in mind, however, that much of what a newspaper might say about a college football player came originally from the desk of someone responsible for publicizing the school's athletes. Ethnic newspapers, moreover, have proven invaluable. They provide background to individuals and teams. Indeed, during past and present research, I would not have known about the existence of many athletes or teams initially without the help of ethnic newspapers.

As I stated in a previously published book on Asian American basket-ball, newspapers can mistake and misspell names, especially Asian and Pacific Islander names. Moreover, I fear that I must have overlooked past Filipino American football players because they often possessed Spanish surnames. And I could well have been confused by surnames shared by Asian and non-Asian people. Lee, for example, might or might not be the surname of an Asian American.

School yearbooks have helped in shedding light on non-elite football players. They often supply more detail about individuals than do news-papers, such as pointing out team captains. What I like best about them is that they published team photographs with the names of the players. Thus, I can avoid the "Lee" problem more effectively. Just as good is that non-varsity teams have been covered and sometimes in depth in year-books. This gives me an opportunity to demonstrate the passion, if not always, the skill that Asian and Pacific Islander Americans have shown for sports. Yet school yearbooks are not always put together well. They can get names wrong, and they do not help with possible Filipino athletes possessing Spanish names.

Microfilmed and digitized U.S. Census manuscripts can suggest social and economic backgrounds of individual football players, especially those born before 1940. They supply insight into the racial and ethnic composition of players and coaches. Moreover, they remind us that peo-ple are not just racially and ethnically positioned in society but that class interweaves with race and ethnicity. Historians and other scholars as well as genealogists can access U.S. census manuscripts up to 1940. Keep in mind, however, these documents are not objective in that they are based upon how the census taker interpreted what he or she saw or heard and what the informant wanted that census taker to know.

I have organized this book topically but each chapter treats the topic matter generally on a chronological basis. Chapter 1 examines football and community among Asian and Pacific Islanders in America. Asian and Pacific Islander experiences differed substantially between the U.S. mainland and Hawai'i over the years. Accordingly, chapters two and three look at Hawai'i. Chapter 2 concentrates on football and intercultu-ral experiences on the islands. Chapter 3 examines Hawaiian football players' journeys to the mainland, usually to play for college teams. Chapter 4 focuses on mainland Asian Americans and how football may have helped them cross cultural frontiers. Chapter 5, likewise, looks at generally mainland Asian Americans who managed to play college foot-ball. Chapter 6 examines the historical experiences of Asian and Pacific Islander Americans in U.S. professional football, while chapter seven fo-cuses on the more contemporary, but ambiguous experiences of Pacific Islanders on American gridirons. The conclusion attends to the uncertain legacy of Asian and Pacific Islander football.

Finally, this is a survey of Asian and Pacific Islander American experiences with football. As such, it runs the risk of underrepresenting and ignoring some of those experiences. If I have overlooked a grandfather who starred on a high school football team or played college ball, I apologize in advance. But I also encourage the offended to find an outlet to let people know about their grandfathers. Football is not the most important thing people need to know about Asian and Pacific Islander history in America. But it has played a role in the making of that history. The more that people know about an omitted grandfather, the more people will know about Asians and Pacific Islanders in the United States and its empire.

NOTE

1. Mark Fainaru-Wada and Steve Fainaru, *League of Denial: The NFL, Concussions, and the Battle for Truth* (New York: Three Rivers Press, 2014).

Acknowledgments

First, I want to thank my colleagues and students at San José State University for support and inspiration. The fine people at San José State's Interlibrary Loan Department have provided me with needed sources. An anonymous reader and Gerald Gems, who edits the "Sports, Identity, and Culture" series for Lexington Books offered many fine suggestions for improving my manuscript. I took them up on many of those suggestions, but, perhaps unfortunately, not all. Finally, I want to thank my wife for putting up with me spending so much time on my laptop and my children and grandchild for just being them.

Introduction

Symbolizing unmatched excellence as a college football player during a given season, the Heisman Trophy reigns as one of the most coveted awards in American sports. In 2014, journalists reporting on college football chose Marcus Mariota, a quarterback for the University of Oregon, as the Heisman Trophy winner. The vote made history. Mariota became the first Hawaiian resident and the first person of Pacific Islander ancestry to get the trophy.

Mariota's acceptance speech clearly recognized his Pacific connections. He declared:

> In Hawaii, if one person is successful the entire state is successful. I'm just grateful to be a part of it. I hope this is just the beginning and that a lot of kids back home are inspired to succeed. . . . It's been a journey, but I couldn't have done it without my boys back home, my family and my teammates. My boys back home were the ones who believed in me. Without them I wouldn't be standing here today. This isn't just a one-person deal, there's a lot of people who have put their heart and their hard work into it. [1]

In closing, Mariota, after unsurprisingly thanking his parents for their support, added, "To the Polynesian community, I hope and pray that this is only the beginning. Young Poly athletes everywhere, you should take this as motivation, and dream big and strive for greatness." Giving thanks in Samoan, he closed with *"Fa'afetai tele lava*, God bless, and go Ducks." [2]

The Heisman going to Mariota and his acceptance speech tell part of an important story about race and ethnicity in clearly the most popular spectator sport in the United States during the early twenty-first century. Since the 1970s, followers of American football have confronted the growing presence of gridders possessing Pacific Islander ancestry on many of their favorite teams. Often bearing names that many in the United States could not easily pronounce, football players who come from or who could trace their ancestry to the indigenous peoples of Oceania have often achieved acclaim as gridiron stars. Yet few in the sports media have tackled the reality that Pacific Islanders have significantly altered the racial dynamics of football; indeed, American sport in general. Most of us have settled for, although not always very comfortably, with the black-white dyad which stipulates that race and sport embraces little but black and white interactions. Yet Marcus Mariota and the many Pacific Islander

1

gridders preceding him, have complicated things more than a bit and not always in a celebratory, "Isn't it grand we gave that Samoan a trophy" sort of way.

But there are other, blatantly disturbing stories, to tell. Junior Seau was arguably the greatest Samoan American football player of his time. An All-American linebacker at the University of Southern California (USC) in the late twentieth century, Seau became a fierce linebacker for the NFL's San Diego Chargers. Not only was he acknowledged as an all-pro defender, but respected for his charitable activities in the San Diego area where he grew up. In 2012, two years after he retired from the NFL, Seau shot himself in the chest. It seems quite clear that all the concussions sustained while hitting and getting hit in all those years in the NFL, not to mention the physical traumas he experienced at USC and before that, Oceanside High School, had much to do with the depression and terror he experienced in his last years and the ultimate choice to put an end to it all.

Seau's tragedy and the physical and emotional breakdown experienced by other elite football players, Pacific Islanders or not, should quiet any celebration of gridiron heroics. The cost accommodating those heroics may just be too high. Moreover, as we will explore later in this book, Pacific Islander football players have had to cope with an excessively masculinized image, imposed from without and within Pacific Islander groups. Perhaps, this image has made it harder for Pacific Islander gridders to handle the emotional and physical consequences of playing football over an extended period. In any event, while we cheer Pacific Islanders as they tackle and block and occasionally run, catch, and throw footballs, where they come from and what they encounter as members of non-white, colonized ethnic groups remains largely invisible to many of us who follow football to any degree.

If the experiences of Pacific Islanders in football have been more troublesome than the American sporting public imagines, the experiences of football players possessing Asian descent have been relatively ignored. For example, it was not all that long ago that a son of Vietnamese refugees, Dat Nguyen, was an All-American linebacker at Texas A&M. Not only that, but he won the prestigious Bednarik Award as the nation's top linebacker and the even more prestigious Lombardi Award as the nation's best defender. Then, he was drafted by "America's Team," the Dallas Cowboys, for which he played solidly as a linebacker until injuries, including head traumas, took its toll and he retired.

Curiously, while many of us were ready to hand over to Jeremy Lin the keys to America's post-racial kingdom in 2012, we have pretty much forgotten about Nguyen, who came from working class, Vietnamese refugee parents to become the leading tackler on America's most famous NFL team. This is not to minimize Jeremy Lin's achievements or his stereotype-busting impact. But Nguyen was a star, certainly at Texas A&M and arguably with the Dallas Cowboys. So, it is curious that while NFL football is America's favorite spectator sport, an Asian American pioneer and solid performer in that sport in relatively recent history largely went unnoticed. There was no "Nguyensanity comparable to the 'Linsanity' generated by Lin's ascendancy in the NBA."[3]

Thus, a critical issue for readers of this book to keep in mind is how racial ideology weaves its way like a Barry Sanders touchdown run through a sport such as football. To help shed light on this matter, this book will focus on Asian and Pacific Islander ethnic groups in the United States. Scholars, activists, and government officials have often placed Asians and Pacific Islanders under the same demographic umbrella as "Asian Pacific Islanders. (API)." While something of a shotgun marriage of relatively disparate groups, the API designation has made some sense in that it has facilitated the construction of alliances among admittedly diverse people but also people who have historically interacted with one another, often intimately, and have frequently confronted at least somewhat similar forms of colonization, labor exploitation, immigration restriction, and racial discrimination.[4]

Nevertheless, the term API has aroused controversy in Asian and Pacific Islander communities, and I will avoid its use whenever possible. Yet by looking at how people of Asian and Pacific Islander descent have embraced football, we can hopefully get an idea of their commonality and their distinctiveness. One place to start is by examining a little historical and cultural context.

INTERNATIONAL MIGRATION AND COLONIZATION

Colonization and international migration have intertwined for Asian and Pacific Islander ethnic groups in the United States. Certainly, colonization played an imposing role in Asian migration at least prior to World War II. British colonization by way of the Opium Wars, in which England imposed the drug trade on China, stirred Chinese international migration in the mid-nineteenth century. The fear of European and American colonization pushed Japan toward modernization, which in turn pushed thousands of Japanese to migrate to Hawai'i and the U.S. mainland in the late nineteenth and early twentieth centuries. British, Japanese, and American colonization fed into migration from British India, Korea, and the Philippines respectively in the early twentieth century.[5]

These immigrants to the United States encountered racial exclusion and labor exploitation, but they and their children also had to maneuver through cultural institutions and practices frequently very different than those found historically in Asia. Sport institutions and practices, over which native born white male Americans claimed ownership, comprised to varying degrees a new cultural landscape for Asian immigrants and their U.S.-born offspring. As did European-based ethnic groups they responded in a variety of ways depending upon a variety of factors such as where they came from and timing of immigration, as well as generation, class, gender, and religion. However, Asian-based ethnic group agency was often hemmed in by the racial ideology and practices prevailing in the United States and confronted less systematically by European-based ethnic groups.

In the United States, government-sponsored restriction of Asian immigration thrived by the early 1900s. The Chinese Exclusion Act, passed in 1882, banned entry into the United States of laborers who comprised the bulk of Chinese immigrants to the United States, while also denying all Chinese immigrants citizenship rights. Combining racial and class hostility to Chinese immigration, this act was renewed in 1892 and 1902 and made permanent in 1904. It would remain the law of the land until 1943. An agreement between the United States and Japanese governments aimed at eliminating the immigration of Japanese laborers to the United States was put into play in 1907. Because it lacked the strength of a federal law, the "Gentlemen's Agreement" did not appease the anti-Asian movement, largely concentrated on the West Coast. However, the first two decades of the twentieth century saw the growing popularity of nativist politics in the United States—a nativist politics which aligned those who believed that immigrants from anywhere that was not western and northern Europe should be barred as much as possible from entering the United States. In 1917, immigration from much of Asia and the Pacific Islands was cut off by Congress. In 1924, Congress enacted a law rendering it difficult for immigrants from southern and eastern Europe, as well as the Middle East, to enter the United States, and casting an eye on Japan, barring "aliens ineligible from citizenship" from the U.S. Filipinos, as residents of a U.S. protectorate, were not "aliens" but U.S. nationals ineligible for citizenship. As such, they could migrate to the U.S. mainland and Hawai'i to provide the labor substantially denied employers by the various efforts to exclude Asian workers. However, in 1934, the Tydings-McDuffie Act put the Philippines on the road to eventual independence, while transforming the status of Filipino migrants from U.S. nationals to aliens, generally barring Filipinos from entering the United States.[6]

Deep into the twentieth century, people of Asian descent in the United States experienced institutional forms of overt racial discrimination, as well as flare-ups of anti-Asian violence and the egregious undermining of Japanese American civil liberties during World War II. One underlying factor was that based on the Naturalization Act of 1790, which deemed only "free white" immigrants eligible for naturalization, Asian immigrants from China, Korea, and India were denied citizenship rights until the 1940s and Japanese immigrants could not become citizens until the early 1950s. Making much of this possible was that the racial science of the time and the courts agreed that people from East Asia belonged to the Mongolian race. And while racial scientists may have designated Indians as Caucasians, the U.S. Supreme Court in the notorious Thind case of 1923 spurned racial science for a "common sense" ruling on race; that is, if one does not look white, one is not white.[7]

A host of factors led to immigration and naturalization reform in the mid-twentieth century in the United States. Race was officially eliminated as an obstacle to enter the United States in the 1960s, while employment qualifications and family reunification became primary factors in welcoming immigrants. By then, moreover, Asian immigrants could enjoy U.S. citizenship. In part, immigration and naturalization reform was instituted out of a concern to do right by people who just sought better lives in America or reunification with loved ones. The devastating consequences of fascist racism combined with global anticolonial and American civil rights movements had, after all, pricked the consciences of many Americans. However, the Cold War also played a role. American policymakers did not relish having to constantly explain racist state policies to Third World people making up their minds about which side of the ideological battle they wanted to join. Ending the most visible patterns of institutionalized racism seemed an obvious step in winning the Cold War, and overtly racist immigration laws struck leaders such as John F. Kennedy as irritating obstacles to such a victory.[8]

Perhaps, too, the comparative prosperity of mid-twentieth century America distracted Americans from political nativism. The greater ability of native-born white Americans to own their own homes and buy cars and television sets based on the earnings of one, typically male breadwinner did not dispel racism and nativism. However, Americans were less inclined to mobilize into anti-immigrant political movements as long as they were sufficiently satisfied with their pieces of the American economic pie.

Immigration reform meant a transformation of Asian America. Whereas before the 1960s the primary Asian-based ethnic groups in the United States were Chinese, Japanese, and Filipino with a smattering of Asian Indians and Koreans, after the 1960s an ethnically diverse population of Asian Americans developed. Moreover, the war in Southeast Asia in the 1960s and 1970s fostered the resettlement of thousands of refugees from Vietnam, Cambodia, and Laos.

Opening the gates to the United States for Asian immigration was all very nice, but it did not eliminate anti-Asian racism within the United States—a racism that fed into anti-immigrant politics in the late 1900s. Yet this anti-Asian racism did not appear and persist in a vacuum. Historically and today, it has been reinforced by fluctuating economic fortunes, fed by deindustrialization and stagflation, and political scapegoating. Asian immigrants and their offspring have served, per historian Al-

exander Saxton, as "indispensable enemies" in America's past—and they
seem to continue to do so.[9]

During the late nineteenth and early twentieth centuries, the United
States built an empire in the Pacific by colonizing the region's indigenous
peoples. It was not always easy and assuredly native populations, especially in Hawai'i and the Philippines, objected as did some Americans
who feared that colonization betrayed American values or feared that
colonization would ultimately lead to U.S. citizenship for thousands of
non-whites. However, by 1940, the United States could claim a political,
economic, and military presence not only in Hawai'i and the Philippines
but parts of Samoa, as well as Guam, Midway Island, and Wake Island.

Because Hawai'i sustained the presence of economically and political
powerful white people of American descent, it could wrangle from the
U.S. territorial status, which provided those born in Hawai'i with citizenship. However, citizenship did not guarantee indigenous or Asian Hawaiians equality—only whiteness could initially do that, although the
struggles of non-white Hawaiians would eventually help democratize
the islands to some degree while leaving the question of indigenous Hawaiian rights unanswered.[10]

The Philippines comprised another matter. Resistance to U.S. occupation by Filipinos provoked a bitter war for liberation that took years for
the occupiers to totally and often brutally suppress. Further, the Philippines did not possess a strong population of Anglo Americans to which
the U.S. government might reserve a semblance of obligation. Thus, considered a land of "little brown brothers" incapable of self-government
and needing Uncle Sam's protection, the Philippines entered the U.S.
empire as a protectorate. Native-born Filipinos were provided with the
status of U.S. nationals ineligible for citizenship until the 1930s when the
Tydings-McDuffie Act turned the Philippines into a U.S. commonwealth
inevitably bound for independence.[11]

The islands of Samoa attracted the imperial ambitions of Germany,
England, and the United States. In 1899, the nations agreed to divide the
islands; the indigenous people were not asked to weigh in on the matter.
American Samoa was largely directed by the U.S. military with Samoans
allowed a certain amount of self-government. Meanwhile, American Samoans have possessed the relegated status of U.S. nationals within the
American empire—a status which Samoans have sought to change in
recent years but so far to no avail even though thousands of Americans
cheer on Samoan-born football players each fall.[12]

A colonial possession of Spain until the Spanish-American War,
Guam was turned over to the winners of that war. Guam was governed
by the U.S. military, and its residents were, like Filipinos and Samoans,
considered U.S. nationals. During much of World War II, Guam was
occupied by the Japanese, but the ultimately victorious U.S. military took
over the islands again in 1944. In the early 1950s, Guam was provided

with territorial status, and its residents became U.S. citizens. In the meantime, historian Bruce Cumings tells us, Guam has become a "'power projection hub' on the edge of Asia" for the U.S. military. Quoting an American diplomat who claims that the United States does not desire to create military presence in a place where it is unwanted, Cumings adds, "The 160,000 residents of Guam are unlikely to [throw the United States out] since the island is an American territory-nor were they ever asked if they wanted to be a 'power projection hub.'" [13]

The island of Tonga has not been directly ruled by the United States, but neither has it escaped the U.S. empire. To be sure, other imperial powers vied with the United States for influence in Tonga—the British and Germans, for example. A king presided over all the many islands of Tonga in the mid-1800s. In 1875, a constitutional monarchy was instituted. However, in the early 1900s, the British pursued a protectorate agreement with Tonga, and although that agreement is no longer in place, Tonga remains a commonwealth member of the British Empire. [14]

A neo-colonial relationship developed between Tonga and the United States largely through the frequently well-meaning efforts of Mormon missionaries. Touting American culture and capitalism, these missionaries encouraged Tongan migration to Hawai'i and the U.S. mainland. Since the early decades of the twentieth century, one could find Tongans as well as Samoans living in La'ie on Oahu, where a Mormon temple and cultural center was created. There, they would serve as "labor missionaries," recruited to help construct and maintain the center. Moreover, when journeying to the mainland, Tongans generally located themselves in and around the Mormon stronghold of Salt Lake City, Utah. [15]

DEMOCRACY

For those of us interested in the complex but often interrelated experiences of people of Asian and Pacific Islander ancestry, football has invited their grit, talent, and support for well over a century. Through American football, Asians and Pacific Islanders living in the United States and its Pacific colonies could initiate and maintain strong and venerable community institutions. They could claim what historian Gaye Theresa Johnson has depicted as "spatial entitlement" of football fields throughout the American empire. Yet they could also reach out to other communities through the sport. That is, on gridirons throughout the American empire, "cosmopolitan canopies" have occasionally been erected. Emerging from the work of sociologist Elijah Anderson, the concept of cosmopolitan canopies might help explain why Americans of Asian and Pacific Islander ancestry could play with and against people of varied racial and ethnic identities during periods of substantial racial exclusion. Moreover, through football some Asians and Pacific Islanders in the United States have gained fame, noteworthy athletic honors, and even a great deal of money.[16]

Yet it has not always been easy and it remains unclear how easy it remains. For decades Asians and Pacific Islanders have encountered unquestionable harm carried out by racialized colonialism and institutionalized racism and nativism. Today, we can argue that most of the more horrendous examples of institutionalized racism have been expunged. Yet have the stereotypes of Asian and Pacific Islanders disappeared as well? Do Asian and Pacific Islander athletes still hear racial taunts from spectators and opponents? Do coaches and others involved in evaluating athletic performances crave Asian and Pacific Islander athletes on their teams as much as athletes from other racial and ethnic groups?

One underlying theme of this book is the interaction of democracy and sport. Democratic political participation would seem linked to at least a semblance of economic and cultural equality. It should not surprise the reader that democracy's growth has been stunted by the "raised hierarchies," explored by the late historian Robert Wiebe. Combining an explosive combination of racial, ethnic, gender, class, and other components these raised hierarchies have been confirmed and contested in all sorts of ways. Sports such as football have helped to both thwart and encourage hierarchical processes in American life.[17]

Colonialism has clearly channeled democracy as a national and transnational endeavor in all sorts of interesting ways. Certainly, any national project aimed at subjugating, exploiting, and even displacing other nations or societies seems at variance with the egalitarian core of democracy. That colonialism has been racialized—often been justified by racism—undermines further the foundations of democratic rule. However, as C. L. R. James and others have pointed out, colonialism can arm the colonized with a new language; a new vision of democratic possibilities, especially if the colonial powers claim, with perhaps some sincerity, that they see themselves as part of a crusading democratic vanguard. Thus, perhaps football has served anticolonial purposes. Yet others can reasonably assert that football has not only failed to serve democracy among colonized people, but has weakened anticolonialism and the more recent struggles against neocolonialism.[18]

IDENTITY

Identity is a great running back—hard to catch and harder to tackle. We should keep in mind that those people of Asian and Pacific Islander ancestry organizing, playing, and watching football games in the United States have identified themselves and been identified in all sorts of ways. In Hawai'i, for example, they might have been perceived by others as primarily agricultural workers or Japanese. They might, indeed, have agreed with such labels, but they also might just as likely have identified themselves by way of neighborhood or as "locals" — working- and lower-middle-class Hawaiians of multiethnic backgrounds. Thus, while this book will explore how various Asian and Pacific Islander ethnic group members have participated in football, we should acknowledge that they have done so not just as Japanese Americans or Samoan Americans but as men and women, as plantation laborers and engineers, as Protestants and Buddhists, and as gays and straights. They have revealed, as borderlands theory argues, that they do not have to be either Asian or American.[19]

Identity has an ascriptive side. That is, we are ascribed certain characteristics by others. In a less than democratic setting, this might mean that voices of authority will assume the power to represent us in the media, churches, and classrooms in such a manner as to justify inequality. Historically, orientalism and primitivism have largely shaped representations of people of Asian and Pacific Islander ancestry. At the same time, Asian Americans have been represented in recent decades as members of a model minority.

Orientalism, according to the late cultural critic Edward Said, surfaced around the time European imperialism ventured eastward into the Middle East and further east to India and China in the eighteenth and nineteenth centuries. Eurocentric, it labeled people of Middle Eastern, South Central Asian, and Eastern Asian backgrounds as Easterners or Orientals. In so doing, the ideology of orientalism stressed that Orientals were notably and often inherently distinct from Westerners or Occidentals. Rudyard Kipling's old verse put it nicely: "East is East/West is West/And Never the Twain Shall Meet." To be clear, orientalists could be hazy on the origins of these distinctions and their consequences. That is, orientalism could feed into a racialism arguing that an innately insurmountable barrier existed between the West and the East as Kipling's words seem to argue. However, orientalism could see that barrier as cultural, surmountable by Orientals willing to accept instruction from the West and Occidentals patient enough to give that instruction. It could, in any event, justify a global hierarchy ruled by Westerners.[20]

Orientalists did not necessarily wrap themselves up in vicious bigotry. Indeed, they could profess admiration for aspects of cultural institutions and practices developed in Asia and affection for individual Asians. Nevertheless, orientalism was often tethered to racism and ethnocentrism. It admonished Westerners to fear Orientals' dishonesty, cruelty, depravity, and lust for miscegenation. In the case of people of East Asian descent, they were often depicted as representatives of a "yellow peril" aimed at dismantling Western civilization. To be sure, as orientalism often urged, Asians and Middle Easterners might seem polite and even intelligent, but, it was all a show—the Oriental's smile hid, that is, a crafty mind. Beyond espousing essentialism, the Oriental/Occidental duality made little geographic sense in a spherical world. To be just, while orientalism permitted Westerners to pigeonhole people of Asian and Middle Eastern ancestry, some Asian and Middle Eastern people have done their fair share of missionary work for orientalism.

The point is that even at its most harmless, orientalism still has exoticized millions and millions of people. In the process, it has tossed about terms such as "exotic," "strange," "mysterious," "inscrutable," and "celestial" to render people of Asian and Middle Eastern ancestry into permanent outsiders to the so-called West; to rob them of their complexity, their humanity.

Asian bodies have often seemingly been targeted by orientalism. For a wide variety of dietary, environmental, and genetic factors Asians generally have been smaller than people possessing European ancestry. Orientalism, in both its negative and positive guises, was put into play, according to historian David Welky during the 1932 summer Olympiad. The games held in Los Angeles witnessed the coming-out party for Japanese athletes, who excelled mainly in swimming. At that time, Americans were feeling more apprehensive about Japanese militarism, especially considering the conflict between Japan and China over Manchuria. Welky maintains that the American press used the Olympics to diminish Japanese athletes and, by extension Japan, through references to their lack of height. Indeed, press accounts of Asian American football players have also employed terms such as "diminutive" and "wee" to describe them. Not knowing the individuals who wrote these accounts, it is easy and probably often accurate for us to perceive them as exoticizing Asian American football players in a condescending manner. However, it is just as easy to assume they were trying to compliment the gridders for transcending their physical limitations and shining in football. Finally, we should also remember that any prominent shorter athlete, regardless of race and ethnicity, will discover his/her size commented upon by the press.[21]

Primitivism comprised a complex of cultural responses by European and European American societies to their contact with indigenous peoples in the Americas, Africa, Asia, and Oceania. To call a culture primitive is not usually meant as a compliment. It stigmatizes a culture as uncivilized—as savage. Yet like orientalism, primitivism meandered different streams of thought. Typically, cultural authorities in Europe and North America used primitivism to demean a group of people as childlike, simple, violent, and blissfully lustful. Often, primitivism stressed culture over race. In other words, primitive people could become more civilized over time if they were willing to heed the lessons of Western civilization. But primitivism also leaned hard toward racialism, arguing that primitives were naturally savage and would always remain out of Western civilization's intellectual reach and rightly so since they had nothing to offer the West except their labor and obedience.

Primitivism evoked the ignoble savage and noble savage. The former was culturally or racially contemptuous of civilization—crafty, lustful, and deadly. Yet a more generous primitivism summoned Rousseau's noble savage as brave, generous, relatively nonviolent, and environmentally sensitive. Here Western civilization often expressed, according to anthropologist Renato Rosaldo, "imperialist nostalgia." In other words, just as many of us fondly remember supposedly simpler, blissful childhoods, Western civilization often represented primitive people as remnants of humanity's idyllic childhood free from modernity's tensions. Primitivism inspired Westerners to re-create humanity's childhood by camping in the woods or vacationing on some Caribbean or Pacific Island. Westerners hoped to approximate, if but for a little while, the lifestyles of people conquered by Western imperialism. To re-create themselves after months in congested public spaces and nine-to-five jobs, Westerners should salvage memories of their simpler pasts by relaxing and enjoying themselves as they did when they were children by temporarily mimicking supposedly happy-go-lucky, albeit simple-minded, natives.[22]

Like orientalism, then, primitivism sought to oversimplify the experiences of millions and millions of people while embracing substantial contradictions. It allowed that primitives could be admired as gracious and affectionate as they performed hula dances and crafted jewelry for tourists, while revering "Mother Earth." But primitivism, as well, warned of savagery's inclination toward primordial violence and lust. The same people who rode surfboards and crafted folk art inspiring Picasso could also pop a white missionary into a pot for a hearty meal. To be fair, primitivism might, as did orientalism, allow a certain amount of cleverness on the part of those it was trying to depict. However, often this cleverness was sneaky, cowardly. It was, that is, the cleverness of the ambush.

Primitivism, at its most generous, could depict primitives as courageous, strong, and even intelligent in warlike settings. Primitive males were seemingly, therefore, capable of manliness by Western standards. If properly disciplined, they might well achieve success in combative sports such as prize fighting, wrestling, or football. By the same token, it was better to sequester primitives from situations which might call upon them using brains, as much, if not more than their brawn. Thus, a primitive might be fine as a down lineman or a linebacker in football, but not as a quarterback even though the most physical positions in football actually require a certain amount of intelligence to excel at the highest levels.

As ideologies, orientalism and primitivism interacted with the often racialized ethnocentricity of Western sport. Yet, it is interesting to note gender working its way into how people got framed by orientalism and primitivism. As many scholars point out, Asian people have long been feminized by European and American dominant cultures. That is, at best orientalism generally esteemed in Asians traits the West has often associated with females—generosity, obedience, cleanliness, and culinary skills. That is, a coach might want an oriental helper; a manager of the football team tasked to pick up balls, do laundry, sort equipment, and treat minor injuries. But that coach would not want an oriental, even an oriental male, to play on that football team.

Gendering of primitive males could be inconsistent. Primitivism often justified imperialism because supposedly savage males were incapable of curbing their violent, lustful dispositions as evidenced by the Massie Affair, which will be discussed later. But Hawaiian scholars Ty Kāwika Tengan and Jesse Makani Markham argue that Hawaiian men have been gendered as more feminine than other indigenous, Pacific Islander males to represent Hawai'i as a soft target for American conquest.[23]

Orientalism and primitivism intertwined with what R. W. Connell calls "hegemonic masculinity" to explain the success of indigenous and Asian American athletes during the early twentieth century. A gendered white supremacy at the time asserted that European and European American males reigned as athletes because they exhibited the proper attributes of manliness in addition to physical strength, endurance, and coordination. That is, they triumphed on the baseball diamond, prize fight ring, and football gridiron the only way men should—through intelligence, hard work, courage, maturity, and honesty. They won "fair and square."[24]

Just as Western military authorities regarded guerilla warfare as "not cricket," because it seemed cowardly and unmanly when armies ought to confront one another in open fields under a barrage of deadly fire, European Americans tended to hail athletes whose manliness inspired them to confront their opponents head on. Early twentieth-century American football was a notable example of this thinking with consequences that I will discuss more in a bit. The idea that an American Indian team could compete with and often defeat the powerhouses of college football at the time might have proved discomfiting to many at the time. Yet that is what Jim Thorpe and his Carlisle Institute teammates did despite the fact they were often undersized compared to their white opponents. In so doing, they employed a variety of tactics viewed as clever by white observers. Getting called clever might seem praise but in the masculine and racialized world of early twentieth-century sport it might get twisted into another way of accusing a team of underhandedness, of engaging in the equivalent of guerilla warfare.[25]

FOOTBALL AND AMERICANS OF ASIAN AND
PACIFIC ISLANDER ANCESTRY

Agency is what people do about the socially structured situations in which they find themselves. Over the years, Americans of Asian and Pacific Islander asserted a sense of agency through sport. As a growing number of historical studies have pointed out, sports such as baseball, basketball, and even prize fighting served Americans of Asian and Pacific Islander ancestry in these matters. However, relatively little has been said of the role of football as a community solidifier, cultural bridge, and producer of joy.[26]

The love of football as both a participatory and spectator sport was nurtured in Asian and Pacific Islander ethnic communities by varied, overlapping influences that affected Americans across social distinctions. Fostered in Victorian Britain, muscular Christianity was one of these influences. Muscular Christianity combined piety and physical exertion. Throughout the late 1800s and early 1900s it found a receptive audience on both sides of the Atlantic among males who worried that Christianity had become too feminized as it seemingly granted more spiritual autonomy to women in the early decades of the nineteenth century. Stressing that there was nothing effete about Christ, muscular Christians supported manly participation in team sports such as American football and rugby, as well as individualized athletic endeavors such as amateur boxing.[27]

Muscular Christianity also helped shaped the thinking of an important blue-blood reformer Theodore Roosevelt. Worried about middle- and upper-class males who worked and enjoyed themselves in relative comfort, Roosevelt advocated the "strenuous life." By hunting elephants or engaging in football or amateur boxing, economically advantaged young men, Roosevelt believed, could overcome the emasculation of their white-collar jobs and their private lives of privilege.[28]

A related influence was the reforming zeal propagated during the early periods of Asian immigration and American imperialism in the Pacific Basin—the late nineteenth and early twentieth centuries. Although often obsessed with cleaning up politics and government while rendering capitalism more equitable in its treatment of workers and consumers, reformers often asserted that a good society required both healthy minds and bodies. These progressive reformers pushed for more playgrounds and organized athletic teams and leagues to rescue young native-born middle-class men from their relatively sedentary yet stressful occupations and divert immigrant and second-generation working class young men from crime and political radicalism while teaching them appropriate Anglo-American values. These reformers, consequently, helped nurture the Playground Movement, which, in turn, called upon public officials to build more playgrounds and gyms accessible to American young people, regardless of gender. On the playgrounds and in the gyms, reformers hoped, team sports could be organized—team sports that would strengthen and Americanize participants by instilling in them the values of physical health as well as mental alertness, diligence, teamwork, and fair play.[29]

The Young Men's Christian Association (YMCA) linked muscular Christianity with progressive reform. English and American physical educators affiliated with the YMCA not only taught youth from diverse class backgrounds and localities the joy of team sports but set up facilities for them (albeit racially segregated ones) to dribble basketballs and hit volleyballs. Subsequently, the Young Women's Christian Association (YWCA) encouraged physical education for females.[30]

Meanwhile, a consumer culture enveloped much of American society in the late nineteenth and early twentieth centuries. Sport proved an integral part of this consumer culture as Americans bought tickets to football and baseball games, sports equipment, and trading cards of athletic celebrities. By the 1920s, observers of the American sporting scene celebrated and feared the advent of "King Football." That is, while baseball may have still reigned as the American national pastime, football, especially intercollegiate football, took over in the fall once the last out was made in the World Series. Accordingly, although many American immigrants, regardless of origins, could have often cared less, their children might well have followed the college football rivalries of the day and the exploits of Bronko Nagurski, and the Four Horsemen of Notre Dame, especially since Nagurski was a child of Eastern European immigrants and Notre Dame proved a source of pride to Roman Catholic immigrants and their offspring.[31]

The use of sport as a vehicle for social engineering and capitalist development globalized. European and American empire builders journeyed to Asia and the Pacific in the nineteenth and early twentieth centuries. They often carried with them a strong belief in sport as an instrument of civilization and pacification. As muscular Christians and playground activists pronounced sport's reforming capabilities in the United States, imperialists hoped to use it to tame potential and actual rebellious colonized people and shape them into consumers of athletic equipment manufactured by American sporting goods companies such as A. G. Spalding, a prominent sporting goods firm in Chicago. To be sure, much of this was done with the best of intent. Physical educators trained in the United States by the YMCA truly believed that if Filipinos hit baseballs and Hawaiians kicked footballs they would be better off. Thus, whether learned from YMCA educators or colonial political and military authorities, the gospel of team sports spread throughout many colonized lands such as India and the Philippines and neocolonized lands such as China and, before it sternly took up colonization itself, Japan.[32]

Yet colonized people frequently asserted a sense of agency in the face of athletic imperialism. They took up the sports of their colonizers not just to please them, but because those sports could be enjoyable. Those sports could as well offer colonized people a certain amount of autonomy from colonial relations. At the same time, they could provide colonized people with the means of subverting colonial rule by defeating the colonizers at rugby, cricket, baseball, or football.[33]

We can view people of Asian and Pacific Islander ancestry in the United States supporting American football as participants and competitors from different perspectives. Perhaps as colonized peoples, they played football to demonstrate a willingness to accept colonial authority. Perhaps, as C. L. R. James reminded us in a somewhat different context, colonized peoples played football to undermine colonial authority. Perhaps, Asian and Pacific Islander Americans sought through football an assimilating passage to mainstream American social and cultural norms. Perhaps, however, they sought through American football a way to evince their cultural citizenship—a desire for full-fledged American citizenship and constructive interaction with mainstream American social and cultural norms without necessarily surrendering their ethnic distinctiveness.[34]

STRUCTURAL OBSTACLES TO ASIAN AMERICAN PARTICIPATION IN FOOTBALL

Conventional thinking on Asian Americans has historically revolved around the stereotyping of them as small and unathletic, especially in those sports that Americans seem to care about the most—sports such as football. Nevertheless, it is important to note the structural impediments to Asian American participation in football, while also acknowledging the surprising ability of some Asian Americans to overcome those obstacles.

Class can influence the ability of a people to engage in and watch athletic competition. For example, French social theorist Pierre Bourdieu argued that laboring class people, possessing relatively little cultural capital except for their ability to engage in physical labor, might be socially predisposed to physically demanding sports such as prize fighting or association football. He called such socialized norms, habitus. Yet the way class and culture have interacted in the United States, it makes sense that it would be easier for participants from more privileged economic backgrounds to play football for community and high school teams than those from less privileged economic backgrounds, although the motivation to do so might not be as strong. Significantly, up until the 1965 Immigration Act, which ultimately fostered the migration to the United States of a sizable number of Asian immigrants from economically privileged backgrounds, Asian immigrants generally came from the lower classes. During the late nineteenth and early twentieth century, Asian immigrants could offer their labor to plantations, mines, railroads, restaurants, or hotels, but not all that much else. To survive and move beyond survival and economic dependence, Asian immigrant families, like other immigrant families, often needed "all hands on deck." In many cases, this would exclude children from spending much time in "organized play." Instead, they were encouraged to focus on doing schoolwork or watch younger siblings for their working parents. If old enough, they might have to earn money themselves or provide unpaid labor in a family business. All of this made it hard for second-generation Asian Americans, as well as European and Latino Americans, to compete in sports, especially a relatively time consuming, expensively staged, and usually daytime sport such as football. Basketball, accordingly, proved more alluring to working class and lower middle-class Asian Americans significantly clustered in urban ethnic enclaves and agrarian labor camps. It required less space and expense and could be played at night, after the work- and school day ended, as well as decidedly encourage more participation of working- and lower middle-class females.[35]

Asian American football was impacted by race-based immigration laws. We should not discount the racial biases of coaches, teammates, fans, and other bigoted individuals, as well as organizations encountered by would-be Asian American football players. Still, the primary way racism inhibited the participation of Asian American in sports was through race-based immigration restriction.

European immigrants confronted bigotry and violence. But the immigration restriction they encountered especially after World War I, while severe, did not reach the harshness meted out to Asian immigrants. Accordingly, European immigrants found it easier to generate a second generation of Knute Rocknes, Benny Friedmans, and Bronko Nagurskis, all of whom gained fame in early twentieth-century American football and were children of European immigrants. Asian immigrants were not so fortunate. A cursory examination of the foreign-born population of the United States in the early twentieth century will underscore the point. In 1900, there were nearly nine million people from Europe in the United States and over 120,000 from Asia. Twenty years later, nearly twelve million European immigrants and nearly 240,000 Asian immigrants lived in the United States.[36]

Thus, instead of asking why Asian American communities did not produce very many great Asian American football players or athletes in general in the twentieth century, we should ask why they produced as many passionate and skilled football players as they did. For in the next chapters, we are going to come across Asian Americans who put together skilled community teams. We will also discover Asian Americans who not only starred on their high school but college teams as well.

These discoveries will hopefully help dent one of the primary arguments for why Asian Americans have not excelled in major American sports. This argument stresses that as members of a "Model Minority," Asian Americans have better things to do than seek excellence as football players. Emerging in the mid-1960s when antiracist social movements were becoming more militant, the model minority thesis was deployed by those defending America's basic political and economic institutions as essentially color blind. Emphasizing brains over brawn, according to the model minority thesis, Asian American youths have overcome the racial injustices of the past and flooded the gates of elite colleges and stormed into labs, operating rooms, and symphony orchestras, as well as shattering the glass ceilings keeping them from running corporations. In the process, they have ostensibly fulfilled the American Dream that other minorities have denied themselves by wasting energy on drugs, sexual profligacy, street crime, welfare, social protest, voting for the wrong political candidates, and sports such as basketball and football. As numerous Asian American Studies' scholars have pointed out, the model minority thesis constitutes a stereotype homogenizing the experiences of millions of people and rejecting the struggles of millions against institutionalized racism. In the process, the model minority thesis has racialized Asian Americans as inherently capable in some areas of human activity but not in others. To some advocates of the model minority thesis, the fact that NFL and Division I football teams have been bereft of Asian American talent has proven the point. [37]

As for Pacific Islanders, it seems as if they have a different problem in terms of football—that is, like African Americans, they are perceived as not just well represented but perhaps even overrepresented in elite football. To some this may be cause for celebration, but to others it seems to suggest that Pacific Islanders prefer tackling and blocking over acing college entrance exams. Thus, through football it has become easier to racialize Pacific Islanders as capable in some areas of human activity but not in others. [38]

Racialization and stereotyping go together. Too many of us effortlessly accept simplistic ways of looking at ourselves and others. Too many of us effortlessly say that certain people behave the way they do because that is just the way they are. Studying history can produce many benefits, but one of the things history does well, when done properly, is defy simplistic thinking. Among my many hopes for this book is that it will offer surprising ways to think about Americans of Asian and Pacific Islander ancestry.

THE "ALL-AMERICAN" GAME

It will surprise few readers to note that the American brand of football grew out of permutations developing between association football or soccer and rugby in the mid- to late 1800s. Americans best enjoyed sports they could somehow claim as their own. The variation of football that rooted itself in many college and high school campuses, as well as parks and playgrounds throughout the United States and its colonies by 1900 could boast of its distinctiveness from either association football or rugby.[39]

American football in 1900 was often a brutal affair. This was the case even though it was substantially played by white young men possessing middle- and even upper-class backgrounds. More violent competitive sports such as prize fighting were typically left to those on the lower rungs of the socioeconomic ladder—those who might consider risking their bodies for a chance at economic gain and at least local celebrityhood. However, thanks to the jeremiads of economically privileged and politically influential spokespersons of American masculinity such as Theodore Roosevelt, American football was widely seen to challenge the manliness of white middle- and upper-class young males. Destined for relatively pampered lives, Roosevelt and his fellow travelers argued, these males needed toughening up if they were going to face off against wily Filipino guerilla fighters trying to stave off American imperialism or immigrant anarchists seeking to unleash an angry American working class.[40]

Yet even Roosevelt was appalled by the fierceness in which middle- and upper-class young men broke each other's limbs and heads on gridirons throughout the United States. He and other reformers called for modifications in the game to limit injuries. Such practices as the flying wedge which cut through defenders like a lawn mower were eliminated. However, the game still encouraged eleven young men on the side to essentially pound each other into submission in part because of Walter Camp, arguably the father of modern American football. A creator of many of the rules that distinguished the American version of football, Camp strongly believed in the controlled mayhem which sent thousands to watch Harvard take on Yale and thousands more to risk their bodies on various gridirons throughout the American empire.[41]

It was not just the violence that provoked critics of American football. The cavalier way in which educational institutions used the sport to promote student body unity and enhance their treasuries proved just as worrisome. Athletes were recruited for their football talents alone. If they bothered to show up in classrooms, that was all well and good but it was not exactly mandatory. Moreover, by the early 1900s, professional coaches were hired to make sure the varsity eleven would bring pride and profits to the old alma mater.[42]

Decades before the NFL grabbed a hold of Americans' pocketbooks, colleges that promoted football offended those who believed that the promotion of elite sports should not be that high on an educational institution's agenda. That cranky social theorist, Thorstein Veblen, was not alone in wondering if college football had distorted that agenda while luxuriating in and helping to foster what Veblen described as "conspicuous consumption."[43]

One hundred years later, critics of American football are fighting many of the same battles, and thanks to the cultural dominance of the NFL, at a greater disadvantage. Yet reformers then and more recently have achieved some success in shedding light on the dangers of the sport. In the early 1900s, this meant changes in the way the game was played. That is, prior to reform, football stressed massive confrontations between offensive and defensive lines. To be sure, speed, quickness, and agility mattered but not as much as large men pounding each other into submission. After reform, the game was eventually opened up, and while strength of muscle and speed would remain important, so did deception and what once was considered sacrilegious in pre-reform football— multiple formations, laterals, reverses, end runs, and forward passes.[44]

The game could still be dangerous to bones, ligaments, tendons, and brain tissue, but the changes helped football to become "King Football," a more dashing, rambunctious sport that fit the needs of a bursting American consumer culture between the wars better than the frequently ponderous game that often prevailed a few decades earlier. In the process, the game became more accessible to male athletes who might be no larger than the typical American man but swifter and nimbler. In other words, the game, even played at its highest level at the time, could welcome Asian Americans and Native Hawaiians, relatively ordinary and even smaller in size.[45]

In many ways, football developed during the middle decades of the twentieth century into a different game than it is now. In the first place, the game did not embrace specialization to the extent it does in the late 1900s and early 2000s. From high school to the pros, players had to compete on both offense and defense. The most publicized gridders were often lauded as "triple threats"—that is, they could carry, pass, and kick the ball with skill. In many cases, one could add to their résumés pass catching, blocking, defensive, and play calling talents. Multiple offensive formations were installed by creative coaches such as Knute Rockne, Glenn "Pop" Warner, and Clark Shaughnessy. The role of the quarterback would vary depending on which formation was used. In the single and double wing formations, the quarterback would stand behind the guard and bark signals, as well as often call the plays in the huddle. The center would then snap the ball a few yards away to a tailback or fullback, who would then initiate the play by handing the ball off to another backfield member, pass the ball, or run with it. The quarterback often then served as an extra blocker, although he might also eventually get the ball on a handoff or a pass. In the T-formation, which gained ascendancy in football in the 1940s and 1950s, the center snapped the ball back to a quarterback squatting closely behind him. Along with his duties of play and signal caller, the quarterback in the T-formation became the primary ball handler—lateraling, handing, and passing it off to others, while occasionally carrying the ball himself. Meanwhile, the quarterback no longer was considered a primary blocker.

Other positions experienced transformations. Offensive guard play, during the heyday of the single and double wing, called for what famed coach Knute Rockne called "watch charm guards"—that is, guards who could lead blockers down field. This meant that guards often had to be as swift as backfield members. Indeed, guards might find themselves switched to quarterback or fullback, as well as vice versa. However, as the T-formation became more engrained and more dependent upon the pass to advance the ball, the role of the guard changed. This was especially the case with the development of the split-T formation in which one halfback was flanked off to the sideline, providing less protection from linemen determined to "sack" quarterbacks dropping back to pass. Guards, then, needed to become larger without, hopefully, losing the athleticism which would allow them to pull in front of the ball carrier as the latter swept around end.

As a game, football seems more democratic in some ways in the mid-twentieth century than in the last few generations. That is, it seems to have been more accessible to ordinary men, possessing relatively ordinary bodies. Perhaps, that is why so many not very large Asian American and Pacific Islander men were attracted to the sport. It helped to stand six feet tall or more, as well as be as close to two hundred pounds as possible, but one could start and star for high school and even college teams and be smaller. Nevertheless, football's inclusiveness was limited. It may not have mirrored the social distinctions present in American society historically and persisting today. It may have even blurred those distinctions when it came to race, ethnicity, and class. But those distinctions remained and were often reinforced to shadow the participation of Asian and Pacific Islanders as they played, coached, and watched American football.

NOTES

1. http://www.heismancentral.com/ (December 19, 2014).
2. http://www.sportingnews.com/ncaa-football/story/2014–12–13/marcus-mariota-heisman-trophy-winner-speech-oregon-ducks-video (December 19, 2014).
3. A son of Taiwanese immigrants who settled in California's Silicon Valley, Jeremy Lin led his Palo Alto High School basketball team to a state championship. Despite being an all-state backcourt standout, he did not receive a single Division 1 scholar-

ship offer. Not even neighboring Stanford was interested. Lin then went on to Harvard, where he played well but went undrafted by the NBA. After a good showing in the NBA summer league, Lin was signed for the 2010–2011 season by the Golden State Warriors, who generally kept him on the bench when he was not shipped out to the franchise's Development League team. Many thought that Lin's signing was merely a publicity stunt to attract Asian American support for the Warriors—a notion seemingly supported when Lin was cut by the Bay Area team before the 2011–2012 season. Subsequently, the Houston Rockets passed on Lin, but the New York Knicks, desperate for background depth, signed Lin and accorded him generally the same kind of treatment the Warriors did a year earlier. However, injuries thinned out an already lean Knicks roster and Lin was pressed into action. Over the next several weeks, Lin surpassed everyone's expectations by consistently scoring significantly over double figures and dishing out many exciting passes for assists.

That Lin was doing all this in the media center of New York, starved for an exciting NBA presence, inspired the media heat of "Linsanity." Meanwhile, many Asian Americans found inspiration in Lin's stereotype-busting performances, while some others used the occasion to racially deprecate Lin.

Since then, Lin has moved on to other teams, demonstrating that he is not the superstar that "Linsanity" seemed to promise, on the one hand, and the bust that his critics predicted. He has turned out to be a good and sometimes great guard, performing well, as of this writing, for the Brooklyn Nets. Lin, while hardly a social activist, is convinced that race has shadowed his experiences in NCAA and NBA basketball. Indeed, he has seemingly had to cope with racialized insults belittling him as an overachieving, intelligent young man who would be better served sitting behind a computer than driving the lanes. He has been accused of lacking the toughness and athleticism to compete with the greatest basketball players in the world, while often fearlessly taking the ball to the hoop as defenders pound his body and referees forget they have whistles. Joel S. Franks, *Asian American Basketball: A Century of Sport, Community and Culture* (Jefferson, NC: McFarland & Company, Inc., Publishers, 2016), 223–231.

4. http://www.apiidv.org/resources/census-data-api-identities.php#identities (December 22, 2014).

5. My discussion of Asian migration to the United States is largely based on Ronald Takaki, *Strangers from a Different Shore: A History of Asian Americans*, (Boston: Little Brown, 1998). Among the many other fine works of Asian American history, I have consulted are Takaki, *A Different Mirror: A History of Multicultural America* (Boston: Back Bay Books, 2005); Helen Zia, *Asian American Dreams: The Emergence of an American People* (New York: Farrar, Straus & Giroux, 2001); Sucheng Chan, *Asian Americans: An Interpretive History* (Boston: Twayne, 1991); Shelley Sang-Hee Lee, *A New History of Asian America* (New York: Routledge, 2014); Gary Okihiro, *American History Unbound: Asians and Pacific Islanders* (Berkeley and Los Angeles: University of California Press, 2015).

6. Ibid.

7. Ibid.; Jean Pfaelzer, *Driven Out: The Forgotten War against Chinese Americans*, (Berkeley and Los Angeles: University of California Press, 2008). The byzantine way in which the concept of race has been used by the state in America is a paramount theme of Michael Omi and Howard Winant, *Racial Formation in the United States: From the 1960s to the 1990s* (London: Routledge, 1994).

8. Cindy I-Fen Cheng, *Citizens of Asian America: Democracy and Race during the Gold War* (New York: New York University Press, 2013); Ellen D. Wu, *Color of Success: Asian Americans and the Origins of the Model Minority* (Princeton, NJ: Princeton University Press, 2015); Lon Kurashige, *Two Faces of Exclusion: The Untold History of Anti-Asian Racism in the United States* (Chapel Hill: University of North Carolina Press, 2016).

9. Alexander Saxton, *The Indispensable Enemy: Labor and the Anti-Chinese Movement* (Berkeley and Los Angeles: University of California Press, 1971); Omi and Winant, *Racial Formation.*

10. Takaki, *Strangers*; Gary Y. Okihiro, *Island World: A History of Hawai'i and the United States* (Berkeley and Los Angeles: University of California Press, 2008); Sally Engle Merry, *Colonizing Hawai'i: The Cultural Power of Law* (Princeton, NJ: Princeton University Press, 2000); Elizabeth Buck, *Paradise Remade: Politics of Culture and History in Hawai'i* (Philadelphia: Temple University Press, 1993).

11. Bruce Cumings, *Dominion from Sea to Sea: Pacific Ascendancy and American Power* (New Haven and London: Yale University Press, 2009), 126–157; Paul A. Kramer, *The Blood of Government: Race, Empire, the United States & the Philippines* (Chapel Hill: University of North Carolina Press, 2006); Gerald Gems, *Sport and the American Occupation of the Philippines: Bats, Balls, and Bayonets* (Lanham, MD: Lexington Books, 2016).

12. http://www.seattleglobalist.com/2012/07/23/samoans-in-seattle-sue-feds-for-citizenship/5580 (July 28, 2015); Paul Spickard, Joanne L. Rondilla, and Debbie Hippolite Wright, (eds.) *Pacific Diaspora: Island Peoples in the United States and Across the Pacific* (Honolulu: University of Hawai'i Press, 2002).

13. Cumings, *Sea to Sea*, 407.

14. Amy Cooper, "Tongan Americans," http://www.everyculture.com/multi/Sr-Z/Tongan-Americans.html (May 9, 2016).

15. Ibid.

16. Gaye Theresa Johnson, *Spaces of Conflict, Sounds of Solidarity: Music, Race, and Spatial Entitlement in Los Angeles* (Berkeley: University of California Press, 2013); Elijah Anderson, *The Cosmopolitan Canopy: Race and Civility in Everyday Life* (New York: W. W. Norton, 2012).

17. Robert H. Wiebe, *Self-Rule: A Cultural History of American Democracy* (Chicago: University of Chicago Press, 1995).

18. C. L. R. James, *Beyond a Boundary* (Durham, NC: Duke University Press, 1993); Gerald Gems, *The Athletic Crusade: Sport and American Cultural Imperialism* (Lincoln: University of Nebraska Press, 2006).

19. Gloria Anzaldua, *Borderland/La Frontera; The New Mestiza* (San Francisco: Spinsters/Aunt Lute, 1987).

20. Edward Said, *Orientalism* (New York: Vintage Books, 1979).

21. David B. Welky, "Viking Girls, Mermaids, and Little Brown Men: U.S. Journalism and the 1932 Olympics," *Journal of Sport History*, 24 (Spring, 1997): 24–49.

22. Renato Rosaldo, *Culture and Truth: The Remaking of Social Analysis* (Boston: Beacon Press, 1989), 68–69.

23. Ty P. Kāwika Tengan and Jesse Makani Markham, "Performing Polynesian Masculinities in American Football: From 'Rainbows to Warriors,'" *International Journal of the History of Sport*, 26 (2009): 2416.

24. R. W. Connell, *Gender and Power: Society, the Person, and Sexual Politics* (Palo Alto, CA: Stanford University Press, 1987; Kristin L. Hoganson, *Fighting for American Manhood: How Gender Politics Provoked the Spanish-American and Philippine-American Wars* (New Haven: Yale University Press, 2000); Gail Bederman, *Manliness and Civilization: A Cultural History of Gender and Race in the United States, 1880–1917* (Chicago: University of Chicago Press, 1996); Clifford Putney, *Muscular Christianity: Manhood and Sports in Protestant America, 1880–1920* (Cambridge, MA: Harvard University Press, 2003).

25. Sally Jenkins, *The Real All-Americans: The Team That Changed a Game, a People, a Nation* (New York: Doubleday, 2007).

26. Linda España-Maram, *Creating Masculinity in Los Angeles's Little Manila* (New York: Columbia University Press, 2006); Kathleen S. Yep, *Outside the Paint: When Basketball Ruled at the Chinese Playground* (Philadelphia: Temple University Press, 2009); Samuel O. Regalado, *Nikkei Baseball: Japanese American Players from Immigration and Internment to the Major Leagues,* (Champaign: University of Illinois Press, 2013); Richard C. King, (ed.) *Asian American Athletes in Sport and Society* (New York and London: Routledge, 2015).

27. Putney, *Muscular Christianity*.

28. Ibid.

29. Ibid.; Dominick Cavallo, *Muscles and Morals: Organized Playgrounds and Urban Reform, 1880–1920* (Philadelphia: University of Pennsylvania Press, 1981); Steven Riess, *City Games: The Evolution of American Urban Society and the Rise of Sport* (Champaign: University of Illinois Press, 1991).

30. Putney, *Muscular Christianity.*

31. Michael Oriard, *Reading Football: How the Popular Press Created an American Spectacle* (Chapel Hill: University of North Carolina Press, 1998); *King Football: Sport and Spectacle in the Golden Age of Radio and Newsreels, Movies and Magazines, the Weekly and Daily Press* (Chapel Hill: University of North Carolina Press, 2001).

32. Putney, *Muscular Christianity*; Gems, *The Athletic Crusade*; Gems, *Sport and the American Occupation*; Robert Elias, *The Empire Strikes Out: How Baseball Sold U.S. Foreign Policy and Promoted the American Way Abroad* (New York: New Press, 2010).

33. Ibid.; James, *Beyond a Boundary.* Joel S. Franks, *The Barnstorming Hawaiian Travelers: A Multiethnic Baseball Team Tours the Mainland* (Jefferson, NC: McFarland & Company, Inc., 2012).

34. Joel S. Franks, *Crossing Sidelines, Crossing Cultures: Sport and Asian Pacific American Cultural Citizenship* (Lanham, MD: University Press of America, 2009); William V. Flores and Rina Benmayor, (eds.) *Latino Cultural Citizenship: Claiming Identity, Space, and Rights* (Boston: Beacon Press, 1997); James, *Beyond a Boundary.*

35. Pierre Bourdieu, *Distinction: A Social Critique of the Judgement of Taste*, Translated by Richard Nice (Cambridge, MA: Harvard University Press, 1984); Joel S. Franks, *Asian American Basketball*; Kathleen Yep, *Outside the Paint.*

36. Takaki, *Strangers*; *A Different Mirror*; http://www.census.gov/population/www/documentation/twps0029/tab02.html (May 16, 2015).

37. Takaki, *Strangers*, chapter 11; http://www.asian-nation.org/model-minority.html (August 13, 2015).

38. Tengan and Markham, "Performing."

39. Julie Des Jardins, *Walter Camp: Football and the Modern Man* (New York: Oxford University Press, 2015); Oriard, *Reading Football.*

40. Hoganson, *Fighting*; Bederman, *Manliness.*

41. Des Jardins, *Walter Camp*, 179–180.

42. John Sayle Watterson, *College Football* (Baltimore: Johns Hopkins University Press, 2000); Ronald S. Smith, *Sports and Freedom: The Rise of Big-Time College Athletics* (New York: Oxford University Press, 1988).

43. Thorstein Veblen, *Theories of the Leisure Class* (New York: Oxford University Press, 2009).

44. Des Jardins, *Walter Camp.*

45. Michael Oriard, *King Football.*

ONE

Community Football

Cultural analyst Raymond Williams once wrote that community is a "warmly persuasive word" deployed to describe all sorts of social relationships. Indeed, political theorist Benedict Anderson has called nations "imagined communities." Marcus Mariota, calling out his "boys" back home in Hawai'i, was representing the Polynesian diaspora as an "imagined community." In this chapter, localized ethnic communities surface as the focus. That is, the chapter will examine the interaction of football and the Chinatowns and Little Tokyos, largely found on the West Coast of the U.S. mainland. A product of racial segregation, on the one hand, and the desire of immigrants to re-create their homelands as much as possible, these enclaves emerged as ethnic islands surrounded by a sea of racialized nativism.[1]

Team sports have furnished minority ethnic groups with a sense of community by linking people together across class, gender, political, spiritual, and other social and cultural differences. Gyms, playgrounds, baseball diamonds, and football fields have offered minority community participants a sense of spatial entitlement—that for a while they could claim autonomy from oppression and exploitation while dribbling basketballs and catching footballs. More concretely, team sports have accorded minority community participants with opportunities to enjoy something that they might not otherwise get to outside of that community. Team sports, in the process, have helped erect cultural bridges between ethnic and nonethnic communities, to share in the benefits of competing under a cosmopolitan canopy. Moreover, since we are discussing competition, team sports have reinforced cultural citizenship when minority community teams performed well against other ethnic or nonminority group's community teams—a community pride enhanced when an individual from the minority community achieved mainstream success and local or even widespread fame in a sport.[2]

By the early twentieth century, people of Asian and Pacific Islander descent were playing football throughout the U.S. empire. As a community endeavor, however, football did not gain as much support among Asian and Pacific Islander ethnic groups or, for that matter, any other largely working-class or lower middle-class, urban-based ethnic group as basketball or even baseball. In the first place, the game required space in which to play. Gaining access to one hundred yards of space on which athletes could punt, pass, tackle, and run was not easy in Honolulu, San Francisco, or New York City. Moreover, given the physical character of football, the playing field was expected to be grassy enough to absorb the blows of hard tackles or blocks. Getting knocked down on concrete or asphalt rarely seemed all that attractive, although touch and flag football proved something of a substitute for children. Second, if participants were bound and determined to tackle and block one another, they were going to have to outfit themselves with relatively expensive protective equipment—equipment that may seem laughably unsophisticated to twenty-first century football fans in the United States but still was expected in the early twentieth century to minimize dangerous head and other injuries. While Asian Hawaiians and indigenous Hawaiians found cleats and pads optional, North Americans generally needed shoes that offered not only protection but warmth and traction in the fall and early winter. Third, if community football was going to reproduce the game as played in myriad schools in the American empire, it would have to lure on to the field eleven players on each side in addition to carrying substitutes in case a participant broke something or got battered in the head a few too many times. Putting together teams of such size in urban ethnic communities could prove difficult, given that most working- and lower middle-class urban youth possessed other responsibilities and other pastimes to take up their time. Nevertheless, creative football lovers took up a six-on-a side variation when prospective participants seemed unavailable.

As team sports, baseball and basketball better suited urban, working- and lower middle-class young people well if those young people had the time and inclination to participate. To be sure, baseball required equipment and relatively large teams but aside from the catcher, no participant needed a great deal of protection. Of course, baseball mandated space and most participants wanted to play baseball on grass—like the big leaguers did—but it could be played on hard surfaces in a pinch. As for basketball, the game was played by five or, if by females, six on a side. It could be played on concrete and asphalt outside, as well as hardwood inside. Uniforms could be T-shirts or blouses and shorts. Accordingly, basketball proved an alluring sport for lower-class urban American youth such as Asian Americans, Italian Americans, and Jewish Americans.

BAREFOOT FOOTBALL

The link between football and community in Hawai'i was forged as much by a sense of place and class as by race and ethnicity; reminding us of the resilience of community. The islands' barefoot football leagues comprise an intriguing case in point. While race and ethnicity have been important markers in Hawai'i, they often merged with class distinctions which frequently threw ethnically diverse people together in various neighborhoods, workplaces, and schools throughout the islands. Working-class areas of Honolulu such as Kalihi, Waipahu, Punchbowl, Kaka'ako, and Palama were represented by barefoot football teams of young men of Portuguese, Native Hawaiian, and Asian descent. The leagues were divided by weight divisions and few of the participants weighed more than 170 pounds. In the 1920s, Hawaiian Japanese journalist George Sakamaki pointed out that "some of the best players in barefoot football, a distinct Hawaiian innovation, are of Japanese descent." In the 1930s, Edwin Burrows asserted that Hawaiian Chinese may have been too small to compete successfully against whites and Native Hawaiians in regular American football. However, he insisted, "they hold their own in the celebrated barefoot leagues." [3]

Barefoot football represented, then, the growth of a transethnic "local culture" among diverse Hawaiians from lower middle- and working-class origins. Historian Franklin Odo has written:

> Barefoot football boasted a long tradition in Hawai'i, with roots probably extending back to sugar-plantation leagues established by management to provide an outlet for the boys and entertainment for themselves. I recall playing in many barefoot games well into high school—we had nothing but old clothes, a football, and a field. Competition was heated and fistfights were not uncommon. Organized barefoot leagues incorporated all the usual football equipment and uniforms except socks and shoes. [4]

Scholar Vicente Diaz confirms the importance of barefoot football for Hawaiian locals.

> Hawaii's barefoot football was a local style of football, multi-"racial" and multi-"cultural" through and through in Honolulu and the rural outskirts. It was also a key player in the emergence of a new, early twentieth-century, multiracial society through the participation of first and second-generation immigrant workers. As such, Honolulu barefoot football also participated alongside the post-overthrow and pre-World War II discourse of Honolulu acculturation and therefore its readiness for (post-war) statehood. [5]

Likewise, Diaz compared barefoot football in Hawai'i to the nurturing of Hawaiian creole or pidgin. Based on the cultivation of sugar and, by the early twentieth century, pineapples, a powerful plantation economy emerged in Hawai'i in the mid- to late nineteenth century. Seeking a hopefully servile labor force, plantation owners and managers recruited thousands of workers from China, Japan, Korea, and the Philippines by 1920. These workers were supplemented by Native Hawaiians, as well as Portuguese and Spanish immigrants frequently employed as *lunas* to supervise non-European laborers. As scholars such as Ronald Takaki have pointed out, plantation management hoped to use ethnic rivalries to divide and control their labor forces and their strategy worked reasonably well in mitigating, if not entirely, eliminating labor conflict.[6]

Yet even if Hawaiian, interethnic, interracial working-class militancy did not approach its full potential until after World War II, non-white, mostly Asian and Hawaiian, laborers and their offspring were difficult to control. They socialized with one another. They married and raised multiethnic families. They moved away from the plantations and congregated in multiethnic neighborhoods of Honolulu and the other more populated areas of the islands. Creole Hawaiian made much of this possible.[7]

Fostered on the Hawaiian plantations, docks, and the working-class neighborhoods of Honolulu and the islands' larger towns, creole Hawaiian developed as a linguistic bridge linking different ethnic groups. Rooted in various languages such as English and Hawaiian, creole Hawaiian helped solidify Hawai'i's multiethnic "local culture." Nevertheless, Diaz did not want to overemphasize the grassroots foundations of barefoot football, which, he argued, still owed a great deal to "American imperialism through the determination of the military."[8]

Scholars Ty Kāwika Tengan and Jesse Makani Markham point out that barefoot football "developed as a site for the performance of a rugged 'local' working class masculinity that Asian American and Native Hawaiian young men laid special claim to. Football was simultaneously a site for the demonstration of American assimilability and a field for eschewing haole [white] domination."[9]

Historian Lauren Morimoto's Ph.D. dissertation is the best single scholarly source on Hawaiian barefoot football. Focusing on the island of Kaua'i, Morimoto argues that barefoot football grew out of diverse factors. For Hawaiians, barefoot football was substantially a matter of "cultural norms, familiarity, and financial need." The children of Kaua'i's plantation workers typically went barefoot, in large measure because of the climate but also because shoes cost more money than they had.[10]

Kaua'i's plantation and cannery management also played a role in cultivating barefoot football. Fearful of labor militancy, Kaua'i's economic elite often deployed organized athletic competition to divert workers from pondering the misery of their working conditions. However, while larger-scale employers may have been willing to finance football leagues to assert a paternalistic relationship with their employees, according to Morimoto, they may have felt that shoes constituted an unnecessary expense given the proclivity of the participants to go shoeless in any event and that those participants tended to be too small to really hurt one another. Accordingly, the uniforms supplied by the plantations and canneries proved often insubstantial. They might include a flimsy helmet that could be folded into competitors' pockets, a T-shirt, and frail shoulder pads if shoulder pads were issued at all. Indeed, some informants told Morimoto they used large grapefruit peels instead.[11]

While Morimoto concedes that barefoot football may have been used by plantation management to offset labor tensions, it was "ultimately a 'local' production." She reminds readers that barefoot gridders expressed pride in representing their communities well. Barefoot football helped nurture the local culture on Kaua'i by recognizing who was "'local,' which had a positive connotation despite its association with those at the lower half of the planation hierarchy." It also helped push participants and supporters across ethnic boundaries. Even though plantation camp housing was largely segregated by ethnicity, labor activist and stellar barefoot football player, Haruo "Dyna" Nakamoto, told Morimoto that "the best thing about barefoot football was that it put him in regular contact with other races."[12]

Weight limits, according to Morimoto, nurtured the relative inclusiveness of barefoot football. Haoles, Hawaiian Portuguese, and indigenous Hawaiians tended to concentrate in the higher weight divisions. However, Hawaiian Japanese clustered in the under 135-pound divisions. When, in 1928, interisland games eventuated between two Kaua'i 135-pound squads and a 135-pound team from Mò'ili'ili in Honolulu, Kaua'i's *Garden Island* noted that nearly all the gridders were *Nikkei*—people of Japanese descent.[13]

Underlying the paternalistic origins of barefoot football on the islands, Morimoto notes, was that initially haoles set up an organization called the Kaua'i Football Association. This organization reflected plantation and cannery hierarchy in that haoles disproportionately held managerial roles on the plantations, while Portuguese Hawaiians were typically *lunas* or overseers. However, Morimoto finds that in the 1930s Japanese and Filipino Hawaiians took on more managerial roles in the organization at a time when field hands and cannery workers were generally Japanese and Filipino. This was especially the case in the 125-pound league. Moreover, during the decade before World War II, the Kaua'i Athletic Union (KAU) assumed much of the organization of barefoot football on the island. KAU members did not always agree on the issue of weight divisions. For example, many wanted greater stress placed on lower weight divisions to accommodate local, mainly Asian, gridders. Morimoto observes, moreover, that at least some of the coaches, possessing Asian ancestry, were plantation workers. Nevertheless, barefoot football allowed them to gain access to leadership positions in the KAU.[14]

Individual barefoot football organizations such as the McBryde Scots paid close heed to local ethnic communities. During the 1930s, the McBryde Scots, staged an "athletic carnival" to help finance the McBryde Plantation's athletic endeavors. To boost Nikkei attendance, the carnival was supplemented with *Ondo* dancing, associated with the late summer *Bon Odori* celebrations held in and near Japanese American communities. Also, to raise money, the Koloa Athletic Association put on a "frolic" in 1939 which included Filipino, Japanese, and Native Hawaiian folk dancing.[15]

Thus, while barefoot football recognized ethnic differences, it sought to transcend those differences as well. In 1938, the Lihu'e Plantation's monthly report claimed that the 115-pound teams were composed "of all nationalities. . . . They play well together and have a good time." Among those competing were boys of Japanese, Filipino, Hawaiian, and Portuguese descent. Moreover, many of the most prominent players and coaches in Kaua'i possessed Asian ancestry.[16]

World War II obviously affected barefoot football on Kaua'i. Significantly, Hawaiian Nikkei generally escaped internment, largely because relocating them would have drastically disrupted Hawai'i's. Still, many Hawaiian Nisei wanted to display their loyalty to the United States and their hatred of European fascism and Japanese militarism. Hawaiian Japanese barefoot players, accordingly, were recruited to join the 100th infantry, which merged with mainland outfits to form the 442nd Regiment, which, in turn, distinguished itself in combat in the European theater of war. In November 1943, one game was dedicated to the memory of Toshiaki "Popeye" Fujimoto, who had previously played for the Koloa Plutes. Fujimoto became Kaua'i's first Japanese American killed in action when he perished in Italy. A couple of weeks later, word reached Kaua'i that another one-time local barefoot gridder, Kairo Naito, had died in action.[17]

After World War II, Kaua'i and other islands were hit by long simmering labor struggles. Seeing its paternalism eventually go unrewarded, the Lihu'e plantation system demonstrated less interest in supporting barefoot football and other athletic endeavors for workers. While some barefooters supported labor militancy, Morimoto points out that others "felt the union disrupted the plantation system, which had been good about meeting the physical and social needs of the workforce. In place of the paternalism that marked the plantation's approach in dealing with labor, the plantation adopted a less 'hands-on,' all-encompassing control of the work force."[18]

Yet while some former barefoot football players point out that the demise of plantation paternalism weakened barefoot football on Kauai, Morimoto posits that up until the last year of the Kaua'i's league existence, in 1955, large crowds showed up for games. In 1948, while labor struggles hit Kauaii's plantations the KAU persísted. In the 135-pound division, union activist Haruo "Dyna" Nakamoto headed the Lihue Plantation AA gridders. Later in life, Nakamoto served as division director for the International Longshoremen's and Warehouse Union. Conceivably, in Nakamoto's case, coaching reinforced his rise to union leadership.[19]

Morimoto maintains there were other factors that eventually stymied participation in barefoot football. She maintains that after World War II more and more Japanese American young men left plantation work. Still, Kaua'i's *Garden Island* reported on league competition consistently through the mid-twentieth century. Moreover, radio stations broadcast games from Kaua'i throughout the islands beginning in 1944 and ceasing in the 1950s. And in December 1955, CBS televised to the mainland a Kaua'i barefoot game. A former barefoot gridder, Taku Akama, provided background information to CBS with the help of other local veterans of barefoot football, Gene Layosa and Mac Kawamua.[20]

Whether inspired by the lack of frigid weather on the islands or the lack of economic privilege, Hawai'i's barefoot gridders proved exciting. Knute Rockne, the legendary Notre Dame coach, visited the islands in 1927 and left impressed with the barefoot athletes. He declared to mainlanders that Hawaiians could easily barefoot kick fifty yards, while local fans regularly jeered participants wearing regulation uniforms. In 1929, an Associated Press (AP) wire story pointed out that without the burden of heavy uniforms and cleats, the barefoot gridders demonstrated speed and dexterity: "Players do spectacular things such as leave their feet to knock runners over."[21]

Prominent journalist Bob Considine visited Hawai'i months before the attack on Pearl Harbor. He noted how much Hawaiians embraced football, whether cleated or barefoot. Considine also observed, "Most of the local teams are made up of a bizarre mixture of races, ranging from the big beautifully pure Hawaiians down to wiry Japanese. . . . They play exceedingly well together, are tough, eager, and clean competitors." Still, while Hawaiians loved sports such as football and were quite willing to buy sports equipment to enhance their enjoyment of various games, Considine wrote, "You can't throw a hunk of coral here without hitting a barefoot gridman. Every available park or vacant lot seems to teem with teams . . . all sizes, nationalities, and shades of dark." Ignoring the class basis for barefoot football, Considine was struck by the skill and sturdiness of its gridders, declaring, "At first blush the islands would seem to be a Utopia for chiropodists." But, Considine enthused, "the barefooters got off prodigious kicks without injuring their feet."[22]

In Honolulu, barefoot games drew relatively large crowds and respectful press coverage from the city's mainstream newspapers. In the late 1920s, the *Honolulu Star-Bulletin*'s sports pages reserved considerable space for barefoot football. If one wanted to find out who was playing barefoot football in Honolulu in 1927, the *Star-Bulletin*'s Loui Leong Hop had to have been a primary source. Representing a working-class neighborhood in Honolulu, the famed and multiethnic Kalihi Thundering Herd, according to Hop, included several key players of Asian and Pacific Islander ancestry. The Kaka'ako Sons, which also originated in a multiethnic, working-class neighborhood, was another notable barefoot contingent.[23]

The coming of World War II to Honolulu could not extinguish barefoot football. One of the more interesting ways in which barefoot teams represented Hawaiian ethnic groups and local culture occurred after the attack on Pearl Harbor. While people of Japanese ancestry on the islands did not face massive relocation, they did encounter widespread suspicion. To help dispel whatever distrust non-Nikkei Hawaiians might have maintained toward them, Hawaiian Japanese young men formed the Varsity Victory Volunteers (VVV) to aid efforts to defend the islands from possible Japanese attacks. The VVV encouraged athletic competition as a way of bolstering the morale of the young men. A magnificent athlete of Chinese and indigenous ancestry, Tommy Kaulukukui served as both an officer and a coach for the VVV. The VVV organized two football teams—one an "unlimited" cleated outfit coached by Kaulukukui and a 130-pound barefoot squad. In heading up the former, Kaulukukui was hailed by one of his players as an "excellent coach [who] believed in conditioning." As for the barefoot contingent, the players took on teams such as the Chow Hounds, Nisei- or second-generation draftees who formed the 1399th Engineering Construction Battalion. On New Year's Day of 1943, the VVV team beat the Chow Hounds, 27–0 at the cavernous Honolulu Stadium. At stake, Franklin Odo writes, was "the mythical Schofield barefoot football championship." Yoshimi Hayashi, a future Hawaiian supreme court justice, was one of the game's stars.[24]

Based in ethnically mixed working-class neighborhoods of Honolulu, as well as plantation fields throughout the islands, barefoot football attracted the pro-labor *Honolulu Record*. Columnist Wilfred Oka informed readers in December 1949 that the Koloa 130-pound team from Kaua'i had been in Honolulu to take on the Chinese Service team. Captained by Bopey Tabuchi, the visitors had won 14–0. Oka was pleased, writing that the Koloa athletes came from "sugar worker families and are all hep to the union movement."[25]

In the 1980s, longtime, working-class Honolulu residents were interviewed by the University of Hawai'i's Ethnic Studies Oral History Project. David Souza was one of those interviewed. Souza played on Kalihi's Thundering Herd contingent. He remembered that in the 1920s Benny Waimau coached the squad, while Frank Anahu played quarterback and Jiro Sato was at guard. Takie Okudara told interviewers he played for a 130-pound squad representing the Kalihi Valley Athletic Club—a team, he purported, that was fervently supported by the Honolulu working-class neighborhood. Okudara recalled that before each game, participants were weighed. He asserted, "If you'd hit 130 pounds . . . you have to sweat it out or sit out." As a Hawaiian Japanese, Okudara was probably typical of the barefoot football player of the post-war era. Eddie Takahara, sportswriter for the Japanese American *Hawaii Herald*, asserted in the early 1950s that most of the players in the lower weight divisions possessed Japanese descent.[26]

CHINESE AMERICAN COMMUNITY FOOTBALL

By permitting and even encouraging community members to play for and support ethnic-based football teams, Asian American ethnic groups asserted cultural citizenship. Through football, they could link their experiences and aspirations to a larger society that was infatuated with football but distrustful of Asian Americans. Through football, as well, they could assert a desire for ethnic community bonding and a sense of ethnic community pride.[27]

Despite the prevalent view that Chinese people held little interest in athletic competition, early twentieth-century diasporic Chinese communities on the U.S. mainland demonstrated a fondness for sports in general and different versions of football. In 1901, the *New York Evening Telegram* observed, "1500 Chinamen Out for Picnic." Engaged in a "Sunday school outing," the celebrants took part in football as well as other enjoyable activities. Within a decade, Chinese Americans in the Bay Area would engage in both American football and rugby.[28]

In the late 1910s, the Kai Kee team surfaced under the leadership of Son Kai Kee, a one-time University of California gridder. During the fall of 1917, the *Oakland Tribune* pointed out that the Oakland Chinese team had just beaten Sacred Heart High School and the San Francisco Chinese elevens. Son Kai Kee led the team even though he remained at Cal. A couple of years later, the *San Francisco Chronicle* reported that the team had trouble finding opponents. Still, the Kai Kee team challenged any squad averaging 145 pounds per player or less. It hoped that a contingent from the "Deaf and Dumb" school in Berkeley might meet its challenge, as well as perhaps a squad of Japanese students from the University of California. Another report, published in the *Oakland Tribune*, asserted that the team managed by "Kai Kee, former University of California pigskinner" sought a game with the best lightweight squad in Vallejo. In the early 1920s, Son Kai Kee organized and coached the Wa Ku football team, which held practices at Davies Field in downtown Oakland and played games at San Francisco's legendary Kezar Stadium.[29]

Across the Bay from Oakland, the Yoke Choy Club organized a football team in San Francisco's Chinatown during the 1920s. Chinese

American historian Thomas Chinn maintained that the Yoke Choy Club promoted Christianity, music appreciation, and athletic competition for young, male Chinese San Franciscans. Its football team opposed other Chinese American elevens in addition to Japanese American squads. In 1931, the Yoke Choy squad competed in the otherwise all European American McNamara Grid League, which scheduled its games at Golden Gate Park.[30]

Early in 1926, a piece in the *San Jose Mercury* announced an impending Chinese New Year's game in San Francisco. Probably taking a cue from what annually occurred on January 1 in Pasadena the event was called the Tournament of Lilies. Reveling in Orientalism, the *Mercury* reported the game would pit an eleven representing San Francisco's Jun Kwan organization against Cal's Chinese Student Club Team. The story promised that thousands of Chinese residents of the Bay Area would show up, while declaring that sportswriters were curious as to whether participants would call signals in English or Chinese and if they would use the "huddle system" in which to determine offensive plays. Nevertheless, the correspondent complained, "With characteristic reticence the participants declined to make this information public."[31]

As it turned out, the Jun Kwan contingent downed Berkeley's "Chinese Gridders," 13–0. Held under rainy skies, the game, readers of the *San Jose Mercury* learned, "gave an interesting Oriental version of how the American gridiron sport should be played." The article stressed that the participants played well, using the cherished huddle system when on offense. But, the *Mercury* asserted, the occasional firecracker popping off lent an exotic air to the contest.[32]

During the decade before U.S. entry into World War I, Chinese Americans evidenced further commitment to representing their communities through football. In 1935, the Chinese Crusaders played out of Oakland. In November of that year, they lost to the Chung Mei Home 100-pound team, 20–2. A few weeks earlier, the latter had shut down the San Pablo Boys' Club, 7–0. According to the *Berkeley Gazette*, the victors played "excellent ball." The *Gazette* added, "Their shift, line play, passing, reverses, kicking, and blocking are extremely interesting." The *Chinese Digest* reported in its December 1937 edition that five hundred people watched the Hip Wo squad whitewash the Chung Wah gridders 24–0 at the Marina Field in San Francisco. The aforementioned Chung Mai Home was represented by decent gridders in the late 1930s. Early in 1938, its 115-pound team beat the Packers, 19–7, at the Chung Mei home's field in El Cerrito. Outside the Bay Area, an eleven called the Panthers represented Sacramento's Chinese American community. The team, the *Chinese Digest*'s Davisson Lee informed readers, barnstormed beyond California's Central Valley. In 1940, a Northern California Chinese Football League played out of San Francisco's Golden Gate Park. The league consisted of elevens such as Sacramento's Black Panthers, Oakland's Young

Chinese, and San Francisco's Unknown Packers, sponsored by China-town's St. Mary's Catholic Church.[33]

The Unknown Packers comprised probably the most famous Chinese American football organization in the San Francisco Bay Area in the years preceding World War II. Organized in the late 1930s, its success demonstrated to the *Chinese Digest* football's appeal Chinese Americans. During the 1937 season, the Packers averaged 130 pounds and won seven games, while losing one. The Packers also had a fine 112-pound team in 1937. Davisson Lee said "Chinatown should be proud" of the squad that had beaten Civic Center, 36–0, the Organized Boys' Club, 33–0, Chung Wah, 19–7, and the Oakland Chinese, 12–8. The Packers not only opposed other Chinese American squads, but beat a Japanese American team, 12–0, inspiring the *Chinese Digest* to regrettably gloat, "Packers 12, Japs 0." The next week, the Packers shut out an eleven of "American lads," who outweighed the victors by five pounds each. The *Digest* boasted that the Packers impressed the "American" spectators.[34]

In Southern California, Los Angeles Chinese Americans also assembled football teams. A onetime Angeleno who had moved to Houston, Texas, Charlie Chan wrote the *Digest* in 1936 that a Los Angeles Chinese eleven had been put together in the early 1930s. He claimed, and the *Digest* confirmed, that he and Joe Yuen coached the squad that nearly beat the "Japanese championship Oliver team."[35]

During the mid- to late 1930s, the Rice Bowl game pitted Chinese American gridders from the Bay Area against Angeleno counterparts. In September 1936, the *Chinese Digest* reported that in Los Angeles Chinese Americans had forged an elite team coached by Cotton Warburton, a former USC football hero, with the assistance of Laurie Vejar, a onetime Notre Dame star. The Bay Area, the *Digest* complained, was slow off the mark in forming a similar elite team of Chinese American gridders.[36]

In October 1936, the Los Angeles Chinese gridders subdued a team from Manual Arts High School. It is difficult to say whether that team was an official varsity or junior varsity squad, but, in any case, the losers were called the Spoilers. A month later, the *Digest* announced that the Chinese Angelenos had blanked a fraternity team from USC, 22–0. In September 1937, the *Los Angeles Times* reported on an impending six-on-a-side matchup between the Los Angeles Chinese and the Los Angeles Cubs.[37]

By the end of 1936, a Bay Area team emerged to challenge the Angelenos. The game, the *Los Angeles Times* declared in December 1936, had become "the Pacific Coast Chinese football championship." The *Times* maintained, "Pasadena has its Rose Bowl—other cities have Sun Bowls, Cotton Bowls, but thanks to the football minded Chinese San Francisco has its Rice Bowl." While Warburton coached the Southern California team in 1936, a lesser known former St. Mary's of Moraga standout, Bill Foster, mentored the Bay Area team. Whether the coaches were volunteers or were paid for their services is unclear. The rival teams, in any event, could call upon the services of experienced gridders such as Ernest Lee, who starred at Hayward High School, played for the San Francisco squad. As it turned out, the Bay Area squad eased past the Angelenos, 6–0. The most exciting play was Charlie Hing's forty-six-yard scamper.[38]

The 1937 Rice Bowl received some, perhaps useful, attention from the *Los Angeles Times*, which still saw the event from an orientalist perspective. In December 1937, the *Times'* sports columnist Bill Henry referred to the Rice Bowl as an "interesting charity game" and an "Oriental fracas" from which "Chinese refugees dip into the proceeds." The *Times* also announced that former Loyola University star halfback Billy Byrnes would referee the "Chinese championship of the Pacific Coast" and that the local "Chinese movie colony" would join the spectators. Indeed, one member of that colony would even play—Roland Got, who had a role in *The Good Earth*, suited up as a fullback for the Chinese Angelenos. Ted Ung, a swift back from Belmont High School, was the Los Angeles team's star. Ung, the U.S. Census manuscript schedules for 1940 disclose, was a lodger in Los Angeles and worked as a butcher. As for the San Francisco eleven, it suited up capable athletes, according to the *Times*. Quarterback Charlie Gunn had been an all-leaguer in high school in the Sacramento area, while George Wong and Harding Leong were all-city linemen in San Francisco and Woodrow Louie had been an outstanding pass receiver at Vallejo High School. The *Times* assured readers that plenty of exoticism would be on hand. It predicted a "spectacular Chinese dragon will dance and parade and a small Chinese New Year's celebration will be in store for the fans." In any event, the *Times* advised, the Los Angeles Chinatown's "Alameda Street gamblers" were wagering on the local eleven.[39]

Based in San Francisco, the *Chinese Digest* extolled the welcome extended to the Bay Area gridders by their Los Angeles counterparts. The visitors were treated to a lunch at the famed Clifton's cafeteria. Then, they were shuttled off to a tour of Twentieth Century Fox, where they saw Chinese American actor Key Luke acting in a movie being shot on set, *Shanghai*. The Bay Area team was subsequently fed a dinner at Los Angeles's Chinatown and given a banquet attended by both squads. And after the game, won by the Bay Area eleven, Frank Young's orchestra serenaded the visitors at a "victory dance."[40]

Early in 1938, the Rice Bowl was played at San Francisco's Ewing Field. Weeks before the game, according to the *Chinese Digest's* H. K. Wong, the Los Angeles Chinese eleven had held a dance at the Wilshire Masonic in order to fund the trip to San Francisco. A wire story announced the upcoming match-up by informing readers that the "Third Rice Bowl" would occur in a "record rainstorm." The author complained that no one seemed to know if the game marked the beginning or end of the football season for Chinese American gridders, but pointed out that the game's proceeds were to help Red Cross workers in war-torn China. The home team won 7–0, thanks to a touchdown scored by Charlie Hing, described in the press as a 150-pound halfback. Several months later, the San Francisco squad shutout the Angelenos, 24–0, in mid-December 1938. The patronizing, orientalist praise of Jack Fong by an *Oakland Tribune* correspondent is noteworthy. Bill Tobitt maintained, "The honorable Jack Fong, a halfback on the San Francisco team, was a scourge of locusts to the red-white-and-blue suited devils from the South."[41]

Clearly, the mainstream press could not always refrain from making light of the Rice Bowl and by extension the ability of Chinese Americans to play football worthy of respect. Writing in February 1938, the *San Francisco Chronicle*'s Bob Stevens declared, "Those little Orientals who ignore the seasons and poo-poo the numbers on the grocer's calendar will haul their honorable selves out to Ewing Field this Saturday afternoon to engage in the most unique football game on the books—The Rice Bowl Business." Nevertheless, Stevens conceded the San Francisco eleven, which he called the "local pigtails," included some fine former high school players.[42]

JAPANESE AMERICAN COMMUNITY FOOTBALL

Historians of Japanese American athletics generally stress baseball and, to a lesser extent, basketball as sports favored in Japanese American communities. Nevertheless, Japanese Americans took up football fervently during the first four decades of the twentieth century. Born from a cohort of immigrants arriving in the United States in the late nineteenth and early twentieth centuries, the *Nisei* or second-generation Japanese residents of the United States matured into adolescents and young adults between World War I and World War II. Many seemingly embraced the idea of forming their own teams on the mainland to represent their ethnic communities while connecting to the larger American society.

During the early decades of the twentieth century, Japanese Americans in the Pacific Northwest organized football teams. In November 1919, the *Seattle Times* reported that "traditional baseball rivals"—the Asahi and Mikados—were going to contest one another at the park operated by the local professional baseball franchise. It announced that "[f]ur will surely fly thick" at the game. Reportedly both teams included former grammar and high school stars—athletes who were light but shifty.[43]

Throughout the 1920s, fired-up Japanese American young men took up football in the Pacific Northwest. In 1921, "the Japanese football team of Portland" traveled to Vancouver, Washington, where it lost to the host Park eleven, 7–0. The next year, a team called the "Japanese students" was scheduled to take on the Woodstock Seniors at the latter's grounds. The *Portland Oregonian* claimed that "[t]his is the first Japanese football team organized in Portland." A few years later, the Japanese Athletic Club eleven visited Portland from Seattle. The *Oregonian* estimated that 2,500 people watched the local Waterfront eleven down the visitors, 13–6. The longshoreman supposedly outweighed the Nikkei squad by fifteen pounds per player. Accordingly, the *Oregonian* surmised, the "Orientals" could not do much on either offense or defense. The next year, the Japanese Athletic Club squad returned to Portland, where it was slated to play the St. John's Bachelors at Wall Street Park. The *Oregonian* averred that "the contest . . . will be out of the ordinary." There were few Nikkei squads in the United States, the *Oregonian* contended, and the Seattleites comprised the only one to gain prominence in the Pacific Northwest.[44]

The late 1920s and early 1930s witnessed more Japanese American community football in the Pacific Northwest. The Nippon Athletic Club squad won "the Japanese football championship of the Northwest" in defeating the Taiyo Club team in November 1927. Played at Seattle's Coast League Park, the game resulted in a 6–0 score, with "Choppy" Minemoto emerging as the big star after scampering for an eighty-yard touchdown. In 1928, two Japanese American elevens, the Nippons and the Taiyos competed in Seattle's Commercial Football League. The *Seattle Times* claimed that a "bitter rivalry" had enveloped the two squads and players cherished a victory in that rivalry as much as a league championship. In any event, by 1930, the Taiyo and Nippon elevens had merged. Playing as the Taiyos, the Seattle team took on the Portland Osei Athletic Club at Portland's Multnomah Stadium "for the Japanese championship of the Northwest." In the mid-1930s, the Taiyo squad participated against whites in Seattle's Commercial League.[45]

Meanwhile, Seattle-based Nikkei gridders participated in the Courier League, initiated in 1929. The *Japanese American Courier* sponsored leagues in baseball, basketball, and football as well, in addition to inviting Chinese ethnic-based teams to compete. In the late 1930s, *Courier* journalist Bill Hosokawa recalled that the league had ceased operating in 1931 because of a lack of interest, but was revived with substantial community support in 1932. However, in 1938, Hosokawa feared that the league was shutting down once again due to community apathy. Although a young man in his twenties at the time, Hosokawa seemed like an old-timer as he recalled the Courier League's "good old days." "The annual Taiyo Red-Waseda Cougar Clash was an event looked forward to and more than just a few fellows lost a lot of sleep thinking about the game the night before. Where is the fight now? Don't the fellows care or are they just (not?) interested in football?" Hosokawa declared that Courier League gridders played because they loved the game, not because they were big stars. Nevertheless, the *Courier*, in mid-October, publicized a community game pitting the Marmots against the University Nippons in a Seattle downpour. The former shut out the latter, 6–0, with running back Paul Uno leading the way.[46]

During the 1920s and 1930s, Japanese American squads sprouted in California. In 1921, "Japanese students" at USC and Stanford planned a football game over Christmas vacation "for the Japanese football championship of the world." In 1930, a team of "Fresno Japanese" headed to San Francisco where they opposed the Chinese American Yoke Choy eleven. One of the Fresno stars was George Domoto, who also played for Fresno State College. In the early 1930s, three hundred people reportedly watched the Fresno Japanese lose to the Showa eleven, 18–0, at San Francisco's Ewing Field. The *Fresno Bee* pointed out that Captain Domoto starred in the losing effort. Down in Santa Cruz County, "1000 rabid fans" watched the "Japanese Kasei football team" lose to the Watsonville Mudhens in what the *Santa Cruz Sentinel* described as a "hard fought game" in Watsonville. In the late 1930s, the *Oakland Tribune* reported on the Sukiyaki Bowl held at the city's Pacific Coast League baseball park on January 1, 1939. The Oakland Tornadoes defeated a team from Brawley, California, 7–0. Former high school standout Moe Domoto was described as the victors' big star and "easily the best back on the field." [47]

Prior to World War II, some of the best Japanese American squads in California were the Berkeley Niseis, Los Angeles Olivers, and Los Angeles Spartans. In 1947, the Japanese American *Pacific Citizen* remembered these teams were not big, but fast. Most of the second-generation players possessed some kind of high school experience. A few might have played in college, but by and large participants were deemed too small for college football. The *Pacific Citizen* lamented that such teams had died out partly because the Nisei were too old to play football while the *Sansei*, or third generation, were too young. [48]

CHINESE VS. JAPANESE AMERICANS

Intriguingly, Japanese and Chinese mainlander teams had been lining up against one another since the early 1900s. Early in January 1909, the *San Francisco Call* published a photograph of members of a team representing Bay Area Chinese called the Imperials and another of their rooters. The occasion was a game pitting the Imperials against a local Nikkei eleven called the Fujis. Played at Oakland's Freeman Park, the game ended in a 10–0 victory for the Imperials. Journalist T. P. Magilligan pronounced the event the first contest of its sort on the West Coast, and declared the Imperials winners because they played an "intrepid and courageous game." [49]

Magilligan exoticized the participants. Referring to writer Bret Harte's famed "The Heathen Chinee'," Magilligan maintained, "Those 11 young Chinese proved Bret Harte's assertions about ways that are dark and tricks that are vain for when they were apparently centering their attentions on rugged center bucks the ball would be quickly passed to Herbert

Chan, and that oocher [sic] youth would circle the end and lope for a 20 or 30-yard gain with the grace and precision of a young gazelle." As for the Fujis, Magilligan was much less enthusiastic. In need of a thesaurus, he called their performance "cold and solid" and their tactics "coldly quiet and suave." Evincing "the chill suavity of ice," they lacked the "abandon and intrepity [sic]" that their opponents featured. Magilligan said the game was fairly played. Unfortunately, he maintained, one Fuji player nearly marred the affair by laying low the Imperial quarterback with "jiu jitsu."[50]

Magilligan estimated that four hundred Imperial rooters showed up to back the victors. He claimed they were as enthusiastic as a college rooting section. Led by a passionate "Yell Leader," they were even-handed enough to render three cheers for the Fujis at the game's outset. The Imperial's rooting section, Magilligan noted, displayed "many pretty little maids of the celestial empire with the soft tinkle of the orient in their voices." Magilligan's condescending yet more complimentary perspective on the Imperials as compared to the Fujis may have reflected that thanks to the Chinese Exclusion Act, the relative diminishing numbers of Chinese immigrants and their offspring no longer represented all that much of a threat to white San Franciscans. Instead, Japanese immigrants were increasingly perceived as representing a more substantial yellow peril, given Japan's growing threat to U.S. imperial ambitions in the Asian Pacific region and the swelling, rancorous calls for Japanese exclusion on the West Coast.[51]

Late in 1909, the *San Francisco Call* acknowledged that "the oriental sports of San Francisco" had engaged in both American football and rugby. However, it added that rugby was growing more attractive because American football proved too rough for "the little brown men." Still, Asian American athletes were practicing assiduously and showing improvement in American football. They would, moreover, play against one another in a game pitting the Chinese "Imperials" against the Japanese Fuji Club in a "battle of nation against nation." A few days later, an AP report published in the *Los Angeles Times* informed readers of a "slit-eyed game" in San Francisco between Japanese Americans and Chinese Americans. The story was headlined "Chino-Jap Footballists" and sub-headlined "Mikado Men Win, but the Chinks Swipe the Ball." The game was reputedly ruined by violence in which players and "oriental spectators" took part. The melee, according to the AP account, was initiated by the Imperials running off with the ball after the game even though the Fuji eleven won, 10–0. In the aftermath, the Fuji team's captain said he was done with playing football against the Chinese. Interestingly, both teams proposed that any future games between them eventuate under rugby rules.[52]

During the 1930s, games between Chinese and Japanese American elevens were often emotionally charged by events in Asia. In San Francisco, the Soko Athletic Club eleven opposed a Chinese American squad in a series of games—the "original" Rice Bowls. These games were well played and publicized, according to both the *Chinese Digest* in the 1930s and the *Pacific Citizen* in the 1940s They occurred regularly until Asia erupted in warfare between Japan and China over Manchuria. Indeed, a story published in the *Washington Post* asserted late in 1931 that the "Japanese-Chinese football game" scheduled for San Francisco on December 13 had been cancelled because of the war clouds gathering over Manchuria. The *Brooklyn Daily Eagle* briefly editorialized about the cancellation, claiming it was due to the fear of excessively aggressive play. The game's cancellation was unfortunate, the *Eagle* opined because both teams were comprised of U.S.-born players who ought to have been "broadminded Americans."[53]

In 1933, the rivalry resumed as the bitterness emanating from the Manchurian war somewhat abated. Neglecting that most, if not all, participants were U.S. citizens, Buddy Leitch, a columnist for the *San Jose News*, asserted, "It is said to be quite amusing to hear the Chinese quarterback call American football signals in his lingo." Leitch, accordingly, found exoticism in the way the Chinese played football, but he admitted, it was no stranger than seeing Americans try their hand at rugby. He added that when Japanese and Chinese Americans confronted each other on the gridiron, the rooting sections were "colorful" and everyone showed up from both communities.[54]

A wire story printed in Nebraska's *Lincoln Star* told readers about the upcoming game between Bay Area Japanese and Chinese American elevens in 1933. It pointed out that Charlie Chan, "a rugged youngster from a local high school," urged patience to his Chinese American teammates. He cautioned them to "wait for mistake—then act." G. Ichiyasu, an "ace end" for the Nikkei squad, was depicted as urging his teammates to be aggressive. While perhaps accurate in reporting Chan's and Ichiyasu's advice, it seems just as likely that the piece was playing off emerging stereotypes of Chinese and Japanese people in light of the war in Manchuria. In other words, Chinese were increasingly represented as quiet, dignified people representing a beleaguered nation that seemingly posed no threat to U.S. interests in the Pacific region, while Nikkei were increasingly perceived as belligerent surrogates for a militaristic Japan.[55]

The Japanese American gridders edged the Chinese Americans in the 1933 Bay Area game, 13–12. Afterward, the losers' team manager, James Lum, threatened to resign and leave San Francisco. Making life more miserable for Lum was that many Chinese San Franciscans had opposed the game because of hostilities in Asia. A former white Cal star, Benny Lom coached the Chinese Americans and claimed that the game was actually a tie after his team achieved a successful conversion after touchdown. However, game officials disagreed that the conversion attempt succeeded and awarded the victory to the Nikkei aggregation. Perhaps out of protest that Chinese Americans should bother with a game against Nikkei, the game itself drew a disappointing number of spectators from the Chinese community and only about eighteen of Lom's original thirty-three players appeared. Lom subsequently announced he would no longer coach the Chinese Americans.[56]

Despite the bitterness the ethnic football rivalry seemingly engendered, Japanese Americans continued to take on Chinese Americans in California. Late in 1934, the *Nevada Journal* printed a photograph of a squad of "Japanese Gridiron All-Stars" scheduled to meet the "Chinese All-Stars" at San Francisco's Kezar Stadium. Tommy Glover, a former Stanford gridder, coached the Nikkei squad. As far away as Cleveland, newspaper readers learned about the rivalry between the Chinese American and Japanese American squads in the Bay Area. The *Cleveland Plain Dealer* in November 1934 ran a photograph of coach Benny Lom, apparently reconciled to coaching Chinese Americans again and pictured with the Chinese American team mascot, a young boy, as well as captain Charlie Hing. Down in Los Angeles, a Chinese American eleven tied a Japanese American team from Pasadena, 6–6. The *Chinese Digest* correspondent complained that not only was the game ragged but that the coach of the Nikkei squad refereed unfairly by calling key penalties on the Chinese American gridders.[57]

Outside of the Bay Area and Los Angeles, Japanese and Chinese Americans played each other. Interestingly, within a week of the attack on Pearl Harbor, a United Press International (UPI) story reported, "oriental rivalries forgotten" when Nikkei and Chinese Americans met in Sacramento's version of the Rice Bowl. The game went on without a hint of turmoil, ending in a tie.[58]

COMMUNITY FOOTBALL DURING WORLD WAR II

During World War II, over 100,000 Japanese Americans from the West Coast were interned in ten concentration camps. In those camps, Japanese Americans engaged in a variety of sports. Much has been written about how baseball bonded people stuck behind barbed-wire fences through no fault of their own. However, given the emergence of "King Football" in American life between the wars, it would be surprising if Japanese Americans did not use football to forge community ties as well.

Before internment in concentration camps, West Coast Japanese Americans were taken to assembly centers, typically fairgrounds and horse race tracks. An August 1942 edition of *Look* magazine published a photo of Japanese American youngsters playing football at the assembly center established at Southern California's Santa Anita Race Track, dubbed "Japanita" by an excessively clever writer. Many of those previously assembled at Santa Anita wound up in Manzanar, where eight-on-a-side football was played in September 1942. Camp authorities insisted that touch football would prevail, arguing that tackle football led to "unsurmountable" injuries. Japanese American recreation leaders cut down the wood themselves for the goalposts.[59]

The Poston camp was in Arizona. There, inmates played plenty of intercamp football. So many boys engaged in "sandlot football," the inmate-run *Poston Chronicle* maintained, that Dr. John Power, who oversaw the camp's Community Management Division, called for curbs on the sport to avoid injuries. Moreover, the camp's high school squad featured several gridders who formerly played prep football. Meanwhile, a nine-on-a-side touch football program was assembled for teenagers.[60]

In Wyoming, the Heart Mountain camp held Japanese Californians from Los Angeles and Santa Clara counties. Soon after arrival at the camp in 1942, internees organized a six-on-a-side football league. Late in September 1942, the *Heart Mountain Sentinel*, which like newspapers in other camps, was run by internees, announced that the Santa Clara Panthers and the San Jose Yankees would meet each other on a newly constructed field in a six-on-a-side game. A month later, the newspaper reported that a league was forming with San Jose Japanese American, Lincoln Kimura, in charge. Among the gridders available was Tosh Asano, a great Southern California junior college player prior to World War II. Asano starred in a Thanksgiving 1943 game between the Center All-Stars and the Jackrabbits. Before two thousand spectators, Asano's Center All-Stars squad blanked the losers 19–0.[61]

A high school was established for Heart Mountain teenagers. Subsequently, Heart Mountain High School assembled football teams that played the regulation eleven-on-a-side game. These teams would take on high schools in the general vicinity of the camp. In early October 1943, the *Sentinel* informed readers that their high school eleven was favored against Montana's Red Lodge squad. The team's big star was Los Angeles tailback, Babe Nomura, who pitched the winning touchdown pass in the previous game against Worland High. During the fall of 1943, the high school squad edged a team of adult all-stars culled from the ranks of Heart Mountain internees with Babe Nomura leading the way. In two years of competition, the Heart Mountain High team went undefeated and unscored upon, demonstrating ethnic pride but also the ability of Japanese Americans to master "King Football" to non-Japanese Americans.[62]

Idaho's Minidoka camp housed internees generally from the Pacific Northwest. In the fall of 1942, the *Pacific Citizen* reported that football was taking over the camp. Interest in the sport seemed spurred by the presence of top-notch former prep talent from Seattle, Portland, and Salem, Oregon. The internee-run *Minidoka Irrigator* could not restrain its excitement about the gridiron prospects at the camp. Thanksgiving 1943, saw Minidoka celebrate football. Two games were featured that day. One was a six-on-a-side, touch female game between young women from "Area A" and "Area B" counterparts. The second game was an eleven-on-a-side tackle game pitting boy "all-stars" from Area A and Area B. In the fall of 1944, the *Irrigator* reported that "400 chilled but enthusiastic fans" watched to the very end a game between the No Names and the Coal Crews. The newspaper, nevertheless, complained that the field was poorly marked and referees had to be recruited out of the stands.[63]

At the Granada camp in southeastern Colorado, the white physical and health director observed in the fall of 1942 that among the internees were several good football players. But he complained that the camp lacked the equipment and facilities for an effective football program. Nevertheless, among the good football players in the camp was John Yamamoto, a former star at San Diego State. He served as athletic director of the camp in December 1942.[64]

Outside of the camps, many Japanese Americans served in the military. Most famously, Japanese Americans from the mainland and Hawai'i were brought together to fight in the 442nd Regiment, which experienced horrendous battle conditions and a corresponding high fatality rate. After the fighting ended, soldiers in the 442nd enjoyed recreational diversion whenever possible while serving as occupying troops in post-World War II Europe. They engaged in all sorts of athletic competition, including taking on other military units in American football. On Christmas Day 1945, the 442nd gridders edged a previously undefeated regimental team at "Yankee Stadium" in Italy. On New Year's Day, they tied a squad from the 88th Blue Devil Division, 13–13. University of Hawai'i linemen Unkei Uchima and Sadao Watasaki were two of the team's stars.[65]

COMMUNITY FOOTBALL IN COLD WAR AMERICA

After 1945, a post-war ideology aimed at assimilating immigrants and their offspring, and a GI-bill– and Cold-War–aided economy capable of pulling people out of their ethnic enclaves and into the suburbs may have hindered the further development of Asian American community football. Other factors perhaps contributed. For example, American-born Chinese and Japanese community gridders were getting too old for the sport, while their children were too young.[66]

Nevertheless, after World War II, Asian American communities continued to support football teams. Chinese American community football thrived in Philadelphia during and right after World War II. The Yu-Pin Chinese Catholic Club sponsored a football team which went undefeated in the fall of 1945. According to a wire story, the team members ranged in age from twelve to eighteen, while averaging 120 pounds. The team used the T-formation and star quarterback Harry Louie reportedly called signals in a "Chinese dialect" to confuse opponents. A Filipino American organization called the Mangoes competed out of San Francisco. The Mangoes were best known for their exciting basketball teams, but they also fielded football squads. In San Jose, an all-Asian American touch football team won a championship in 1947. The San Francisco Eagles represented San Francisco's Chinese community in 1949, while the Sacramento Chinese organized the Sacramento Panthers. That same year, the *Pacific Citizen* informed readers that the Chicago Indians had entered a semi-professional league in the Windy City. The weekly hailed the Indians as the first all-Nisei eleven organized east of the Rockies. George Kita, who starred at San Diego State and Drake, was on the team.[67]

The China Clippers comprised a relatively well-known community squad in post-World War II Seattle. In late September 1949, the *Seattle Times* introduced the team to readers. It pointed out that no one stole signals from the Clippers because "the glib quarterback" barked signals in Chinese. Hank Haugh, a former Gonzaga star, coached the team sponsored by local businesswoman Ruby Chow. Carrying twenty-two players, the Clippers apparently needed to fill their schedule because a phone number was provided to those teams who wished to oppose them. A few days after the *Times'* article, "Seattle's Oriental football team" shut out Holly Park, 19–0. Clipper Ed Chow tossed two touchdown passes and scored a third. Around the same time, the *Times* published a photograph of team members donating blood to a seriously ill Chinese "war wife," Julie Yip. In November 1956, the *Times* told readers about an upcoming game between the Beacon Hill-based Clippers and the Grizzlies from the Queen Anne section of the city. To be contested at the West Seattle Stadium, the 135-pound league title was at stake and each team had lost but one game out of seven.[68]

Other Pacific Northwest Nikkei community teams surfaced after World War II. On December 5, 1949, the *Seattle Times* published a photograph of a Nisei youth team losing a game against the Ballard Associated Boys' Club. In early October 1951, an eleven representing Nisei veterans in Seattle defeated a squad from the White Center Boys' Club. Charlie Chihara, who had competed for O'Dea High School in Seattle, and Toby Watanabe, a former Franklin High School gridder, starred for the victors. Eddie Sato captained the Adna All-Stars, a Japanese American eleven that beat a Centralia Junior College squad in the fall of 1951. Around the same time, the Nisei-Vets–sponsored squad defeated the Adna All-Stars in Chehalis, Washington.[69]

CONTEMPORARY COMMUNITY GRIDIRON EXPERIENCES

Since the latter decades of the twentieth century, the organization of ethnic-based football teams and leagues declined, especially in comparison to basketball. Yet, in the Minneapolis-St. Paul area, Hmong American women have organized a flag football league in recent years. An agrarian people inhabiting Laos, Hmong collaboration with the United States in the Southeast Asian War put them in the crosshairs of the ultimately victorious Communist forces. Many Hmong attained refugee status in the United States and were dispersed by American authorities to places like Minnesota and Wisconsin. Given their lack of cultural capital, Hmong did not fit the model minority narrative as easily as other Asian immigrants and refugees.[70]

One athlete, twenty-seven-year-old Christine Yang, asserted that she and other participants had been advised in their community that they "should stay in the house and kind of cook." A law student, Yang declared, "[Hmong American] Girls don't usually like to go out and things, and be independent, but flag football gives us independence." Further, it offered participants a sense of community. Yang pointed out that women in her community tended to feel isolated, but flag football "builds a community, and there are role models you can look up to. A lot of our members, we hang out with each other outside of the field, and this is a great opportunity to learn what you can do outside of what you've been taught." Articulating an optimistic perspective on cultural citizenship in the United States, one participant told scholar Chia Youyee Vang, "We play football because we can! This is America. We can do anything we want. It's a free country!"[71]

Since the mid-twentieth century, Asian American communities frequently exhibited affection for football aside from getting themselves bloodied and muddied on various gridirons. Realizing this, professional franchises have not ignored promoting themselves in such communities. In 1949, the San Francisco 49ers sought to extend and sustain a fan base in Chinatown. Only a few years old and seeking to overcome Bay Area sport fans' predilections toward the college game, the 49ers were sparked by Bay Area hero and former Stanford great, Frankie Albert. It was no coincidence then that the clever quarterback appeared at several San Francisco Chinatown functions, including a banquet celebrating young Chinese American athletes.[72]

Recognizing the growing demographic importance of Asian Americans, professional teams reached out to local Asian American communities in the twenty-first century. In October 2008, the Oakland Raiders staged the first-ever NFL "Filipino Heritage game." *Asian Journal* journalist, A. J. Press, commented:

> It was another milestone indeed for the Filipino-American community, as the day itself reaffirmed our existence and significance in the mainstream. We were able to share to Americans and other ethnic groups our culture through the cultural performances given by our Filipino dance groups. We were able to show how we, as a community, unite as one. We believe that there'll be more Filipino Heritage days, nights or

games in the mainstream. First of all, we are a big community that continues to contribute in making this nation a great one. Most of us may still have to learn how to understand American football, but having a whole day to recognize the Filipino community is a total touchdown.[73]

Still, the interactions between Asian American communities and professional football show that the NFL had not entered the much-vaunted era of post-raciality, supposedly ushered in by the election of President Obama. NFL player Richie Incognito was the focal point in 2013 of an investigation leading to the league disciplining him for bullying Miami Dolphin teammate Jonathan Martin. However, this investigation revealed that Incognito and some of his teammates also harassed a trainer of Japanese ancestry. The trainer was abused with verbal harangues referring to him as a "Jap" and a "Chinaman." Upon the anniversary of the Pearl Harbor attack, Incognito and a couple of his teammates wore headbands adorned with the Japanese rising sun emblem and, in a lame exhibition of humor, threatened the trainer that they would avenge "the Day of Infamy."[74]

In 2014, sportswriter Jacob Cruz told readers that controversial pass receiver Rob Gronkowski was enjoying himself at a fan gathering when he noticed a person possessing Asian ancestry wearing his jersey and, perhaps, like most at the gathering inspired by alcohol, enthusiastically dancing. A miked-up Gronkowski announced to the crowd, "They told me he could only cook fried-rice." Unfortunately, Cruz writes, Gronkowski "was not done with his racist remarks as he referred to the guy as 'Leslie Chow.' Chow is the flamboyant character played by Ken Jeong in *The Hangover* movies." Event organizers, aware that they and the Patriots were facing public relations problems, urged partygoers to turn over cell phone footage to them once the festivities ended. As Cruz put it, "I guess the organizers were not successful as Gronkowski's remarks made it to the internet."[75]

On a couple of occasions, the San Francisco 49ers have displayed organizational and personal insensitivity to the large Asian American communities inhabiting the Bay Area. In 2005, the 49ers assembled a training film showing a person "with buck teeth" and speaking "with a mockingly Asian faux accent." Belatedly cognizant of its multicultural fan base, the franchise apologized when Asian Americans in the Bay Area protested. But *Asian Week* columnist Samson Wong insists that the public relations blowback may have been one reason why the 49ers left San Francisco for nearby Santa Clara.[76]

The 49ers tried to mend fences with the Bay Area's Asian American communities. Two town-hall meetings were held, one in San Francisco's Chinatown. Then 49ers president, Dr. John York apologized on behalf of the organization. But some community activists were not mollified. They demanded the 49ers implement, in the words of journalist Bill Picture, "a zero-tolerance policy regarding harassment and discrimination, and in-creased outreach to affected communities in the Bay Area." Yvonne Lee of the Asian and Pacific Islander American Health Forum felt the 49ers believed Asian and Pacific Islander communities in the Bay Area could be easily bought off. She maintained, "This isn't about money. They have a responsibility to know and support their neighbors, just like we've been supporting them. So we need to educate them about the different com-munities they serve, which will require an ongoing commitment from both sides." Hinting at a boycott, the Chinese Progressive Association's Leon Chow said that his organization "wants to see how these changes are implemented and how they're enforced. I want to see the [anti-dis-crimination] language written into the multimillion dollar contracts that the players sign, not just in a handbook. Then I'll believe it."[77]

The threatened boycott did not occur. Yet if Samson Wong is right about a legacy of embittered feelings between at least some Asian Americans and the 49ers, what happened in 2014 did not help. In 2014, the 49ers, playing the first year in Santa Clara's Levi Stadium, found itself ensconced in a controversy surrounding talented but troubled defensive lineman Aldon Smith. According to Wong, the *San Jose Mercury's* Tim Kawakami pushed then 49er head coach Jim Harbaugh to explain what the 49ers were going to do with Smith, after a recent scrape with the law. Harbaugh replied, "You can take bamboo shoots and stick them under my fingernails, and there still wouldn't be any more I could add further to the discussion." Perhaps, it was coincidental that Harbaugh was allud-ing to a torture widely identified with World War II Japanese imperial forces while responding to the Japanese American sports columnist. Wong and others in the Bay Area Asian American communities believed otherwise. At any rate, Wong admitted that Harbaugh had not been near-ly as insulting as Bill Parcells, who, when coach of the Dallas Cowboys in 2004, described tricky plays as "Jap plays."[78]

CONCLUSION

While seemingly not as useful as a community solidifier as baseball and especially basketball for Asian Americans, Asian and Pacific Americans used football to represent their communities. In the case of barefoot foot-ball, not just their ethnic communities, but the multiethnic neighbor-hoods or workplaces in which largely working-class Hawaiians lived and labored. Football could provide them with a claim on spatial entitlement as they briefly took over playing fields throughout the U.S. empire. In the 1930s, San Francisco's Kezar Stadium was the domain of generally white college and high school football players, but during the decade a Chinese American football team played there as well. However briefly, football also ushered them across racial and ethnic boundaries to play with and against whites and other racial and ethnic groups. In the process, Asian Americans could assert a cultural citizenship that both recognized their ethnic distinctiveness and a desire for inclusion in what political theorist Rogers M. Smith has called "a collective civil identity" in the United States—an identity historically denied them.[79]

NOTES

1. Raymond Williams, *Keywords: A Vocabulary of Culture and Society* (New York: Oxford University Press, 1983), 71–72; Benedict Anderson, *Imagined Communities; Reflections on the Origins and Spread of Nationalism* (London: Verso, 1983).

2. Johnson, *Spaces of Conflict*; Anderson, *Cosmopolitan Canopy*; Flores and Benmayor, *Latino Cultural Citizenship*.

3. George Sakamaki, "Japanese Athletes in Hawaii" *Bulletin of the Pan-Pacific Union* (August, 1931), 12; Edward Burrows, *Hawaiian Americans: An Account of the Mingling of Japanese, Chinese, and Polynesian People* (New York: Archon Books, 1970), 83.

4. Franklin S. Odo, *No Sword to Bury: Japanese Americans in Hawai'i During World War II* (Philadelphia: Temple University Press, 2003), 208.

5. Vicente M. Diaz, "Fight Boys, 'till the Last . . . : Islandstyle Football and the Remasculation of Indigeneity in the Militarized American Pacific Islands," in *Pacific Diaspora: Island Peoples in the United States and Across the Pacific*, edited by Paul Spickard, Joanne L. Rondilla, and Debbie Hippolite Wright (Honolulu: University of Hawai'i Press, 2002), 187.

6. Ronald Takaki, *Pau Hana: Plantation Life and Labor in Hawaii, 1835–1920* (Honolulu: University of Hawai'i Press, 1984); Moon-Kie Jung, *Reworking Race: The Making of Hawaii's Interracial Labor Movement* (New York: Columbia University Press, 2010).

7. Ibid.

8. Diaz, "Fight Boys," 187.

9. Tengan and Markham, *Performing*, 2415.

10. Lauren Shizuyo Morimoto, "The Barefoot Leagues: An Oral (Hi)story of Football in the Plantation Towns of Kaua'i" (Ph.D. dissertation, Ohio State University, 2005), 2.

11. Ibid., 3–4, 8, 28.

12. Ibid., 118, 119, 124.

13. Ibid., 4, 24–25.

14. Ibid., 37, 57 67.

15. Ibid., 59, 65.

16. Ibid., 53, 56, 62, 66, 67, 85, 86, 87, 99, 115, 124; U.S. Census Bureau, Kaua'i, 1940, Manuscript Census Schedules, www.ancestry.com, (August 18, 2015).

17. Morimoto, "Barefoot," 77; Takaki, Strangers, 379–406.

18. Ibid., 101, 111.

19. Ibid., 6, 111; Honolulu Record, September 30, 1948; http://thegardenisland.com/news/local/obituaries/obituaries-for-jan/article_87f06d3e-9637–11e4-bc92-fb23a2ae4818.html (July 26, 2016).

20. Morimoto, "Barefoot," 6, 111; *Honolulu Record*, December 8, 1955.

21. *New York Times*, November 17, 1927; *Dallas Morning News*, November 13, 1929.

22. Bob Considine, "Barefooters in Majority in Hawaii," *Springfield Republican*, January 24, 1941.

23. Loui Leong Hop, "Many Stars on Squads, Coaches Working With Teams," *Honolulu Star-Bulletin*, September 27, 1927; Hop, "Thundering Herd to Make Strong Bid for Honors," September 28, 1927; Hop, "Veterans Back with Team," September 29, 1927; October 1, 1927; Hop, "Thundering Herd Wins 6–0 Thriller from Kakaako Sons," October 10, 1927; Honolulu Record, October 31, 1957; U.S Census Bureau, Manuscript

Census Schedules, City and County of Honolulu, 1940, www.ancestry.com (July 10, 2015).

24. Odo, "No Sword," 208–209.

25. *Honolulu Record*, December 22, 1949.

26. Ethnic Studies Oral History Project, Kalihi: Place of Transition, Social Science Research Institute, University of Hawai'i, Manoa, June 1989, vol., 3, 430–432; *Hawaii Herald*, January 3, 1951.

27. Flores and Benmayor, *Latino Cultural Citizenship*.

28. *New York Evening Telegram*, July 29, 1901; *San Francisco Chronicle*, December 23, 1911; Mark Dyreson, *Making the American Team: Sport, Culture, and the Olympic Experience* (Urbana: University of Illinois Press, 1997), 54.

29. *Oakland Tribune*, November 17, 1917; November 2, 1919; *San Francisco Chronicle*, November 14, 1919; Eve Armentrout Ma and Jeung Hui Ma, *The Chinese of Oakland: Unsung Builders* (Oakland: Chinese History Research Committee, 1982), 54.

30. Thomas Chinn, *Bridging the Pacific: San Francisco Chinatown and Its People* (San Francisco: Chinese Historical Society, 1989), 125–128; *San Francisco Chronicle*, December 13, 1931; *San Francisco Examiner*, February 8, 1932.

31. *San Jose Mercury*, February 13, 1926.

32. Ibid., February 14, 1926.

33. *Chinese Digest*, November 22, 1935; December, 1937; February, 1938; October, 1938; January, 1939; *Berkeley Daily-Gazette*, November 9, 1935; Franks, *Crossing*, 122.

34. *Chinese Digest*, January, 1937; December, 1937; October, 1938; January, 1939.

35. *Chinese Digest*, October 9, 1936.

36. *Chinese Digest*, September 4, 1936, 12; September 25, 1936, 13.

37. *Chinese Digest*, October 9, 1936; November 6, 1936; *Los Angeles Times*, September 26, 1937.

38. *Los Angeles Times*, December 20, 1936; *Hayward Review*, December 16, 1936; *Santa Cruz Sentinel*, December 22, 1936.

39. *Los Angeles Times*, December 16, 1937; December 17, 1937; December 19, 1937; U.S. Census Bureau,, Manuscript Census Schedules, City and County of Los Angeles, 1940, ancestry.com., (May 21, 2015).

40. *Chinese Digest*, February, 1938.

41. *Chinese Digest*, December 1937; January 1939; *Lawrence Daily Journal-World*, February 12, 1938; *Seattle Times*, February 13, 1938; Bill Tobitt, "North Wins Rice Bowl," *Oakland Tribune*, December 18, 1938.

42. *San Francisco Chronicle*, February 8, 1938.

43. *Seattle Times*, November 16, 1919.

44. *Portland Oregonian*, December 6, 1921; October 15, 1922; November 17, 1924; November 26, 1925.

45. *Seattle Times*, November 21, 1927; November 9, 1928; September 13, 1930; September 15, 1935; *Portland Oregonian*, November 15, 1932.

46. *Japanese American Courier*, September 24, 1938; October 8, 1938; October 15, 1938; Shelley Sang-Hee Lee, *Claiming the Oriental Gateway: Prewar Seattle and Japanese America* (Philadelphia: Temple University Press, 2011), 164–166.

47. *Decatur Review*, November 23, 1921; *Fresno Bee*, December 27, 1930; January 4, 1931; *Santa Cruz Sentinel*, December 7, 1932; Avrum Stoll, "East Bay Wins Sukiyaki Bowl, *Oakland Tribune*, January 2, 1939.

48. *Pacific Citizen*, October 4, 1947.

49. T. P. Magilligan, "Oriental Kickers Indulge in One-Sided Game," *San Francisco Call*, January 9, 1909.

50. Ibid.

51. Ibid.

52. *San Francisco Call*, December 23, 1909; *Los Angeles Times*, December 27, 1909.

53. *Chinese Digest*, September 4, 1936; *Pacific Citizen*, October 4, 1947; *Washington Post*, December 22, 1931; *Brooklyn Daily Eagle*, December 13, 1931.

54. *San Jose News*, December 20, 1933.

55. *Lincoln Star*, December 23, 1933.

56. *Modesto Bee* and *Herald News*, December 24, 1933; *Seattle Times*, December 25, 1933.

57. *Nevada Journal*, December 6, 1934; *Cleveland Plain-Dealer*, November 17, 1934; *Chinese Digest*, October 30, 1936.

58. *Oakland Tribune*, December 1, 1941.

59. *Look Magazine*, August 24, 1942, 56; *Manzanar Free Press*, September 21, 1942; October 8, 1942.

60. *Poston Chronicle*, December 2, 1944; November 26, 1943; *Pacific Citizen*, November 19, 1943.

61. *Heart Mountain Sentinel*, September 26, 1942; October 24, 1942; November 21, 1942; January 1, 1943; November 6, 1943; November 20, 1943; August 12, 1944.

62. Ibid., October 8, 1943; September 9, 1944; Jack Kumitomi, "Prepsters Stave Off All-Star Threat," November 6, 1943; *Topaz Times*, November 15, 1943.

63. *Pacific Citizen*, October 1, 1942; *Minidoka Irrigator*, October 14, 1942; November 20, 1943; November 18, 1944.

64. *Granada Bulletin*, October 17, 1942; *Granada Pioneer*, December 5, 1942.

65. 442nd Regimental Monthly Report, September 3, 1945; January 21, 1946; February 20, 1946; Franks, *Crossing*, 123–124.

66. Franks, *Crossing*, 123.

67. *Northwest Arkansas Press*, December 13, 1945; Juanita Tamayo Lott, *Common Destiny: Filipino American Generations* (Lanham, MD: Rowan and Littlefield Publishers, 2006), 44; San Jose Mercury, November 9, 1947; Franks, *Crossing*, 123; *Pacific Citizen*, November 12, 1949.

68. http://www.historylink.org/index.cfm?DisplayPage=output.cfm&file_id=8063 (May 20, 2015); http://www.legacy.com/obituaries/seattletimes/obituary.aspx?pid=152442853 (May 20, 2015); *Seattle Times*, September 29, 1949; October 3, 1949. October 6, 1949; November 9, 1956.

69. *Seattle Times*, December 5, 1949; October 2, 1951; October 27, 1951; November 20, 1951.

70. Chia Youyee Vang, "Hmong Youth, American Football, and the Cultural Politics of Ethnic Sports Tournaments," in *Asian American Sporting Cultures*, edited by Stanley I. Thangaraj, Constancio R. Arnaldo, Jr., and Christina Chin (New York: New York University Press, 2016), 201.

71. Ibid., 214; http://www.nprnews.org/story/2013/06/28/news/for-hmong-american-women-flag-football-breaks-barriers (January 29, 2016).

72. *Chinese Press*, June 2, 1950.

73. http://asianjournal.com/editorial/american-football-filipino-style/#sthash.5FZLs0CG.dpuf (June 23, 2015).

74. Jason Cruz, "The Layup Drill: Racism Alive in the NFL, Baseball is Back, and Good News for UW Golfer," http://www.nwasianweekly.com, March 28, 2014 (April 15, 2015).

75. Ibid.

76. www.asianweek.com, May 29, 2014 (April 11, 2015).

77. Bill Picture, "Looking for Change, Not a 49er Bandaid," www.asianweek.com (July 8, 2005).

78. www.asianweek.com, May 29, 2014 (April 11, 2015).

79. Rogers M. Smith, *Civic Ideals: Conflicting Visions of Citizenship in US History* (New Haven, CT: Yale University Press, 1997), 30–31.

TWO

Playing Well with Others

Hawai'i

To cling overly tenaciously to the tenets of white supremacy was a luxury Hawaiian football teams could not afford if they wished to remain competitive. The pool of potential athletes was largely comprised of non-white Asian and indigenous Hawaiian and other Pacific Islanders. In 1920, over 60 percent of the Hawaiian population was comprised of people of Asian and Pacific ancestry and that demographic reality has remained in play. The quest for inexpensive, reliable, and controllable labor by white plantation owners and managers brought thousands of Chinese, Japanese, Korean, and Filipino workers to Hawai'i when Native Hawaiians proved too few and too resistive. Hawaiian economic and political leaders, unlike their counterparts on the U.S. mainland, encouraged spouses and children to join their workers to produce more plantation laborers. Hawai'i's relative tolerance of interracial and interethnic marriage meant a larger pool of Hawaiian Asian workers and ultimately a larger pool of Hawaiian Asian young people excited to play all sorts of sports on the islands. Thus, football and other sports proved cosmopolitan canopies for the islands' diverse population of athletes of indigenous Hawaiian, Chinese, Japanese, Filipino, Portuguese, Spanish, and other European ancestries. Yet, as Elijah Anderson points out, cosmopolitan canopies, at best, offer social spaces of relative civility for those black and white Philadelphians who enter urban parks and shopping malls. Beyond them, the incivility of race persists.[1]

Well over one hundred years ago, Hawaiian football coaches customarily suited up squads representing the islands' developing multiethnic local culture. Aloy Soo played quarterback for Oahu College in 1906, while Honolulu High School's Ah Chieu ran for an eighty-yard touchdown to key a victory over the famed private school, Punahou. Subsequently, Solomon H. Hoe, a brilliant, versatile athlete, competed for Honolulu High School from 1908 to 1910.[2]

Founded on the island of Oahu, Kamehameha (Kam) Prep School represented the educational ambitions of Hawaiians of indigenous ancestry, many of whom possessed European and Asian parentage as well. At the dawn of the twentieth century, it engaged in interscholastic athletic competition with other secondary schools in Hawai'i's largest city of Honolulu. School authorities, according to scholar Margaret Jolley, used sports such as football to discipline young men of Hawaiian ancestry to counter the widespread haole association of them with the Waikiki "beach boys"—as "lazy, unduly sexual, and rebellious." In 1911, however, Kamehameha's administration banned students from interscholastic football, believing there was not enough gridiron material on campus to compete effectively against other schools. Instead, school officials and students deemed rugby a suitable option as had mainland universities such as Stanford and California, although the latter schools were more motivated by intercollegiate football's violence and disdain for academic integrity. Kam did, however, sponsor an intramural football game between a team called Reliance and another squad, the Boys of Eleven. By 1915, Kam had returned to interscholastic football in Honolulu. In 1920, the Kam eleven's haole or white coach wrote home to Chicago, claiming that his team played in bare feet and without much equipment. Mainland squads, he insisted, could learn a thing or two about physical courage from his Native Hawaiian gridders.[3]

Originally established to serve the generally privileged haole population, Punahou opened its doors to culturally diverse Hawaiians—a policy reflected on its football teams' rosters. Joe Pa was a running back for the private school in 1905. In 1908, Mon Yin, Che Bui, and Goo On played for Punahou. Two years later, Hawaiian Chinese Coy Zane lettered at Punahou. In 1915, Hawaiians Noble Kauhane and Bill Nahipaa, competed for Punahou. The next year, Bill Kanakanui and Ki Fuk Zane, Coy's brother, suited up for the private school.[4]

McKinley High School eventually took over from Honolulu High as the city's sole public secondary school in the early twentieth century. In 1911, the school had one of Hawai'i's most remarkable all-around athletes, Lai Tin, later known on the mainland as a skilled baseball player, Buck Lai. In 1912, Jiro Morita and En Choi were McKinley gridders. In 1917, Walter Akana and Peter Chang were quarterbacks; Wilfred Tsukiyama, the first Japanese American state supreme court justice, was at halfback; and Chinese surnamed athletes were on the line.[5]

Other secondary schools engaged in football with Asian and Pacific Islander athletes. In 1911, St. Louis College was actually a prep school which suited up Yeichi Yamashiro and David Paaluhi. In 1915, it fielded an eleven featuring "a speedy end," A. Amoy. Competing for Mills Prep in 1915 were Lan Nam and Hin Char. The next year, August Puuki captained the Mills eleven and played fullback.[6]

In 1917, Mills School gave up football apparently because its generally Asian student body could not summon a team large enough to compete effectively in interscholastic football. The *Honolulu Star-Bulletin*, put it another way, claiming that the "Oriental boy is not adopted to the game of football." According to the *Star-Bulletin*, K. Muratsuka, who once captained the Mills eleven, agreed with the decision.[7]

In the 1920s, high school teams represented Hawai'i's diverse population on not only the territory's most populated island of Oahu but other islands as well. On the Big Island of Hawai'i around the same time, Kenichi Hiraoka captained and starred on the Waena High School squad. On the same island, Kohalu High was represented by Ah Choy and Ah Sun at quarterback, while on the line were gridders such as center Tadao Okube and end Mitsuo Wataoka.[8]

Propelled largely by Asian and Native Hawaiian gridders, high school football in Honolulu received plenty of press attention and fan support during the 1920s. Clarence "Shorty" Lee Chong quarterbacked for St. Louis in the early 1920s. A historian of Hawaiian Chinese has written, "It was said that Shorty was built so low to the ground that he was almost impossible to stop." One of Hawai'i's greatest running backs at the time, Hiram Kaakua illuminated football at St. Louis Prep in the early 1920s. Possessing Hawaiian ancestry, "Ducky" Swan was an all-league performer for St. Louis in 1922, 1923, and 1924. During the decade, Noble Kauhane returned from mainland football exploits to coach St. Louis Prep. Among his top players were guard Lum Wai; part-Hawaiian tackle and three time all-leaguer, Barney Joy, Jr.; and Henry Oana, a Hawaiian of indigenous and Portuguese ancestry who would carve out an interesting professional baseball career on the mainland in the 1930s and 1940s. When St. Louis decisively defeated Punahou in mid-October 1927, Oana stood out. *Star-Bulletin* correspondent Frank Belles described him as "a rugged laddie."[9]

In the 1920s and 1930s, Kam teams were competitive in Honolulu prep football and even traveled to the mainland to play on the West Coast. Three Kam backfield stars made all-league three times in a row— Rusty Holt from 1924 through 1926, John Wise from 1925 through 1927, and Jonah Wise from 1927 through 1929. Coached by Bill Wise, a former star for the University of Hawai'i, Kamehameha's 1927 squad featured two sons—Jonah Wise was an end, while brother John was the team's leading ground gainer. In 1928, the *Dallas Morning News* told readers that a Kam football team had arrived in San Francisco to oppose a Pasadena Junior College (JC) squad. According to the wire story, this was the first Hawaiian prep team to trek to the American mainland. After Kam downed the mainland squad at the famed Pasadena Rose Bowl, sports columnist Don Watson of the *Honolulu Star-Bulletin* declared that all of

Hawai'i expressed pride in the victory. Four years later, a Kam squad journeyed to the mainland to play Chaffey JC. The Hawaiians won the game, played in the Southern California town of Oxnard, 12–0. When an all-league team was chosen in Honolulu in 1934, Kamehameha contributed center Joe Anuhea, guard James Nakapaahu, tackle William Toomey, and quarterback Charles Mahoe. Other Kam stars of the 1930s included Moses Hanohano, who, the 1930 U.S. Census manuscripts tell us, was the eleven-year-old son of Hawaiian parents. His father worked as a machinist for a power plant.[10]

Pulling from a largely multiethnic working- and lower middle-class population, McKinley High was a public school that frequently competed well for football laurels in Honolulu between the world wars. In 1927, the *Honolulu Star-Bulletin* published a photo of "Flashy Mick Halfback" Imamoto toting the ball helmetless against Kamehameha. Kam proved vastly superior to McKinley that day, winning 46–0, but Imamoto emerged as a star of the game. A part-Hawaiian and future mayor of Honolulu, Neal Blaisdell coached the 1930 squad. Among the standouts playing for him were Moses Moepono and Soo Bok Kim. When McKinley High won the 1933 prep championship of Honolulu, Charley Ah Sui emerged as one of the team's stars. In 1934, Charley Ah Sui captained the McKinley High team, becoming in the process one of the handful of Hawaiian prep gridders to make all-league for three years.[11]

Like the Kam gridders a decade earlier, the McKinley squad journeyed to the mainland in the 1930s and early 1940s. Expeditions of Hawaiian athletes to the mainland had been going on for a couple of decades. Going back to 1912 when the still relatively unknown Duke Kahanamoku and a team of ballplayers of Chinese descent were dispatched to the mainland, Hawaiian commercial interests and political leaders sought to promote the islands to potential mainland tourists and investors. They believed that putting largely non-white Hawaiian athletes on display in competition with largely white mainlanders would ease racial anxiety in Sacramento and Salt Lake City about visiting and investing in Hawai'i.[12]

Thus, late in October 1931, a team of McKinley High School football players found themselves in Idaho to take on a "Gem State" eleven. The Micks lost 12–6 but a substitute halfback called "Midget" Kim sparkled for the Hawaiians. In Ogden, Utah, McKinley opposed the Utah University junior varsity team in the mid-1930s. The *Ogden Standard-Examiner* extolled the "Micks" backfield as "fast but small." It claimed that McKinley's "Mankoa is said to be the only Filipino to make a first team in football." The *Standard-Examiner* was talking about Crispin Mancao, who at 128 pounds was considered a fine all-around football player. Subsequently, he gained fame on the islands as an excellent left-handed pitcher. In the fall of 1937, McKinley High's eleven returned to the mainland, where it encountered a team from Lakeside High in Seattle. The *Seattle*

Times informed readers that McKinley High suited up Sadao Watasaki at left tackle, Kai Bong Chung at center, and left half Wan Lum Ho. The team also featured "broken field specialist," John Naumu. About a month before Pearl Harbor was attacked the Micks were back in Utah, opposing the East High School Leopards in Salt Lake City. The starting lineup included several Hawaiian-, Chinese-, and Japanese-surnamed players. Among Mick gridders of note who played in the late 1930s and early 1940s were Ken Nunogawa and end Bill Apau, who captained the team in 1940.[13]

Other Honolulu high schools featured Asian and Pacific Islander football in the decade before the war. Joining McKinley as a public secondary school, Roosevelt High assembled a top-notch team in the mid-1930s. One of the major reasons was Joe Kaulukukui, who had transferred to the Honolulu high school after, according to the *Honolulu Record*, "he came out virtually unheralded from Hilo's barefoot ranks." Kaulukukui, as we will find out, was a member of a Hawaiian family well known for its athletic skills. In 1940, Punahou was co-captained by Eddie Ching, credited in the school yearbook for "consistent, inspirational playing." Another public school, Farrington High in 1939 was represented by a varsity team coached by an alumni standout Francis Aiwohl. The 1940 school yearbook identified Quarterback Vernon Taguba as the "spark plug of the team." Lawrence Iwabashi and Vernon Chang were also team leaders. The yearbook described Chang as a fullback who was a hard tackler and good receiver, while Iwabashi ranked as "one of the best linemen of Farrington." In the years before Pearl Harbor was attacked Iolani suited up several Asian and Pacific Islander standouts, such as Packard, also known as Pat Harrington, Stan Kamakana, Al Lolotai, Nelson Moku, Francis Sing, Saburo Takeyasu, Ed Hulihee, and Charlie Yee Hoy. The *Star-Bulletin's* Don Watson hailed Harrington as the best drop kicker in the league and Charlie Yee Hoy as one of Honolulu's best backs. As for Francis Sing, he was, according to 1940 U.S. census data, a son of a Hawaiian Chinese locksmith and a Native Hawaiian mother. St. Louis College in 1940 had Herman Wedemeyer, deemed a "capable understudy" at the time. Sadly, the young Wedemeyer broke his arm and had to sit out a chunk of the 1940 season, but he would make up for lost time in 1941 and 1942, emerging as a legendary Honolulu high school hero.[14]

High schools in more rural Oahu, as well as Maui, Hawai'i, and Kaua'i had teams with plenty of Asian and Pacific Islander grid talent in the decade before World War II. On Oahu, Leilehua High School usually fielded competitive elevens. The 1937 varsity squad was captained by Wilfred Minn, who starred at end, while Stanward Kim excelled in the backfield. In early October 1940, Maui's Lahainaluna took down Baldwin, 19–6, thanks to the "brilliant open field running" of halfback Masayoshi Otake and fullback Akira Yonamine, the older brother of the great Wally Yonamine. Akira eventually won the Maui Interscholastic Outstanding

Player Award. The next year Wally joined the team as a freshman. In his first game for Lahainaluna, he came off the bench to heave a touchdown pass, scored on an eleven-yard touchdown run, and then tallied again on a seventy-yard jaunt with an intercepted pass. In 1942, the *Maui News* pronounced Yonamine a first team all-leaguer. Thanks largely to Yonamine, known then as Kaname, Lahainaluna copped two league championships. When Hilo beat Baldwin 13–6 in early October, Rodney Miyamoto's seventy-eight-yard touchdown run with an interception proved vital. [15]

Despite World War II, Hawaiian high school football fields kept busy in the fall. The early years of the war saw Herman Wedemeyer, possessing Native Hawaiian and Chinese ancestry, in his ascension as a high school legend at St. Louis Prep. After Wedemeyer headed to the mainland for college football stardom, backfield aces Tommy Low and Richard Mamiya shined for St. Louis in 1943. When St. Louis downed Maui's St. Anthony's in November 1943, the *Star-Bulletin's* Mickey Mapa wrote, "Right half Dick Mamiya played his usual steady game." A week later, Low starred in a losing effort against Kamehameha. [16]

McKinley and Roosevelt had their gridiron moments during the war. In the fall of 1943, Shigeki Yamada scored on a one yard run for the victorious Micks in a game against Punahou. Al Minn, Mickey Mapa declared, "play[ed] like an all-star" in the same contest. Meanwhile, Roosevelt downed Farrington thanks in part to the all-around performance of quarterback George Hong. [17]

Henry Kusonaki coached Farrington High School during the war. Farrington suited up some of the more talented players in Honolulu such as halfback Joe Tom. After a loss to Roosevelt, Mickey Mapa pronounced "Joe Tom . . . one of the greatest backs of the season." Indeed, Tom made all–league in 1943. Farrington High School in 1944 had the elusive, versatile Wally Yonamine. The latter had transferred from Lahainaluna and was declared ineligible in his first year at Farrington in 1943. In 1944, Yonamine scored all ten points when Farrington beat Kam, 10–7. Against McKinley later in the season, he scored all fourteen of Farrington's points in a 14–6 victory over McKinley. At the end of the season, Yonamine was voted the league's MVP. He carried the ball eighty-five times for 557 yards and completed twelve of twenty-one passes. Author Robert Fitts claims Yonamine was a source of pride to Hawai'i's beleaguered but generally not interned Nikkei population. [18]

Kam had some good gridders, as did high schools on Maui during the war years. Part-Hawaiian Earl Fernandez proved an all-around star for Kam in the fall of 1943 and an all-leaguer. Other Kam all-leaguers in 1943 included tackle Waldeman Durachelle, guard Rowland Melim, center Howard Benham, and end Moses Paianina. On Maui, running back Johnny Dang illuminated the gridrion for St. Anthony's eleven, co-coached by Henry Ah Sui. [19]

After World War II, Hawaiian high school football seemed the islands' favorite spectator sport. Former Kansas University athlete, Bert Itoga helped Henry Kusonaki coach Farrington after World War II. In 1948, the *Honolulu Record* extolled the way the two coaches prepared their team against Punahou. The *Record* was also impressed with their quarterback Ken Kahoonei, described by the weekly as one of the best passers in Honolulu history. While associated with the educational aspirations of wealthy haoles, Punahou "interracial" football team after World War II caught the attention of the *Honolulu Record*'s Wilfred Oka. Indeed, the great Charlie Ane was Punahou's largest star in the late 1940s. Possessing Hawaiian, Samoan, and Chinese ancestry, Ane's "sterling line play" was hailed by the *Honolulu Record*. In 1953, Samoan Allen Harrington starred for Punahou when it clinched the league championship in a game against Kam. Sticky fingered Native Hawaiian Alfred Ainoa Espinda was Harrington's teammate. In 1947, McKinley High won a league championship with quarterback Henry Lum, as well as Abe Kaihenui and Dave Kikau among those leading the way. Iolani also fielded fine football players of Asian and Pacific Islander ancestry. In 1948, future mainland college gridders such as halfback Allen Napoleon, tackle Charlie Ka'aihue, and a "hard driving fullback" named Harold Han played for Iolani. A few years later, Iolani's Noboru Yonamine, Wally's brother, did well as a halfback. When the *Pacific Citizen* informed readers that several Nikkei had made all-league in Honolulu, it especially lauded Yonamine as a back who "combined ruggedness with speed." Another Iolani standout on the all-league team with Yonamine was center Walt Nobuhara, while halfback Dave "Dynamite" Yamashiro made the second team.[20]

During much of the mid-twentieth century, mainland teams and their coaches were predominantly white. Like their players, in contrast, Hawaiian coaches came from disparate racial and ethnic backgrounds. In so doing, they reflected the Hawaiian local culture which sought to transcend ethnic borders. Former Punahou and St. Mary's of California gridder Native Hawaiian Noble Kauhane coached at St. Louis Prep in the mid-1930s. Hawaiian Japanese Henry Masato Kusonaki coached outstanding Farrington High School elevens in Honolulu during the mid-twentieth century. In the late 1940s, the superb all-around athlete and record-breaking swimmer, Hawaiian Japanese Keo Nakama, coached football at Leilehua High School, Hawaiian Korean Peter Kim coached at Kaimuki High, and Hawaiian Korean Philip Minn and Native Hawaiian Charles Kalani assisted at Iolani. Even if they had wanted to teach and coach on the mainland, it is doubtful that these men would have been given the opportunities afforded them by Hawaiian local culture.[21]

During the 1950s, Allen Nagata and Joe Tom headed prep football teams in Honolulu. In 1951, the *Honolulu Record*'s Wilfred Oka tried to come to the rescue of Nagata, who was apparently beleaguered by alumni for the job he was doing at St. Louis Prep. Oka argued that Nagata deserved praise for stressing sportsmanship and character rather than victory in the face of "shortsighted" critics. Among those who assisted Nagata at St. Louis were Native Hawaiian and former mainland college standout, Leon Sterling, and Jyun Hirota, who had starred as a running back at UH and would play major league baseball in Japan. Joe Tom, a Chinese Hawaiian who quarterbacked for the University of Oregon, coached McKinley High School's varsity squad. University of Hawai'i alum, Harry Kahuanui, was his assistant in the mid-1950s. Wilfred Oka was so impressed with the Micks' triumph over Farrington in the fall of 1955 that he speculated Tom could be coach of the year.[22]

Coach Eddie Hamada of Iolani left good memories for many former players possessing diverse ethnic and racial backgrounds. Competing for Hamada in the late 1960s, Sidney Sadowski told reporter Cathy Chong, "The thing that stands out in my mind, above all else, is Eddie Hamada. . . . He was all about character building. We didn't have the biggest players, the fastest players, but Coach knew what it took to bring a team together." Hamada was assisted by former San Jose State star, Charley Ka'aihue, and John Kai. Elroy Chong was an all-league quarterback for him.[23]

In the later twentieth century, Hawaiian high school grid teams depended even more on Asian and Pacific Islander coaches. This was not just a product of the locals recruiting locals. By 2000, less than a quarter of the islands' population claimed to be white. The rest were Asian, Pacific Islander, or people of mixed ancestry. Calvin Chai, a stalwart performer for the University of Denver, returned to his alma mater, Kamehameha to coach football and serve as athletic director in the early 1970s. Former pro standout Charlie Ane coached at Damian, Radford, and Kaimuki. His son, Kale, coached many years at Punahou, recruiting his dad as an assistant. Like his father, Kale Ane starred as a lineman at Punahou and in big time college football on the mainland. He also played professionally for several years. In the 2010s, he recruited his son Teetai to help him coach Punahou.[24]

INDEPENDENT TEAMS

Independent of educational institutions, Hawaiian adult amateur, youth, and semi-professional squads could hardly exist without Asian and Native Hawaiian gridders. As early as 1895, Hawaiian surnamed athletes competed for a team called the Defenders in Honolulu. Native Hawaiian Barney Joy performed well as a tackle and kicker for the Honolulu Athletic Club in the early twentieth century. He also earned plaudits as a good ball carrier. In 1930, Barney Joy's son was competing for the Honolulu Athletic Club along with Native Hawaiians who made names for themselves on the mainland—"Ducky" Swan and Sam Hipa. In 1917, Boy

Scout troops in Honolulu were represented by multiethnic football teams. Late in the year, the *Star-Bulletin* reported that Boy Scout Troop XVIII had downed troop VIII. Honolulu's Outriggers Club was originally organized in the early twentieth century by haoles passionate about Native Hawaiian water sports such as surfing and outrigger canoeing but not so passionate about recruiting Native Hawaiians. Yet by the 1910s, it had reached out to prominent "watermen" such as Duke Kahanamoku and his brothers. Moreover, in 1919, it sponsored a football team, which, indeed, included Duke's brother, Dave.[25]

During the early twentieth century, the Honolulu Town Team assembled formidable, multiethnic elevens proving capable of giving visiting mainland gridders a rough time. In 1917, a brilliant Native Hawaiian running back, Noble Kauhane starred for the Town Team against a U.S. Marine contingent. In the early 1920s, Hawaiians of Asian Pacific Islander ancestry such as Willie Wise, Nick Hoopi'i, and F. H. Tong competed for the Honolulu Town Team. Part-Hawaiian Herman Clark, Sr. played for the Town Team as well. *Los Angeles Times* sports reporter Dick Hyland remembered Herman Clark, Sr., as "one of the toughest linemen I ever saw." In 1927, the team featured back Hiram Kaakua, a growing Native Hawaiian football legend on the islands.[26]

Meanwhile, the mainland press picked up on the remarkable story of Frank Kanae, renowned on the islands for playing twenty-five years on independent elevens such as the Honolulu Athletic Club, the Honolulu Town Team, the First Hawaiian Infantry eleven, and the Palama Settlement House squad. Born on Molokai, the eighteen-year-old Kanae was living with his parents in Honolulu at the time of the 1900 U.S. Census. According to the census schedules, both his parents were Hawaiians. His father was a police officer, while he was listed as a driver. Kanae generally played tackle, but was known as well as a hard charging ball carrier. Indeed, 1905, the *Honolulu Evening-Bulletin* dubbed Kanae one of the best ball carriers around. Reportedly forty years old and a father of sixteen in 1923, Kanae earned the nickname of "Cannonball." In 1930, the U.S. Census manuscripts depict the forty-seven-year-old Kanae as racially Hawaiian and working as a watchman.[27]

Throughout the 1920s and 1930s, mainland elevens shipped themselves off to the islands to compete against various Hawaiian squads. Doing so, might have given youthful mainland football squads a reward for a hard season. But such trips could also promote mainland educational institutions, commerce, and culture in Hawai'i, while Hawaiians could see hosting mainland teams as a way of promoting their educational institutions, commerce, and culture to visitors, perhaps expecting to see plenty of primitivism on display. In late 1927, Santa Clara College beat the Honolulu Town Team, led by Hiram Kaakua and Henry Oana. On New Years' 1933, the professional Green Bay Packers were in Honolulu where they easily handled a team called the McKinley Alums. However, on the home team was "Hiram Kaakua, Hawai'i's foremost triple threat star." Around two years later, the Cal football squad traveled to the islands, where it was beaten on Christmas Day by the Honolulu Town Team, led by halfback Kaakua who performed "brilliant feats" such as a forty-four-yard touchdown jaunt. Racially identified as a Hawaiian in the 1930 census, the then-twenty-two-year-old Kaakua worked as a clerk. In 1935, Kaakua carried the ball twenty-eight times for a stunning 239 yards against the Kam Alums. The next year, a squad of college all-stars beat the Honolulu Town Team, but went away admiring the play of Kaakua, dubbed the "Black Grange," in reference to the great running back of the 1920s, Red Grange. The *Star-Bulletin* remembered Kaakua made the all-star team headed by Stanford great, Bob Grayson, "look silly." In an interview with University of Hawai'i oral historians, Minoru Kimura recalled the exhilaration of Hawaiian football in the 1930s. He particularly remembered exciting gridders of Hawaiian descent such as the "Kalihi boy," Hiram Kaakua.[28]

However, there were not enough mainland visitors to keep Hawaiian gridirons busy. Therefore, the more elite Hawaiian grid squads played each other. In October 1929, the University of Hawai'i eleven downed the Honolulu Athletic Club team. Performing well for the losers was John Kerr. Wooed by major league baseball teams in the 1930s, Kerr possessed Hawaiian and Chinese ancestry. In 1936, a team composed of McKinley High alums downed UH easily 26–0. Starring for the victors were Part-Hawaiian Toots Harrison and Ben Ahakuelo, both of whom scored touchdowns in the rout. That same year, the multiethnic Honolulu Town Team had to overcome the dazzling performance of UH halfback Tommy Kaulukukui to carve out a 13–6 triumph. The irrepressible Hiram Kaakua scored the go-ahead touchdown for the Town Team.[29]

The 1940 census data described the previously mentioned Ben Ahakuelo as a twenty-nine-year-old, part-Hawaiian "utility man." More than that, however, Ahakuelo, who also stood out in barefoot football and amateur boxing, was one of five non-white, working-class Hawaiians falsely accused of raping the wife of a U.S. Naval officer in Honolulu in 1931. When a hung jury led to their freedom, the mother-in-law and husband of the alleged victim conspired to kidnap and then murder one of the accused, Joseph Kahahawai, well known in Honolulu athletic circles as a high school and barefoot football player as well as an amateur boxer. The subsequent Massie-Kahahawai Trial proved controversial in more ways than one. Kahahawai's murderers were let off with little punishment (as little as one hour's detention in the governor's residence). Fed by the publicity emerging from both trials, anti-Hawaiian racism became more pronounced on the mainland. Perhaps, many mainlanders feared, Hawai'i was not such a colonial paradise after all. However, Kahahawai's murder and the disappointing results of the second trial results mobilized working-class Hawaiians across racial and ethnic lines and nurtured the continued development of the Hawaiian local culture. Yet sports such as football also seemingly advanced the local culture. Two barefoot teams, the Hui Eleus and the Kaka'ako Sons sent floral wreaths to Kahahawai's funeral, attended by working-class locals, while the Honolulu Town Team and other independent, cleated elevens seemingly represented the kind of people who mourned Kahahawai's death.[30]

On the eve of World War II and during the conflagration, Hawaiian football fans were entertained by a variety of local teams. In Honolulu, the Hawaii Senior Football League fielded many of the islands' best gridders. In 1940, the Bears suited up Native Hawaiian, Sam Kapu at center. In a few years, Kapu would take over the coaching reins of the Bears. Guards included Hawaiian Korean Philip Minn and Sam Shibuya. In the backfield, Ken Nunogawa was a halfback and George Hao played fullback.[31]

One eleven representing the Rainbow Athletic Club in the Hawaii Senior Football League boasted a backfield that included the Kaulukukui brothers. Tommy Kaulukukui, who starred for UH in the mid-1930s, was at halfback, alongside Joe and Sol. In 1943, the Rainbows beat the Bears, and the *Star-Bulletin's* Don Watson praised the work of quarterback Sol Kaulukukui as well as backs Packard Harrington and John Naumu. Harrington, according to the *Star-Bulletin*, was an "ace passer." The Rainbows were coached at the time by Harold Kometani, with Chin Do Kim as an assistant.[32]

Comprised of a mixture of Kamehameha alumni and members of the "old town team," the Healanis had former pro Harry Field as coach and Herman Clark, Sr., nicknamed "Big Hoiman" as an assistant. Native Hawaiian David Trask served as team president. Playing for the Healanis were Hawaiian legends such as Tony Morse and Hiram Kaakua in the backfield. The latter, the *Star-Bulletin's* Loui Leong Hop maintained, was in his eighteenth year of competitive football on the islands. In mid-October 1940, the *Star-Bulletin* detailed the Healanis' roster. For example, there were at least three Korean Hawaiians on the squad. Kaye Chung was a center as well as Nikkei Harold Kometani. Guard Chin Do Kim was another Korean Hawaiian on the squad as was quarterback Y. S. Ko. Others on the squad included halfback John Naumu, quarterback Ben Ahakuelo, and halfback Henry Wong. When the Healanis opposed the Bears in early October 1940, Kaakua scored the only touchdown in a 7–0 victory. Sam Kapu and George Hao stood out for the losers, however. In 1943, Neil Blaisdell coached the Healanis. Joe Kaulukukui was a big star, averaging over six yards per carry in 1942. In mid-November 1943, the Healanis lost to the Bears augmented by mainland stars such as Edgar Jones. Still, Joe Kaulukukui carried the ball for 137 yards in but twelve attempts.[33]

Hawaiians of Asian and Pacific Islander backgrounds proved integral to the Hawaii Senior Football League. A Hawai'i-Japanese, Harold Kom-

etani, served as a player-coach for the Manoans. Coached by Neal Blais-
dell in 1940, the Hawaiian Pine included halfback Masa Takeba and full-
back Ken Kauka. At that time, the 1940 U.S. Census manuscripts tell us,
Takeba worked as an assistant foreman for a pineapple company. His
Issei father was a mason, while his Hawaiian-born mother worked as a
laundress for a private family. The part-Hawaiian Kauka was the son of
Hawaiian father who worked as a machinist and a white mother. Part-
Hawaiian Tony Morse handled the coaching reins of the Kaalas with
Kaye Chung as an assistant in 1943.[34]

The Hawai'i Senior League attracted considerable support for much of
the 1940s, but the league suffered a setback with the public when the
Hawaiian Warriors were organized into a professional team affiliated
with the professional Pacific Coast Football League after World War II.
Nevertheless, a gambling scandal destroyed the Warriors' credibility
with island football fans, and various Asian Hawaiians such as Philip
Minn, Chin Do Kim, Tommy Kaulukukui, and Iwao Miyake sought to
revive the Senior League with some success. In 1950, the Leilehua Vandals won the Senior Football League championship. The team was
headed by Japanese Hawaiian player-coach Masa Gunda. According to
the 1930 census data, Gunda was a Nisei son of a father who worked in a
sugar mill.[35]

Other independent teams popped up on the islands. In 1950, the
Record complained that UH's frosh team had been beaten by the Kawai-
loa independent squad, coached by Andrew Choo. In 1952, the *Pacific
Citizen* reported that Noboru Yonamine led the Keiki Ali'i eleven to a
21–0 whitewashing of the Keiki Kanes at the Aloha Bowl.[36]

In the meantime, the University-Armed Forces Football Conference
emerged to include a Tommy Kaulukukui-coached team called the Hawaiian 49ers. Playing for Kaulukukui were prominent Hawaiian gridders
Ken Kahoonei and Johnny Dang. Subsequently, Johnny Dang and Sal
Naumu, who had performed well for USC, suited up for an eleven called
the Hawaiian Rams, which opposed UH in the mid-1950s. In 1957, another former USC standout, Harold Han, ran for a twenty-nine-yard
touchdown which helped the Rams upset the University of Hawai'i elev-
en. The Hawaiian Athletic Club also had a team in the conference.
Owned by Philip Minn, it was coached by Chin Do Kim. The former was
greatly involved in the Hawaiian world beyond the gridiron. In 1948, he
ran for Honolulu supervisor as a Democrat, advertising his campaign in
the militantly pro-labor *Honolulu Record*, and eventually he became the
first Korean American elected to the Hawaiian legislature. Moreover,
when the *Honolulu Record* listed prominent Hawaiians in favor of imme-
diate statehood, Philip Minn was one of those named, as well as Noble
Kauhane. Wounded during World War II, Minn also was active in the
Disabled American Veterans organization in the 1950s.[37]

World War II slowed competition between mainland and independent Hawaiian teams, but that changed after V-J day. In the fall of 1947, the Moiliili Bears, representing a notable working-class neighborhood in Honolulu, journeyed to Southern California, where they played Pepperdine College at Inglewood's Sentinel Field. One of the many talented Kaulukukui brothers, Dick, starred for the Bears. In December 1947, the University of Montana traveled to the islands. There they beat a team called the Olympics, 28–14. The Olympics' roster included Bill Kaulukukui and Joe Corn, a superb running back possessing indigenous Hawaiian ancestry.[38]

Hawaiian all-star elevens trekked to the mainland after World War II. Out from the shadows of war, many ethnically diverse Hawaiians sought statehood. However, opposition emerged on the mainland—a racially based opposition mostly focused on the large population of Nikkei on the islands. Given the popularity of football in the United States, those commercial and political interests favoring statehood could well hope the promotion of traveling teams of multiethnic Hawaiian gridders would foster mainland support for statehood.[39]

In 1946, a team called the Hawaiian All-Stars, also known as the Leilehua Alums, visited the West Coast. Among the Hawaiian All-Stars was the superb Wally Yonamine. Coached by Chin Do Kim, who was said to have barefooted a 78-yard field goal for the University of Hawai'i, the squad also suited up other talented gridders of Asian and Hawaiian descent. As for Kim, he was eulogized upon his death in the late 1990s by veteran *Star-Bulletin* writer, Bill Kwon. Kim, according to Kwon, was a five-foot-six and 160-pound guard for Leilehua High and then UH, serving as co-captain his last year on the Manoa campus. As a player, Kwon said, Kim was a "bulldog in temperament and in built [sic]." As a coach, Kwon maintained, "Kim might have stressed basics. But he was no dummy. He made sure he had the players. And he got one of the best at the time, Wally Yonamine, to play for him."[40]

In late September 1946, Portland University hosted the Hawaiians. While practicing, Yonamine and his teammates impressed observers in the "City of Roses" with their fancy ball-handling drills. The *Portland Oregonian* told readers that the Hawaiians "play strictly for distance with passes and tricky ball-handling their main forte." The game itself produced a rout as the visitors won, 54–13. Bruce Hamby wrote for the *Portland Oregonian* that the Hawaiians displayed the "fanciest" offense ever seen in Multnomah Stadium. Despite watching the home towners humbled, eight thousand spectators apparently enjoyed the Hawaiians' style of play. One example of the Hawaiians' cleverness occurred when their offense was on its own twenty-eight yard line. Quarterback Marco Takata lateraled the ball to Yonamine who sprinted to his left. Rather than dash up field, Yonamine suddenly stopped and quick kicked the ball to the Portland ten yard line. Meanwhile, Jim Asato scored on a seven-yard touchdown for the Hawaiians, and Yonamine carried the ball for one touchdown and after dropping back twenty yards heaved the "pigskin" over the goal line for a touchdown pass. The *Portland Oregonian* asserted that the Hawaiians accumulated an outstanding 538 yards in offense.[41]

Several days later, San Jose State had to fight off the Hawaiian gridders' stunning comeback to come away from the fray with a 19–19 tie. Yonamine distinguished himself for the visitors as the *San Jose Mercury* displayed him in a photo and called the Maui native "the southpaw halfback." But backs Joe Tom, Marco Takata, Jim Asato, and center Henry Hosea contributed as well. After their season ended, the San Jose State gridders picked Hosea and Yonamine for their all-opposition squad at the end of the season.[42]

Essentially the same squad of Hawaiian gridders toured the U.S. mainland again in 1947. Yonamine was gone, but the team gave mainland elevens all they could handle. Before the Hawaiian All-Stars took on San Jose State in September, the *San Jose News* announced that Wally Yonamine's loss would be covered in part by the recruitment of his brother, Akira, called a "brilliant prospect" by the *News*. Masa Gunda captained the team. Fred Merrick of the *San Jose Mercury* praised Gunda as well as linemen Bill Apau, John Kapuinai, and Isao Ito, a "141 pound might atom guard." San Jose State beat the visitors easily 35–18, although Spencer Kamakana managed to return an interception for a sixty-five-yard touchdown. In October, the Hawaiians beat Portland University, 14–6. An article in the *Nevada State Journal* hailed the performances of the Asato brothers, Jim and Richard, against the larger Portland squad, claiming that the former figured in practically every major play.[43]

UNIVERSITY OF HAWAI'I FOOTBALL

The University of Hawai'i has been the islands' most constant source of football entertainment for over a century. For many years in the twentieth century, however, the UH football team was substantially confined by geography to playing local elevens. In 1910, the Oahu campus at Manoa was known as the College of Hawai'i. In November 1910, the school's football team played Fook On Yap at right end, Tse Tau Le at left end, and Sing Hung at left half. Throughout the twentieth century's second decade, the College of Hawaii fielded gridders of Hawaiian and Asian ancestry. In 1917 the College of Hawai'i experienced the first gridiron death in Hawai'i when Nikkei Mariuchi Kawamoto died of a fractured vertebra. Among his teammates was the Native Hawaiian captain, Lionel Brash.[44]

The College of Hawai'i became the University of Hawai'i in 1920. Within a decade, a few mainland squads journeyed to Oahu to oppose

UH teams. The results were usually but not always pleasing to the visitors. Early in 1920, the *Wichita Beacon* published a photograph of the UH squad. The caption described the roster as carrying players possessing eleven different "nationalities," including Korean, Chinese, Japanese, Hawaiian, and part-Hawaiian. When the University of Nevada battled the UH squad in 1920, the Nevadans found Peter Hanohano at left tackle and Francis Kanahele at right end. In previewing an upcoming game pitting the University of Oregon against the UH eleven in the fall of 1921, the *Portland Oregonian* gushed over Hawaiian fullback Sam Poenoe in terms familiar to Lamarckian biology. A former star at Punahou, Poenoe was "[a]Hawaiian of magnificent proportions, he has the ability to plow through a stone wall line. . . . It is almost impossible to knock his feet from under him, for he has pedal extremities that are large and ground-gripping—an Hawaiian heritage from his ancestors who never wore shoes." A couple of years later, the *Nevada State Journal* informed readers that Pomona was about to encounter UH gridders, among whom were two "Hawaiian-Americans," one Hawaiian, one Chinese, one Japanese, and "one negro." Part-Hawaiian Neal Blaisdell captained the team. The *Portland Oregonian* dubbed him the "brains" of the eleven. Subsequently, Blaisdell would coach on the islands, but more memorably he would carve out a successful political career in Hawai'i, becoming a Republican mayor of Honolulu. As it turned out, UH downed the visitors from Southern California on January 1, 1923. UH student journalist, Yasuo Goto, praised the performances of Blaisdell and Native Hawaiian Willie Wise.[45]

UH football squads proved troublesome to visiting mainland teams in the 1920s. In 1925, Willie Wise helped lead UH to an easy victory over Colorado Agricultural College, which later became Colorado State. Wise was also the son of a prominent former athlete, Hawaiian clergyman and politician named John Wise. That same year, the UH squad journeyed to California. There they opposed Occidental College in Southern California. Before arriving in Los Angeles, the Hawaiians dropped in on Santa Clara Valley, where they practiced at Santa Clara College's Mission Field. The *San Jose Mercury* noted that Willie Wise was both star halfback and captain. Subsequently, UH shut out Occidental 13–0. Turnovers proved productive for the winners. For example, Willie Wise intercepted a pass and carried the ball for an eighty-five-yard touchdown.[46]

A few years later, Lemon Holt, described as a Caucasian-Hawaiian, or part-Hawaiian, in the U.S. census in 1930 stood out, with his brother Walter, when UH edged the University of Utah eleven in December 1927. Later, Lemon Holt scored a touchdown in a losing effort against Santa Clara in early January 1928. Native Hawaiian Bill Kaeo, meanwhile, captained the UH squad. Neil Blaisdell's brother, Bill, who starred on the mainland previously for Bucknell, joined UH in 1927.[47]

Meanwhile, UH gridders showed up in Los Angeles to take part in a doubleheader staged on Thanksgiving Day, 1927, at the relatively new Los Angeles Coliseum. Pre-game publicity included a photo in the *Los Angeles Times* of UH's David Wong standing with a white player for Hollywood High, which would also participate in the doubleheader. Manifesting a racial liberalism, much too rare in pre-World War II America, the *Times'* caption described the two gridders as "brothers under the skin." A crowd of forty thousand watched the Hawaiians subdue Occidental, 20–0. According to the university yearbook, Lemon Holt proved "spectacular," while Wong "played a remarkably fine game." In 1929, Lemon Holt was still an offensive force. When UH took down the Honolulu Athletic Club squad, he, Willie Wise's brother, John, and Hiram Kaakua led the way. [48]

The 1930s witnessed plenty of action between UH and mainland gridders. In early January 1930, Washington State handled UH relatively easily, 28–7. Still, observers were impressed with the play of Lemon Holt and Hiram Kaakua in the backfield and Norman Kauhahilo on the line. In 1931, Bill "Sonny" Kaeo, who formerly was a lineman as well as captain on the 1928 UH squad, served as assistant for head coach Otto Klum. The UH yearbook of 1932 described Ernest Chan as "a promising Rainbow quarterback," while touting William Ahuna as a halfback and William Kishi as a tackle. One of the 1931 team's biggest victories was over the Drake University squad, which visited the islands from Iowa. Guard Norman Kauaihilo proved vital in the 19–13 victory as he knocked down and intercepted a Drake pass and then proceeded to run the ball into the end zone for a touchdown. The 1931 team also played the University of Oklahoma tough, as George Indie, a Native Hawaiian fullback, stood out. A highlight of the 1933 season was UH's upset of Denver, 7–6, on the mainland. Playing in the mile-high city, Masao Sone helped lead the drive for UH's sole touchdown and took the ball into the end zone for his team's only touchdown. [49]

Fred Dawson, who coached the University of Denver, heaped praise on a Hawaiian Japanese gridder for UH. After his team played UH in 1933, Dawson maintained "Hawaii has a little guard who is as good as any I have seen . . . I sent three men into the game Saturday with specific instructions to break through [Isao] Toyama—to get him out of there. But they could not move him. He deserves a great deal of credit for keeping us from scoring that time we had three downs on the one-yard line." [50]

In the mid-1930s, UH football attracted national publicity. A traditional powerhouse from the West Coast, Cal was upset by UH when the Bears journeyed to Oahu. Bill Ahuna scored a touchdown for the home team as did Native Hawaiian Maynard Pilitz. Several months later, the *Salt Lake Tribune* columnist Jimmy Hodgon purported that the first thing the UH players did when they got off a train in Salt Lake City in November 1935 was ask, "Where can we get some chop suey?" After leaving

Utah, UH gridders traveled to Denver where Denver University upended them 14–7 despite the sterling performance of Tommy Kaulukukui. Then they backtracked to Los Angeles to play UCLA at the Los Angeles Coliseum. The *Los Angeles Times* sportswriter, Jack Sanger, marveled at the diversity of the UH football team: "Five Hawaiians, two Japanese, two American Indians, and one Scotchman will be in . . . [the] . . . starting lineup." Aside from star Hawaiian Chinese Tommy Kaulukukui, Tony Morse, who possessed Irish, Indian, and Native Hawaiian ancestry, stood out at halfback, while George Aki played fullback. The Hawaiians lost to UCLA. However, after returning to the islands, UH managed to edge the visiting University of Utah eleven, 21–20. Kaulukukui and Morse starred for the victors, but it was Aki who gathered in an eighty-three-yard touchdown pass. Another visiting team was less generous. USC pounced on the home team, 38–6, in the Poi Bowl. Morse, Ahuna, and Aki, nevertheless, performed well.[51]

Excelling in baseball and basketball as well as football, Tommy Kaulukukui stunned mainland squads with his talents. In 1934, UH drubbed Denver 36–14. Kaulukukui scored a touchdown and tossed two more. He was not the whole show, however. Hawaiian Chinese George Zane blocked a Denver punt, which led to a safety, and Kenichi Hayakawa added some finishing touches by throwing a touchdown pass toward the end of the game. The next year, UCLA beat UH rather handily, 19–6. Still, Kaulukukui shined as one of the game's biggest stars after he took off on a 100-yard kickoff return for a touchdown. Before the game, however, the *Los Angeles Times* lauded Kaulukukui's passing ability, claiming he "throws-em and with accuracy." After the game, the *Times'* Jack Sanger called Kaulukukui "Cookie," because "he looked mighty sweet" and, more likely, because it was easier to type. Exoticizing Kaulukukui, Sanger insisted that "Cookie had learned to shake his hips [to avoid tacklers] from the native Hawaiian hula dancers." America's most famous sportswriter at the time, Grantland Rice was inspired by an insipid popular song about the islands to tout Kaulukukui as "Grass Shack." In December, 1935, a visiting Utah University squad saw its lead over UH evaporate before seventeen thousand fans at Honolulu Stadium. Kaulukukui heaved the winning touchdown pass to put the Rainbows up for good. According to one press account, "[T]he tiny Hawaiian ran back with towering Ute linemen swarming after him . . . [and] . . . calmly flipped the ball over the enemy secondary to Ernest Moses, who fell over the goal." Also impressed with Kaulukukui, the *Salt Lake Tribune* published a photo of the backfield star and hailed his "dazzling running and passing," adding that he was "as hard to stop as a greased pig in a picnic crowd."[52]

Tommy Kaulukukui's brothers were also great athletes who excelled in football at UH. Late in 1937, the *Seattle Times* asserted that when the University of Washington encountered UH, it had better be prepared not only for Tommy Kaulukukui, but his freshman brother, Joe. The brothers apparently did the bulk of the running and passing for UH. In 1938, the San Jose State football squad was riding high on an eleven-game winning streak. Then, the Spartans journeyed to the islands where they were upset by the UH squad, 13–12. Joe Kaulukukui was the big star for the home team. Later in December, UH traveled to Utah where the University of Utah barely beat the Hawaiians despite the heroics of Joe Kaulukukui.[53]

In 1939, UH continued to irritate mainland elevens. The *San Diego Union*'s sports editor, Ted Steinman, complained that UH's John Naumu riddled San Diego State's pass defense by completing seven of twelve passes. A few weeks later, the UH eleven was in Utah to take on the University of Utah. The home team won, but the *Salt Lake Tribune*'s John F. Chandler praised Joe Kaulukukui as the game's brightest star. Kaulukukui "had the hardest name to pronounce and was the toughest to stop as he ran the ball, passed, and booted it for sixty minutes." Center Kaye Bong Chung stood out as well for blocking a Utah PAT attempt.[54]

John Naumu remained an important fixture of UH's backfield in the early 1940s. In 1941, John Nanumu's arm led UH to another victory over a mainland team in September, when the Hawaiians easily downed Portland, 33–6. Naumu even passed for a conversion after a touchdown as he flung the ball successfully in Min King Wong's direction. Aside from his passing, Naumu also scored on a ten-yard carry. Some weeks later, UH whitewashed the College of Pacific (COP), 14–0. Naumu crossed the goal line on a seven-yard run and kicked the conversion. Moreover, Chin Do Kim, ordinarily a lineman, managed to use his passing ability to keep COP in the doghouse. After the United States entered the war, UH played a schedule of games against local teams in 1942. In October, John Naumu was still in the backfield when UH edged the Hawaiian Pines, 7–6. Naumu, praised as the "backfield ace" by *Ka Leo O' Hawaii,* tied the score up in the last moments of the game with a touchdown run.[55]

UH teams often inspired exoticization and some respect from mainland journalists. In 1938, the *Los Angeles Times* noted the arrival of the Rainbow Warriors in Los Angeles as the squad made its way to Denver. The daily observed the cultural diversity of the twenty-four athletes on the traveling squad, captained by Kaye Chung and "representing fifteen distinct racial groups—including Koreans and Scandinavians." Late in 1940, readers of the *Charleston Daily Mail* published a photograph of two UH gridders, Joe Kaulukukui and Nolie Smith. The two were pictured receiving pineapple juice and a bowl of poi from Gertrude Kamakau and Martha Levy, described as "Hula-dancing coeds at the university." The occasion was the Pineapple Bowl, then an annual event in Honolulu. Several months later, the UH squad arrived in Portland to take on the University of Portland eleven. The *Portland Oregonian* proclaimed that the Hawaiian gridders had come from the "islands of pineapple and poi." The *Oregonian* also pointed out that hula dancers had journeyed with the football team to lend it an exotic aura.[56]

The Honolulu press seemingly took the UH team and its unique diversity more in stride. On the day before Pearl Harbor was attacked, the *Honolulu Star-Bulletin* praised a couple of Japanese American linemen for UH. "[H]usky Unkei Uchima" was extolled as a mainstay on the UH line. As for Sadao Watasaki, he was the team's "star tackle."[57]

After interruption by World War II, games between UH and mainland colleges revived. Coached by Tommy Kaulukukui, the postwar UH teams did not always beat mainland elevens but they were entertaining. The *San Francisco Examiner*'s Harry Borba wrote in 1946 that "they say Tommy Kaulukukui's boys do more tricks with a football than a distiller with the prices of bootlegged liquor." In 1946, UH upset a visiting team from Fresno State. Starring for the home team were lineman Unkei Uchima, as well as backs Wallace Lam Ho, described in the 1930 census data as racially an Asian Hawaiian son of a police officer father, and Sol Kaulukukui, Tommy's and Joe's younger brother. Uchima had blocked a Fresno State punt, which set up Lam's winning touchdown.[58]

The 1947 squad had enough talent to beat some mainland elevens. Sol Kaulukukui was described by the *Honolulu Record* as UH's "ace 'T' master," alluding to his command of the still relatively novel T-formation offense. Against a respected Michigan State squad in 1947, Kaulukukui heaved "two beautiful touchdown passes" before he was hurt in a 58–19 loss. Richard Asato threw another touchdown pass. Moreover, Michigan State players praised the performances of Wallace Lam Ho and Bob Shibuya. UH later took an even greater shellacking from the University of Nevada, 73–12. However, according to the *Ka Leo O' Hawaii*, "diminutive, dynamic Jimmy Asato" proved troublesome to the victors. Before falling to Michigan State, UH had shut out Montana, 14–0. Part-Nikkei Charley Bessette crossed the goal line once for UH, while Jyun Hirota, the "little scatback" ran the ball in for a thirty-three-yard touchdown. In December 1947, UH beat Fresno State at the Shriner's Aloha Bowl, 27–13. Jyun Hirota, who would later play Japanese major league baseball, provided one of the game's highlights by scoring on a sixty-eight-yard jaunt for which Unkei Uchima led the interference. Johnny Dang and Richard Mamiya, described by UH's student newspaper as a master of the bootleg play, added touchdowns for the victors. Also performing well for the 1947 was guard Saburo Takeyasu, praised in the *Ka Leo O' Hawaii* as "185 pounds of sheer power and strength." Part-Hawaiian and a son of a sugar boiler father on Maui in 1940, end Philip Haake contributed to the team's success. The "lanky" Haake was nicknamed Tarzan. According to UH's 1948 yearbook, Wally Lam Ho, the team's "block busting fullback" was MVP (Most Valuable Player). Hirota was voted the most improved player on the squad, while Saburo Takeyasu was named the best lineman.[59]

In 1948, Jyun Hirota and Louis Collins, co-captained the squad. Five foot seven and 165 pounds when he played for UH, Hirota, the 1930 U.S. census manuscripts tell us, was the seven-year-old son of Japanese immi-

grants living in Honolulu. His father was a post office clerk, while his
mother was a servant for a private family. The 1940 U.S. census manuscripts tell us that Collins was the part-Hawaiian son of a father who
worked as a road construction laborer in Maui. When UH met Redlands
in Southern California, the *San Bernardino County Sun* promoted the
game. In one article, the *Sun* asserted the UH's standout Harry Kahuanui
was the only "full-blooded Hawaiian" on the team and passing to Kahuanui was the "sweet tossing" Sol Kaulukukui. Accompanying Kaulukukui
in the backfield were "swivel-hipped" running backs such as Louie Collins, Johnny Dang, Richard Mamiya, and Jyun Hirota.[60]

During the 1948 season, the UH squad traveled to East Lansing, Michigan. The promotion of Hawaiian statehood and tourism clearly hovered
over the excursion. Yet attracting support for Hawaiian statehood meant
demonstrating how familiarly American Hawai'i was despite its large
population of non-white, Asian and Pacific Islander people, while attracting tourism meant demonstrating Hawaiian exoticism. Suiting up and
dispatching to the American Midwest, a multiethnic, multiracial group of
young men competent in one of the United States' favorite sports might
help reconcile mainlanders to Hawaiian statehood. Yet exoticizing the
Hawaiian experience to expedite tourism might deter efforts to make
Hawai'i the fiftieth state.

Accompanying the team to East Lansing was UH athletic director,
Iwao Miyake. A few days before the game, Miyake and several UH gridders made a presentation on behalf of Hawaiian statehood and tourism.
The players, ukuleles in hand, strummed and sang "Hawaiian song."
Moreover, Hawaiian Olympic swimmer Thelma Kalama was recruited to
perform the hula. Miyake lectured the audience on Hawaiian history and
translated the songs and dances for the audience.[61]

In 1949, the UH team took on mainland squads such as Texas Western
and Fresno State. In Texas to play Texas Western, the Hawaiians were
greeted by press coverage which included a brief poem about running
back Johnny Dang: "A good back is Dang/And that's no slang." The *El
Paso Herald-Post* then told readers that the "Chinese youth" combined
"speed and power" as a fullback. The *Post* advised readers further to
keep an eye out for the passing of Sol Kaulukukui and Richard Mamiya,
as well as the pass catching of Harry Kahuanui. Several weeks later,
Fresno State again dispatched an eleven to the islands, where they met
defeat by the University of Hawai'i and stars, Johnny Dang, Jimmy Asato, and Sol Kaulukukui. The same team edged a visiting squad from
Redlands on New Year's 1950, 33–32. Quarterback Sol Kaulukukui
proved the game's big star, tossing touchdown passes to Hirota and
Francis Lum, along with also kicking three conversions. Meanwhile, Harry Kahuanui was picked to play in the East West Shrine game in 1949.
Indeed, he wound up in the starting lineup.[62]

After World War II, the *Pacific Citizen* noted that Nisei significantly powered University of Hawai'i grid teams. The 1947 squad not only included several Hawaiian Japanese, but Harold Kometani served as a team assistant coach. Hawaiian Japanese were also prominent on the 1949 team. On that squad, the *Pacific Citizen* acknowledged athletes such as Jimmy Asato, Mansfield Doi, and Richard Mamiya. According to a *Los Angeles Times* report, Jimmy Asato and Sol Kaulukukui both shined for the home team despite a devastating 74–20 loss to Stanford. Saburo Takayasu was chosen the MVP of the 1949 squad, while Kiyoshi Matsuo was honored as the most promising gridder, and Jimmy Asato, the most inspirational. Takayasu, a veteran of the valiant all Nikkei 442nd regiment during World War II, was team captain in 1949, while Mansfield Doi earned election as captain for the 1950 season. Doi's brother Herbert was also a starting center for the team in 1949. Moreover, an older brother, Wally, played for UH in 1940 and 1941. The Doi brothers' father was Hawaiian-born, declared racially Japanese by the U.S. Census manuscripts of 1940, and a warehouse clerk. Their mother was also a Hawaiian born Nikkei. During the 1950 season, Mansfield Doi and Jimmy Asato excelled in a game against Fresno State. Later, the players on that California squad named them to their all-opponents' eleven.[63]

Remembered as one of Hawai'i's most remarkable athletes, Tommy Kaulukukui coached postwar UH squads through 1950. Then, after too many unprofitable, losing seasons to suit UH administrators, he was given a "leave of absence," which turned out to be permanent. A student columnist for the *Ka Leo O' Hawaii* defended Kaulukukui, insisting that he had an insufficient supply of local talent with which to work. Rather than staying home and putting their skills on display for UH, capable Hawaiian gridders were heading to the mainland. UH alumni could help keep local gridders at home, but, the columnist lamented, they had failed to do so. A patronizing mainland sportswriter at the time told readers that Kaulukukui was a "likeable little island native."[64]

Tommy Kaulukukui Jr., a judge on the islands, wanted to remind islanders in the early 2000s that his father "led a life of service and tried to instill that in others. He was a spiritual man and well balanced. I think he was most proud of his work as a teacher and coaching, molding young people." Aside from coaching and teaching, Kaulukukui owned an insurance agency in the 1950s, was appointed a U.S. Marshal, and served several years in the Office of Hawaiian Affairs (OHA). Steve Kuna, who played for UH while Kaulukukui coached and served with him on the OHA, told the *Honolulu Star-Bulletin*'s Dave Reardon, "I was always in awe of him as a coach because he was so soft-spoken but commanded so much respect. I trusted everything he said. He told you your job and how to do it. None of that Vince Lombardi rah-rah stuff, but he gave you the confidence you needed."[65]

In the 1950s, UH football occasionally held surprises for unsuspecting mainland elevens. In the early 1950s, Sadoa Matsukawa was a fine quarterback for UH. Halfback Jim Asato, guards Henry Ariyoshi and Eric Watanabe, tackle Charley Araki and end Richard Ueoka also shined, as did Hartwell Freitas and George Fujiwara at linebacker. Thanks largely to Asato and Matsukawa, UH beat the University of Denver, while the latter's passing undid Lewis and Clark. According to the university's 1956 yearbook, linemen Dick Ueoka, Bruno Ariyoshi, and Charles Araki were chosen to compete in the Hula Bowl all-star game. Ueoka served as cocaptain of the 1955 squad along with part-Hawaiian Hartwell Freitas. The latter, in 1940, was found by the census taker as a six-year-old residing at Honolulu's Kalihi Orphanage. Ed Kawawaki was the team's total offense leader, Fred Nagata excelled as the best passer, and Christy Mamiya achieved the highest per carry average. Bruno Arioshi and Bill Tam starred as guards. Kaye Chung and Sus Tanaka were assistant coaches.[66]

In 1955, UH pulled off a major upset by beating the University of Nebraska on the Cornhuskers' own field in Lincoln. To be sure, the game was relatively close, 6–0, but Hawaiian running back Eddie Kawawaki proved vital to the victors. For much of the game, Kawawaki had been "dazzling" at halfback. However, regular quarterback Fred Nagata got hurt, and Nagata's usual replacement, Dick Hadama, had been previously sidelined by an injury. Thus, Kawawaki was moved over to quarterback where he performed well, guiding UH to within a yard of the goal line. From there, Hartwell Freitas, a fullback replacement for Clayton Ching, plunged for the only touchdown. Meanwhile, Charles Araki excelled on the line. Kawawaki remembered his victorious team as "locals. We represented Hawaii." If so, the UH gridders were complicating, as well as reinforcing Hawai'i's bid for statehood given localism's tense relationship to nation-building and globalization.[67]

UH football experienced ups and downs in the late 1950s. In 1957, UH demolished Lewis and Clark, 40–7, thanks to the work of backfield standouts and Native Hawaiian brothers, Nolan, Talbot, and Henry George, as well as pass receiver Ben Holokai. Against Willamette, Colin Chock scored on two passes of twenty-seven and ninety-two yards. The George brothers excelled for the 1958 team. Henry scored UH's only touchdown against Arizona State on a ninety-five-yard "breathtaking" kickoff return. When UH easily downed Idaho State, 40–19, all the Georges did well, but Henry scampered for an eighty-three-yard touchdown. In the Aloha Classic, Nolan George caught a touchdown pass in a loss against Utah.[68]

Tennyson Lum was described by the *San Jose Mercury* as a "145 pound scatback" for UH. Lum, who had tried his hand at mainland football with Oregon's little Linfield College in the late 1950s, dazzled for UH. When UH beat Los Angeles State in 1959, Lum tallied on a fifteen-yard run. A couple of weeks later, UH lost to Fresno State but Lum managed to toss a touchdown pass to Nolan George. In September 1960, Lum ran amuck against Los Angeles State. In thirteen carries, he chalked up 152 yards, including a sixteen-yard touchdown run. The next week, a wire story maintained, "Tiny Tennyson Lum, a 140-pound sophomore from Honolulu, ran the [Utah] Utes dizzy in the first half." Utah prevailed, 33–6, but Lum scored UH's only touchdown on a ten-yard run. The next month, he crossed the goal line three times against COP. The *San Jose Mercury* maintained Lum proved the "big man in the attack."[69]

For much of the mid-twentieth century, UH retained a relatively small-time football program. In the early 1960s, Jim Asato joined Kaulukukui as UH's second head coach possessing Asian or Pacific ancestry. Asato coached three years from 1961 to 1963. Curiously, despite the relatively large numbers of Asian and Pacific Islanders playing UH football, the school would not hire another coach possessing Asian or Pacific Islander ancestry until Norm Chow was brought on board in 2012. By the late twentieth century, UH was granted elite Division I status in the NCAA, while suiting up many competitive teams. Honolulu sportswriter Bill Kwon told the *Sporting News* in 1993 that the football team reflected the islands' diversity. He said that twenty UH gridders were either Hawaiian or part-Hawaiian. Nineteen possessed Samoan ancestry, while others could boast of Tahitian and Tongan descent. Kicker Ampay Champathong came from a Laotian background.[70]

Indeed, late twentieth-century multiethnic, multiracial UH football could indeed boast of talented football players. Nationally prominent gridders such as Mark Tuinei, Jesse Sapolu, Falina and Al Noga, and Ma'a Tanuvasa donned UH uniforms on the way to the pros. There were other lesser known but still fine UH football players of Asian and Pacific Islander descent. In 1971, Elroy Chong was the regular quarterback for UH, tossing 156 passes, while completing 71. That same year, Don Mahi carried the ball 95 times for a respectable 379 yards as a backup running back. A few years later, Morgado was on the Manoa campus after a stint at Michigan State. In 1974, he gained 436 yards in 129 attempts. At quarterback, Alex Kaloi completed half of his 240 pass attempts. Backing Kaloi up was future pro and UH coach, June Jones. In the mid-1990s, UH suited up a quarterback named Glen Freitas, possessing indigenous Hawaiian and Filipino ancestry. Born in Western Samoa, Tuu Alalu was a running back around the same time. Teammates included linebacker Danny Katoa who came to UH by way of Hawthorne, California, but was born in the Philippines and, possessing East Indian ancestry, talented 300-pound Bobby Singh was born in Fiji. During the early 2000s, UH nurtured standout defenders such as linebacker Vince Manuwai and Isaak Sapanoga.[71]

Levi Stanley was one of the more respected UH gridders in the late twentieth century. Scholars Tengan and Markham describe Levi Stanley as "a football star-cum-educator." Growing up in a lower class, predominantly Native Hawaiian district of Wai'anae, Stanley's football skills rendered him a star on the UH football team in the 1970s. At that time, Coach Larry Price challenged Stanley and teammates to achieve academically as well as in football. Stanley subsequently earned his BA and MA and took up an honored career as an educator.[72]

In the early 2000s, Hawaiian Chinese Timmy Chang broke passing records as former NFL quarterback June Jones introduced a wide open, pass happy offense to the university on Oahu. In 2000, Chang was named the WAC's freshman of the year. When he took part in San Francisco's East-West Shrine game in 2005, the Bay Area's Asian Americans noticed. At a luncheon for Chang, Steve Louie, chair of the Asian Women's Resource Center, acknowledged that "other Chinese" had tried to play professional football, but none had succeeded. Louie hoped that Chang would change all that and maintained that Chang had the talent to do so. James Fang, president of *Asian Week*, gushed over Chang's pro prospects, claiming that none other than Bill Walsh saw Chang's potential.[73]

Chang was greeted enthusiastically by students at Newcomer High School in San Francisco, a school designed to serve the city's large population of English as Second Language (ESL) families. The *Asian Week* reported that the students practiced their English before they participated in a rally to welcome Chang. They also read an earlier *Asian Week* piece published about Chang. A Korean immigrant student and a Russian immigrant student spoke of the inspiration they have taken from Chang's success. Chang was introduced by Newcomer principal Herb Chan, who was accompanied by three Chinese American members of San Francisco's Board of Education. The Hawaiian quarterback responded, "I am very proud to be Asian American and to be representing a lot of us over here today, and it's a dream come true to play football at such a high level—and I believe that if you work hard, anything can come your way. I've tried to work very hard at football and tried to make it my career, and I'm just very proud to be here."[74]

Subsequently, Bryant Moniz had some good seasons quarterbacking UH. Possessing Hawaiian and Chinese descent, Moniz was an all-conference choice in 2010. During that season, he connected on 248 of 397 passes for 2,733 yards. An all-around athlete who started at point guard for UH's basketball team, Moniz was also the second leading ground gainer on the team.[75]

CONCLUSION

When mainland Americans think of football, they rarely think of Hawai'i. Nevertheless, football fans in Berkeley in 1950 may have been surprised to note that Hawaiian Elizabeth Pa had been chosen "Miss Football of 1950" over several European American competitors. Accordingly, she presided over Cal's "Football Festival," and the *Chinese Press* subsequently displayed a photo of the "part Hawaiian, part Caucasian and part Chinese" Pa waving to thousands of football fans in Berkeley. Historian Shirley Jennifer Lim maintains that post-World War II important segments of Asian American ethnic communities looked upon young women such as Pa demonstrating "ideal female citizenship." as key in gaining acceptance by the dominant white American culture. And what could be more acceptable in a post-World War II United States seeking to contain feminist ambitions than serving as a football festival beauty queen?[76]

Yet Pa's hybrid ancestry reveals another story that football helped narrate on the Hawaiian Islands. A sport nurtured on the mainland by largely native-born, white, and economically privileged men prospered among the island's multiethnic population. Not only has it encouraged the skills of Pacific Islander Hawaiians, which may not surprise mainlanders, but Hawaiians of Asian ancestry as well. In the process, football reinforced Hawaiian local culture—a culture which does not erase racial and ethnic borderlands so much as render them easier to traverse. Yet football has proven a ragged cosmopolitan canopy in Hawai'i. As Tengan and Markham point out and as we will discuss in a further chapter, football, and its obsession with hypermasculinity, may not have contributed all that much to the welfare of Pacific Islander Hawaiians.

NOTES

1. Takaki, *Strangers*, chapter 4; Morimoto, "Barefoot"; Joel S. Franks, *Hawaiian Sports in the Twentieth Century*, (Lewiston, ME: The Edwin Mellen Press, 2002; *Hawaiian Travelers*; Anderson, *Cosmopolitan Canopy*.

2. *Pacific Commercial Advertiser*, November 11, 1906; December 2, 1906; *Honolulu Evening Bulletin*, November 7, 1908; September 16, 1911; Franks, *Hawaiian Travelers*.

3. Margaret Jolley, "Moving Masculinities: Memories and Bodies across Oceania," *The Contemporary Pacific* (Spring, 2008), 6; *Pacific Commercial Advertiser*, November 12, 1905, 11; November 14, 1916, 14; *Honolulu Evening-Bulletin*, September 2, 1911, 9; September 25, 1911, 9; November 29, 1911, 9; *Honolulu Star-Bulletin*, September 11, 1915, 15; October 11, 1915, 11; *Fort Worth Star-Telegram*, November 3, 1920, 17; Des Jardins, *Walter Camp*, 193–194.

4. *Honolulu Evening Bulletin*, November 7, 1908; November 14, 1908; *Pacific Commercial Advertiser*, November 21, 1905; October 26, 1912; November 4, 1916; *Honolulu Star-Bulletin*, October 14, 1916; T. C. Goo, "Wonderful Athletes when They Want to Be," in *Chinese in Hawaii: A Historical Sketch*, edited by Robert M. Lee (Honolulu: Advertising Publishing Company, 1961), 71

5. *Pacific Commercial Advertiser*, November 4, 1911; October 26, 1912; *Hawaiian Gazette*, October 21, 1913; *Honolulu Star-Bulletin*, September 11, 1915; October 7, 1915; October 9, 1915; October 5, 1917; Franks, *Hawaiian Travelers*.

6. *Honolulu Evening Bulletin*, September 25, 1911; *Pacific Commercial Advertiser*, October 4, 1915; November 4, 1915; *Honolulu Star-Bulletin*, September 30, 1916.

7. *Honolulu Star-Bulletin*, September 10, 1917.

8. Ibid., September 24, 1927; September 28, 1927. October 22, 1927.

9. Ibid., October 13, 1927; Don Watson, "St. Louis Athlete Can Perform in Exhibition Game," October 26, 1927, 8; Frank Belles, "Noted Star of Grid in States Exclusive Services, September 24, 1927, 8; "Oana Was Good But He Was Not the Whole Show," October 17, 1927, 8; October 13, 1927; Franks, *Hawaiian Sports*, 134–135; Goo, *Chinese*;

http://www.hawaiiprepworld.com/football/ilh-football-first-team-all-stars-1920-present/ (June 18, 2016).

10. Albert Chee, "Kam Warriors Set for First Grid Struggle," *Honolulu Star-Bulletin*, September 24, 1927, 8; January 8, 1929; December 7, 1934, 12; *Dallas Morning-News*, December 25, 1928, part 2, 13; *Nevada State Journal*, December 27, 1932, 9; *Honolulu Record*, October 24, 1957, 4; U.S. Census Bureau, Manuscript Census Schedules, 1930, 1940, City and County of Honolulu, www.ancestry.com (July 16, 2015). http://www.hawaiiprepworld.com/football/ilh-football-first-team-all-stars-1920-present/ (June 18, 2016).

11. *Honolulu Star-Bulletin*, October 6, 1927, 10; October 10, 1927; December 4, 1934, 10; December 7, 1934, 12; *Honolulu Record*, October 24, 1957, 4; McKinley High School Yearbook, 1934, 1936, www.ancestry.com (November 3, 2013); http://www.hawaiiprepworld.com/football/ilh-football-first-team-all-stars-1920-present/ (June 18,2016).

12. Franks, *Hawaiian Travelers*.

13. Al Warden, "Idaho Ekes out 12 to 6 Decision over Hawaii Grid Eleven, *Ogden Standard-Examiner*, October 29, 1931; November 10, 1935, 9; October 1, 1940; October 21, 1940; McKinley High School Yearbook, 1936, www.ancestry.com (November 3, 2013); Joel S. Franks, *Asian Pacific Americans and Baseball: A History* (Jefferson, NC: McFarland & Company, 2008), 91–92; *Seattle Times*, December 10, 1937, p. 31; Marlow Brangan, "6,000 Fans Expected to See Colorful Micks in Action," *Salt Lake Tribune*, November 8, 1941, 24; *San Francisco Chronicle*, October 6, 1941; *Honolulu Record*, October 24, 1957, 4; http://obits.staradvertiser.com/2014/03/21/ (December 10, 2015); Franks, *Hawaiian Sports*, 67, 195.

14. *Honolulu Star-Bulletin*, October 1, 1940; October 4, 1940; October 5, 1940; October 12, 1940, October 15, 1940; *Honolulu Record*, October 1, 1953, 6; October 24, 1957, 4. Punahou Yearbook, 1940, 1941, www.ancestry.com.,(November 12, 2014); Farrington High School Yearbook, 1940, www.classmates.com (December 29, 2014); U.S. Census Bureau, Manuscript Census Schedules, 1940, City and County of Honolulu, www.ancestry.com (July 29, 2015).

15. Leilehua High School Yearbook, 1938, www.ancestry.com (September 27, 2014); Hilo High School Yearbook, 1941, www.ancestry.com (September 26, 2014); *Honolulu Star-Bulletin*, October 3, 1940; October 9, 1940; Robert K. Fitts, *Wally Yonamine: The Man Who Changed Japanese Baseball* (Lincoln: University of Nebraska Press, 2008), 15, 16, 18; U.S. Census Bureau, Manuscript Census Schedules, City of Lahaina and Island of Maui, www.ancestry.com (July 29, 2015).

16. *Honolulu Star-Bulletin*, November 10, 1943; Mickey Mapa, "Best Not Too Good for St. Louis Team," November 12, 1943; November 20, 1943.

17. Mickey Mapa, "They're Kittens No Longer," in *Honolulu Star-Bulletin*, November 15, 1943; November 22, 1943.

18. Ibid., November 1, 1943; Mickey Mapa, "Raiders End Prep Season Undefeated," November 22, 1943; November 27, 1943; Fitts, *Yonamine*, 19–24, 26, 27.

19. *Honolulu Star-Bulletin*, November 10, 1943; November 12, 1943; November 20, 1943; November 25, 1943; November 27, 1943.

20. *Honolulu Record*, October 14, 1948; November 18, 1948; October 12, 1950; October 19, 1950, September 27, 1951; Dick Brome, "Honolulu Gridders to Invade Mainland," *Santa Cruz Sentinel*, September 14, 1946; *Pacific Citizen*, December 9, 1950; November 28, 1952; December 30,, 1952; Goo, *Chinese*, 71; Kaimuki High School Yearbook, 1946, www.ancestry.com (April 25, 2016); Punahou High School Yearbook, 1949, www.ancestry.com (September 8, 2010); Iolani High School Yearbook, 1949, www.ancestry.com (May 21, 2014); Kamehameha Yearbook, 1956, www.ancestry.com., (July 14, 2016) ; U.S. Census Bureau, Manuscript Census Schedules, City of Waimea, island of Hawai'i, 1940, www.ancestry.com., (April 20, 2015); http://obits.staradvertiser.com/2015/03/15/alfred-ainoa-eki-coach-espinda-jr/, (October 3, 2016); http://content.lib.utah.edu/utils/getfile/collection/uuath2/id/100/filename/76.pdf, UCLA /Utah program (June 9, 2016).

21. *Honolulu Advertiser,* April 16, 1935; *Pacific Citizen,* January 14, 1950; Honolulu *Record,* October 14, 1948; *Honolulu Star-Bulletin,* December 6, 1949; Iolani High School Yearbook, 1949, www.ancestry.com (May 21, 2014).

22. *Honolulu Record,* October 11, 1951; November 18, 1952; October 6, 1955; McKinley High School Yearbook, 1956, 1959, www.ancestry.com (April 1, 2011); St. Louis School Yearbook, 1951, www.ancestry.com (September 21, 2016).

23. Cathy Chong, "Golden Time for Football and Friendship," https://www.iolani. org/files/pdfs/coverstory_winter08.pdf (July 20, 2015).

24. https://factfinder.census.gov/faces/tableservices/jsf/pages/productview.xhtml? src=bkmk (September 16, 2017); Miliani High School Yearbook, 1988, www.ancestry.com (September 27, 2014); Michael Lasquero, "Wong to Take over Kailua Football Program," http://scoringlive.com/story.php?storyid=11242 (March 7, 2015); *Honolulu Star-Advertiser,* January 2, 2015; Tom Shanahan, "Kale Ane Followed His Father's Footsteps Back to Coaching in Hawaii," http://footballmatters.org/kale-ane-followed-his-fathers-footsteps-back-to-coaching-in-hawaii/ (February 2, 2016); http://www.punahou.edu/alumni/community-groups/athletic-hall-of-fame/profile/ index.aspx?linkid=648&moduleid=101 (February 2, 2016); Nick Abramo, "Roosevelt Hires Kahooiihala as Football Coach," http://www.hawaiiprepworld.com/football/ roosevelt-hires-kahooilihala-as-football-coach/ (June 30, 2016).

25. *Hawaiian Gazette,* November 29, 1895; *Pacific Commercial Advertiser,* November 8, 1902; December 13, 1905; *Honolulu Evening Bulletin,* December 28, 1905; February 14, 1906; December 31, 1917; *Honolulu Star-Bulletin,* November 7, 1919; *Ka Leo O' Hawaii,* November 5, 1930; Franks, *Hawaiian Sports,* 42, 43; Michael Nevin Willard, "Duke Kahanomoku's Body: Biography of Hawai'i," in *Sports Matters: Race, Recreation and Culture,* edited by John Bloom and Michael Nevin Willard (New York: New York University Press, 2002), 30.

26. *Pacific Commercial Advertiser,* December 20, 1911; December 3, 1916; December 4, 1916; *Hawaiian Gazette,* October 24, 1916; Franks, *Crossing,* 118; Dick Hyland, "Hyland Tabs Beavers as Upset Boys," *Los Angeles Times,* September 8, 1951; *Honolulu Star-Bulletin,* December 17, 1917; September 21, 1927; October 20, 1927; Don Watson, "Deans Win From Oahu Blues," October 24, 1927.

27. *Honolulu Evening Bulletin,* December 28, 1905; *Charleston Daily Mail,* January 5, 1923; U.S. Census Bureau, Manuscript Census Schedules, City and County of Honolulu, 1900, 1930, www.ancestry.com (May 21, 2015).

28. *San Jose News,* December 27, 1927; *Reno Evening Gazette,* January 3, 1933; December 26, 1934; *Salem Daily Capital Journal,* December 26, 1934; *San Francisco Chronicle,* February 10, 1936; *Honolulu Star-Bulletin,* October 2, 1940; Franks, *Crossing,* 118; Ethnic Studies Oral History Project, *Kalihi,* vol. 1, 271, 346; Goo, "Wonderful Athletes," 71; U.S. Census Bureau, Manuscript Census Schedules, City and County of Honolulu, 1930, (May 21, 2015).

29. *Ka Leo O' Hawaii,* October 18, 1929; *Honolulu Star-Bulletin,* October 1, 1940; Franks, *Asian Pacific American Baseball,* 90–91, 151; University of Hawai'i Yearbook, 1937, www.ancestry.com (May 19, 2016); U.S. Census Bureau, Manuscript Census Schedules, City and County of Honolulu, 1940 (May 19, 2016).

30. John P. Rosa, *Local Story: The Massie Kahahawai Case and the Culture of History* (Honolulu: University of Hawai'i Press, 2014).

31. *Honolulu Star-Bulletin,* October 1, 1940.

32. Don Watson, "Rainbows Too Bright for Bears," *Honolulu Star-Bulletin,* November 1, 1943; November 18, 1943.

33. Ibid., October 1, 1940; October 2, 1940; October 15, 1940; November 5, 1943; November 16, 1943; U.S. Census Bureau, Manuscript Census Schedules, City and County of Honolulu, 1940, www.ancestry.com (July 29, 2015); *Honolulu Record,* October 24, 1957.

34. *Honolulu Star-Bulletin,* October 1, 1940; October 2, 1940; October 3, 1940; October 15, 1940; Mickey Mapa, "Names Starters for Healanis," November 5, 1943; November

12, 1943; November 16, 1943; U.S. Census Bureau, Manuscript Census Schedules, City and County of Honolulu, 1930, www.ancestry.com (July 17, 2015).

35. *Honolulu Star-Bulletin*, November 17, 1949; Franks, *Hawaiian Sports*, 106; U.S. Census Bureau, Manuscript Census Schedules, City of Wailua and Island of Kaua'i, 1930, www.ancestry.com (April 29, 2016).

36. *Honolulu Record*, September 2, 1948; October 5, 1950; *Pacific Citizen*, December 30, 1952.

37. *Honolulu Record*, September 23, 1948; October 23, 1952; October 30, 1952; *Kansas City Times*, August 24, 1953; University of Hawai'i Yearbook, 1953, 1956, 1958, www.ancestry.com (May 29, 2015); U.S. Census Bureau, Manuscript Census Schedules, City and County of Honolulu, 1940, www.ancestry.com (July 3; 2015); Roberta Chang and Wayne Patterson, *The Koreans in Hawai'i: A Pictorial History, 1903–2003* (Honolulu: University of Hawai'i Press, 2003), 155.

38. *Los Angeles Times*, October 18, 1947; *Helena Independent Record*, December 26, 1947.

39. Opposition to Hawaiian statehood also existed on the islands after the war. To a strong extent, fear of Nikkei empowerment among haoles, Native Hawaiians, and other Asian ethnic groups stoked this opposition. Wu, *Color of Success*, 210–242.

40. *San Jose Mercury*, October 8, 1946; October 10, 1946; October 11, 1946; *Portland Oregonian*, September 29, 1946; *Honolulu Star-Bulletin*, June 27, 1997.

41. *Portland Oregonian*, September 28, 1946; September 29, 1946.

42. *San Jose Mercury*, October 11, 1946; *Ogden Standard Examiner*, December 6, 1946.

43. Frank Bonanno, "Operation Ordered for Cheim," *San Jose News*. September 13, 1947; Fred Merrick, "6 New Stars in State Line-Up," *San Jose Mercury*, September 26, 1947; September 27, 1947; *Pacific Citizen*, October 11, 1947; *Nevada State Journal*, October 7, 1947; U.S. Census Bureau, Manuscript Census Schedules, City and County of Honolulu, 1940, www.ancestry.com (April 29, 2016).

44. *Honolulu Evening-Bulletin*, November 14, 1910; *Pacific Commercial Advertiser*, November 12, 1911; November 4, 1915; November 14, 1916; *Honolulu Star-Bulletin*, October 5, 1917; *San Jose Mercury*, November 22, 1917.

45. *Wichita Beacon*, November 3, 1920; *Reno Evening Gazette*, December 13, 1920; *Portland Oregonian*, October 9, 1921; June 22, 1923; *Nevada State Journal*, November 21, 1923; Yasuo Goto, "Clean Fast Plays Characterize Game at Alexander Field," *Ka Leo O' Hawaii*, January 3, 1923.

46. *San Jose Mercury*, November 19, 1925; November 27, 1925; *Helena Independent*, December 13, 1925.

47. *Portland Oregonian*, December 19, 1927; *Berkeley Daily Gazette*, November 17, 1927; January 3, 1928; U.S. Census Bureau, Manuscript Census Schedules, 1930, City and County of Honolulu, www.ancestry.com (February 7, 2014); Don Watson, "Blaisdell Strengthens Dean Team," *Honolulu Star-Bulletin*, September 30, 1927; University of Hawai'i Yearbook, 1928, www.ancestry.com (July 9, 2015).

48. *Los Angeles Times*, November 23, 1927; University of Hawai'i Yearbook, 1928, www.ancestry.com (July 9, 2015); *Ka Leo O' Hawaii*, October 18, 1929.

49. *Bellingham Herald*, January 2, 1930; *Portland Oregonian*, January 2, 1930; University of Hawai'i Yearbook, 1932, 1934, www.ancestry.com (November 13, 2009).

50. William Carlson Smith, *Americans in Process: A Study of Our Citizens of Oriental Ancestry* (New York: Arno Press, 1970), 341.

51. *Nevada State Journal*, January 2, 1935; *Salt Lake Tribune*, November 4, 1935; *Los Angeles Times*, November 15, 1935; University of Hawai'i Yearbook, 1935, 1936, www.ancestry.com (November 13, 2009).

52. *Los Angeles Times*, November 14, 1935; November 16, 1935; *Ogden Standard Examiner*, December 15, 1935; *Salt Lake Tribune*, December 15, 1935, Franks, *Crossing*, 116, 117; University of Hawai'i Yearbook, 1935, www.ancestry.com (November 13, 2009).

53. *Seattle Times*, November 30, 1937; *Los Angeles Times*, December 4, 1938; *Salt Lake Tribune*, December 18, 1938.

54. *San Diego Union,* November 17, 1939; John F. Chandler, "Redskins Vanquish Hawaiian Machine Before Big Crowd," *Salt Lake Tribune,* December 11, 1939; *Ka Leo O' Hawaii,* October 7, 1939; U.S. Census Bureau, Manuscript Census Schedules, City and County of Honolulu, 1940, (July 28, 2016).

55. *Oregon Statesmen,* September 21, 1941; *Nevada State-Journal,* September 25, 1941; *Corvallis Gazette-Times,* September 25, 1941; *Ka Leo O' Hawaii,* October 14, 1942.

56. *Charleston Daily Mail,* December 27, 1940; *Portland Oregonian,* September 14, 1941; Franks, *Crossing,* 117; U.S. Census Bureau, Manuscript Census Schedules, Island of Molokai, 1930, www.ancestry.com (August 13, 2014).

57. *Honolulu Star-Bulletin,* December 6, 1941.

58. *San Francisco Examiner,* November 1, 1946; November 12, 1946; *New York Times,* November 12, 1946; U.S. Census Bureau, Manuscript Census Schedules, City and County of Honolulu 1930, www.ancestry.com (September 24, 2011).

59. *Honolulu Record,* December 9, 1948; *Fresno Bee,* December 7, 1947; *Ka Leo O' Hawaii,* October 14, 1947; December 5, 1947; January 1, 1948; University of Hawai'i Yearbook, 1948, www.ancestry.com (July 28, 2016); U.S. Census Bureau, Manuscript Census Schedules, City of Wailuku and Island of Maui, 1940, www.ancestry.com (April 22, 2016).

60. *San Bernardino County Sun,* October 6, 1948; October 8, 1948; Franks, *Asian Pacific Americans,* 187–188. University of Hawai'i Yearbook, 1949, www.ancestry.com., (July 20, 2015); U.S. Census Bureau, Manuscript Census Schedules, City and County of Honolulu, 1930, www.ancestry.com., (July 30, 2015); U.S. Census Bureau, Manuscript Census Schedules, City of Hana and Island of Maui (July 20, 2015).

61. *Honolulu Star-Bulletin,* October 1, 1948.

62. *El Paso Herald-Post,* September 26, 1949; *Honolulu Star-Bulletin,* December 3, 1949; *San Jose Mercury,* December 29, 1949; *San Bernardino County Sun,* January 2, 1950;

63. *Pacific Citizen,* October 11, 1947; January 7, 1950; January 28, 1950; March 11, 1950; December 30, 1950; *Los Angeles Times,* January 3, 1950; U.S. Census Bureau, Manuscript Census Schedules, City of Koloa and Island of Kaua'i, 1940, www.ancestry.com (March 3, 2013).

64. *Ka Leo O' Hawaii,* January 14, 1949; *Salem Statesmen,* February 13, 1951.

65. Dave Reardon, "Island Sports Legend Defined Wisdom of Warrior," http://archives.starbulletin.com/2007/03/10/news/story06.html (May 7, 2010); *Honolulu Record,* October 5, 1950.

66. *Hawaii Herald,* January 2, 1951; *Honolulu Star-Bulletin,* September 24, 1953; *San Francisco Chronicle,* December 6, 1953; Dan Cisco, *Hawai'i Sports: History, Facts, and Statistics* (Honolulu: University of Hawai'i Press, 1999), 149; University of Hawai'i Yearbook, 1953, 1956, www.ancestry.com (May 29, 2015); U.S. Census Bureau, Manuscript Census Schedules, City and County of Honolulu, 1940, www.ancestry.com (May 29, 2015).

67. Lyle E. Nelson, "A Real Upset," *College Football Historical Society,* May 1996, 11; Dennis Anderson, "UH Pulled Upset of Ages," honoluluadvertiser.com September 19, 2002, (September 8, 2007); Anderson, *Imagined Communities.*

68. Pat Frizzell, "Hawaii Wallops L.C. with Second Half Surge," *Portland Oregonian,* September 22, 1957; Ralph Chaotian, "Spartan Grid Squad Prepares for Hawaii," *Spartan Daily,* September 24, 1958; "Spartan Gridders to Open At Home," September 26, 1958; *San Francisco Chronicle,* September 21, 1958; University of Hawai'i Yearbook, 1958, 1959, www.mocavo.com (December 17, 2014).

69. *San Jose Mercury,* September 14, 1960; December 2, 1960; *Troy Times Record,* November 14, 1959; *San Rafael Daily Independent,* November 28, 1959; *Salt Lake Tribune,* September 12, 1960; *Arizona Republic,* September 18, 1960; *Santa Cruz Sentinel,* October 2, 1960; Goo, "Wonderful Athletes," 71.

70. Cisco, *Hawai'i Sports,* 157; *Sporting News,* October 4, 1993.

71. www.Hawaii.edu (June 7, 2000); Cathy Chong, "Golden Time," http://www.sports-reference.com/cfb/schools/hawaii/1971.html (March 29, 2016); http://www.sports-reference.com/cfb/schools/hawaii/1974.html (March 29, 2016).

72. Tengan and Markham, "Performing," 2424.

73. Franks, *Crossing*, 117–118; Ryan Leong, "A Down-to-Earth Superstar," www.asianweek.com., January 14, 2005 (March 8, 2005).

74. Leong, "Superstar."

75. http://asianplayers.com/football, (May 25, 2016); http: //hawaiiathletics.com/roster.aspx? rp_id=8921 (May 26, 2016).

76. *Chinese Press*, September 29, 1950; Shirley Jennifer Lim, *A Feeling of Belonging: Asian American Women's Public Culture, 1930–1960* (New York: New York University Press, 2006), 137; Elaine Tyler May, *Homeward Bound: American Families in the Cold War Era* (New York: Basic Books, 1988).

THREE

Hawaiian Gridders, Mainland Teams

Around 1890, John Wise was a Native Hawaiian who played football at Oberlin College in Ohio. Indeed, the 1892 Oberlin Yearbook claims that "J.H. Wise" was on the "rush line" for the school football team. Created in Ohio out of the nexus of the second Great Awakening and the abolitionist movement, Oberlin had long seen its mission in part as educating non-white students in the name of Christianity and social justice.[1]

That Wise made his way to Oberlin for a higher education did not just stem from the fact that institutes of post-secondary education did not exist on the islands in the late nineteenth century. Idealistic, if culturally chauvinistic, missionaries flocked to Hawai'i from mainly New England in the early nineteenth century. Spreading the gospel of Protestant modernity, these missionaries found allies among more privileged Native Hawaiians and could influence not only the way Hawaiians were educated but the way Hawai'i was governed. Consequently, they and their descendants wound up with large chunks of Hawaiian land. While the missionaries set in motion an educational system designed to provide some Hawaiians of indigenous descent access to a "classical education" aimed at westernizing them, much of the lesser privileged Hawaiians were educated for dependency—just as American Indians and African Americans were on the mainland.[2]

While Wise was studying at Oberlin, the independent nation of Hawai'i was under attack. Hoping to ultimately join the United States, politically and economically powerful haoles, many of whom were descendants of missionaries, diminished the power of the Native Hawaiian king, as well as Native Hawaiian voting rights. When King Kalakaua died in 1891, and was replaced by his highly nationalistic sister, Queen Liliuokalani, these haoles feared she would restore the power of the Hawaiian monarch and the voting rights of the Hawaiian people. Therefore, they staged a coup and placed Liliuokalani under house arrest. A Hawaiian nationalist, Wise was imprisoned by the haole-backed Republic of Hawaii after he returned to the islands. His crime was his support for Queen Liliuokalani and Native Hawaiian sovereignty. Wise was subsequently freed, but he did not forget his allegiance to his Hawaiian identify. Wise served as a senator in the territorial legislature, in which he often spoke out for the rights of common Native Hawaiians, in the process revealing a troubling belief that they were not only embattled by land-hungry haoles but by job-seeking Asian immigrants. The 1920 U.S. census data describes him as the son of a German immigrant father and a Hawaiian mother. At that time, he worked as a building contractor. During the next decade, his sons, John, Jr., Bill, and Jonah, would emerge as talented football players.[3]

Yet just as American missionaries and later secular educators, businesspeople, and military personnel spread the varying and conflicting gospels of Christianity and Western, capitalist modernity to Hawai'i, Wise and other Hawaiians spread the varying and gospels of Hawai'i. From the late nineteenth century onward, Hawaiian athletes, musicians, and dancers performed Hawai'i throughout the mainland. The Hawai'i performed by singers and dancers may have struck mainlanders as one of warm, tropical breezes; beautiful ocean vistas; and a generous, albeit exotic and primitive, non-white people, seemingly content in their colonized status. The Hawai'i performed by athletes such as those who played football for various colleges on the mainland was that of a land undergoing modernization under American colonial guidance. To be sure, it could all be more complicated. For example, during the 1910s, the multiethnic Hawaiian Travelers baseball team entertained mainlanders with ukuleles and Hawaiian songs, while the great Duke Kahanamoku did not just competitively swim for mainlanders, but expertly displayed his mastery of the traditional, and to mainlanders at the time, highly exotic pastime of surf boarding. As these athletes, traversed geographic and political boundaries, they also had to traverse cultural boundaries.[4]

As it turned out, those who installed the haole-dominated Republic of Hawaii in the hopes of opening the door to quick American annexation were disappointed. For good reasons and bad, many Americans were reluctant to colonize Hawai'i. Some believed that building an American Empire in the Pacific was a betrayal of what the nation should stand for. Others did not want to introduce thousands of non-white people into an expanding United States. This controversy would not find resolution until 1898, when a pro-imperialist Republican Party, in control of Congress and the White House, successfully pushed for U.S. annexation of Hawai'i. In 1897, the controversy over what to do about Hawai'i was still going on. At that time, the *Hawaiian Gazette* reprinted a story from the *San Francisco Examiner*. Entitled "We Must Annex Hawaii," the story was about Henry Beckley, a "brunette" Stanford freshman who helped Stanford beat Cal. The 1910 U.S. Census manuscript describes a Henry Beck-ley as living in Waimea village with a wife and daughter. Racially, the manuscript reports, Beckley was a thirty-two-year-old "Caucasian Ha-waiian" with an indecipherable occupation. In 1930, Beckley, then in the army in Hawaii, was depicted as "Hawaiian" in the census manuscript, while his wife and children were called Caucasian Hawaiian, which meant that they possessed Native Hawaiian and white ancestry.[5]

Before becoming one of the first Asian Americans to play organized professional baseball on the mainland, Andrew Yamashiro suited up for Temple Preparatory School in Philadelphia. For a few years, Yamashiro played for a team of Hawaiian ballplayers that barnstormed the U.S. mainland from 1912 to 1916. Since this team was widely promoted as "Chinese," Yamashiro appeared in the box scores as "Yim" to disguise his Nikkei background. After the 1916 tour, Yamashiro decided to follow the advice of team leader Buck Lai and remain on the East Coast. The son of a prominent Japanese Hawaiian hotel owner and community leader, Yamashiro entered Temple in Philadelphia with an eye on a career in dentistry. His appearance in a Temple football uniform fostered publicity from the Philadelphia press as well as a nationally published wire story. The *Philadelphia Public Ledger* headlined a story on Yamashiro—"'Yim,' Oriental Football Player, Temple Regular." The Philadelphia daily pro-claimed the Nikkei as the first "Chinese player" to win a regular spot on a gridiron team. Then, as if to confuse readers, the *Ledger* maintained that the athlete's real name was "Yamashire," identified him as a right guard in a game against La Salle and as "the only player of Japanese descent on a local football team." The Hawaiian was quoted as saying, "I like foot-ball very much. . . . Baseball, though, I think is better. You can use your hands in baseball but not in football. I don't quite get the idea." Given the popularity of football on the islands, it seems doubtful that Yamashiro was that ignorant of how the game worked.[6]

In the latter stages of the 1910s, Hawaiian gridders appeared in the San Francisco Bay Area, playing for St. Mary's, located then in Oakland. Catholicism had made inroads in Hawai'i, thanks, in part, to the recruit-ment of laborers from Portugal, Spain, Puerto Rico, and Mexico. On the islands, Catholic post-secondary education did not exist. Thus, young people who could find the financial means to do so went to schools like St. Mary's in California and Dayton University in Ohio.

In 1918, Hawaiian football players were accorded attention by Ed Hughes of the *San Francisco Chronicle*. Hughes wrote that Kauhane, Nahi-paa, and Correa were "boys . . . well-groomed in football. . . . They are fast, tricky runners and know how to protect themselves in the open field." In addition, St. Mary's suited up a gridder from Guam called Herrero. An *Oakland Times* sportswriter called James Herrero the hardest worker on the Gaels' eleven. All three Hawaiians, Hughes stressed, gained experience on the islands by playing plenty of football and rugby.

As for Herrero, he had family members who had previously attended St. Mary's. Hughes described him as small but good.[7]

Tony Correa possessed Portuguese ancestry, but the other two Hawaiian gridders for the Gaels could claim indigenous descent. Kauhane was particularly good. He struck the *San Francisco Chronicle* as a "streak in the broken field." Before St. Mary's eleven encountered the University of California football squad in 1918, Herbert Hauser described Kauhane as a "tricky runner" who would prove less effective against the powerful, larger Bears than the bigger Correa. As predicted, Cal humbled St. Mary's, 40–14. As was not predicted, St. Mary's big star was "little Kauhane." Kauhane scored all of St. Mary's points. He rushed for two touchdowns, including one of ninety yards, and kicked both extra points. St. Mary's had little better luck against a service team representing nearby Fort Baker. In that game, Kauhane managed an eighty-yard touchdown pass. Meanwhile, Nahipaa's career with St. Mary's was limited by a broken leg in 1917.[8]

On and off the gridiron, Kauhane seemed to have lived a varied and interesting life. In 1920, Noble Kauhane, portrayed by the *Oakland Tribune* as the "shifty Hawaiian half back," coached high school football in the East Bay. In 1922, Kauhane was back on St. Mary's campus and playing on a team which included two other Hawaiians, both possessing indigenous ancestry, Nick Hoopi'i and Clarence Lane. By this time, Kauhane had been moved to end and unfortunately suffered an injury which kept the "Hawaiian flash" out of action for a couple of months. Nevertheless, in late November St. Mary's trekked to Hawai'i. There, the Gaels beat an eleven called the Hawaii All-Stars. The press credited the victory, in part, to Kauhane's and Hoopi'i's contributions. By the end of the 1920s, Kauhane was back on the islands. In 1930, the U.S. Census depicts Kauhane as racially Hawaiian and occupationally a "draftsman." In 1944, sports columnist Dan McGuire told readers of the *Berkeley Daily Gazette* that Kauhane had been elected as a city supervisor in Honolulu as a Democrat. When he died in 1960, the *Oakland Tribune* printed a column by Arch Ward, who wrote that in Hawai'i "[h]is popularity was extensive, his name an inspiration to every Hawaiian kid who aspired to football prominence." Hoopii and Lane were backfield standouts. The former was remembered by *Los Angeles Times* columnist Al Wolf in the early 1940s as a halfback who scored a winning touchdown against Stanford. In 1921, the *Oakland Tribune*'s Ralph Hosler praised Lane as a St. Mary's halfback.[9]

While not reaching the fame of Red Grange or Ernie Nevers, a perhaps surprising number of Hawaiians became well-publicized members of King Football's fraternity during the years between World War I and World War II. Bill Blaisdell, identified as part-Hawaiian in the U.S. Census manuscripts of 1930, was a "wonder boy" for the Bucknell University squad during the mid-1920s. Blaisdell was described as a "Honolulu lad" as he took over as quarterback for Bucknell. Later in November 1924, he starred in a game against Rutgers. The 1927 Bucknell Yearbook reveals that in the fall of 1926 the school played to a 0–0 tie with Haskell, a famed Native American institution. Nevertheless, Blaisdell "made one of his famous dashes" to provide a rare offensive highlight. After he died, Bucknell would name him to the school's Hall of Fame.[10]

Hawaiian Chinese Walter Tin Kit Achiu starred at Dayton University in the early and mid-1920s. According to a newspaper account published after he died in Eugene, Oregon, in 1989, Achiu's father was a Chinese immigrant who worked in the California gold fields before moving to Hawai'i, where he married an indigenous Hawaiian woman and settled down as a rice farmer. A wire story published in 1940 depicted Achiu as a "formidable chap" who acquired the nickname of "Sneeze" at Dayton University.[11]

Achiu attended Kamehameha, but wound up heading to Dayton, in part because of its Catholic orientation. Moreover, Achiu's football coach at Dayton, Harry Baujan, told the press that he was responsible for bringing Achiu "to this country" after seeing him play on the islands. Yet Achiu got no scholarship. His father reportedly could only afford to help his athletic son out a little financially, but borrowing money from his older siblings cleared a monetary path for Achiu to Dayton.[12]

Baujan and other athletic coaches at Dayton were probably glad to have Achiu on campus. In the fall of 1922, *Cincinnati Enquirer* advised that Achiu "will be a real novelty" for local football fans when Dayton visited the hometown Xavier eleven. But he was more than just exotic, the *Enquirer* added, he was also a very good halfback. Around the same time, the *Cleveland Plain Dealer* published a photograph of the Dayton University gridder and described him as "one of the few Chinese players in America." The daily added that the Hawaiian was an "excellent line plunger." In 1924, the press portrayed Achiu as a "one man wrecking crew" as Dayton shut out Cincinnati, 21–0. Nearly a year later, an advertisement promoting an upcoming game between Dayton and John Carroll counseled readers to keep an eye on Achiu. Ignoring his Hawaiian birth and U.S. citizenship, the advertisement added that Achiu was "one of the fastest men on the gridiron and one of the best all-around athletes The Flower Kingdom (China) has given us."[13]

Early in 1926, significant press coverage headed Achiu's way. In February, readers of Wisconsin's *Appleton Post-Crescent* could run across Achiu's photograph and an article on him. The photograph showed the Hawaiian in a Dayton track outfit. Underneath, an Orientalist illustration displayed a "queued" runner. Called a "Chinese student," Achiu was the elected captain of Dayton's track team. The article also pointed out Achiu's athletic versatility by asserting that he shined in both baseball and football as well as track and field for Dayton. The next month, Ohio's *Hamilton News-Journal* called Achiu "one of the greatest athletes to compete at Dayton." It declared that upon commencing football at the Ohio school, the Hawaiian was given the nickname of "Sneeze" and when he started to excel at rounding end with the ball, he became known as the "Almond-eyed Speed Demon." In any event, he was the first "Oriental" accorded All-American mention by the great Walter Camp. At the end of the 1925–1926 academic year, Dayton's yearbook acclaimed Achiu as a "popular . . . Chinese-Hawaiian athlete and star halfback." Eventually, he graduated from Dayton with a degree in electrical engineering. In 1974, the University of Dayton selected Achiu as a member of the school's athletic Hall of Fame.[14]

Sam Hipa was Achiu's teammate at the University of Dayton. Before journeying to the mainland, the Hawaiian born Hipa competed for the Catholic preparatory school, St. Louis, in 1919. Once on the mainland, Hipa stood out athletically. In 1925, Dayton beat Bucknell, led by Bill Blaisdell at quarterback. Hipa, who started at right end, blocked a punt--a feat which fostered a key Dayton touchdown. Achiu, by the way, started at right half for the Flyers. The versatile Hipa also starred on Dayton's basketball team.[15]

When Dayton took on John Carroll in October 1926, the game's program listed not only Hipa as starting right end, but Swan as starting left half. Identified in the 1920 U.S. census as a part-Hawaiian, Robert "Ducky" Swan was a son of an Ohio-born clerk and the brother of a talented Hawaiian baseball player, Fred Swan. Before the 1928 season began, Ohio's *Wilmington News-Journal* announced that the Dayton squad had unanimously named him captain of the team, making Swan the most popular choice in school history. Called a "tall Hawaiian" by the *News-Journal,* Swan had made the all-conference team the year before, partially because his play had helped Dayton overcome Wittenberg in a crucial game. Swan could not only run with the ball but was talented as a punter and passer. In mid-October 1928, Swan ran for a 71-yard touchdown against Brown. In late October, Grantland Rice, America's most revered sportswriter at that time, insisted, "Swan is the only Hawaiian football leader in the United States and is classified among the best." The *Pittsburgh Press* added that Swan was the first Hawaiian named captain of an "American" grid team. The *Press* also noted the existence of seven Hawaiians in all on Dayton's 1928 squad. After leaving Dayton, Robert Swan returned to the islands where he worked as a civil engineer by the time of the 1930 U.S. Census.[16]

A Punahou graduate possessing indigenous ancestry, Henry Hughes departed Hawai'i for Oregon State in the late 1920s. In 1927, the *New York Times* represented Hughes as a barefoot kicking "phenom." The daily learned that as a freshman Hughes had drop-kicked a fifty-five-yard field goal. The *Times* supported the veracity of the story since Knute Rockne had come from Hawai'i, telling tales of barefoot gridders capable of kicking fifty yards and Hawaiian crowds jeering those athletes daring to wear regulation cleats. In April 1928, sportswriter Lawrence Perry claimed that

Hughes stood in the vanguard of other Hawaiian players heading to the mainland. He added, "It is expected that he will prove a worthy representative of the best of the Hawaiian football guild." Exoticizing Hughes, the *Montreal Gazette* told readers in the fall of 1928 that he was a "football novelty," incapable of kicking well with cleats. It added that Paul Schlisser, Oregon State's coach, was looking for shoes that Hughes could easily slip on once the punt was away and the Hawaiian had to turn his attention to blockers and tackling punt returners. Sportswriter Ben Titus admired Hughes's barefoot, booming punts and the *Portland Oregonian* praised "Honolulu Hughes" and his ability to kick not only far but accurately. When Oregon State played rival Oregon at the end of the 1929 season, Hughes, according to the Oregon State's yearbook, performed "spectacularly." After the 1930 season, Oregon State's yearbook averred that "Honolulu Hughes" had become "one of the most outstanding right halfs in the conference."[17]

Around the same time, Harold Yap also played big-time college football in the Pacific Northwest. But unlike Hughes, Yap showed up at Washington State, where he put together a fine career as a lineman. Yap also seemed intent upon making his mark in Pullman, Washington, as more than just a football player. While Yap was a frosh during the 1927–1928 academic year, the *Portland Oregonian* acknowledged that "[p]roving he can handle king's English . . . the fleet lineman" on the freshman squad was trying out for Washington State's debate team.[18]

A son of a father who worked as a commission agent for a dry goods store and a mother who worked as a teacher in Honolulu, the Hawaiian Chinese Yap performed well on the Washington State varsity. The readers of the *Riverside Daily Press* could discover praise for the "work of Harold Yap, bronze Hawaiian" late in 1930. They would find out that Yap "is a fiery, eager worker, not exceptionally good on defense, but excellent at the helm of the Cougar interference." A book about Hawaiian Chinese remembered Yap as the first Hawaiian to play in the Rose Bowl.[19]

The U.S. Census manuscripts of 1930 tells us that Naval Academy standout Gordon Chung-Hoon was the son of "Asian Hawaiian" parents. Suggesting how different Hawai'i was for Asian Americans than the mainland, the father was a deputy treasurer in Honolulu's government. The mother worked as a playground director. Perhaps his comparatively privileged background helps explain why the Naval Academy, which did not admit an African American until after World War II, opened its doors to Chung-Hoon.[20]

Orientalism stalked Chung-Hoon's football career. Early in the 1931 football season, a fanciful Associated Press story on Gordon Chung-Hoon reported that the recruit to the Naval Academy's football team had never seen a football until he came to the United States three years earlier. Aside from exoticizing Hawai'i as foreign to American football, the story claimed that Chung-Hoon never wore shoes and had foresworn cleats whenever he punted or drop-kicked. Before entering the Naval Academy, the story maintained, Chung-Hoon attended the Severn Academy in Maryland to make up for some academic deficiencies. There, it seems he learned to play football well enough to become an effective back. Upon joining Navy's varsity squad, the five-foot ten-inch, 175-pound Hawaiian emerged as a "speedy and hard hitting runner."[21]

Chung-Hoon proved more than just a cultural curiosity. Described as a "reserve halfback" for the Naval Academy in mid-October of 1931, Chung-Hoon completed a touchdown pass which helped Navy overcome the University of Delaware. In 1932, Navy easily downed Washington & Lee, 33–0. In describing the game, a wire story enthused, "Chung-Hoon, Navy's brilliant triple-threat Hawaiian" paved the way, scoring a touchdown in the process. Navy also handled Maryland easily, thanks in part to Chung-Hoon's two touchdowns. Navy lost against its traditional rival—the eleven from West Point, 20–0. However, Chung-Hoon starred for the losers. Sportswriter Alan Gould argued that Chung-Hoon almost single-handedly kept Navy in the game. Meanwhile, the *New York Evening Post*'s Robert Harron incorrectly informed readers that the Naval Academy football team had America's only Hawaiian gridder. Gordon Chung-Hoon, Harron wrote, "is a triple-threater, and a nifty performer, although inclined to be brittle." In 1933, Chung-Hoon continued to excel for Navy. Against Pittsburgh University, "the slippery little back from Hawaii" scored Navy's only touchdown—a nineteen-yard jaunt. In early November, Navy upset Notre Dame and Chung-Hoon's play was accorded a great deal of credit for the victory. Around the same time, a wire story called Chung-Hoon one of the fastest backs in the nation. Late in 1933, readers of the *Aberdeen Daily News* discovered a photograph of Gordon Chung-Hoon, captioned "Hawaii's Gift to Navy Football." Forgetting Walter Achiu, the *Daily News* described Chung-Hoon as "the first of his race to get All-American mention." A wire story published in early 1934 claimed that Chung-Hoon performed "brilliantly" for Navy. Chung-Hoon, conceded the school's 1934 yearbook, was not an academic wonder. Nevertheless, it described him as popular and a good musician. Moreover, he was apparently something of a "social satellite."[22]

Famed columnist Westbrook Pegler brought Chung-Hoon up in a column in January 1934. Pegler was discussing how Americans seemed confused about racial identification when it came to Asians and Pacific Islanders. This particularly bothered Pegler at the time because he was hoping that the United States would grant the Philippines independence while shoring up the latter's ability to withstand Japanese aggression. But Americans struck Pegler as indifferent, in part because they were worried about the depression, but also because they had a tough time caring about or differentiating the peoples of Asia and the Pacific. Thus, Chung-Hoon found himself amid a controversy stirred up during the Navy-

Columbia game of 1933. Identifying Chung-Hoon as Hawaiian, Pegler told readers that when taking on Columbia, the halfback was not playing outright dirty football, but was engaging in something the journalist called "not parlor football." Apparently, the Columbia sideline was not happy with the Hawaiian's tactics and a player and coach shouted over to the Navy coach, "Hey, Rip, tell that damn Chinaman of yours this isn't that kind of football game."[23]

After leaving the Naval Academy, Chung-Hoon remained in the service. Promoted through the ranks to Commander, he was awarded with the Navy Cross and Silver Star "for conspicuous gallantry and extraordinary heroism" during World War II. Subsequently, a guided missile destroyer, the USS Chung-Hoon was named in his honor. Given the racially exclusive nature of military service at the time for especially African Americans and, during World War II, Japanese Americans, Chung-Hoon's career suggests that some non-white individuals, particularly those of relative economic privilege, could negotiate racial borders more easily than others.[24]

A Hawaiian of indigenous, Chinese, and Irish ancestry, Walter "Mickey" McGuire played for the University of Wisconsin in the early 1930s. According to the 1930 U.S. Census manuscripts, McGuire was racially an "Asian Hawaiian." His white father worked as a collector for a milk company in Honolulu, and his mother, possessing a Chinese immigrant father and a Hawaiian-born mother, was a teacher.[25]

McGuire made an impact on rugged, Midwest college football. In 1931, he carried the ball effectively in a game against Purdue and led Wisconsin to a 12–0 triumph over Chicago. Called a "Hawaiian Irishman" in a newspaper report on the game, McGuire not only tallied two touchdowns, but as quarterback helped his team strategically. One of McGuire's touchdowns against Chicago was a thirty-two-yard jaunt with a short pass and another was a thirty-eight-yard return of a punt. An AP report in 1932 maintained that if cleats and socks were banned from college football, McGuire would do even better. McGuire insisted he never wore football shoes until he got to Wisconsin. Called the only Hawaiian in the Big Ten conference, McGuire earned a reputation as a swift and versatile back, characterized by a modest personality. In November 1932, Wisconsin beat Minnesota 20–13 with McGuire scoring three times during the game. One of his touchdowns was an eighty-five-yard run. At the end of the 1932 season, McGuire was named second team all-conference by the UPI.[26]

McGuire returned to the islands after leaving Wisconsin. The U.S. Census manuscripts of 1940 tell us that he was a thirty-year-old athletic director for a steam railway company in Honolulu and that he was racially part Hawaiian. Later, McGuire got involved in public affairs in Hawai'i as a territorial representative, administrative assistant to the president of the Honolulu Transit Authority, vice president of the Hawaii Baseball League, and administrator of Honolulu Stadium.[27]

In the fall of 1932, a wire photo appeared in the *Reno Evening Gazette*, constructing an exoticized link between Chung-Hoon and McGuire. Individual shots of Chung-Hoon and McGuire were displayed, accompanied by the headline, "Football from the South Seas." The caption asserted that the two stars originated "[f]rom the land of shimmy-shaking maidens."[28]

Bill Anahu headed eastward to Santa Clara College from the islands in the late 1930s. The *Dallas Morning News's* Gordon White revealed that the gridder's original surname was Machado, but he had changed it to Anahi to honor his Native Hawaiian grandmother, "one of the wealthiest women on the islands." When Anahu entered Santa Clara, a Jesuit-run college near San Jose, it played big time football and often quite well. In 1937, Anahu's first year on the varsity, he made a key interception of a University of San Francisco (USF) pass, helping Santa Clara roll to a 13–0 victory. Santa Clara put together a fine season in 1937 and wound up in the prestigious Sugar Bowl in January 1938, and during that game, Anahu was credited with playing "vicious football" for the Broncos. In October 1938, his pass catching helped Santa Clara subdue Arizona, 27–10. Against USF later in 1938, Anahu's fifteen-yard reception keyed Santa Clara's drive for the only touchdown in the game. At the end of the 1938 season, Charles Burton of the *Dallas Morning News* reported that the University of Arizona football squad named "Bill Anahu, Santa Clara's Hawaiian" on its all-opponent team. Moreover, the Associated Press selected him as an honorable mention member of the all-Pacific Coast team.[29]

In 1939, Anahu had another fine season. His coach, the respected Buck Shaw, hailed Anahu as the best end on the Pacific Coast. A *Salt Lake Tribune* writer agreed that Anahu was one of the best ends in the nation, outstanding as a blocker and a fast, clever receiver who could also defend capably. The *Tribune's* Phil McLeese exoticized Anahu's pass catching expertise. In probably an apocryphal story, McLeese insisted that Anahu learned how to catch passes while throwing and catching a football on the shores of a Hawaiian beach. Yet when the football got worn out, Anahu and a companion supposedly used a pineapple. During the 1939 season, Anahu snagged a pass against Stanford and then raced fifty yards for a touchdown. Columnist Doug Baldwin of the *Santa Cruz Sentinel* called Anahu's romp the best run of the game. After his touchdown, Anahu, the team captain, kicked the point after touchdown as the Broncos undid the neighboring eleven, 27–7. Against Michigan State, Anahu received a touchdown pass and made several other important receptions as the Broncos bettered the Midwesterners, 6–0. At the end of the 1939 season, Anahu was named to the all-Pacific Coast team by the United Press. Picked to play for the West squad in San Francisco's East-West Shrine game, Anahu excelled. Readers of the *Portland Oregonian* discovered that on January 1, 1940, "Big Bill Anahu, who learned his football fundamentals in Hawaii's barefoot leagues" ran twenty-five yards for a touchdown after catching a pass.[30]

After the Hawaiian graduated from Santa Clara, he still had some football to play. He was named to play in Chicago's annual College All-Star game. A noted Chicago sportswriter, Arch Ward, identified Anahu as a "Hawaiian boy" and a former Kamehameha student. His presence, the sportswriter purported, inspired the lame joke, "What's the matter Anahu?" Anahu, Ward's readers were told, learned his football in the barefoot leagues and was "like most Hawaiians . . . an excellent swimmer." A few days later, Ward insisted that Anahu favored poi around meal time. After the Pearl Harbor attack, Anahu joined the military. But like many college stars who entered the armed services during World War II, Anahu continued to play football. In late August 1942, Anahu was at end on an Army all-star eleven that lost to the NFL Washington Redskins, 26–7. Unlike many college stars who entered the armed services during World War II, however, Anahu did not come home, dying as a fighter pilot in the Philippines.[31]

The sons of a Hawaiian Chinese father who worked as a bank auditor, according to the 1930 census data and a part Hawaiian mother, Francis and Conkling Wai competed for UCLA in the late 1930s. Prior to attending UCLA, Francis, Conkling, and another brother, Bob, stopped in at Sacramento Junior College to play football. A quarterback, Francis suited up for Sacramento in 1935 and 1936. Conkling, an end, arrived on campus in 1936 and played in 1937, during which Bob joined him. In 1937, Bob not only quarterbacked the Sacramento JC squad but served as a place kicker and punter as well. When Sacramento downed the Santa Clara frosh, 7–0, Bob Wai's punting kept the losers penned up in their own territory. Meanwhile, Conkling started at end for Sacramento.[32]

The *Sacramento Bee* exoticized the Pacific connection between Hawai'i and Sacramento Junior College. In late September 1937, it published a photo of Sacramento's small contingent of Hawaiians, describing the gridders as "Barefoot Boys with Cheeks of Tan" and "Swivel Hipped Grid Players from the Beach at Waikiki." It maintained that Francis Wai had helped recruit his brothers and other Hawaiian gridders to California's state capital, although why Francis Wai journeyed to Sacramento remains unclear.[33]

Francis moved down to Westwood in 1937. The *Los Angeles Times* branded him as a "Native Hawaiian quarterback" when he speared on the Bruins' practice field. However, the *Times* reported that in a preseason intersquad game, Wai displayed "fire" while playing with the regulars. Although not normally a regular, Francis got minutes off the bench. In his first game as a Bruin in September 1937, he reportedly impressed as a blocker and tackler. In one game in 1938, the *Los Angeles Times* listed Francis as the Bruins' starting quarterback, while Conkling played as a reserve end. Interestingly, both brothers, shadowed by the Chinese Exclusion Act, had to show a certificate of U.S. citizenship to be allowed off the U.S.S. Matsonia when the brothers arrived in Los Angeles before the 1939 season. After UCLA played Cal in 1940, Conkling Wai's defense was applauded by the press. As for his older brother, Francis Wai sadly died in the Philippines in World War II. His courage earned him the Congressional Medal of Honor in 1999, yet only after voices from the Asian American communities convinced Congress to investigate whether Asian American military personnel were not accorded the honors they deserved for the sacrifices they made during World War II.[34]

Honolulu Advertiser journalist, Lee Cataluna, tells an interesting story of when the Wai brothers returned to the islands with UCLA to play in the 1939 Pineapple Bowl. Cataluna writes that Francis and Conkling helped make the UCLA team "the most diverse in the country." However-er, Cataluna adds, the paramount roles of African American Woody Strode and Kenny Washington on the Bruins truly brought national at-tention to the Westwood eleven. As an end, Strode was good. Washing-ton, though, was legendary, but was denied the Heisman Trophy. Many at that time and for years later would say he was the greatest backfield star ever on the Pacific Coast.[35]

Whether black or Hawaiian Chinese, the non-white gridders for UCLA encountered discrimination despite their football prowess. The Wai brothers, according to Cataluna, formed a close friendship with Washington and Strode "in a kind of shared outsiderness." Moreover, when UCLA journeyed to the islands for the Pineapple Bowl, held on January 2, 1939, against UH, the eleven from Westwood discerned hostil-ity from islanders stemming less from race and ethnicity than the fact that talented gridders like the Wai brothers had carried their skills to the mainland rather than remaining in Hawai'i. Both the Wai brothers were taken out of the game by injuries caused presumably by vengeful UH players. However, an angry Woody Strode apparently got some payback by punching out a few UH gridders before referees chased him from the field.[36]

Sons of a Honolulu chamber of commerce clerk father, Leon and Wayne Sterling were part-Hawaiians who played for Pacific Northwest college teams—216-pound Leon for Oregon State in the late 1930s and Wayne for the University of Washington in the late 1930s and early 1940s. In 1941, the *Honolulu Advertiser*'s Red McGuire commemorated Wayne Sterling's last game with Washington by telling readers that the lineman was known as the "Happy Hawaiian." McGuire also quoted Royal Brougham, a Seattle-based sportswriter. Brougham called Sterling "a poi-eating fat boy from the beach of Waikiki." Alluding to the famed American humorist of the 1920s and 1930s, Brougham claimed, more-over, that Sterling was both the "Will Rogers of the squad" and "a great talker." In any event, the UPI acknowledged Sterling as an honorable mention member of its All-American squad. After returning to the islands, Wayne Sterling coached high school football, and became a minister at the Healani Congregational Church. Leon, moreover, was active in public affairs in Hawai'i.[37]

In pre-World War II Southern California, a couple of Hawaiian Asians were featured on small college teams. A Hawaiian Nikkei named Kazuma Hisanaga was considered one of the better all-around players in the conference when he suited up for Cal Poly Pomona. As a frosh, Hisanaga started as a guard, but his varsity coach moved him to the backfield. The *Chino Champion* hailed Hisanaga, subsequently, as a "star quarterback." The *Los Angeles Times* portrayed him in 1938 as a "chunky sophomore from Hawaii." Cal Whorton of the *Times* also praised "Benny Hisanaga [as] a clever blocking quarterback." In 1940, Hisanaga was an all-conference backfield member. During the 1940 season, Hisanaga served as team captain and managed to score a touchdown in a 33–0 rout of La Verne. A graduate of Hilo High, Hisanaga was named to Pomona's Hall of Fame. Not only were his athletic accomplishments based on winning three letters in football and baseball contributing factors in his alma mater honoring him, but Hisanaga also earned a Silver Star and Purple Heart for his World War II service in the famed Hawaiian-based 100th battalion, which was eventually merged in to the 442nd regiment. Moreover, he was community oriented, working as a counselor in Hawai'i for the National Youth Corps in 1969.[38]

Hawaiian Chinese Al Chang shined in Redlands College's backfield before the onset of World War II. While on Redlands' frosh team in 1938, Chang ran for a forty-five-yard touchdown and passed for another as his squad pummeled Cal Tech, 79–0. The 1940 Redlands yearbook tells us that in 1939 Chang scored a touchdown against the San Diego Marines, heaved a twenty-yard touchdown pass against Laverne, and connected on a key pass to help Redlands overcome Cal Tech. Before Redlands was to meet Pomona in 1939, Eugene Giedt of the *San Bernardino County Sun* proclaimed Chang as one of Redlands' "stellar backs." As the 1940 season began, the *Sun*'s Becky Burris asserted that "Alvin Chang, shifty little Hawaiian quarterback" keyed Redlands' offense. In mid-October, Redlands lost to San Diego State, but Chang's performance drew praise from the *San Diego Union*. "Hawaiian halfback Al Chang" tossed three touchdown passes in a victory over Pomona, 27–6, in late October, impressively targeting thirteen of seventeen passes in the process. A week later, Chang's threw two important touchdown passes to help Redlands defeat Occidental. Towards the end of November, Redlands fared less well against New Mexico A&M. Nevertheless, Chang heaved one touchdown pass and completed another to a receiver who lateraled the ball to a teammate who then scampered across the goal line. Against New Mexico A&M, Chang passed the ball thirty-four times and completed eighteen. His coach gushed that Chang, called by the *Sun* Redlands' "diminutive football star" was all-conference material. Indeed, he joined Hisanaga as an all-conference back after the 1940 season.[39]

Chang proved more than just a star athlete who excelled in basketball as well as football. He also served as Redlands' student body president. Indeed, in June 1941, the school's president, Elam J. Anderson, used the occasion of Chang's election to assert Redlands had demonstrated its loyalty to America by exhibiting "justice for all." The proof, Anderson added, was the election of a Hawaiian Chinese to the student body presidency. Upon his graduation in June 1942, the *San Bernardino County Sun* pointed out that Chang had earned three coveted awards as a Redlands' student—one for athletic sportsmanship, a second for student service, and finally "cum laude" for his academic prowess.[40]

After graduating, Chang's marriage to a European American woman received attention in the society pages of the *San Bernardino County Sun*. Chang, according to the wedding announcement, had been coaching football at Redlands High School, and was hoping to return to Hawai'i to continue coaching. In fact, the 1945 Kamehameha Yearbook pointed out that Chang coached baseball for the school. Chang tried his hand in minor league professional football after the war, but he mainly concentrated on nurturing a career as an educator in Hawai'i and California.[41]

HERMAN WEDEMEYER AND WORLD WAR II FOOTBALL

During World War II, college football saw tough times as many fine athletes were off to war and many fine gridiron programs shut down. Few gridders, however, added more glitter to wartime football than Hawaiian Herman Wedemeyer. A son of a Pearl Harbor crane operator, Herman Wedemeyer was a college "phenom" in the mid-1940s for St. Mary's in the Bay Area. Remembering his early years for veteran San Francisco sportswriter Ron Fimrite, Wedemeyer said:

> I was born on the Big Island (Hawaii) in an area so remote that we had no paved roads. We used cornstalks for goalposts, and we played a type of touch football with as many as 30 on a side. Let me tell you, you learned to dodge with that many people trying to catch you. And we threw the ball around all the time. According to our rules, you could pass the ball forward or backward whenever you pleased. It was chaotic. But I took that style of play with me to St. Mary's.[42]

Wedemeyer called himself a "walking United Nations," claiming he possessed indigenous Hawaiian, Chinese, German, English, and Irish ancestors. The 1940 census manuscripts designate Wedemeyer's parents as part Hawaiians. At that time, his father worked as an engine man for the U.S. Navy in Honolulu. Wedemeyer subsequently remembered that his father was a good athlete, who among other sports competed in barefoot football. After his family moved to Honolulu, Wedemeyer starred in both football and baseball at St. Louis Preparatory, earning all-league honors for his sterling backfield performances in Honolulu prep circles.[43]

Thanks to Bill Smith, an illustrious Hawaiian swimming star attending Ohio State, Wedemeyer was set to trek to Columbus, Ohio, after high school. However, Wedemeyer wanted Ohio State's assurances that a Hawaiian friend of his would also attain a roster spot on the Big Ten team's football squad. Ohio State was reticent about making such assurances. St. Mary's, having established its own pipeline to Honolulu's athletic world since the days of Noble Kauhane, stepped in. Coach Jimmy Phelan expressed not only a willingness to recruit Wedemeyer but his friend, Red Mauk. St. Mary's administrators were far less enthused about the Hawaiian lads, given their apparently unimpressive academic credentials. Thus, St. Mary's refused to pay Wedemeyer's and Mauk's way to Northern California. Yet Honolulu boosters established a donation drive which eventually financed the young men's journey to California.[44]

Crossing regional and cultural borders, Wedemeyer spread the conflicting gospel of Hawai'i as both exotic and modern. At St. Mary's, sportswriter Mal Florence recalled, "Squirmin' Herman received his most lasting recognition as the leader of a band of beardless wonders, some Hawaiian like himself, who dazzled the nation with their daring—impromptu laterals, ahead of their time spread formations, and plays made up in the huddle." Wedemeyer remembered Jimmy Phelan "used to tell us that we were just a bunch of entertainers, so go out and put on a show." Ron Fimrite asserted that Wedemeyer's "timing was marvelous." Because World War II depleted the talent available to Bay Area college football programs, the region's football fans were desperate for a gridiron hero they could embrace. However, Wedemeyer's appeal, Fimrite maintained, transcended region. Fimrite wrote in the late 1960s that Wedemeyer's "combination of . . . Hawaiian ancestry and truly remarkable versatility captured an entire nation of football freaks."[45]

Soon after Wedemeyer's arrival at St. Mary's Moraga, California campus, Jimmy Phelan figured he had something special in the Hawaiian, according to Grantland Rice. Phelan maintained, "It took me less than two minutes to see that I had the football player every coach dreams about, but seldom gets. . . . Here was a kid who had everything—speed of foot and body and hands, speed of brain, perfect coordination, amazing flexibility, and the ability to be at his best when you needed him the most."[46]

During World War II, colleges overlooked the rule excluding first year students from varsity play to enhance their otherwise diminished rosters. Thus, as a frosh at St. Mary's the Hawaiian became a football hero in the San Francisco Bay Area. Indeed, even before his first varsity game in 1943, Wedemeyer impressed Bay Area sportswriters. After watching the Gaels in practice, Will Connolly of the *San Francisco Chronicle* wrote that the "dark complexioned [Wedemeyer] is rugged and elusive and laughs throughout practice." Against Cal, St. Mary's built its offense around Wedemeyer, who ran a punt back forty-seven yards and then lateraled the ball to teammate John Ryan. The tackle then carried the ball the remaining twenty-five yards for a touchdown. Coach Jimmy Phelan now had six Hawaiians on his squad, inspiring a *Los Angeles Times* writer to joke about St. Mary's using a "Hula-Shift." Indeed, St. Mary's Hawaiians seemingly transported the local culture to the Bay Area. Phelan maintained, "I like to coach the Hawaiian boys. . . . [T]hey have a good sense of humor, have played the game since they crawled out of the cradle, and are they durable." [47]

Wedemeyer shined throughout the 1943 season. Before the Gaels met the UCLA Bruins, Al Wolf of the *Los Angeles Times* declared that Wedemeyer "does everything and does it superlatively, although he's only 170 pounds." Late in November, St. Mary's shut down Utah, 34–0. Wedemeyer helped the Gaels' cause by returning a punt sixty yards. Prescott Sullivan, a columnist for the *San Francisco Examiner*, lamented at the end of the season that Wedemeyer had not been picked on any All-American team. He cited the words of respected Bay Area coach Buck Shaw, who remarked that Wedemeyer was "so good it's hard to believe he's playing his first year of college ball." Even though Wedemeyer was just a nineteen-year-old frosh, he was chosen to play in the East-West Shrine game in 1943. Moreover, his performance helped the West team tie the East, 13–13. [48]

Wedemeyer missed the 1944 season due to a stint in the Merchant Marines. However, he was back in Moraga by the fall 1945 season. In the meantime, professional football teams were reportedly proposing contracts of over $20,000 a year to Wedemeyer, who worked in an Oakland bar in the summer of 1945. Because Wedemeyer spurned those offers, Bill Leiser rejoiced that the "21-year-old Hawaiian-Chinese boy" had made it back to St. Mary's. Coach Phelan was happy too, acclaiming Wedemeyer as the "champion of all boys I have coached." In 1945, Wedemeyer and St. Mary's assembled a dream season, ending in a Sugar Bowl confrontation with the heavily favored Oklahoma A&M eleven. [49]

Joining Wedemeyer in the St. Mary's backfield was another Hawaiian, Skip Cordeiro, an elusive halfback of Portuguese descent. Hal Wood of the UPI wrote that together Wedemeyer and Cordeiro constituted a "pair of genuine, non-skid, super duper Hawaiian backfield stars"—stars who propelled the Gaels to an upset victory of Cal before eighty thousand at Berkeley's Memorial Stadium. A few days later, Wood pronounced "the 21-year old Honolulu star" as not only the best college player in the West, but, as Coach Jimmy Phelan insisted, improving. Writing for Cal's student newspaper, Warren Mangels called Wedemeyer a "Hawaiian-Chinese halfback with the crazy legs." After St. Mary's downed USC in the Los Angeles Coliseum, the *Los Angeles Times* columnist Dick Hyland extolled the Hawaiian's versatility, asserting that "[h]e hit the Trojans with everything but the goalposts."[50]

St. Mary's, while hardly a perennial, national powerhouse, made its way to New Orleans's prominent Sugar Bowl game, where it lost to Oklahoma A&M on January 1, 1946. Nevertheless, Wedemeyer and the Gaels staged an unforgettable show. Wedemeyer, for example, was heading for a touchdown when, on nearing the end zone, one of his lineman started yelling for the ball. Wedemeyer commented, "You know how lineman always want to run with the ball. So I turned around and lateraled to him. Then I put a block on the last defensive man and he went in for the touchdown. The crowd went wild." Grantland Rice was enamored by Wedemeyer's Sugar Bowl performance. He wrote:

> Wedemeyer looked smaller than he was. But I noticed that in addition to good legs and a halfbarrel chest, he had a pair of great-looking hands, developed from pushing hand trucks loaded with cases of pineapples, a job that called for both strength and dexterity. This work undoubtedly helped him to get that firm grip on a football, so that he seems almost to palm it as he roves around looking for a pass opening.[51]

In naming Wedemeyer a 1945 All-American, the All-America Board of Review explained that his "statistics and technical skill cannot be discounted but it's the utter nonchalance and wizardry that keeps customers jumping up and down." Although young, Wedemeyer's leadership and courage were praised by the board. It declared, "win, lose or tie, the youngster is a born leader and doer. The harder they hit him, the cooler he bounces from the ground to the huddle." As for the prestigious Heisman Trophy, Wedemeyer ranked fourth in the voting.[52]

The 1946 season began with hope for St. Mary's. The Bay Area–based Bill Leiser proclaimed, "Hawaiian-born Herman, so small it's impossible to believe when you see him off the field he can do what he does on it, takes his place as the greatest Coast-developed player of all time, a distinction previously owned by the big U.C.LA. back, Kenny Washington." The *Hayward Daily Review*'s Joe Wilmot dubbed the local hero a "tan tornado." However, there were fewer moments of glory in 1946 than the previous year for Wedemeyer. Still, he remembered fondly a game at New York City's Polo Grounds against Fordham. Playing on defense, he was disconcerted when Fordham quick kicked the ball over his head from its own five-yard line. Wedemeyer retrieved the ball at the Gaels thirty-yard line, but noted he was surrounded by Fordham gridders. He then kicked the ball himself. Wedemeyer's booming punt was finally downed on Fordham's own seven-yard line. On Fordham's first play, St. Mary's intercepted a pass and scored. Wedemeyer declared, "The crowd couldn't get over it. They hadn't seen anything like that." During the 1946 season, the *San Francisco Examiner* depicted Wedemeyer's seventy-three-yard jaunt against Santa Clara as the "run of the year." Wedemeyer, moreover, "electrified the throngs with a 70-yard touchdown" against Cal. Still, Wedemeyer fell from the ranks of the All-American elite, partly because St. Mary's was a decidedly weaker team in 1946 than in 1945. However, Wedemeyer still made *Look Magazine*'s third team All-American and the All-Pacific Coast first team. He was named Northern California's gridder of the year for the second season in a row.[53]

Wedemeyer, despite his non-white identity, was often perceived in Hollywood leading-man terms. Indeed, columnist Dave Lewis of the *Long Beach Independent* speculated in the fall of 1946 that Wedemeyer could be tempted into a movie career. Lewis added that Hollywood seemed interested, too, given that Wedemeyer was a "handsome black-haired Hawaiian," although likely the roles offered him would not have been those offered Ronald Reagan, let alone Gregory Peck.[54]

Convinced of Wedemeyer's gridiron credentials, the NFL's Los Angeles Rams drafted the Hawaiian after the 1946 season. Upstate from Los Angeles, the All-American Football Conference's San Francisco 49ers were pursuing West Point's well-publicized backfield stars—Glenn Davis and Doc Blanchard. Perhaps too parochial, the *San Francisco Examiner*'s Prescott Sullivan called on the 49ers to concentrate instead on recruiting Wedemeyer. The columnist wrote, "In our book, Wedemeyer has more to offer than either Blanchard and Davis or, for that matter, both of them put together." Even so, the halfback decided to return instead to St. Mary's for his last year of college eligibility. One professional football executive confided that Wedemeyer's decision cost the Hawaiian money. After the 1946 season, he might have been able to shake out of a pro football franchise a relatively sizable $25,000 a year contract. However, after a frustrating 1947 season in Moraga, Wedemeyer's professional services were acquired with a $9,000-a-year contract.[55]

The 1947 season, indeed, proved something of a disappointment to Wedemeyer and St. Mary's fans. Yet Wedemeyer soldiered on while supported by a generally weak Gael team. A lack of unity, moreover, reportedly accelerated St. Mary's decline. A *Chronicle* columnist feared that Wedemeyer had become something of a lone wolf on the Gaels' squad. But Will Connolly of the *San Francisco Chronicle* felt moved to write that the "mild mannered Hawaiian [was] the most exciting player we ever laid eyes on—anytime, anywhere, on any team." For Connolly, Wedemeyer appeared "destined to become a legend in these parts." In any event, Wedemeyer was selected for the second string All-Pacific Coast team at the end of the 1947 season.[56]

Before Wedemeyer's last season with St. Mary's ended, he and the Gaels traveled to Hawai'i to play the UH eleven. The game had been long awaited by Hawaiian football fans. Several years later, *Honolulu Advertiser* sportswriter Ferd Lewis maintained, "[I]t had been Hawaii's fortune to have the greatest exploits . . . of the man who put Hawaii football on the map . . . 2,500 miles away from those who celebrated his wondrous gifts the most." Locals grabbed up tickets in a matter of hours. Fired up by a chance of seeing four Hawaiians, Wedemeyer, Packard Harrington, Spike Cordeiro, and Henry Van Giesen, working out as Gaels, three thousand watched the Gaels practice. Playing before an overflow crowd at Honolulu Stadium, St. Mary's won decisively, 27–7. While not spectacular, Wedemeyer's performed well. Tommy Kaulukukui, who coached UH at the time, remembered, "He put on quite a show. He did things other people never would have thought of doing."[57]

Aside from Wedemeyer, other Hawaiians competed for mainland college elevens during the war. Possessing Samoan descent, the 220-pound Al Lolotai suited up for Weber College in Utah in the early 1940s. In 1940, the U.S. Census manuscript schedules list the teenaged Lolotai as living with his Samoan-born stepfather and Samoan-born mother. The father worked in road maintenance, while the future professional labored on a sugar plantation. Joining Lolotai on Weber was halfback Nelson Moku. After the 1941 season, in which both Lolotai and Moku made the all-conference team, the Pearl Harbor attack seemingly changed plans for the two. According to a wire service report, they were both in Hawai'i when the Japanese struck and planned on not returning to Weber even though both were slated to be co-captains in the 1942 season. Moku was quoted as declaring, "Uncle Sam needs us," thus assuring mainlanders of Hawaiian loyalty to the United States. Nevertheless, Lolotai and Moku were back on the Weber campus in 1942 and had successful seasons.[58]

HAWAIIANS ON POSTWAR MAINLAND GRIDIRONS

Immediately after World War II more and more Hawaiians made their way to mainland football rosters. Pacific Northwest campuses drew several fine Hawaiian gridders. The *Illustrated Football* of 1946 described Honolulan Charley Liu "as a magician among T-formation quarterbacks" as he performed for the University of Portland. When Portland University hosted Wally Yonamine and the Hawaiian All-Stars in late September 1946, the *Portland Oregonian* lamented that Liu, "the 150-pound fireball from Hawaii" was hurt and could not perform. Herbert Imanaka was a Hawaiian Nisei who played for the College of Idaho in the late 1940s and early 1950s. After the 1950 season, he was honored as an all-conference quarterback for among other accomplishments, leading his team to a victory over Pacific College. Willamette College suited up quarterback Al Minn, halfbacks Bill Kuhahiko and Bill Ewaliko, tackle Newt Kehahio, and guard Charles Nee. Early in October 1949, Willamette downed Chico State, 7–0. Ewaliko scored on a touchdown pass, and Minn added the conversion. Charles Nee, described as "spirited" in the school's 1950 yearbook, was not only the squad's smallest lineman but made second team all-conference in 1949. The next season, Al Minn, Bill Ewaliko, and Nee were all credited for helping Willamette whitewash East Washington, 21–0. At the end of the season, Ewailiko was an all-conference halfback. In addition, Al Minn was named an all-conference defensive back, while Charles Nee earned honorable mention as a lineman.[59]

Quarterback Joe Tom played behind the great Norm Van Brocklin at Oregon University in the late 1940s. The 1940 U.S. Census manuscript schedules reveal that the bi-ethnic Tom's father was a Hawaiian Chinese radio salesperson, while his mother was Hawaiian Japanese. Soon after the 1948 season began, "little Joe Tom" became Oregon's second-string quarterback after impressing the Ducks' coaching staff. Columnist Charles Burton reported in late 1948 that Oregon coach Jim Aiken had discovered Tom playing intramural football at the Eugene school. A former member of the Leiluhua Alums, Tom declared at the time that he did not think he was good enough to play varsity football at Oregon and had not even bothered to try out for the frosh squad. Tom's teammates swore, Burton asserted, that the Hawaiian called signals "one, twoee," although Burton thought they undoubtedly exaggerated Tom's accent. In any event, Burton maintained that Tom was popular among his Duck teammates. Moreover, according to the *Portland Oregonian*'s L. H. Gregory, a "Joe Tom for Quarterback Club" surfaced among Duck fans while the "little Hawaiian" labored behind Van Brocklin. Labeling Tom a "Japanese boy," Will Connolly described him as a clever ball handler and faker, but disadvantaged by his size of five feet eight.[60]

Norm Van Brocklin left Oregon for a long and illustrious NFL career in 1949. Joe Tom was reportedly in line for his job. Ruminating over Tom's chances to become a first stringer, *Portland Oregonian* sportswriter Don McLeod called him a "half-pint Chinese Hawaiian from Honolulu." Tom never got to be the starting quarterback for the Ducks, although he did stand out as a varsity baseball player for Oregon. He subsequently became a coach and teacher in Honolulu.[61]

Following in Wedemeyer's footsteps, talented Hawaiians showed up on Bay Area gridirons after World War II. Raised on the Hawaiian Islands but possessing Samoan ancestry, Packard Harrington was initially perceived in the Bay Area as a worthy successor to Herman Wedemeyer at St. Mary's. Not nearly as charismatic on the gridiron as Wedemeyer, Harrington proved a solid performer, especially on defense. Born in 1923 on a small island called Pupi, Harrington entered the military in World War II after distinguishing himself as a Honolulu high school grid sensation. After a couple of years of inadequately working out as Wedemeyer's heir in St. Mary's backfield, Harrington concentrated on developing into a "stellar linebacker" — good enough to get drafted by the Cleveland Browns. The *San Jose Mercury*'s Fred Merrick extolled Harrington in 1949 as "[b]rilliant," and another *Mercury* writer, Louis Duino, commended his performance in a losing effort against Santa Clara. Harrington consequently coached a semi-pro team in the Bay Area. Based in South Alameda County town of Fremont, it briefly suited up Herman Wedemeyer.[62]

Abe Dung was a fine player for Santa Clara University after World War II. The U.S. Census manuscripts describe him in 1930 as the two-year-old son of a Hawaiian Chinese father who managed a music store in Honolulu and a Hawaiian born mother. In 1945, sportswriter Hal Wood suggested that St. Mary's should recruit Dung, who, as a St. Louis Prep gridder, had broken Wedemeyer's scoring record in Honolulu. *Fresno Bee* reporter Ross Newland declared that Dung could be some West Coast team's prize recruit. The "little elusive halfback" had scored an impressive 101 points in but seven Honolulu prep games. Bill Leiser expected that Dung and another Hawaiian halfback, Johnny Dang, would join St. Mary's and their All-American, Hawaiian Herman Wedemeyer. Leiser wrote, "A Ding-Dang-Dung combination . . . may boost the Gaels . . . Abraham Dung of St. Louis High in Hawaii will personally provide one-third of the aforementioned combination. Johnny Dang of St. Anthony's will do ditto. This leaves Wedemeyer to add the ding, of which same he has a very large supply." Leiser cited Honolulu sportswriter Loui Leong Hop to the effect that both Dang and Dung were better prep gridders than the renowned Wedemeyer. Sadly, for St. Mary's, Dung not only ended up at a rival college but Dang remained on the islands to compete for the University of Hawai'i.[63]

In April 1946, Braven Dyer told Southern California readers that "Santa Clara gets Abe Dung, flashy Chinese-Hawaiian halfback, who burned up the [high school] hula-hula circles last season." Dung was reportedly attracted by Santa Clara's law school. However, he had to serve in the military before joining the Bronco football squad. Prior to the 1947 season, the *San Jose News* opined that Santa Clara was looking forward to the "classy Hawaiian" arriving on campus. When a frosh, Santa Clara Yearbook's praised Dung as "the sensational left half from Honolulu" and "swivel-hipped Hawaiian star."[64]

By the time, Dung moved up to the varsity, he encountered a squad with several skilled backfield players. Thus, Dung came off the bench on offense, although he apparently got into plenty of action on defense, where he shined, according to the *San Jose Mercury*'s Louis Duino. Nevertheless, in 1949, Hal Wood pronounced the "shifty Hawaiian" the best understudy in the nation. Indeed, during the 1949 season, Dung ran for a touchdown against Fresno State and intercepted a St. Mary's pass and took off for what Duino called an "outstanding" ninety-three-yard touchdown. When the Broncos upset the Bear Bryant–coached Kentucky team in the Orange Bowl of 1950, Dung was considered one of the game's big stars. The yearbook boasted that Dung excited spectators with his "zig-zag" punt returns.[65]

Before the 1950 season began, coach Dick Gallagher considered switching the "speedy" Abe Dung to quarterback. During the 1950 season, moreover, Dung scored the first opposition touchdown ever at Rice Stadium, on a twenty-two-yard pass reception. Against Nevada in 1950, he ran the ball three times for forty-two yards, while completing five of seven passes, including one touchdown heave. Santa Clara routed Nevada 55–0 in the game in which Dung operated as a T-formation quarterback for the first time in his college career.[66]

Unfortunately, for reasons not entirely clear, Dung slipped out of the football headlines for most of his senior year in 1951. In November 1951, however, Dung was elected captain for Santa Clara's game against Marquette. During that game, which Santa Clara won 27–14, Dung managed to return a punt twenty-eight yards. Moreover, Dung was honored with an invitation to play in the North-South Shriners All-Star Game held at Miami's Orange Bowl. Competing for the victorious south, Dung was shown in a nationally syndicated photograph helping to tackle an opposing ball carrier. Meanwhile, the Bay Area's Chinese American community expressed pride in Dung's achievements by way of the San Francisco-based *Chinese Press*. The weekly hailed Dung as one of the best punters in Santa Clara' s long history and "175 pounds of dynamite."[67]

In Southern California, former UH standout Johnny Naumu inspired some to declare him Wedemeyer's equal when he showed up at USC. "But," said a story in the *Oxnard Press-Courier*, "all this astonishment at 'finding' the dark-skinned, wiry touchdown-running Mr. Naumu is bringing a lot of laughs from the barefoot leagues of Honolulu" as the twenty-six-year-old was a star in Hawai'i before Herman Wedemeyer. Naumu had attended McKinley High School and stood out for the University of Hawai'i prior to World War II.[68]

Naumu was initially described by the *Pacific Citizen* as a Hawaiian of indigenous and Japanese ancestry, although the weekly later pointed out that he did not really possess Japanese descent. In 1946, Naumu's ball carrying helped USC triumph over Stanford and the University of Washington. Against Stanford, Naumu scored on a one-yard touchdown and helped drive the Trojan ground game. In USC's cross-country rivalry game against Notre Dame, Naumu's one-yard touchdown run prevented the Trojans from getting blanked when they lost 20–6. Naumu also kicked points after touchdowns for USC in 1946. Impressed with his "Honolulu halfback," Naumu's head coach at USC, Jeff Cravath, likened his running style to that of a "hula girl." Naumu won a starting job early in 1947 when he scored two touchdowns against Washington State, inspiring one wire story to call him the "Hawaiian boy." One touchdown went for seventeen yards and, according to the *San Bernardino County Sun*, the Hawaiian proved the Trojans most consistent ground gainer against the Cougars. Unfortunately, he broke his arm against Ohio State. Yet while he could not play in USC's big game against UCLA, his teammates named Naumu as an honorary captain.[69]

Leroy Ka-ne was one of the best running backs in the nation in the late 1940s and early 1950s. The 1930 U.S. census manuscripts tell us that his father Solomon, a public works clerk, was part-Hawaiian and his mother Elizabeth, Hawaiian. In 1948, Ka-ne scored three touchdowns against Marshall and ran back a fifty-five-yard interception for a touchdown against St. Louis. In September 1949, Xavier beat Dayton. However, "Leroy Ka-ne, Hawaiian halfback" scored on a forty-seven-yard touchdown. Ka-ne subsequently tallied three touchdowns against Miami of Ohio. He made two touchdowns against Toledo, including one on a fifty-eight-yard pass and run. An Ohio daily hailed Ka-ne as an "explosive runner." Ka-ne then tallied two touchdowns as well against Marshall and ran the ball for 137 yards and two touchdowns against St. Bonaventure. At season's end, "the great Hawaiian back" set the Dayton scoring record by making two touchdowns, one a ninety-four yarder, against Scranton. In all, Ka-ne accumulated seventy-two points. For his 1949 season, Ka-ne was named to the second team all-Ohio squad.[70]

The next year, Ka-ne was plagued by injuries. At season's outset, the *Olean Times Herald* published a photo of Ka-ne and the caption called him the "happy hyphen," "high powered hyphen," and the "sensational Hawaiian halfback." He did manage to carry the ball past the goal line for one touchdown in a victory over Marshall. Moreover, at the end of the 1950 season, Ka-ne became the first Hawaiian chosen to compete for the East all-star squad in San Francisco's vaunted Shrine All-Star Game. Consequently, the *San Jose Mercury* described Ka-ne as a "hard running Hawaiian back." *Mercury* readers learned that while his real name was reportedly Peter Patrick Wialaahea Ka-ne, Dayton teammates dubbed him, "the Savage," "Cocoanut," "Pineapple," and "Hyphen." Playing in the Hula Bowl in Honolulu shortly after the Shrine game, Ka-ne, "Dayton's Hawaiian halfback" scored on a seventy-nine-yard catch and run with a pass from the legendary Sammy Baugh in January 1951. Twenty-five thousand Hawaiian fans cheered his feat. [71]

A few years after leaving Dayton, Ka-ne was in Honolulu, working as an assistant hotel manager. And when he died in Hawai'i in the mid-1990s, Dayton sportswriter Ritter Collett complained that it took weeks before local football fans knew about his demise. Playing on the same team as the great NFL lineman Jim Katcavage, Ka-ne was remembered as a "great runner" by Collett.[72]

Jim Akau proved more than an adequate replacement for Ka-ne at Dayton. U.S. census data tells us that in 1940, Akau was the nine-year-old son of a part Hawaiian father, whose occupation was that of a tax collector. His mother was Hawaiian Chinese. The 1950 Dayton yearbook asserts that Jim Akau performed well for the frosh squad in 1949. But after spending his first year on the varsity primarily as a defender, Akau turned into a topflight running back. In 1951, Hall of Fame coach, Chuck

Noll, was a star lineman for Dayton. But the Hawaiian was the team's leading rusher, helping to propel Dayton into the Salad Bowl.[73]

When Dayton appeared in the Salad Bowl in Phoenix, the *Tucson Daily Citizen* pointed out that Akau represented Dayton's "second jarring runner in three years" to emerge out of Hawaiian barefoot football. "Jimmy Keeaumoku Akau," according to the Citizen, was the "smiling Hawaiian" and a light but "fast stepping fullback." Akau reportedly told the press that he preferred playing barefoot because he could run faster, but he knew those days were gone. Polishing Akau's credentials further, the *Citizen* reported that Akau had been named the INS all-Ohio fullback, while the AP had relegated him to the all-Ohio third team.[74]

In the Rocky Mountains and Great Plains, Hawaiians performed for college elevens in the early 1950s. Cal Chai was an all-conference guard for Denver University in the early 1950s. The 1940 U.S. census data describe him as the ten-year-old son of a Chinese immigrant clerk for an iron works in Honolulu and a part-Hawaiian mother. In 1949, the *Tucson Daily Citizen* hailed Chai as a "stellar" 168-pound guard. After leaving Denver, he would serve as a frosh defensive coach for Colorado State before returning to Hawai'i and a career in education. Part-Hawaiian Tom Hugo also stood out for Denver in the early 1950s. The 1940 census data indicates that Hugo's father worked as a Honolulu bus driver. Before the 1950 season began, Salt Lake City sports columnist, Jim Mooney, predicted the 210-pound Hugo would be the finest lineman in Denver's history. In 1951, both Hugo and Chai were all-conference guards. Another Hawaiian, Charles Kalani made third-team all-conference as a University of Utah representative. Meanwhile, William Chai, a guard for College of Emporia in Kansas, made first team All American for small colleges in 1951.[75]

In the Pacific Northwest, the remarkable Ken Kimura stood out as an excellent football and basketball player for Southern Oregon College in the early 1950s. The *Klamath Falls Herald and News* acclaimed Kimura the "Hawaiian flash" in early fall of 1950. At that time, he ran for a touchdown against Oregon Tech in a 19–12 victory. In the fall of 1953, Southern Oregon lost to Chico State, 26–7. But Kimura, who played quarterback and halfback, scored all his team points on a thirteen-yard touchdown run and a kicked PAT.[76]

On the West Coast in the early 1950s, the image of Hawaiian football was getting changed from that of dazzling running backs like Wedemeyer to that of hulking Pacific Islander linemen. Herman and Jim Clark were sons of a Honolulu police officer and a formidable athlete himself. As for the Clark brothers, they were large, skilled athletes who possessed Hawaiian ancestry. In analyzing the Oregon State prospects in 1950, the *San Jose Mercury* described "Jim and Herman Clark [as] two husky brothers from Hawaii." Both, as it turned out, starred at Oregon State. The *Los Angeles Times'* Dick Hyland remembered their father as a tough lineman for the Honolulu Town Team and said that Herman was his "true son. No one is going to push him around." In October 1951, Oregon State was set to take on USC, featuring a promising and very hefty Hawaiian lineman, Charlie Ane. The *Los Angeles Times'* Braver Dyer pointed out that the USC's "mammoth . . . tackle" was outweighed by "Herman Clark, gargantuan Beaver tackle." However, Clark's coach said he was not just big but the best tackle on the Pacific Coast.[77]

Both Clarks earned postseason honors. Herman received honorable mention on the International News Services' All-Coast team and was named to the West Shrine squad after the 1951 season. An East-West Shrine Football game program notified readers that Herman was a 295-pound tackle who ranked as the largest lineman on the Pacific Coast. An expert swimmer, Clark, the program elaborating on the narrative of Clark representing exotic Hawai'i while competing in a modern sport, asserted he also enjoyed playing ukulele and "singing Hawaiian style." As for brother Jimmy, he was a comparatively svelte, 235 pounds. After his senior year, he too played in the East-West Shrine game, as well as the Hula Bowl and the College All-Star game.[78]

Charlie Ane gained national recognition as an outstanding lineman for USC in the early 1950s. According to the U.S. Census manuscripts of 1940, Ane was the son of Tuitai and Eva. The father, born in British Samoa, worked at the time as a stevedore in Honolulu, while his mother, described as having no occupation, was born in Hawaii. In 1949, Ane left the islands to play on Compton Junior College's eleven in Los Angeles. When Compton beat San Diego Junior College, the college's yearbook enthused that the defense was "bulwarked by Charlie Ane, huge Hawaiian tackle."[79]

Indeed, Compton proved a prime destination for Hawaiian gridders of various Asian and Pacific Islander ethnic backgrounds, hoping seemingly to further their college football careers at some mainland four-year school. More than likely, this school was USC as Compton's football program was, according to the *Honolulu Advertiser's* Red McQueen, widely perceived as a "farm" for the Trojans. A Hawaiian of Chinese ancestry, Roy Hiram was a running back for Compton in 1950. In 1951, Rex Pahoa caught a touchdown pass against Ventura JC in October. Later in the year, Joe Kahahawai blocked a Pasadena JC punt and recovered the ball for Compton's only touchdown. That same year, the *Los Angeles Times'* Don Snyder hailed center Famika Anae as one of the team's brightest stars. He wrote that Anae came to Compton as a good single wing quarterback. As it turned out, Anae did not spend all his time at center in 1951 as he ran for a touchdown in Compton's 58–0 blowout of Glendale.[80]

In 1952, the Compton football roster included several players of Asian and Pacific Islander ancestry, not all of whom came from the mainland. Hawaiians Charlie Ka'aihue, Famika Anae, and Dave Yamashiro made the "All-Southland" eleven. The 1940 U.S. manuscript census schedules disclose that Dave Yamashiro was the Hawaiian-born ten-year-old son of a carpenter father working for a plantation on Kaua'i. His mother and his father were both immigrants. Lineman Joe Kahahawai was described in the school yearbook as a "murderous tackle" and junior college All-American. That he bore the same name as a young man murdered because of a controversial court case in Honolulu in 1931, the yearbook's choice of wording was, at the very least, unfortunate. As we will discuss in future pages, Compton was not the only Southern California junior college suiting up Hawaiian football players. Pasadena JC included former Punahou standout Darwin Chang in 1950 and would later field slippery running back Al Napoleon. The quest for football supremacy among Southern California's junior colleges had seemingly compelled them to engage in recruiting efforts that might have looked like mainland colonialism to Hawaiian locals.[81]

After leaving Compton, Ane proved a standout at nearby USC. Before his first season at USC began in 1951, the *Los Angeles Times'* Braven Dyer paid plenty of attention to the "massive Charlie Ane," extolling Ane's "bear-hug tackles" in practice sessions and predicting he would get action as an offensive guard and defensive tackle. After the season began, Dyer called the Hawaiian "Tugboat Ane" in reference to not only his size but a famed movie character, "Tugboat Annie." Once the 1951 season began, Dyer further declared Ane had struck "holy terror" into Washington from his defensive left tackle spot. At the end of the 1951 season, Ane made UPI's All-American team as an honorable mention member.[82]

In 1952, Ane's coach switched him, at least occasionally, from the offensive line to a single wing quarterback. *Los Angeles Times* columnist Al Wolf said Ane had the "speed [and] agility" to do the job. Wolf expected he might even catch some passes. When USC shut out Wisconsin, 31–0, Ane indeed captured a pass for sixteen yards. In a game against Oregon, Ane's blocking from the quarterback position helped USC march to an important, fifty-seven-yard touchdown in the second half. Ane also played sterling defense. After the UCLA rivalry game, a wire photo appeared in the *Salem Daily Capital Journal* showing Ane tackling a Bruin ball carrier with a caption acclaiming the Hawaiian was vital to a Trojan triumph.[83]

In December 1952, Rube Samuelson introduced Ane to *Sporting News* readers. His article was much too cleverly headlined "Hawaiian Ane One Hula-Va Tackler USC Foes Learn." It described the usually "bespectacled" Ane as the most famed Hawaiian gridder since Wedemeyer. Claiming that the 256-pound lineman possessed Chinese and English, as well as Samoan ancestry, Samuelson asserted that Ane's wife, Marilyn, combined Irish and Native Hawaiian descent. Unreported by Samuelson was the fact that Marilyn was Neal Blaisdell's daughter.[84]

During the 1951 season, the *Los Angeles Examiner* exoticized Ane, along with Hawaiian USC teammates, Sal Naumu and Harold Han displaying them in a photograph adorned with large straw hats, while one played the ukulele. Though not as famous as Ane, Sal Naumu and Harold Han contributed to USC's success in the early 1950s. Sal Naumu was John's younger brother and a leading ground gainer at Compton prior to his short journey to USC. Before the 1951 season, he was listed as one of five fullbacks on the Trojan roster. Described by Braven Dyer as a "capable performer" and a "doughty Hawaiian," Han got into more action for the Trojans than Naumu. He even played for the West all-star team in San Francisco's Shrine game in 1953 and made the PCC's all-conference as an honorable mention selection.[85]

Another Hawaiian of Samoan descent, Al Harrington caused quite a stir when he joined the Stanford squad in the mid-1950s. Born Al Ta'a in the Samoan village of Malaemi, he took his white stepfather's surname in Hawai'i. A star at Punahou, Harrington was urged by school head, Dr. John Fox, to head to Stanford. However, before officially entering the university, Harrington's deficient academic preparation compelled him to spend a year at nearby Menlo Junior College.[86]

While prominent non-white athletes were still all too rare at even Pacific Coast Conference schools in the mid-twentieth century, they were rarer still at Stanford, which had yet to field a black athlete on its football team by the mid-1950s. In any event, Harrington was ready to enter Stanford in the fall of 1955. Will Connolly told *San Francisco Chronicle* readers that Harrington was the sensation of the Stanford football team's "Picture Day" before the 1955 season began. Connolly asserted that "it did not take long for the cameramen to discover Harrington, a 195-pound brunet and a fine figure of a boy." Despite his 195-pound frame, the *Chronicle* called Harrington a "little Samoan" and featured more from Connolly on the Hawaiian. The sports columnist asserted that Stanford authorities were miffed that the "handsome Polynesian" had injured himself slightly while performing a "ceremonial sword dance" in his dormitory. Unconcerned, Harrington insisted he would continue to do his "Samoan dance." He claimed, "[M]y people pay respect to the war weapon and the work tool." Yet Connolly indicated that Stanford should express gratitude to Harrington, since "his exotic background" would attract fans to Stanford Stadium. Moreover, in away games "the Samoan," Connolly wrote, would serve as an "ornament to Stanford." Probably unintentionally, Connolly even poured gasoline on the sexual fears of some white supremacists when he predicted that once Stanford's fall quarter began, Harrington would "slay coeds."[87]

As for football, Harrington could play. An AP story informed readers that Harrington was "fast and hits hard." Sportswriter Chris Edmonds speculated that the "full-blooded Samoan" would add zip to the Stanford backfield. It turned out that Harrington wound up coming off the bench for Stanford in 1955. In a game against San Jose State, won easily by

Stanford, 34–18, Harrington scored on a short run. However, an ankle injury slowed Harrington down for most of the 1955 season.[88]

Harrington spent much of the 1956 season on the bench. He told the *Stanford Daily* he was "philosophical" about his lack of playing time. In November, though, he had a chance to show off his skills against USC, running the ball six times for thirty-eight yards. This led the *Stanford Daily* to headline a story about him: "Al Harrington, Card halfback, Best Example of the Word, 'Desire.'"[89]

Harrington would finally become a regular until 1957. An often dazzling, elusive running back, Harrington also punted and placekicked for Stanford. Moreover, he was a fine pass receiver. One of his best and worst games had to have been against Oregon. He ran for over 106 yards and, stressed coach Chuck Taylor, "played his heart out." Unfortunately, he missed two touchdown conversions, allowing Oregon to gain a narrow victory. Before facing Stanford, USC coach Don Clark expressed concern about what Harrington might do to the Trojans. When Stanford played USC, however, Harrington suffered a cracked jaw and broken molars. With the Hawaiian out of the backfield, Stanford followers feared that their team's chances for a conference title and a Rose Bowl bid were greatly dimmed. Indeed, Stanford did not make it to the Rose Bowl, but Harrington with his jaw wired shut, put on a cardinal red and white uniform and kicked two extra points against rival Cal, giving his team the margin of victory in a 14–12 game. In general, Harrington was exceptional in 1957, gaining honorable mention recognition in the Pacific Coast Conference for his play.[90]

Yet the exoticization of Harrington often overshadowed his gridiron achievements. After one game in which the halfback excited the crowd, the *Stanford Daily* beamed, "Allan Tausau Harrington can really put on a sword dancing act." Before a game against Washington State, the *Daily* published a photograph of Harrington and promised readers that the halfback would "Luau Cougars." In early November, Jack Bluth, a sportswriter for the *San Mateo Times*, declared that "Harrington hula danced for much of Stanford's yardage against the [Oregon] Ducks." Jack Winkler of the Associated Press reported that the American History major danced with "murderous looking Samoan ceremonial sword," and boasted that "Samoan music has more of a beat than American music." Yet Winkler added that Harrington was a good all-around player who led Stanford in ball carrying. The handsome and gregarious Harrington even appeared on national television, "sword dancing" on shows such as "To Tell the Truth" and "You Asked for It."[91]

Seemingly pushed and pulled across daunting cultural frontiers in mid-twentieth-century America, Harrington reveals mixed feelings about his Stanford experiences. In a recent interview, he remembers Stanford as "challenging," but not so much because of its classroom demands. Indeed, Harrington claims he was more comfortable in a Stanford classroom than on a football practice field. His coaches, he insists, just could not get beyond the fact that he "was the darkest guy on the team." Harrington subsequently became an actor and entertainer, appearing regularly on *Hawaii Five–0.* [92]

Not as publicized as Harrington, Hawaiian Al Napoleon played halfback for Stanford in the 1950s. A part-Hawaiian son of a prison guard, Napoleon competed for Pasadena Junior College before heading up to the Farm. At the time, Pasadena Junior College vied with Compton for Hawaiian talent. In October 1951, the "hippity . . . halfback" was named Southern California's "TV player of the week" for his performance against Los Angeles JC. In that game, Napoleon tallied two touchdowns. Napoleon later "sparked" Pasadena as it triumphed over Fullerton JC by scoring three touchdowns. Against Compton, Napoleon scored on what Don Snyder of the *Los Angeles Times* called a "sensational" ninety-one-yard run. In another game, he ran for three touchdowns against Muir College at the Rose Bowl. Little wonder that Don Snyder acclaimed Napoleon as one of Pasadena's "main offensive sparkplugs." In the Junior Rose Bowl, pitting a Southern California junior college against a top-rated JC eleven from another region, Napoleon gained over two hundred yards. Moreover, at the end of the 1951 season, Napoleon earned junior college All American recognition. [93]

After leaving Pasadena, the "swivel hipped broken field runner" helped Stanford upset the powerful UCLA Bruins squad in 1953 by nabbing the winning touchdown pass. He also had a fine game against Washington State, putting his broken field running on display. He carried the ball five times for twenty-seven yards against the Cougars, caught a touchdown pass, and weaved through defenders for a thirty-six-yard kickoff return with little blocking help. Then, unfortunately, he got into trouble with the U.S. Selective Service for allegedly evading the draft. Napoleon maintained that he thought he had a deferment, but would gladly serve Uncle Sam if called upon. Napoleon wound up serving in the military only to return to Stanford football in 1956. He got hurt and was out for that season, but in 1957 he left the bench a bit, carrying the ball four times for thirty-nine yards. His best game was against San Jose State early in the season—a game in which he scored on a dazzling twenty-eight-yard touchdown run. [94]

Joe Francis starred as a single wing tailback at Oregon State in the middle to late 1950s. The two-year-old Francis was described in the U.S. Census Manuscripts of 1940 as a part Hawaiian son of a Honolulu police officer. Francis prepped at Kamehameha, where his gridiron performances attracted mainland recruiters. However, a back injury suffered at Kam caused some mainland college programs to shy away from recruiting him. Oregon State, nevertheless, brought Francis eastward. It was a wise decision as Francis helped the Beavers compete against perennial southern conference powerhouses such as USC and UCLA. Sportswriter

John Eggers exoticized Francis as "a hula-hipped Hawaiian." Eggers confided, "Honolulu Joe . . . like all Hawaiians . . . loves his native music and in moments of relaxation packs a mean baritone imparting island tunes." A more subdued, respected football writer, Harold Classen, dubbed Francis, "as fine a tailback as you'll ever see." [95]

Francis starred from the outset of his varsity career with Oregon State. In his first varsity game against BYU, Francis, the "sophomore halfback from Honolulu," ran twenty-five yards for a touchdown as the Beavers shut down the Utah squad 33–0 in 1955. In 1957, Francis led Oregon State to the Rose Bowl, where his team lost but he accumulated an impressive 203 yards in running and passing. Because of his great 1957 season, Francis was named MVP of his Oregon State eleven and won the Pop Warner Award as the year's outstanding Pacific Coast gridder. [96]

Trying to break into the elite strata of Pacific Coast football, San Jose State recruited a relatively impressive cadre of Hawaiians in the 1950s. Early in September 1954, the *San Jose Mercury* published a photograph of Miss Santa Clara County Fair presumably receiving hula lessons "from four Hawaiian boys on the San Jose State football team." The "boys" included running backs Mel Soong, Roy and Pat Hiram, as well as end Merv Lopes. [97]

Possessing Chinese ancestry, brothers Roy and Pat Hiram, as well as Mel Soong, played considerably in the backfield for the Spartans in the early and mid-1950s. The 1940 U.S. Census manuscript schedules depicted the Hirams' father as a part-Hawaiian construction worker in Honolulu, whereas their mother possessed Chinese ancestry. Early in the 1954 season, the *San Jose Mercury* dubbed Roy Hiram a "speedy little back." Subsequently, Roy crossed the goal line four times to lead the Spartans to a 38–7 victory over Idaho in 1954, gaining eighty-seven yards on but eight carries. His performance also proved vital in San Jose State's stunning upset of Stanford that year. Called "a 155 pound halfback from Honolulu" in a wire story, Pat Hiram's forty-three-yard scamper to pay dirt helped the Spartans beat the College of Pacific in 1952. Military service interrupted Pat Hiram's San Jose State career. But, in 1956, he gained 158 yards in just twenty-eight carries. Before the 1954 season began, the *San Jose Mercury*'s notified readers that "Mel Soong, a relatively unheralded junior transfer from Denver University" stole the show at a scrimmage, in which Pat Hiram also shined. Considered a good running back by the *San Jose Mercury*, Soong, in 1955, scored on a four-yard touchdown as San Jose State blanked the University of Hawai'i in San Jose, 34–0. San Jose State's 1955 yearbook displays a photograph of Soong carrying the ball with Japanese American Tom Yagi trying to clear a path for him. [98]

Charlie Ka'aihue was a fine guard for the Spartans in the mid-1950s. A Native Hawaiian son of a bus driver father, he captained the team in 1956. In 1960, the fledgling Oakland Raiders would give Ka'aihue a tryout. Indeed, he even got the football card treatment from the Fleer Company. Ka'aihue's football card described him as five feet eleven, 235 pounds and twenty-five years old. He was further depicted as a guard who "thrives on rugged play."[99]

As Hawai'i was nearing statehood in the late 1950s, two Hawaiians ranked high among the best linemen in college football. Oregon State's Ed Kaohelaulii, called a "gentle Hawaiian" by the *Portland Oregonian*, earned a berth on the Honorable Mention All-Coast squad as a tackle in 1958. The next year, he was named co-captain of the Beavers. In 1959 John Kapele was described by *Sports Illustrated* as an all-conference, "220-pound Hawaiian tackle" for Brigham Young University in Utah. According to columnist Roy Schwartz, Kapele's coach claimed before the 1959 season that "[n]obody can play football like John Kapele when he puts his mind to it," intimating that Kapele did not consistently "put . . . his mind to it." When BYU downed Colorado State in 1959, the school's yearbook applauded his line work.[100]

Several other Hawaiians performed and excelled for big-time and not so big-time college programs in the late 1950s and early 1960s. In 1961, the *Portland Oregonian* reported that former Iolani High star Hugh Yoshida was a solid linebacker and short gain ball carrier for Linfield. Yoshida eventually earned National Association of Intercollegiate Athletics (NAIA) All-American honors as a linebacker. Moreover, Tony Ah Yat emerged as a fine defensive end for Linfield. Ah Yat's coach pronounced the Kamehameha grad "aggressive and hard-nosed." His accolades included all-Pacific Coast and NAIA All-American honors. After leaving Linfield, Yoshida took up coaching in Hawai'i at Wailua High on rural Oahu and then Leilehua, where he had greater success. Indeed, Leilehua High's football stadium is named after Yoshida. Moving on from high school coaching, Yoshida became UH's associate athletic director and then eventually athletic director, a position from which he retired in 2002. Ah Yat turned to a career in coaching and teaching too after graduating. One of Tony Ah Yat's sons would become a prominent quarterback for Montana University in the late 1990s, and the other would pitch minor league baseball.[101]

Another Pacific Northwest small college, Willamette, suited up Hawaiians. In the early 1960s, Stan Solomon earned honors as a Willamette running back. A son of a Native Hawaiian father and a Hawaiian Japanese mother, Solomon was largely raised by the latter. A superb all-around athlete at McKinley, Solomon journeyed eastward to Oregon after graduation. The running back earned all-conference, first team honors three times. In 1960, he was a National Association of Intercollegiate Athletics (NAIA) first team All-American selection. The *Oregon Journal* also honored him as the state's small college player of the year. Also a track standout at Willamette, Solomon was named to the school's Hall of Fame. After leaving Willamette, Solomon remained in Oregon where he became a high school teacher and coach of not only varsity football teams but also female basketball squads.[102]

During the 1950s and 1960s, Hawaiians became quite prominent in the powerful Midwest Big Ten Conference. The son of a well-known Hawaiian athlete in the 1930s, John Kerr Jr., possessed Hawaiian and Chinese ancestry. In 1940, the U.S. Census manuscripts tell us, John Kerr, Sr. was a clerk for an electric utility company in Honolulu, while his wife worked as a grocery store clerk. John Kerr played end for Purdue in the early to mid-1950s. A Punahou graduate, Kerr headed to Pasadena City College upon leaving the famed Honolulu school. After a year in Pasadena, he transferred to Purdue. Sportswriter Jim Vanheel praised Kerr in 1954 as Purdue's "prize receiver." In early October 1954, Kerr snagged a touchdown pass against Notre Dame from all-time great quarterback Lenny Dawson. At the end of the 1954 season, Kerr made the AP All-Big Ten second team and the 1955 East Shrine team. After getting drafted by the San Francisco 49ers and serving in the military, Kerr enjoyed a lengthy career as a classroom teacher, vice-principal, and football coach on the mainland and in Hawai'i.[103]

Kerr was not the only Hawaiian to boost Purdue's football fortunes in the 1950s. The part-Hawaiian son of a Honolulu office clerk father, John Simerson proved an excellent lineman for the Boilermakers in the mid-1950s. Another part-Hawaiian, Alfred Espinda was a fine pass receiver for Purdue in the late 1950s. His father, Alfred Espinda Sr., had played football for UH in the 1930s. In a 1936 loss to San Jose State, he scored UH's only touchdown after a blocked punt. According to the 1940 census data, his father was an athletic director for a plantation. After graduating from Purdue, Espinda carved out an extensive career as a teacher and coach at Farrington High for years.[104]

Beginning in the 1950s, Michigan State surfaced as a major destination for Hawaiian football players, partly because Tommy Kaulukukui had gotten his Ph.D. at the university and served briefly as an assistant coach in East Lansing. Five-foot-eight-inch halfback, Bill Kaae, was the smallest player on the Michigan State team in 1956. Tommy Kaulukukui's nephew Dick Kenney found his way to East Lansing in the 1960s. A son of a European American Navy veteran father from Kansas, Kenny's mother was Tommy Kaulukukui's sister. In the mid-1960s, Kenney's barefoot kicking not only won national publicity exoticizing him but helped the Spartans win games, although coach Duffy Daugherty complained that Kenney scratched footballs with his toenails. Around the same time, Michigan State also recruited fine gridders such as Bob Apisa and lineman Jim Nicholson in Hawai'i. The press extolled Apisa as a "215 pound line-cracking Hawaiian." Making a stab at humor, one Associated Press article depicted Apisa as able to "run . . . as if he were chasing a hula girl." In 1965, Apisa piled up an impressive 715 yards and 5.7-yards-per-carry average, while crossing the goal line ten times.[105]

Apisa had grown up in Samoa, which he and his family left because his father had taken a military post in Hawai'i. Apisa recollected for the *Los Angeles Times'* Bill Dwyre that "[w]e didn't have electricity in Samoa then. . . . I left in a boat, looked back and saw all the kerosene lamps, lighting the island. . . . When we got to Honolulu, about two weeks later [it is a 2,500-mile trip north], we came in at night and I was amazed at the electricity, of how aglow the city was." Upon arriving in Hawai'i, Apisa spoke no English but eventually starred in high school football and emerged as a "target of Duffy Daugherty's pioneering attempt to lure hefty Hawaiians to Michigan State." After leaving East Lansing, Apisa settled in the Los Angeles area, where he worked as an actor for many years, appearing in Polynesian roles in *Hawaii Five-0* and *Magnum P.I.*[106]

Charlie Wedemeyer, Herman's younger brother, proved a prime recruit for Duffy Daugherty. Prior to journeying to East Lansing, Charley Wedemeyer starred at Punahou and wound up as one of *Sports Illustrated* "Faces in the Crowd" in 1965 because of his prowess as a prep. Indeed, he made all-league three years in a row. Once in East Lansing, the versatile Wedemeyer played his way onto the East all-star squad that competed in the East-West Shrine game in San Francisco in the late 1960s after carrying the ball twenty-one times for 147 yards and catching nine passes for 108 yards. His wife accompanied him to the Bay Area, where they fell in love with the region and hoped to stay. Happily, Wedemeyer landed a job as head coach of Los Gatos High School in Santa Clara County. The Hawaiian had been coaching there for several years, when he learned that he suffered from ALS and was given three years to live. Wedemeyer, however, remained as coach of Los Gatos High School long enough to be named California's high school coach of the year in 1985 and see his son, Kale, play for him. Indeed, Kale accomplished two outstanding seasons as a running back for Los Gatos High, carrying the ball for over one thousand yards in his junior and senior years. Sadly, Wedemeyer's illness forced him to eventually leave his head coaching post, but he continued to advise the Los Gatos coaching staff and continued to inspire with his bravery and endurance until his death in 2010. Meanwhile, Kale put together a fine career at the University of Pacific in the early 1990s before becoming a respected physician.[107]

HAWAIIAN GRIDDERS, MAINLAND TEAMS IN THE LATE TWENTIETH AND EARLY TWENTY-FIRST CENTURY

Several other Hawaiians stood out on the mainland in the 1960s and 1970s. A fine lineman, Mel Tom played college ball first at USC and then starred at San Jose State in the early to mid-1960s. Kam grad Rockne Freitas was a fine lineman for Oregon State in the mid-1960s. In the late 1960s, Utah University's Norm Chow was hailed by the *Tucson Daily*

Citizen as one of the WAC conference's best linemen. Chow's coach, Mike Giddings, considered him one of the best guards in the land. When the 1967 season ended, Chow earned all-WAC honors. In the next decade, Kale Ane, the lineman son of Charley, was a stalwart center for the Michigan State eleven. [108]

Dubbed "Pineapple Milt," Milt Holt not only possessed indigenous Hawaiian ancestry but performed well at quarterback for Harvard in 1974. Indeed, he was described in the press as a "Japanese looking" quarterback. Against Princeton, Holt ran for two touchdowns and threw for three more, completing sixteen of twenty-four attempts for 234 yards. In the rivalry game against Yale, he connected on twenty of thirty-two passes and scored one touchdown, leading Harvard to a victory. At the end of the season, Holt made all-conference. [109]

In 1997, the University of Montana's ability to recruit talented Hawaiian gridders sparked an article in the *Sports Illustrated*. Written by Ivan Maisel, the piece centered on the exploits of quarterback Brian Ah Yat, the son of previously mentioned Tony Ah Yat. According to Maisel, the University of Montana had six Hawaiian players on the squad, but "Ah Yat may be the best player to come through a pipeline that, on and off for decades, has sent football players from the islands to the Big Sky country." One major reason why Montana could bring in Hawaiian players was assistant coach Tommy Lee, a Hawaiian who later moved on to the University of Utah and helped the Utes suit up twelve Hawaiians in 1997. Lee told Maisel, "You sign one or two [Hawaiians], they enjoy it, and by word of mouth, more kids get interested." [110]

In the twenty-first century, Division 1 college programs on the Pacific Coast counted upon the contributions of Hawaiian gridders. The University of Oregon emerged as a consistent power in the PAC-10, which subsequently expanded to twelve teams. Hawaiian quarterback Marcus Mariota proved invaluable to Oregon's success in the early 2010s. By the time he ended his college career in 2014, Mariota had won practically every major individual award a college quarterback could get. Not only was he considered an expert passer, but his running ability constantly kept defenses on their toes. During his Heisman winning year of 2014, Mariota completed 68 percent of 445 passes for 4,454 yards and 42 touchdowns. At the same time, he ran the ball for 707 yards in 135 carries, scoring 15 touchdowns. [111]

HAWAIIAN COACHES ON THE MAINLAND

Hawaiians have made their way onto mainland college coaching staffs. After his professional football career, Al Lolotai signed up to coach linemen at Colorado A&M in 1950. As mentioned earlier, Tommy Lee served as an assistant at the University of Montana and University of Utah.

Moreover, he headed small college programs at Willamette and Montana Western. Prior to taking up coaching, Lee went to Oregon's Willamette College, where he became a small college All American. After leaving college, Lee spent a year in the Canadian Football League (CFL). Aside from coaching college gridders, Lee also served on the staffs of professional teams such as the CFL Toronto Seahawks and the World Football League's San Antonio franchise. Duane Akina is another Hawaiian who served as an assistant coach for several years. At the University of Washington, Akina backed up the great Warren Moon as a quarterback. After he turned to coaching, Akina became an assistant at the University of Hawai'i and the University of Arizona. For many years, Akina was an assistant at the University of Texas, but most recently he has been a defensive back coach at Stanford.[112]

For years, Norm Chow was expected to eventually take over a mainland college program. A son of a Chinese Hawaiian father and a mother possessing Portuguese and Native Hawaiian ancestry, Norm Chow even approached getting a NFL head coaching job when he became offensive coordinator for the Tennessee Titans. Before that, Chow put together an extensive résumé at the college level, and many expected that he would become the first Asian American Division I head coach after serving as USC's offensive coordinator in the early 2000s. During one game in which USC's potent offensive obliterated Oregon State, 55–28, analyst and former quarterback great Dan Fouts insisted several times on air that Chow deserved a head coaching position of a big-time college program. Chow previously starred as a guard for the University of Utah in the mid-1960s. He then competed in Canadian football before starting his coaching career at Waialuha High School in Hawai'i. Chow's talents as an offensive teacher and strategist gained widespread recognition at Brigham Young University, when that institution stunned the college football world to win the National Title in 1984. By the early 2000s, Chow clearly hoped to pin down a head coaching job, although he stressed he was not job hunting while serving as Pete Carroll's offensive coordinator at USC. He claimed that becoming a head coach was "very important to me. . . . People can say what they want, but I would like that opportunity to do that." As to why, he stressed, "Because you're the first! There are not that many of us that are in this profession. I have seen the good things. I have seen the bad things. I have seen the prejudices. All you can do is work as hard as you can. If you get caught up in that, you're in big trouble. I was taught a long time ago, just to do the best that you can and whatever happens will happen."[113]

While crossing cultural frontiers, Chow also hoped he could emerge as something of a role model by eliminating derogatory racial stereotypes. He told an *Asian Week* journalist, "I take great pride [in tearing down racial stereotypes. . . . As a young person you always looked up and admired and tried to follow someone. If we're doing something that others aspire to and want to do and can maybe follow through with, then it's all well worthwhile."[114]

While few have accused Chow of oversensitivity on racial matters, he left BYU in 1999 because of a racial stereotyping incident involving a school administrator. Chow recalled:

> The guy stood up in front of us and talked about a new building that was going to be built. . . . Said. . . . "We have all of the Chinamen lined up ready to work on it." As far as I was concerned, this was the 20th Century. That comment didn't have to be made. I saw very little remorse after that. There was a form letter that came out apologizing to everybody. I just happen to be the only "Chinaman" sitting there.

Chow thought the media glossed over the issue, but to the Hawaiian "[t]his was not a minor incident. It made me realize how important it was to work in the proper environment. I went home and told my wife it was time to go. We were working with people that I didn't prefer to deal with. I didn't have a problem, but that guy sure did."[115]

After leaving USC, Chow inked an approximately $1,000,000 contract to become the Titans offensive coordinator. Before heading to Tennessee, however, Chow was honored as Grand Marshal for a Los Angeles Chinatown parade. At that time, Chow stressed he sought "to be a good football coach who happens to be Asian or Hawaiian or whatever the heck I am." Chow declared that he was proud of his ancestry, "but I don't want to wear it on my sleeve. If I can be of help and an example, as other people were to me, it's all right."[116]

Chow did not stay in the NFL. The Titans' offense sputtered and he moved on to UCLA and Utah. Finally, in 2012, he became the first Asian American coach at a Division 1 school, when he took the helm of UH's football team. His UH teams had a rocky time of it, but they achieved an all-time high in graduation rates. The former proved more important to those in authority at UH than the latter, and Chow was fired in November 2015.[117]

As it turned out, the honor of becoming the first Pacific Islander to head up a Division 1 football team goes to Ken Niumatalolo. Born in Samoa and raised in Hawai'i, Niumatalolo starred as a quarterback for Radford High School in Honolulu. Niumatalolo then quarterbacked at UH. Turning to coaching after his UH career, Niumatalolo eventually became offensive coordinator for the Naval Academy squad. When Navy had a head coaching vacancy, Niumatalolo filled it in 2007. Since then, he has become the winningest coach in the history of the Naval Academy.[118]

After the 2015 season ended, BYU named alumnus Kalani Sitake as head coach. Possessing Tongan descent, the one-time resident of Laie, Hawai'i was a stellar fullback for BYU in the late 1990s. Sitake subsequently became an assistant coach at Oregon State, Utah, Southern Utah, Eastern Arizona, and BYU. Sitake chose Harvey Unga to assist him as a running backs coach. As a running back for BYU in the 2000s, he ran for over 1,000 yards in his second through fourth years for the Cougars.[119]

CONCLUSION

For over a century before Marcus Mariota passed and ran his way to a Heisman Trophy season in 2014, Hawaiians of diverse and blended ethnic backgrounds contributed as players and now as coaches to "King Football" on the mainland. What football analysts called "pineapple pipelines" linked the islands to college programs, big and not so big, such as those found at St. Mary's, Michigan State, Dayton, University of Montana, San Jose State, and Whitman. Many of these players proved vital to their college elevens. Indeed, some like Herman Wedemeyer, Charlie Ane, and, most recently, Mariota were stars. They mastered a game that despite its atavistic, violent features was often hailed by advocates such as Walter Camp for its modernity. Yet they were often exoticized into non-white, cultural others. In the process, they negotiated the cultural frontiers formed by the colonialism directed by the U.S. government and the neocolonialism-fostered American economic and cultural institutions.

NOTES

1. Oberlin College Yearbook, 1892, www.ancestry.com (July 14, 2015); Ronald Williams, "The People's Champion," http://www.hanahou.com/pages/magazine.asp?MagazineID=&Action=DrawArticle&ArticleID=1124 (July 13, 2015).

2. Okihiro, *American History Unbound*, 221–223.

3. U.S. Census Bureau, City and County of Honolulu, 1920, www.ancestry.com (July 16, 2015); J. Kēhaulani Kauanui, *Hawaiian Blood: Colonialism and the Politics of Sovereignty and Indigeneity* (Durham, NC: Duke University Press, 2008).

4. Okihiro, *Island World*; Buck, *Paradise Remade*; Adria L. Imada, *Aloha America: Hula Circuits through the U.S. Empire* (Durham, NC: Duke University Press, 2012); Franks, *Barnstorming*; Willard, "Duke Kahanamoku's Body."

5. *Hawaiian Gazette*, November 12, 1897; U.S. Census Bureau, Manuscript Census Schedules, City of Waimea and Island of Hawai'i, 1910; City and County of Honolulu, 1930, www.ancestry.com (March 8, 2010).

6. *Honolulu Star-Bulletin*, November 21, 1916; Franks, *Barnstorming*.

7. *San Francisco Chronicle*, October 19, 1918; Ed Hughes, "A1 Americans Star to Show Speed Today," *San Francisco Chronicle*, October 26, 1918; Herbert Hauser, "St. Mary's and California Football Teams Ready for Fray," *Oakland Tribune*, November 8, 1918.

8. *San Francisco Chronicle*, October 13, 1918; Ed Hughes, "Bears Winners over St. Mary's," November 10, 1918; October 19, 1928; Herbert Hauser, "St. Mary's and California Football Teams Ready for Fray," *Oakland Tribune*, November 8, 1918; *Sausalito News*, November 30, 1918.

9. Doug Montell, "Saints and Santa Clarans Renew Rivalry," Ralph Hosler, "St. Mary's and Stanford Meet at Palo Alto, *Oakland Tribune*, October 7, 1921; November 29, 1922; May 22, 1960; December 6, 1920, p. 12; *Sacramento News*, December 25, 1922; *Los Angeles Times*, November 19, 1943; *Berkeley Daily Gazette*, November 25, 1944; *Hon-*

olulu Record, October 2, 1952; U.S. Census Bureau, Manuscript Schedules, City and County of Honolulu, 1930, www.ancestry.com (September 18, 2007).

10. *Washington Post,* December 7, 1924; U.S. Census Bureau, Manuscript Census Schedules, City and County of Honolulu, 1920, www.ancestry.com (November 8, 2009); *Reading Eagle,* November 4, 1924; *Dallas Morning News,* November 24, 1924; http://www.isr.bucknell.edu/Collections_and_Borrowing/Spe-cial_Collections_University_Archives/Yearbooks/pdf/1927/1927_Part_3.pdf (April 2, 2010); http://www.bucknellbison.com/sports/hallfame/spec-rel/hall-of-fame-football.html., (April 2, 2010).

11. Ron Bellamy, "From Tackling to Takedowns," *Eugene Register-Guard,* March 31, 1989; *Marion Star,* April 5, 1940.

12. Bellamy, "Tackling"; *El Paso Herald-Post,* November 8, 1939.

13. *Cincinnati Enquirer,* October 14, 1922; *Cleveland Plain Dealer,* October 22, 1922; *Mansfield News,* November 2, 1924; *Hamilton Journal-News,* October 15, 1925.

14. *Appleton Post-Crescent,* February 23, 1926; *Hamilton News-Journal,* March 16, 1926; Dayton University Yearbook, 1926, 1927, www.ancestry.com (April 29, 2015); *Los Angeles Times,* February 22, 1974.

15. http://www.hawaii.edu/uhwo/clear/HonoluluRecord/articles/v10n20/Like%20Father%20Like%20Son%20Footballs%20In%20The%20Blood%20Of%20Scrappy%20Willie%20Croziers.html (July 31, 2010); *Honolulu Record,* December 12, 1957; *Reading Eagle,* November 29, 1925; *Youngstown Vindicator,* January 13, 1927.

16. John Carroll University vs. Dayton University Program, Luna Park Stadium, University Heights, Ohio, October 9, 1926; U.S. Census Bureau, Manuscript Census Schedules, City and County of Honolulu, 1920, 1930, www.ancestry.com (August 7, 2008); Franks, *Barnstorming; Wilmington News-Journal,* September 19, 1928; *Providence News,* October 15, 1928; *Binghamton Press,* October 24, 1928; *Pittsburgh Press,* November 17, 1928.

17. *New York Times,* November 17, 1927; Lawrence Perry, "Oregon State Discovers Two Football Stars for Eleven to Use Next Fall," *Utica Observer,* April 10, 1928; *Montreal Gazette,* October 8, 1928; Ben Titus, "Indian, Hawaiian Star on Oregon Elevens," *Pittsburgh Press,* October 25, 1928; *Portland Oregonian,* October 29, 1928; Oregon State University Yearbook, 1930, 1931, www.ancestry.com (May 25, 2016).

18. *Portland Oregonian,* January 8, 1928.

19. U.S. Census Bureau, Manuscript Census Schedules, City and County of Honolulu, 1920, 1930, www.ancestry.com (August 23, 2014); *Chinese Digest,* September 24, 1936; *Portland Oregonian,* December 12, 1929; University of Montana vs. Washington State, Rogers Field, Pullman, Washington, October 25, 1930; *Riverside Daily Press,* December 27, 1930, 9; Goo, "Wonderful Athletes," 71.

20. U.S. Census Bureau, Manuscript Census Schedules, City and County of Honolulu, 1930, www.ancestry.com (September 22, 2014);

21. *Augusta Chronicle,* October 4, 1931.

22. *Dallas Morning Daily News,* October 18, 1931; *Trenton Evening Times,* October 18, 1931; December 4, 1932; October 15, 1933; *Kingsport Times,* October 9, 1932; *Brooklyn Eagle,* November 13, 1932; Robert Harro "Review of Series Finds Army, Navy in Close Battles," *New York Evening Post,* December 1, 1932; Alan Gould, "Versatile Attack Sweeps by Midshipmen in Great Battle before 79,000," *Montana Butte-Standard,"* December 4, 1932; *Seattle Times,* November 5, 1933; *Danville Bee,* November 1, 1933; *Aberdeen Daily News,* December 1, 1933; *Massillon Evening Independent,* March 21, 1934; U.S. Naval Academy Yearbook, 1934, www.ancestry.com (May 14, 2016).

23. *El Paso Herald-Post,* January 6, 1934.

24. *Asian Week,* July 8, 2009.

25. U.S. Census Bureau, Manuscript Census Schedules, City and County of Honolulu, 1910, 1930, www.ancestry.com (May 29, 2015); *Ironwood Daily Globe,* December 1, 1932.

26. *Oshkosh Daily,* November 23, 1931; *Charleston Gazette,* October 16, 1932; *Ironwood Daily Globe,* November 13, 1932; December 1, 1932; *Chicago Tribune,* November 17,

1934; Wisconsin Football Facts: Season of 1947 and Athletic Review of 1946–1947 School Year, University of Wisconsin Sports News Service; University of Wisconsin Yearbook, 1932, (May 25, 2016).

27. U.S. Census Bureau, Manuscript Census Schedules, City and County of Honolulu, 1940, www. ancestry.com., (May 29, 2015); *Chicago Tribune*, April 23, 1945.

28. *Reno Evening Gazette*, November 22, 1932.

29. Will Connolly, "Broncs Overpower Dons, 13 to 0 Despite Fumbles," *San Francisco Chronicle*, October 11, 1937; *Dallas Morning News*, December 27, 1937; December 23, 1938; *San Francisco Examiner*, January 6, 1938; *San Jose Mercury*, October 16, 1938; November 17, 1938; *Los Angeles Times*, December 3, 1938.

30. *Los Angeles Times*, September 14, 1939; December 6, 1939; *Salt Lake Tribune*, September 29, 1939; "Phil McLeese, "Bronco Followers Claim Injuns Have Edge in Kicking 'Bureau,'" September 30, 1939; *Seattle Times*, November 5, 1939; *Santa Cruz Sentinel*, November 5, 1939; Don Caswell, "Santa Clara Tops Michigan State, 6–0," *Eugene Register-Guard*, November 12, 1939; *Portland Oregonian*, January 2, 1940;

31. *Chicago Tribune*, June 1, 1940; August 13, 1940; August 16, 1940; *San Jose News*, August 8, 1940; *New York Times*, August 31, 1942; Franks, *Crossing*, 126.

32. U.S. Census Bureau, Manuscript Census Schedules, City and County of Honolulu, 1930, www.ancestry.com (August 3, 2009); *Sacramento Bee*, September 2, 1937; Wilbur Adams, "Forward Pass Gives Locals Win over Visiting Gridders," October 18, 1937; *San Francisco Chronicle*, November 6, 1937.

33. *Sacramento Bee*, September 29, 1937.

34. Ethen Leiser, "A War Hero Remembered," *Asian Week*, July 27, 2002-August 2, 2002; *Los Angeles Times*, September 11, 1937; September 15, 1937; October 22, 1938; *Sacramento Bee*, September 11, 1937; September 26, 1937; *Honolulu Star-Bulletin*, October 19, 1940; University of California, Los Angeles Yearbook, 1939, www.ancestry.com (March 7, 2010); http://interactive.ancestry.com/7949/cam1764_91–0027/2611309?backurl=http%3a%2f%2fsearch.ancestry.com%2f%2fcgi-bin%2fsse.dll%3findiv%3d1%26db%3dsfpl%26gss%3dangs-d%26new%3d1%26rank%3d1%26msT%3d1%26gsfn%3dConkling%26gsln%3dWai%2 6MSAV%3d0%26cp%3d0%26catbucket%3drstp%26uidh%3dqc9%26pcat%3d40%26fh %3d0%26h%3d2611309%26recoff%3d7%2b8%26ml_rpos%3d1&ssrc=&backlabel= ReturnRecord, (August 12, 2015); Duane Vachon, "Honor Overcomes Prejudice—Captain Francis Brown Wai, U.S. Army, WW II, Medal of Honor (1917–1944)," http://www.hawaiireporter.com/honor-overcomes-prejudice-captain-francis-brown-wai-u-s-army-ww-ii-medal-of-honor-1917–1944/ (October 17, 2017).

35. Jackie Robinson would join UCLA's football squad the next fall. Lee Cataluna, "Isle Families Trace Ties to '39 Pineapple Bowl," *Honolulu Advertiser*, May 23, 2010.

36. Ibid.

37. Ed Hughes, "Great Joy Folks in Ol' New York," *San Francisco Chronicle*, November 1, 1937; *Honolulu Advertiser*, December 5, 1941; *Honolulu Star-Bulletin*, December 23, 1941; U.S. Census Bureau, Manuscript Census Schedules, City and County of Honolulu, 1930, www.ancestry.com (August 17, 2015); http://archives.starbulletin.com/2000/04/06/news/obits.html (September 16, 2016); *Honolulu Star-Bulletin*, September 7, 1946.

38. Franks, *Crossing*, 125; *Santa Ana Register*, October 8, 1938; *Chino Champion*, October 21, 1938; *Los Angeles Times*, October 22, 1938; Cal Whorton, "Aztecs Rate over Bulldogs," October 20, 1938; October 6, 1940; *San Bernardino County Sun*, December 6, 1940; *Pomona Progress Bulletin*, April 24, 1969.

39. Franks, *Crossing*, 131; *San Bernardino County Sun*, November 13, 1938; Eugene Giedt, "Redlands to Battle Pomona Sahegans," October 14, 1939; Becky Burris, "Bulldogs Given Chance against Loyola," September 14, 1940; October 29, 1940; Becky Burris, "Redlands Beats Oxy to Take Loop Lead," November 3, 1940; November 24, 1940; December 6, 1940; December 13, 1940; *San Diego Union*, October 20, 1940; Redlands University Yearbook, 1940, www.mocavo.com (January 24, 2015).

40. *San Bernardino County Sun*, May 29, 1941; June 11, 1941; June 11, 1942.

41. *San Bernardino County Sun*, November 3, 1943; Kamehameha School Yearbook, 1945, www.ancestry.com (June 7, 2016); http://lmtribune.com/obituaries/alvin-k-chang-lewiston/article_1ff602b5–0f4f-5c88-bf92–6b0e0e6f55a3.html (June 13, 2016).

42. Ron Fimrite, "Little St. Mary's Big Star," *Sports Illustrated*, October 26, 1996.

43. *Honolulu Advertiser*, November 25, 1941; Ibid.; U.S. Census Bureau, Manuscript Census Schedules, City and County of Honolulu, 1940, www.ancestry.com (September 14, 2015).

44. Franks, *Hawaiian Sports*, 91.

45. *Los Angeles Times*, December 22, 1978; *San Francisco Chronicle*, October 17, 1968.

46. Grantland Rice, "Who Is America's Top Athlete," *Sport Magazine*, http://www.wedey.usanethosting.com/rice.htm., (November 3, 2005).

47. *San Francisco Chronicle*, September 10, 1943; September 23, 1943; *Los Angeles Times*, September 26, 1943; September 30, 1943; Rice, "Top Athlete."

48. *Los Angeles Times*, November 16, 1943; *Berkeley Daily Gazette*, November 26, 1943; *San Francisco Examiner*, December 3, 1943; *St. Petersburg Times*, January 2, 1944.

49. Rice, "Top Athlete"; *San Francisco Chronicle*, September 9, 1945.

50. Hal Wood, "Hawaiian Backfield Stars Shine for St. Mary's Team" *Oxnard Press Courier*, September 24, 1945; "Wedemeyer Is West's Idea of 1945 Best," October 1, 1945; *San Francisco Examiner*, September 23, 1945; *Daily Californian*, September 21, 1945; *Los Angeles Times*, November 4, 1945.

51. *Los Angeles Times*, December 22, 1978; Rice, "Top Athlete."

52. Bernie McCarty, "Squirmin' Herman and the Whiz Kids," *College Football Historical Society* (November, 1987), 4; Rice, "Top Athlete."

53. Bill Leiser, "The Coast," *Illustrated Football 1946*, 46; *Hayward Daily Review*, September 27, 1946; *Los Angeles Times*, December 22, 1978; *San Francisco Chronicle*, October 13, 1946; Emmons Byrne, "80,000 See Bears Score Win," *Oakland Tribune*, October 13, 1946; *San Francisco Examiner*, November 18, 1946; *Los Angeles Times*, December 22, 1978; *Look*, December 24, 1946, 34; *Portland Oregonian*, November 28, 1946; *San Francisco Examiner*, November 19, 1946.

54. *Long Beach Independent*, October 28, 1946.

55. *San Francisco Examiner*, February 1, 1947; *Los Angeles Times*, December 29, 1946; *San Francisco News*, November 6, 1947.

56. *San Francisco Chronicle*, October 14, 1947; October 21, 1947; *Reno Evening Gazette*, November 25, 1947.

57. Ferd Lewis, "'Squirmin' Was Sight to Behold," *Honolulu Advertiser*, January 31, 1999.

58. *Ogden Standard-Examiner*, January 15, 1942; July 5, 1945; *Oakland Tribune*, April 9, 1946; U.S. Census Bureau, Manuscript Census Schedules, City of Laie and County of Honolulu, 1940, www.ancestry.com (April 29, 2015); Weber Normal College Yearbook, 1943, www.ancestry.com (April 29, 2015); *Charleston Daily Mail*, October 29, 1943; *Honolulu Star-Bulletin*, October 1, 1948; October 7, 1948; November 12, 1948; Franks, *Crossing*, 131.

59. Leiser, "Coast," p. 54; *Portland Oregonian*, September 28, 1946; October 2, 1949; September 24, 1950; November 26, 1950; *Pacific Citizen*, September 13, 1947; January 14, 1950; *San Bernardino County Sun*, October 8, 1948; *Nevada State-Journal*, September 2, 1950; *San Jose Mercury*, October 14, 1949; December 3, 1949; Franks, *Crossing*, 131; *Honolulu Star-Bulletin*, December 2, 1949; April 6, 1950; Willamette University Yearbook, 1950, www.ancestry.com (March 25, 2015); *Seattle Times*, May 26, 1949; *Idaho State Journal*, September 23, 1959.

60. U.S. Census Bureau, Manuscript Census Schedules, City and County of Honolulu, www.ancestry.com (March 3, 2011); *Portland Oregonian*, September 22, 1948; March 12, 1954; *Dallas Morning News*, December 7, 1948; *San Francisco Chronicle*, August 7, 1949.

61. Don McLeod, "Jim Aiken Says Ducks Will Give Foes Trouble, *Portland Oregonian*, September 2, 1949; March 12, 1954; McKinley High School Yearbook, 1965, www.ancestry.com (May 26, 2015).

62. U.S. Census Bureau, Manuscript Census Schedules, City and County of Honolulu, 1940, www.ancestry.com (January 7, 2007); *Portland Oregonian,* October 28, 1949; Louis Duino, "Santa Clara Bottles Up Gaels, Win 19–6," *San Jose Mercury,* November 14, 1949; Fred Merrick, "Sparts Roar to 40–13 Win in Game Here," November 19, 1949; September 28, 1950; Harold Sauerbrei, "Harrington Is Lineman Who Quit Role of Back," *Cleveland Plain Dealer,* August 2, 1950.

63. *Nevada State Journal,* December 23, 1945; *Fresno Bee,* January 3, 1946; Leiser, "The Coast," p. 49; U.S. Census Bureau, Manuscript Census Schedules, City and County of Honolulu, 1930, www.ancestry.com (September 18, 2015).

64. *Los Angeles Times,* April 13, 1946; *Nevada State Journal,* March 17, 1946; United States Veteran's Gravesites, www.ancestry.com (April 24, 2010); *San Jose News,* June 26, 1947; Santa Clara University Yearbook, 1948, www.ancestry.com (October 13, 2014).

65. *Nevada State Journal,* September 19, 1949; Louis Duino, "Broncos Plan Air Attack, Cook Up New Plays," *San Jose Mercury,* November 12, 1949; "Santa Clara Bottles Up;" Santa Clara University Yearbook, 1950, www.ancestry.com (January 13, 2014); Franks, *Crossing,* 132.

66. *Nevada State-Journal,* September 2, 1950; October 24, 1950; https://bill37mccurdy.wordpress.com/2013/09/16/first-game-at-rice-stadium-september-30–1950/ (May 18, 2015); *San Diego Union,* October 23, 1950.

67. *Nevada State-Journal,* November 23, 1951; *Los Angeles Times,* November 26, 1951; *Chicago Tribune,* December 26, 1951; *Chinese Press,* November 10, 1950; San Jose Mercury, October 16, 1950.

68. *Oxnard Press-Courier,* November 2, 1946.

69. *Pacific Citizen,* September 13, 1947; October 11, 1947; November 29, 1947; Russ Newland, "Trojans Facing Defeat Charge from Behind to Nip Stanford," *San Bernardino County Sun,* October 27, 1946; September 28, 1947; *Eugene Register-Guard,* November 3, 1946; *Mansfield News,* December 1, 1946; *San Francisco Examiner,* September 7, 1947; *San Jose Mercury* September 28, 1947.

70. *Sporting News,* December 26, 1951; U.S. Census Bureau, Census Manuscript Schedules, City and County of Honolulu, www.ancestry.com (March 3, 2008); Dayton University Yearbook, 1949, 1950, www.ancestry.com (March 31, 2015); *Toledo Blade,* September 28, 1949; *Bradford Era,* September 28, 1949; *Mansfield News-Journal,* October 16, 1949; November 20, 1949; *Logan Daily News,* December 14, 1949; *Zanesville Signal,* December 14, 1949.

71. *Olean Times Herald,* September 28, 1950; *Mansfield News-Journal,* November 19, 1950; *San Jose Mercury,* December 10, 1950; *Shamokin News Dispatch,* December 20, 1950; *Ludington Daily News,* January 8, 1951; *Dallas Morning News,* January 8, 1951.

72. *Dayton Daily News,* October 27, 1994; Bucky Albers, "Six Football Greats Going into UD Hall of Fame," September 24, 2004; Ritter Collett, "UD Football Greats Pass Away," April 12, 1995; http://interactive.ancestry.com/2469/16081953/1309975328?backurl=http%3a%2f%2fsearch.ancestry.com%2f%2fcgi-bin%2fsse.dll%3findiv%3dtry%26db%3dUSDirectories%26h%3d1309975328&ssrc=&backlabel=ReturnRecord (July 10, 2015).

73. Dayton University Yearbook, 1950, www.ancestry.com (March 31, 2015); *Tucson Daily Citizen,* December 25, 1951; Bucky Albers, "Flyers Revive Rich Playoff History," *Dayton Daily News,* November 17, 2001; U.S. Census Bureau, Manuscript Census Schedules, City and County of Honolulu, 1940, www.ancestry.com (August 12, 2015).

74. *Tucson Daily Citizen,* December 25, 1951.

75. *Tucson Daily Citizen,* September 23, 1950; *Tucson Daily Citizen,* October 29, 1949; *Salt Lake Tribune,* September 8, 1950; *Ogden Standard-Examiner,* September 10, 1951; November 20, 1951; *San Bernardino County Sun,* December 6, 1951; *Big Spring Daily Herald,* May 4, 1969; U.S. Census Bureau, City and County of Honolulu, 1940, www.ancestry.com (August 8, 2016).

76. *Greeley Daily Tribune,* August 5, 1950; *Klamath Falls Herald and News,* September 28, 1950; *Pacific Citizen,* December 9, 1950; *Roseburg News-Review,* September 28, 1950; October 19, 1953; *Medford Mail Tribune,* September 17, 1953; September 17, 1953.

77. U.S. Census Bureau, Manuscript Census Schedules, City and County of Honolulu, 1930, www.ancestry.com (March 3, 2006); Dick Hyland, "Hyland Tabs Beavers as Upset Boys," *Los Angeles Times,* September 8, 1951; Braven Dyer, "Giant Tackle Foes Collide in Coliseum," October 10, 1951.

78. *San Jose Mercury,* November 23, 1951; East-West Shrine Football Game Program, Kezar Stadium, San Francisco, California, December 19, 1951; *Seattle Times,* October 31, 1951; http://www.osubeavers.com/sports/2011/3/9/208343623.aspx (December 13, 2016).

79. U.S. Census Bureau, Census Manuscript Schedules, City and County of Honolulu, 1940, www.ancestry.com (October 4, 2014); Compton Junior College Yearbook, 1950, www.ancestry.com (March 8, 2013).

80. Compton Junior College Yearbook, 1951, www.ancestry.com (May 28, 2015); *Honolulu Advertiser,* August 26, 1951; *Los Angeles Times,* October 14, 1951; October 27, 1951; Don Snyder, "Tartars Loom Large on Jaysee Horizon, September 7, 1951; "Pasadena Thumps Compton, 21 to 6," November 3, 1951; "Tartars and Bulldogs Meet in Rose Bowl," November 2, 1951.

81. U.S. Census Bureau, Census Manuscript Schedules, City of Makaweli, Island of Kaua'i, 1940, www.ancestry.com (June 11, 2015); Compton Junior College Yearbook, 1953, www.mocavo.com (January 24, 2015); Pasadena Junior College Yearbook, 1951, www.ancestry.com (May 28, 2015); Rosa, *Local Story.*

82. Braven Dyer, "Hill Expects 100 at Trojan Grid Turnout Today," *Los Angeles Times,* September 1, 1951; Braven Dyer, "Jess Hill's Experiments Under Way," September 2, 1951; September 11, 1951; Braven Dyer, "Giant Tackle Foes Collide in Coliseum, October 10, 1951; November 29, 1951; *San Jose Mercury,* November 23, 1951.

83. *Los Angeles Times,* September 15, 1952; September 27, 1952; October 19, 1952; *Salem Daily Capital Journal,* November 24, 1942.

84. Rube Samuelson, "Hawaiian Ane One Hula-Va Tackler USC Foes Learn," *Sporting News,* December 3, 1952.

85. http://digitallibrary.usc.edu/search/controller/view/examiner-m5845.html?x=1321723638467, (December 7, 2011); Compton Junior College Yearbook, 1949, www.ancestry.com (June 7, 2014); *Los Angeles Times,* September 2, 1951; Braven Dyer, "Troy Loaded with Talent at Fullback," *Los Angeles Times,* September 11, 1952; *Nevada State Journal,* December 24, 1953; Franks, *Crossing,* 133.

86. http://www.pbshawaii.org/ourproductions/longstory_transcripts/LSS%20611%20%20Harrington%20-%20A%20Life%20of%20Gratitude%20-%20Transcript.pdf (March 3, 2010); *San Francisco Chronicle,* September 4, 1955.

87. Indeed, California's supreme court had but a few years earlier terminated the state's anti-miscegenation law. This law did not apply to Pacific Islanders, although it did apply to white marriages to people of African, Asian, and Malay (Filipino) ancestry. Nevertheless, its existence reveals the strong current of white supremacy running through mid-twentieth century California. Mark Brilliant, *The Color of America Has Changed: How Racial Diversity Shaped Civil Rights Reform in California 1941–1978* (New York: Oxford University Press, 2010); *San Francisco Chronicle,* September 1, 1955; September 2, 1955; September 4, 1955.

88. *Spokane Daily Chronicle,* September 6, 1955; Chris Edmonds, "UCLA Team to Beat," *Tri-City Herald,* September 7, 1955; November 3, 1955; Stanford vs. San Jose State Football Program, Stanford Stadium, Palo Alto, California, October 29, 1955; *Sarasota Herald-Tribune,* October 30, 1955.

89. Jack Runnels, "Al Harrington, Card Halfback, Best Example of the Word 'Desire,'" *Stanford Daily,* November 6, 1956.

90. It was not unknown at the time for non-white football stars to get targeted by opposing defenses. During the early 1950s, Johnny Bright of Drake was put out of a game because he was black. There is, however, no evidence that USC, more willing to

recruit non-white football players in the 1950s than Stanford, was targeting Harrington because of his racial background. *Sacramento Bee*, November 5, 1957; *Ellensburg Daily Record*, November 6, 1957; *Spokane Daily Chronicle*, November 12, 1957; *Bend Bulletin*, November 25, 1957; *Stanford Daily*, October 21, 1957; January 6, 1958; http://www.sports-reference.com/cfb/players/tauasu-harrington-1.html (September 12, 2013).

91. *Stanford Daily*, October 29, 1957; October 31, 1957; Jack Bluth, "Rose Bowl Menu, Duck Soup," *San Mateo Times*, November 5, 1957, 17; August 8, 1958; Jack Winkler, "Samoan Harrington Dances His Way through School and Foes' Defenses," *Walla-Walla Union Bulletin*, November 6, 1957, 19.

92. http://www.pbshawaii.org/ourproductions/longstory_transcripts/LSS%20611%20%20Harrington%20-%20A%20Life%20of%20Gratitude%20-%20Transcript.pdf (December 20, 2014).

93. U.S. Census Bureau, Manuscript Census Schedules, City and County of Honolulu, 1940, www.ancestry.com (March 3, 2014); *Los Angeles Times*, October 13, 1951; Don Snyder, "Aoki Leads Jaysee Scorers," October 17, 1951; October 20, 1951; Don Snyder, "Pasadena Thumps Compton, 21 to 6," November 3, 1951; Don Snyder, "Pasadena Gets Bid to Little Rose Bowl," November 27, 1951; *San Jose Mercury*, November 23, 1951; Pasadena Junior College Yearbook, 1952, www.classmates.com (August 10, 2016); http://the.honoluluadvertiser.com/article/2004/Nov/23/sp/sp12p.html., (August 11, 2016).

94. *San Francisco Chronicle*, November 1, 1953; *Lodi News-Sentinel*, November 19, 1953; *Deseret News*, November 20, 1953; *San Jose Mercury*, October 12, 1956; http://www.sports-reference.com/cfb/schools/stanford/1957.html (June 3, 2015); Stanford University Yearbook, 1954, www.ancestry.com (August 13, 2016).

95. U.S. Census Bureau, Manuscript Census Schedules, City and County of Honolulu, www.ancestry.com (June 3, 2010); Bill Miller, "Hawaii Volcano Named 'Joe' Accustomed to Unexpected Eruptions," *Pasadena Star-News*, December 27, 1958; *Sports Review Football Annual, 1957*; Harold Classen, "Classen Opens Another Season, *Owosso Argus-Press*, September 18, 1957.

96. *Long Beach Independent Press*, September 18, 1955; *Milwaukee Journal*, January 28, 1958; February 20, 1958; *Pasadena Star-News*, January 19, 1958.

97. *San Jose Mercury*, September 6, 1954.

98. Wes Mathis, "SJS Defense Sharp," in *San Jose Mercury*, September 12, 1954; September 24, 1954; Wes Mathis, "Roy Hiram Paces Spartans to 38–7 Over Vandals," October 3, 1954; November 1, 1955; October 2, 1956; October 4, 1956; U.S. Census Bureau, Manuscript Census Schedules, City and County of Honolulu, 1940, www.ancestry.com (April 20, 2015); San Jose State College Yearbook, 1955, www.ancestry.com (April 20, 2015); *Los Angeles Times*, October 19, 1952; http://www.sports-reference.com/cfb/players/pat-hiram-1.html (May 27, 2015); *Reno Evening Gazette*, September 24, 1955; October 13, 1956.

99. *San Jose Mercury*, October 12, 1956; San Jose State College Yearbook, 1957, www.ancestry.com (March 3, 2011); U.S. Census Bureau, Manuscript Census Schedules, City and County of Honolulu, 1940, www.ancestry.com (September 3, 2015); https://www.google.com/search?q=Charlie+Kaaihue+football&biw=1366&bih=667&tbm=isch&imgil=6JVpjIutMBk7rM%253A%253BaV2RzAxT95ICUM%253Bhttp%25253A%25252F%252552Fwww.tradingcarddb.com%25252FGalleryP.cfm%25252Fpid%25252F10976%25252FCharlie-Kaaihue&source=iu&pf=m&fir=6JVpjIutMBk7rM%253A%252CaV2RzAxT95ICUM%252C_&usg=__1BQfNrqIMmzFzI8bfn9Dub__whQ%3D&ved=0CFYQyjc&ei=ebJzVLXbIo7koAT47oCYCA#facrc=_&imgrc=6JVpjIutMBk7rM%253A%3BaV2RzAxT95ICUM%3Bhttp%253A%252F%252Fwww.tradingcarddb.com%252FImages%252FCards%252FFootball%252F3203%252F3203–104Bk.jpg%3Bhttp%253A%252F%252Fwww.tradingcarddb.com%252FGalleryP.

126   *Chapter 3*

cfm%252Fpid%252F10976%252FCharlie-Kaaihue%3B350%3B247 (June 29, 2015); U.S. Census Bureau, City and County of Honolulu, 1940, www.ancestry.com (July 20, 2015).

100. *Portland Oregonian*, November 1, 1958; December 5, 1958; September 2, 1959; *Provo Daily Herald*, April 19, 1959; Jack Rickard, "Three Named by Oregon State Eleven," *Corvallis Gazette-Times*, September 4, 1959; *Sports Illustrated*, October 28, 1959; Brigham Young University Yearbook, 1960, www.ancestry.com (March 11, 2016);

101. Honolulu City Directory, 1958, www.ancestry.com (June 15, 2015); http://www.yoteathletics.com/hof.aspx?hof=13&path=&kiosk= (June 22, 2015); *Pacific Citizen*, December 9, 1950; *Hayward Daily Review*, October 29, 1957; *San Jose Mercury*, September 1, 1957; Brigham Young University Yearbook, 1955, www.ancestry.com (February 13, 2016); University of Washington Yearbook, 1957, www.ancestry.com., (August 27, 2014); U.S. Census Bureau, City of Wailuku, Island of Maui, 1940, www.ancestry.com., (July 24, 2015); San Francisco State College Yearbook, 1954, www.ancestry.com (July 24, 2015); http://www.sfstategators.com/sports/2008/8/6/HOF.aspx?tab=halloffame, (September 7, 2015); Honolulu City Directory, 1973, www.ancestry.com (February 13, 2016); UCLA vs. Utah University Football Program, Ute Stadium, November 26, 1960, https://collections.lib.utah.edu/details?id=768666&q=Uyeshiro&page=1&rows=25& fd=title_t%2Csetname_s%2Ctype_t&sort=&gallery=#t_768666, (June 9, 2016); http://sltrib.utestats.com/players.php?id=12661, (June 9, 2016); *Idaho State Journal*, September 23, 1959; *Oregon Statesman*, September 13, 1959; *Portland Oregonian*, August 27, 1959; November 12, 1961; December 9, 1961; Rod Ohira, "Leilehua Honors Former Coach," *Honolulu Advertiser*, September 17, 2004; Linfield College Yearbook, 1963, www. ancestry.com (September 21, 2016); http://the.honoluluadvertiser.com/article/2008/ Jun/13/br/hawaii80613055.html (October 28, 2016); http://www.linfield.edu/sports/hof-member.html?m=105&y=18 (October 28, 2016).

102. *Portland Oregonian*, August 27, 1959; Don Fair, "Cats Eyeing Early Foes," September 10, 1964; Willamette University Yearbook, 1956, 1961, www.ancestry.com (August 13, 2016); http://www.legacy.com/Obituaries.asp?Page=LifeStory&PersonId= 123103565 (August 19, 2016).

103. U.S. Census Bureau, Manuscript Census Bureau, Census Manuscript Schedules, City and County of Honolulu, 1930, 1940, www.ancestry.com (May 2, 2015); *San Jose Mercury*, October 3, 1954; *Waterloo Daily Courier*, November 5, 1954; Jim Vanheel, "Hawkeyes Win 4th Big Ten Game: Purdue Halted 25–14," *Mason City Globe-Gazette*, November 9, 1954; *Kokomo Tribune*, November 22, 1954; http://www.purdueexponent.org/sports/article_2a48d7d4–0eb9–11e0-b766–00127992bc8b.html (May 2, 2015); http://obits.staradvertiser.com/2016/04/07/john-m-kerr-jr/, (July 26, 2016).

104. *Ogden Standard-Examiner*, December 12, 1936; http://www.pro-football-reference.com/players/S/SimeJo20.html., (July 26, 2016); U.S. Census Bureau, Manuscript Census Schedules, City and County of Honolulu, 1940 (July 26, 2016); http://obits.staradvertiser.com/2015/03/15/alfred-ainoa-eki-coach-espinda-jr/, (July 26, 2016); http://archives.starbulletin.com/96/06/10/sports/kwon.html (July 26, 2016).

105. *Los Angeles Times*, December 20, 1956; *Sporting News*, September 25, 1965; *Oneonta Star*, October 1, 1965; *St. Joseph Herald-Press*, November 18, 1965; *Marion Star*, September 6, 1968; http://www.sports-reference.com/cfb/schools/michigan-state/ 1965.html (March 24, 2015).

106. Bill Dwyre, "Marcus Mariota Has a Kindred Hawaiian/Samoan Spirit in Bob Apisa, http://www.latimes.com/sports/la-sp-rose-bowl-dwyre-20150102-column.ht (May 25, 2015).

107. *Sports Illustrated*, January 4, 1965; http://www.sports-reference.com/cfb/schools/ michigan-state/1968.html (March 24, 2015); Bob McCoy, "Wedemeyer Hanging Tough against Some Overwhelming Odds," *Sporting News*, February 16, 1987; http://www. sports-reference.com/cfb/players/kale-wedemeyer-2.html (May 27, 2015); http://www. hawaiiprepworld.com/football/ilh-football-first-team-all-stars-1920-present/ (March

25, 2016); Dick Sparrer, "Kale Wedemeyer Enters Los Gatos Hall of Fame," http://www.mercurynews.com/hssports/ci_9028017 (June 30, 2016).

108. Leroy Bearing, "Giddings Predicts Better Grid Teams at Utah," *Albuquerque Journal*, September 7, 1967; *Provo Daily Herald*, December 5, 1967; *New Orleans Times-Picayune*, August 17, 1970; Franks, *Crossing*, 135; Cathy Chong, "Golden Time for Football and Friendship," http://www.iolani.org/files/pdfs/coverstory_winter08.pdf (July 20, 2015); Shanahan, "Kale Ane."

109. *Bridgeport Post*, November 10, 1974; *Berkshire Eagle*, November 25, 1974; Heshell Nissonson, "Yale Has 3 Repeaters on All Ivy Team," *Hazelton Standard-Speaker*, December 4, 1974; Franks, *Crossing*, 135;

110. Ivan Maisel, "Beach Ball," *Sports Illustrated*, August 25, 1997.

111. http://www.sports-reference.com/cfb/players/marcus-mariota-1.html (May 27, 2015).

112. *Salt Lake Tribune*, September 9, 1950; Franks, *Crossing*, 140; http://hawaiiathletics.com/coaches.aspx?rc=1073 (June 17, 2014); http://espn.go.com/college-football/story/_/id/10581659/stanford-cardinal-hires-texas-longhorns-assistant-duane-akina-secondary-coach (July 7, 2015).

113. Sam Chu Lin, "Norm Chow Leads USC's National Football Title," *Asian Week*, January 10, 2004; "Norm Chow Kicks Off Career as NFL Offense Coordinator," September 30, 2005.

114. Lin, "Norm Chow Leads."

115. Ibid.

116. *Asian Week*, February 11, 2005; Lin, "Norm Chow Kicks."

117. Ian Scheuring, "Norm Chow Fired as University of Hawaii Football Coach," *Hawai'i News Now*, November 4, 2015.

118. Franks, *Crossing*, 142; Stephanie Loh, "Niumatalolo Makes History," http://www.utsandiego.com/news/2014/dec/21/poinsettia-bowl-navy-ken-niumatalolo-makes-history/ (May 28, 2015).

119. http://byucougars.com/staff/m-football/kalani-sitake, (April 4, 2016); http://byucougars.com/athlete/m-football/harvey-unga (May 4, 2016).

FOUR

Playing Well with Others

The Mainland

Asian Americans have been more geographically and socially isolated on the mainland than on the islands. Thus, for much of the twentieth century, mainland high school football coaches, for example, could safely assemble squads free of Asian Americans and other people of color thanks largely to housing discrimination which, in turn, buttressed educational discrimination. This was the case even in cities and towns possessing a relatively considerable number of Asian Americans. However, in some neighborhoods of West Coast cities such as pre-World War II Seattle and Los Angeles, it became impossible to amass football teams without at least a few Asian Americans and other non-white gridders. Moreover, Asian American gridders occasionally showed up in perhaps surprising places outside of the Far West. Mainland football fields, therefore, could emerge as sites of spatial entitlement for some Asian Americans as early as the first half of the twentieth century—as social spaces where they asserted a sense of belonging.

The fruits of the Immigration Act of 1965 have been many. Perhaps among the least consequential has been its impact on youth and high school sports in the United States. Accordingly, in the late twentieth and into the twenty-first century, we can find Asian Americans popping up on suburban football teams throughout the United States. In addition, gridders of Pacific Islander descent also have made their way on to high school programs on not only the West Coast in the late twentieth and early twenty-first century but, in Utah and even Texas. However, we will explore this in a future chapter.

YOUTH AND INDEPENDENT FOOTBALL

It may not have happened often, but Asian American youngsters played football with and against non-Asian Americans on the mainland during the early-twentieth century. According to a 1903 edition of the *Oakland Tribune*, youthful football players in Berkeley's Ashby district were disappointed that "Wing, the Chinese football player of their team" had been too injured to compete with them. Wing, the *Tribune* claimed, lived with the "Americanized Chinese" family of Joseph Tape, who, along with his wife Mary, initiated a famous legal case in Chinese American history. Determined to integrate San Francisco's public schools in the 1880s for their children, Mamie and Frank, Joseph and Mary Tape won their legal challenge, but it was something of a Pyrrhic victory. San Francisco's Board of Education admitted the Tape children but created an Oriental School to accommodate and segregate Mamie and Frank and other Chinese American students. The Tapes subsequently moved to Berkeley.[1]

The instances of Asian American youths playing with and against non-Asian Americans grew more prevalent in the mid-twentieth century. In 1950, the *Pacific Citizen* announced that a youth team, the International "Fighting Irish," had just won the Seattle championship. It showed a photograph originally published in the *Seattle Post-Intelligencer* of Takashi Aoki running with the ball. Supported by the Nisei Veteran's Committee of Seattle and coached by former high school varsity player Charley Chihara, the multiethnic team's big star was Akira Moriguchi. North of San Francisco, Joey Wong starred for the Petaluma Chicks Pop Warner team in the early 1960s. Down in the South Bay Area, San Jose operated a touch tackle league for boys after World War II. In early October, the *San Jose Mercury* reported that the Cubs had vanquished the Rockets, 40–0. Three of the big stars were Japanese Americans. Kent Ikeda starred on the Conway-Culligan Cougars in Pop Warner football in San Mateo County in 1950, and around the same time, Bill Kogura and Wes Dobashi stood out in a touch football league in San Jose. Nearby in Mountain View in 1951, Crittenton Elementary School downed Jefferson Elementary School, 26–13. Hiroshi Ueno's long run highlighted the game for the victors, while Bob Tachibana was one of Jefferson's leading lights. Tackle Dick Shigemoto stood out in Pop Warner football for the San Jose Hornets in the mid-1950s. Around ten years later, John Kitazumi scored on a six-yard touchdown in a Hornet game. Within a few years, the Almaden Argonauts beat the San Jose Hornets in youth football in the late 1960s. Steward Sugimoto excelled for the victors.[2]

Older Asian Americans played football with and against non-Asian Americans beyond the school yards and college campuses. Seattle, before World War II, hosted a relatively lively contingent of independent, adult teams, which may have been more semi-professional than amateur. According to the *Japanese American Courier's* sports columnist Bill Hosokawa, Nob Yoshida joined the Tacoma Alt Heidelberg eleven in 1938. Former all-city Garfield standout, Harry Yanagamichi competed for the West Seattle Athletic Club team. The Enumclaw eleven was enlivened considerably by George Hirai. The *Seattle Daily Times* offered in 1936 that the "little Japanese quarterback" was Enumclaw's sparkplug. It added that most of Enumclaw's offensive plays were designed to get Hirai out in the open "where he could use his swivel hips to greatest advantage." In one game in 1936, Hirai scored all thirteen points for Enumclaw on two touchdowns and one conversion. In 1938, Hosokawa extolled Hirai's "splendid performance" as a back for Enumclaw and was distressed that mainstream newspapers in the Seattle area continued to call him Harai after years of excelling on local gridirons. Rhino Nakamura, remembered by Bill Hosokawa as "a powerful ex-Garfield tackle," performed for a predominantly black team in the late 1930s. Mike Hirahira, who previously captained the local Garfield High's varsity, played for the Ubangi eleven as well. Competing in the Seattle Community League, this squad was owned by a local nightclub owner, "Noodles" Smith, and won the league championship in 1937.[3]

SCHOOL FOOTBALL BEFORE WORLD WAR II

Some, mostly Pacific Coast, schools served as "cosmopolitan canopies" for Asian American gridders during the early and mid-twentieth century. Unlike Hawaiian elevens, mainland secondary school teams could typically thrive without the contributions of Asian Americans. One factor limiting Asian American gridders even at mainland schools with comparatively large Asian American populations had to have been European American perceptions. White physical educators capable of praising Asian American athletes doubted them as gridders. Ed Williams, a coach of Poly High School in San Francisco, informed the *Chinese Digest* in the 1930s that he knew of several fine Chinese American athletes but he declared, "Chinese boys are not cut out for football." Gendering Chinese American males as insufficiently masculine, Williams believed they were not big enough or tough enough for the game.[4]

Yet somehow athletes of Asian descent wound up on school football teams as early as the first decades of the twentieth century. In 1902, a young man named Kuroshiwa played a "strong right guard" for Santa Clara High School against San Jose High School. Toy Lowe, described by the *San Francisco Call* as a "full-blooded Chinese," competed for San Francisco's Poly High School in 1903. A year earlier, the youthful Lowe achieved national recognition. A wire story appearing in Montana's *Anaconda Standard* informed readers that in San Francisco "a Chinese giant and a hammer down Jap" would oppose each other in a grammar school game. Toy Lowe was described as a six-foot-tall and 143-pound fullback for Clement School. "A full blooded Chinese," he was reportedly the son of a prominent merchant father. Because of his ability as a "line plunger," Lowe was dubbed the "demon fullback." Facing him was the "Jap" star of the Crocker school team, "C Ockada," described in the wire story as a small but effective tackler.[5]

Outside of California, gridders of Asian descent attracted press notice in the early twentieth century. In 1912, the *Portland Oregonian* reported that Wing Wang was a tackle in the local Grammar School Football League. A few years later, the *Portland Oregonian* announced that James John High School had a "Chinese boy" at quarterback. In 1919, the *Oregonian* publicized the Atkisson Grammar School team comprised of players from "five nations." Included in their ranks were Willie H. Wong, Him Wong, Sue Chan, Yoichi Okabe, Wong Wing, Chikashi Fukuda, Ding Chang, and captain Lawrence Chinn, who reportedly stood out as fullback. In Washington in 1913, Issei Morimitsu Kitamura played guard for West Seattle High. *Seattle Times* columnist Vince O'Keefe claimed in 1973 that he was a "spunky guard." Later, Kitamura would return to Japan and become a correspondent for the *Osaka Mainichi*. His antiwar writings caught the attention of the militaristic Japanese government, which imprisoned the former gridder. In the Midwest, according to the *Kalamazoo Gazette*, an athlete named Ourubia played end for Ann Arbor High School in Michigan. He was called "a full-fledged Filipino, [who], they say, can play football." On the East Coast, in 1914, Burlington High School in Vermont suited up Mariono S. Solit, a Filipino 160-pound halfback, known as "Solit the bullet." In Philadelphia, the *Philadelphia Evening Ledger* announced that Leonia High School's Koh Am Wee was not only an exceptional basketball player but competed in football and baseball as well in the mid-1910s.[6]

Asian Americans appeared on California high school rosters during the 1920s. In 1920, readers of the *Los Angeles Times* learned about Sakamoto, a "Japanese end," who played for Poly High. Across town, Santa Monica High had a guard named Tojo. The *Times* claimed he was "aggressive and can hold his own in the best of company." In 1921, the *San Jose Mercury* reported that an athlete with the Chinese surname of "Moy" was a "Japanese gentleman" who scored a touchdown for Palo Alto High School against San Jose High School. Later in the 1920s, Harold Fong won a football letter while attending Commerce High School in San Francisco. In 1924, the Commerce High Yearbook pointed out he was new at the game, but very good at handling the guard position. A few years later, Chinese Americans such as George "Tiny" Leong and Charlie Chan were linemen for San Francisco's Commerce High School. The *Chinese Digest* remembered the former as one of the best linemen in Commerce's history. The school's 1928 yearbook hailed Leong's return to the starting lineup as a tackle in 1927 after an apparent absence in 1926. As for Chan, he was described in the 1929 Commerce yearbook as a "marvelous pastimer on defense." Frank Ichishita was a valuable fullback for San Jose High School. The U.S. Census Manuscripts disclose that Ichishita's parents were Issei and his father a laundryman in 1920. In California's Central Valley, Albert and Ernest Yee played quarterback for Marysville High in the late 1920s. The 1930 U.S. Census manuscript schedules reveal that the California-born Yees lived with their brother Samuel in a home headed by a Chinese American pharmacist in Marysville. At Lodi High, Masuo Osaki played for Lodi High's "first team" in 1929. When Bakersfield High took on Merced for the San Joaquin Valley Championship in 1929, Lum, the "Chinese star," spearheaded Bakersfield's ground game. To the south, Orange County's Anaheim High suited up Tanaka in 1927. Against Woodrow Wilson High, he ran for a seventy-four-yard touchdown.[7]

During the decade before U.S. entry into World War II, Asian American gridders popped up on varsity squads in California's Central Valley. In the fall of 1930, Elk Grove High was represented by two Nikkei running backs. Early in October, Elk Grove shut down Grass Valley, 33–0. During the game, 118-pound Al Tsukumoto scored on a forty-yard run. In October 1930, Elk Grove humbled San Juan, 52–0. Al Tsukumoto crossed the goal line for the victors on a long run. Playing for Elk Grove High School in the mid-1930s were Frank Yamada, George Noda, and Shigeo Ishi. In the fall of 1934, George Uyeda performed for Stockton High. Courtland High's championship team in 1935 included several Asian Americans. During the fall of 1936 and 1937, Ed Fugitani served as a lineman on Lodi High's varsity. The *Sacramento Bee*'s Tom Kane praised Fugitani's defensive performance against Sacramento High in October 1937. Edison High's Henry Wong drew acclaim from a *Fresno Bee* writer in 1937. Gayland Miller testified that Wong was not only strong on offense but his team's most consistent defender.[8]

The Kuwabara brothers stood out for Sacramento High in the years before World War II. Five-foot-eight and 210 pounds, Paul was an all-league guard and captain on the 1938 team. A year earlier, he had been elevated to first string after a sterling performance against Fresno High. He later captained Sacramento Junior College. Hailed as the best defensive guard in the conference by his coach, Paul was named to the all-conference team in 1940. The younger and larger George was six foot and 240 pounds. Called a "giant tackle" by the *Sacramento Bee*, he captained Sacramento High's team in 1939 and was named all-league. He planned on going to Arizona State before both the brothers were interned at Poston.[9]

Chinese Americans gridders glittered in varsity football in San Francisco during the depression and pre-World War II years. In the late 1930s, Marshall Leong earned all-league honors for Mission High School. The *Chinese Digest* averred that Leong proved especially adept on defense. However, he could do damage on offense as well. Against Commerce in

1937, Leong scored on a one-yard plunge and set up another Mission touchdown with an interception and run. He participated in the 1937 all-star game for San Francisco. In the process, the *Chinese Digest* pointed out, he was "the first Chinese to play in the DeMolay all-star classic." In the same all-star game matching the best of San Francisco preps against East Bay standouts in 1938, Leong managed to rush for a seven-yard touchdown. Called "China" in Mission's 1938 yearbook, Leong was described in the 1937 yearbook as a "pile-driving fullback." The yearbook also pointed out that his "ear-to-ear grin comes from a Chinese family with a pigskin craze." A "grand fellow," Leong apparently loved movies but had no favorite—not even, the yearbook stressed, Anna Mae Wong, the first Chinese American film star. Ed Leong, his brother, also played for Mission. Another brother, Harding started as a guard and fullback at Commerce. U.S. Census data tells us that in 1930, the Leong brothers' father was born in California, while the mother was a Chinese immigrant. The father worked as a taxi driver.[10]

San Francisco prep football seemed to embrace a handful of Asian American gridders in the fall of 1940. At Washington High, Al Lum played as a "135-pound guard." On the same squad, Joe Chun and Henry Tom served as reserve halfbacks. The presence of three Chinese Americans on the Washington squad helped inspire the *San Francisco Examiner*'s Dick Toner to remark, "The Chinese are doing all right this year." Not only did he reference Lum, Chun, and Tom, but he told readers that Commerce had two Chinese Americans—one of which was Gene Louie, who, though only 135 pounds, was the best downfield blocker on the team. Moreover, Toner added, Poly had George Fong. A stellar performer for Poly, Fong, the *San Francisco Chronicle*'s Bob Stevens reported, threw a "mean football." Fong's 1941 season was tainted somewhat when he was kicked out of game against Mission for fighting. And not all Asian American varsity gridders in San Francisco in the years before World War II were Chinese Americans. The athletically versatile Filipino American, John "Babe" Samson was a halfback for Commerce in the early 1940s. Before the 1940 season began, Toner acclaimed him as a "sprinter" and "a threat at right half." Described as one of the "Commerce comets," Samson helped his eleven beat Mission 8–0. Late in September 1940, Samson proved pivotal in a victory over St. Ignatius. Among other things, he threw a touchdown pass. The five-foot-five, 145-pound Samson subsequently starred in Commerce's 6–0 victory over Sacred Heart in 1940.[11]

Outside of San Francisco, Asian Americans gridders appeared on Bay Area and Central Coast varsity squads between 1930 and 1940. North of San Francisco, end Woodrow Louie and quarterback Leslie Fong played for Vallejo High. The former, the *Chinese Digest* declared, was one of the best in the school's history. It cited the *Vallejo Times-Herald*, which lamented that due to Louie's graduation Vallejo High could no longer count on his gridiron services. The *Times-Herald* asserted, "[Louie's] loss dealt the team a severe blow. Whenever he was in the game, he had a steadying influence because of his coolness." The son of a California-born court interpreter father and a Chinese immigrant mother, Louie subsequently played football at Sacramento Junior College. In the East Bay, Moe Domoto quarterbacked Oakland's Castlemont High squad in 1932. Ernest Lee merited all-Alameda County recognition as a tackle for Hayward High School. Berkeley High suited up all-league tackle Tak Katayanagi in the late 1930s. In 1941, Bryant Wong was an all-league guard for Alameda High. In Santa Clara County, Mountain View High School's 1933 yearbook declared that Harry Hamasaki "supplied the brain work" as quarterback, adding that [n]one in the league was his equal at this tough job." A few years later, the school's yearbook maintained that Charles Hamasaki was the best end in the league. [12]

Monterey County Asian Americans were represented by high school gridders in the years before Pearl Harbor was attacked. In Salinas, Union High School suited up talented Frank Chin. The *Chinese Digest* speculated that Chin would have starred had Union High not been blessed with so many skillful gridders. York Asami starred as a fullback for Watsonville's unbeaten team in 1936. During that season, Asami put together some gaudy numbers, carrying the ball over fourteen yards per attempt, completing thirty-two of forty-seven passes, and punting an average of forty-four yards. In one game, he returned a kickoff of fifty-seven yards for a touchdown against Santa Cruz High. In 1939, Roy Mori captained the Watsonville varsity. [13]

In Southern California, Orange County gridirons hosted plenty of fine Asian American football players in the 1930s. In 1930, the *Santa Ana Register*'s Eddie West stated that Anaheim High School's varsity squad included Kioshi Shigekawa, the "best Japanese football player we've ever seen." In 1935, Anaheim High fielded backfield standout Harry Tanaka, who helped his team topple Garden Grove High, 25–0, with a sixty-yard touchdown run. Called a "line-smashing hero" by the *Los Angeles Times*, Tanaka tallied three touchdowns against Huntington Beach in November 1935. In 1936, Jim Sakamoto co-captained the Anaheim varsity, while also making an all-division squad as a halfback. At nearby Santa Ana High, Hideo Higashi starred at end in 1930, and Mits Nitta distinguished himself as both an excellent football player and an honor roll student in the mid- to late 1930s for Santa Ana. Described by sports columnist Ed West as an all-conference end at Santa Ana High, Nitta excelled on both offense and defense. [14]

Throughout Los Angeles County Asian American high school gridders emerged in the pre-World War II era. In southeast Los Angeles County, Leuzinger High School had "Tokio Nitahara," identified by the *Los Angeles Times* as a "flashy left half [who] sparkled with a number of long runs" when his team downed Jordan in 1937. Belmont High in Los Angeles featured numerous Asian Americans. Among those on the 1936 team were captain William Hirata and center Robert Shibuya, as well as Carl Kim. A couple of years later, Dick Ung was a second team all-league lineman for Belmont. A U.S. census enumerator described Ung's family as racially Japanese in 1940. Both parents were U.S.-born. His father worked as chef in a restaurant, in which a couple of his older siblings worked. Subsequently, when Ung enlisted in the military, his papers categorized him as racially Chinese. In 1938, a *Los Angeles Times* writer described Venice High's Izumi Itsuki as "the toughest Japanese backfield man seen in these parts in many moons." Around the same time, Art Omori stood out as a fullback at San Bernardino High and San Fernando High, suited up several Asian American gridders in the fall of 1938, including the skilled Tom Woo. Akigee Shimatsu was a fine fullback for Torrance High School, while 195-pound Allen Dong was a standout guard for Lincoln High School in Los Angeles. The 1930 U.S. census data tells us that Allen Dong was the nine-year-old son of Chinese immigrants. His father worked as a restaurant cook. The *Los Angeles Times'* Carl Blume claimed Dong "has a world of fight." Blume reported that when Dong joined the Lincoln varsity the coach considered him a "chicken," but kept calling plays in his direction until he "wound up a fighter." Described by Blume as a "Japanese lad" and "slippery" ball carrier, Teizo Koda was one of Dong's teammates in 1939. Roosevelt High's Dave Komatsu played center and captained his squad in the fall of 1940. In the months before U.S. entry into World War II, Sam Kim performed well for Manual Arts in Los Angeles. The 1942 school yearbook praised his play against Gardena and Roosevelt.[15]

According to a 2016 posting in *Discover Nikkei*, high school football helped solidify the Japanese American community in the Imperial Valley, located in southeastern California. Isamu "Sam" Nakamura recalled for journalist Tim Asamen that Brawley High's football field stood across the street from the Japanese Methodist Episcopal Church and the Brawley High football roster included many Japanese American players. Nakamura and his Nisei friends religiously attended home games and afterwards "the boys would walk through the chilly air to Nihonmachi (Japantown). At Fat's Café, they reported to Mr. and Mrs. Kuramoto on how their son, Eichi, played in the game that night."[16]

Nikkei football in the Imperial Valley could also build bridges to other cultural groups. Asamen maintains, "That so many Imperial Valley Nisei excelled in football is a local phenomenon. . . . In football, we had the closest thing to a meritocracy that existed in Imperial Valley." Thus, while Japanese Americans often felt isolated in the region, Brawley High football star, Hank Sasaki, remembered that football "helped quiet down the racism," because of its popularity in and around Brawley. But Sasaki insisted that playing football was not about making white people happy: "We played for the pure enjoyment of the game."[17]

Asamen, moreover, reveals that Nikkei football participation could only do so much to tame racism. He asserts that when a bus carrying released concentration camp prisoners crossed into Imperial County from Riverside they found themselves unwelcomed despite the Japanese American heroics on local gridirons. Indeed, many Brawley residents staged a mass protest on the high school gridiron in opposition to Japanese Americans returning to Imperial Valley—the very gridiron on which many Nikkei football players had sacrificed their bones and brain matter for the local high school.[18]

Brawley High School, to be sure, offered a home to Japanese American football heroes in the 1930s. End Tom Sasaki captained the 1933 squad and was the older brother to halfback Hank Sasaki. Tom Sasaki earned some national publicity that year. A wire story published in the *Baton Rouge Advocate* described him as a fine pass catcher for Brawley. But during the 1933 season, he began to have trouble latching on to footballs thrown in his direction. Apparently, his eyesight was slipping. Sasaki, accordingly, was outfitted with a special helmet that could accommodate his newly acquired glasses.[19]

Hank Sasaki was one of the best Japanese American gridders in the pre-war Imperial Valley. The 1940 U.S. census data discloses that he was twenty-two years old, living with an Issei father who operated a grocery store in Brawley. His mother, who clerked in the store, was a Hawaiian-born Nisei. Illuminating Brawley High football in the mid-1930s, Sasaki was extolled by the *San Diego Union* as an excellent passer. The "diminutive Japanese quarterback" was especially accurate on short throws. Sasaki led his team to a thrilling victory over Coronado High in October 1935. The *Brawley News* extolled him in a story entitled, "Henry Sasaki Stands Out as Great Football Star in One of the Best Games Ever Seen Here." Author Paul Post claimed that "Sasaki virtually ran, passed, and kicked the Brawley team to victory and established himself as one of the best high school backs in Southern California if not the entire country." Few gridders in the Imperial Valley were as feared by opponents as Sasaki. Moreover, younger brother Ray also illuminated Brawley football. In October 1937, the *San Bernardino County Sun* reported that he led Brawley to a victory over Redlands High. In any event, the Sasaki family were incarcerated at Poston, a concentration camp in Arizona.[20]

Japanese Americans competed for other high schools in the largely agricultural Imperial Valley of the 1930s. George Kita was a "whipcord-strong lineman" and captain of the Calexico High grid team. Asamen describes him as possibly the best player in Calexico High's history. The *Calexico Chronicle* raved that while Kita was small for a guard, "he makes up for his lack of weight by smart and aggressive playing." According to Asamen, 120-pound center Noboru Morose drew people to Central High's football games because so many doubted that such a light weight gridder could do so much damage to opposing teams. A white teammate remembered, "[E]veryone marveled at how such a light fellow could snap the ball then take out one of the opposing players. It was sheer determination."[21]

Junior colleges in Southern California offered Asian Americans opportunities to shine as football players between the wars. At Santa Ana Junior College, Hideo Higashi stood out in the early 1930s. In 1935, Powell Lee scored on a four-yard touchdown run after carrying the ball for thirty yards in a game in which Los Angeles Junior College beat UCLA's frosh squad. A son of Korean immigrants, Lee's father ran a vegetable market in 1940, while he served as a playground director. A left guard, 178-pound Bob Shibuya performed for the same school, becoming an all-conference guard in 1940. Playing with Jackie Robinson on Pasadena Junior College's football squad in 1937 were Shig Kawaii and Shiz Kunihiro. Tad Iwata quarterbacked Fullerton JC in 1939. After 127-pound Johnny Takahashi played quarterback for Long Beach High School, he went on to start for Long Beach Junior College in the fall of 1941.[22]

In the late 1930s and early 1940s, Chaffey Junior College's Kobei Shoji led the Orange Empire Junior College League in scoring and Citrus Junior College's Tosh Asano was an all-conference halfback. When Chaffey blanked Citrus in 1938, 33–0, Shoji stood out, tossing a thirty-three-yard touchdown pass. The *Santa Ana Register* referred to Shoji in the fall of 1938 as a "sensational Japanese halfback." According to the 1940 census data, Shoji was the son of a widowed Japanese immigrant mother who operated a ranch in San Bernardino County. At that time, Shoji labored on the ranch. In the late 1990s, Shoji was named to Chaffey's Hall of Fame. In September 1941, Asano scored a touchdown against San Bernardino J.C. leading the *Los Angeles Times* to acclaim him as his eleven's "star right half." Asano, moreover, led all junior college gridders in America in scoring with 103 points; subsequently he was honored as a second team all-Southern California gridder. Sadly, like many Japanese American students on the West Coast, his education was interrupted by internment. Nevertheless, a ninety-one-year-old Asano received his delayed diploma from Citrus College.[23]

Seattle provided a home for a good number of Japanese American varsity gridders between the wars. Broadway High School's 1926 yearbook acclaimed Toshi Tsukono as a "brainy quarterback." The school's 1934 yearbook tells us about Isamu Kozu. Next to a photograph of the young man, the yearbook asserted, "Sam was a quiet, serious young fellow to whom football meant a lot. He played the brand of football we're proud to speak of." A few years later, Broadway suited up Shiro Tenma and, according to Bill Hosokawa, the "powerful Jim Yoshida." Tenma, the 1938 school yearbook purported, stood out against West Seattle in 1937. In 1940, Pete Fujino gained honorable mention all-city for Broadway. Harry Yanagamichi was an all-city center at Seattle's Garfield High in the early to mid-1930s. The school's 1932–1933 yearbook described Yanagamichi as a good blocker. In 1933, the *Seattle Times* pointed out that Harry Yanagamichi starred in Garfield's triumph over Lincoln, 19–7. When Yanagamichi graduated from Garfield, he left, the *Seattle Times* fretted, a big hole in Garfield's line. Nicknamed "Pianolegs" Mike Hirahira starred as a guard for Garfield in 1937. Against Franklin, he blocked two punts, which helped furnish Garfield with a victory. A few years later, Harry Yanagamichi's brother, Bill, played for Garfield along with George Okamura. Bill Yanagamichi, according to Hosokawa, was a "backfield ace," and Okamura was the team's "hardest man to stop past the line of scrimmage."[24]

While many scholars have addressed the liminal experiences of the second generation, Jim Yoshida lived those experiences in a more dramatic way than most. Mostly playing guard, Jim Yoshida was a "Japanese football star" at Seattle's Broadway High School in the late 1930s. In November 1938, the *Seattle Times* praised Yoshida's performance against Cleveland. In 1939, Yoshida, although usually a lineman, managed to score Broadway's only touchdown in two years against Garfield High. Yoshida enjoyed all-city honors while performing for Broadway. But too soon after his high school playing days, Yoshida' Japanese immigrant father died, and he would have to make the sad journey to Japan with his father's ashes. Yoshida was in Japan when World War II erupted. Forced to remain in the land of his father's birth, Yoshida was conscripted into the Japanese army. Unlike so many young Japanese men of his generation, the Japanese American Yoshida survived the war.[25]

In Arizona, the versatile Bill Kajikawa surfaced as a prep standout in the 1930s. In 1930, the *Arizona Republic* praised him as a "fleet, little reserve back" for Phoenix High. When Phoenix High knocked off Arizona State, Flagstaff's frosh squad, Kajikawa starred, demonstrating that he was "fast as a flash." The *Republic*'s George Moore in 1940 remembered Kajikawa as one of the best blockers and signal callers in Phoenix High School history. That so many Japanese Americans such as Kajikawa shined on pre-World War II football fields in the west seemed to belie a popular racial stereotype of people of Japanese descent.[26]

To the east, Chinese Americans emerged as high school gridders between the wars, thus exposing the perception of them as disinterested and unskilled in sports such as football. During the early 1920s, a wire story told readers that "Charlie Lumm, full-blooded Chinese" quarterbacked a Chicago high school team. Lumm's parents apparently lived in China, where his father was an exporter. Described as a triple-threat, Lumm, according to his coach, was college football material. During the mid-1930s, a story appeared in the *Binghamton Press* notifying readers that "[a] native born full blooded Chinese" played left tackle for Central High in St. Louis. The account described Lee Wing as five foot seven but tipping the scales at 216 pounds. His coach expected him to emerge as a "savage" lineman.[27]

Buck Lai, Jr., the son of a prominent Hawaiian Chinese baseball player who had settled on the East Coast, carved an enviable career in athletics. In the mid-1930s, he starred on the Audubon High School squad in New Jersey. Sportswriter John Grange asserted that Lai played halfback on a team that won the south New Jersey championship three years in a row. The 1935 school yearbook reported that in the previous fall "Bucky Lai" was named second team all-South New Jersey as a halfback. World War II interrupted his athletic career at Long Island University, where he mainly played baseball. However, during the war Lai managed to play football for the Pensacola Naval Station. Several years later, while serving as athletic director for the U.S. Merchant Marine Academy, Lai took over as football coach for a couple of games. Meanwhile, Lai had put together a lengthy career as a baseball and basketball coach, as well as athletic director at Long Island University.[28]

WORLD WAR II

World War II interrupted the football careers of many young men, but Asian Americans took to the grid as high schoolers and junior college students during the period of global combat. Japanese Americans in the Los Angeles area faced internment. But non-Nikkei Asian American players proved capable gridders. Early in the 1940s, Bobby Balcena, a pioneering Filipino American baseball player, starred at end for San Pedro High School. In 1943, San Fernando High's Willie Wong was an all-league guard and second string all-Los Angeles player. The Helms Athletic Foundation press release in December 1943, described the five-foot-five, 175-pound Wong as a lineman who "defends, blocks, [and] leads." In 1945, Willie Wong was an all-league guard for Los Angeles Junior College.[29]

Elsewhere in the West, Asian American high schoolers often performed well for various elevens. In California's central valley, Korean American Luther Hahn captained the Delano High School eleven. Moreover, Nikkei gridders played high school football outside of the Pacific Coast war zone. The big Japanese American star in Spokane was Frank Miyaki, a backfield standout who made all-city in 1944. The year before he made second team all-city and was named the "most inspirational" member of North Central High's squad. In Arizona, Jimmy Kajikawa, brother of the more famous Bill Kajikawa, was named captain of the Tempe High School football team. At East High School in Salt Lake City, Toby Sasaki surfaced as an all-city tailback. The *Salt Lake Tribune* hailed him as "the Japanese powerhouse" and "the best open field runner in the city." The *Tribune* pointed out that he was versatile as well—capable of running, passing, and kicking well for East High. In Wyoming, Ray Saito quarterbacked for Worland High School. The *Pacific Citizen* dubbed Saito a "brainy field general and a triple threat player." Howell Ujifusa was a teammate and co-captain. Ujifusa, according to the *Pacific Citizen*, was a "savage blocker and fine defensive player." [30]

Meanwhile, Sam Nakaso had been released from Utah's Topaz camp to attend high school on the East Coast. Despite the harshness of the camps, the U.S. government had shown a willingness to allow some internees to go to school or work outside of the Pacific Coast war zone. This was done partly because some government officials deemed it the right thing to do but also because lowering camp populations would cut costs. In 1940, Nakaso lived with his Japanese immigrant mother and his older siblings in Alameda, California. His mother performed housework for a private family, while his older sister and brother cooked and gardened respectively for probably the same private family. After leaving camp, Nakaso wound up in Connecticut where he enrolled at Hillview High School, for which he starred in basketball and football. In the latter sport, he set a state record by intercepting four passes in back-to-back games. Because of this feat, Hillview High's 1945 Yearbook hailed him as a "mighty mite" and "defensive star." A few years later, Hillview High's 1948 yearbook remembered Nakaso as a "shining star" on the football team. [31]

POSTWAR YEARS

After World War II, Asian Americans showed up on several high school football rosters on the West Coast and elsewhere. In Southern California, within weeks of V-J Day, Wayne Tsukahira played center for Belmont High. The next year, he made all league. In the fall of 1940, the *Los Angeles Times'* John De La Vega maintained that San Fernando High depended on "Larry Woo, 140-pound Chinese quarterback to engineer T-attack." In November 1945, Woo keyed San Fernando's whitewash of Canoga Park, 26–0. A few weeks later, he scored the only touchdown in a San Fernando loss. To the south, Garden Grove High School was captained by Tak Matsunaga in 1949. A 165-pound guard, Matsunaga also made second team all-league. [32]

In the early to mid-1950s, several Japanese Americans illuminated Southern California's prep gridirons denied them almost a decade earlier by internment. Ralph "the Rabbit" Kubota glittered as a 135-pound halfback for Compton High School in the late 1940s and early 1950s. In 1950, Kubota ran for touchdowns of seventy-one and seventy-three yards against Excelsior. He also staged a brilliant performance in Compton's CIF (California Interscholastic Federation) championship game against Fullerton. Indeed, he was named to the first string all-CIF team two years running, leading all Southern California backs in yards gained as he accumulated over 1,100. The *Pacific Citizen* pointed out that Kubota was the smallest back to make the all-CIF squad. In late summer of 1951, Kubota shined in a high school all-star game when he "scooted 40 yards around end" to set up a touchdown.[33]

Kubota then moved up to Compton Junior College, a perennial powerhouse in Southern California junior college grid circles. Some of the greatest players of postwar American football such as running backs Joe Perry and Hugh McElhenny, as well as the aforementioned Charlie Ane, had performed for the Tartars. Early in October 1951, Kubota scored two touchdowns of fourteen and twenty-five yards as Compton walked over Joliet Junior College, 59–0. A couple of weeks later, Kubota ran a touchdown in from fourteen yards as Compton beat Ventua, 21–7. The same month, Kubota scampered for two touchdowns of sixteen and seventeen yards when Compton edged San Angelo College, 14–13.[34]

While Kubota performed well for Compton, Benny Aoki was doing even better as a running back for Long Beach Junior College. Aoki was the son of Japanese immigrant parents living in Torrance at the time of the 1940 census. His father was described in the census manuscript schedules as a farmer. Prior to attending Long Beach JC, Aoki had sparked Long Beach High School's backfield. The high school's yearbook described him as a "speed merchant," who, in 1948, tallied twice with runs of over fifty yards against San Diego's Hoover High. Aoki also scored twice against Orange County's Excelsior High. One of the touchdowns was a "sensational run" of thirty-two yards. Aoki, moreover, was given the General George S. Patton Award as the varsity's Most Inspirational Player.[35]

Out of high school, Aoki sustained his football heroics. Early in October 1951, he scored five touchdowns and kicked five PATS when Long Beach Junior College clobbered Santa Ana, 41–7. A week later, Aoki tallied three more touchdowns as Long Beach Junior College crushed San Diego JC, 54–20. In mid-October 1951, Don Snyder called Aoki "Benny the Bunny" and described him as "[i]tty-bitty Benny, who tips the Toledo at 152 pounds and looks like he's standing in a hole when he sizes up his five feet seven inches." Backing up Snyder's enthusiasm, Aoki scored a touchdown and kicked two PATs as Long Beach downed Bakersfield, 32–28. In early November, Aoki caught a thirty-yard touchdown pass against El Camino JC. Around the same time, Snyder pointed out that Aoki was competing for the league scoring title. He told readers that the "itty-bitty 150 pound back" had accumulated eleven touchdowns and twenty-three PATs. Before Long Beach took on Santa Monica Junior College, the latter's newspaper pointed out that Aoki helped make Long Beach's running attack the best in junior college ranks. Subsequently, Aoki scored his one hundredth point when he kicked a PAT against Santa Monica in a 32–7 triumph.[36]

Despite the relatively numerous Nikkei gridders in the region, the *Pacific Citizen* complained that no Japanese American got all-star honors in Southern California in high school football after the 1952 season. After 1953, the *Citizen* proudly pointed out that several Japanese Americans gained postseason honors. Mitch Yamamoto earned all-league honors as a center. Poly High's Jim Sakoda was an all-league linebacker. Westchester's halfback Ken Matsuda was an all-leaguer, too, while tackle Jim Nakaoka from Gardena and Dorsey guard Bill Saito made second team all-league. Moreover, Japanese Americans would continue to receive all-league honors in highly competitive Southern California high school football circles into the mid-1950s.[37]

Antelope Valley's Dennis Ekimoto had an incredible year in 1957. An "ace fullback," Ekimoto averaged 7.4 yards per carry and accumulated over 1,300 yards and twenty touchdowns. He was not only all-league, but all-Southern California. He was purportedly a "student leader" to boot. Against Oxnard, Ekimoto crossed the goal line five times. Calling Ekimoto a "great fullback," sportswriter Hal Totten reported that Ekimoto gained 209 yards in addition to scoring five touchdowns against Oxnard. The next week, "Dennis the Menace," as sports columnist Stan Hochman nicknamed him, managed to run for another five touchdowns in a game against Muir.[38]

Not all of Southern California's best Asian American players were Japanese Americans in the 1950s. Possessing Filipino and African American ancestry, Joe Agapay shined at Chaffey High in the early 1950s. When a junior varsity player in 1951, Agapay was dubbed "[s]ensational" after he led his team to a 45–0 stomping of San Bernardino. During the game, he ran for an eighty-yard touchdown. Early in the 1953 season, Chaffey's varsity downed Alhambra, 20–7. Sportswriter Jerry Boyd claimed that Agapay "ran like a Democrat in Dixie" in that game, scoring all three Chaffey touchdowns. "The powerful Tiger fullback" carried the ball eleven times for seventy yards. In mid-October 1953, Agapay threw a touchdown pass and ran for another score in a losing effort to Colton. Agapay did more than just play football at Chaffey. Aside from starring and captaining Chaffey's football team, he was a Boys' State representative. In March 1954, he was declared Upland, California's "Boy of the Year."[39]

A contemporary of Agapay's, Dick Dagampat starred at Belmont High in Los Angeles. Like Herman Wedmeyer, Dagampat seems to have been the product of the interethnic relationships nurtured under the aegis of Hawaii's developing local culture. His father, Claudio, according to census data, worked as a barber and was born in the Philippines but was described in the 1940 census as racially Polynesian as was his Hawaiian-born mother. Several years earlier, Claudio arrived in Hawai'i from Guinan. In 1952, Dick made second team all Los Angeles and was named the most valuable player in the league. Against Lincoln High, the "ace half-back," the school yearbook raved, tallied two touchdowns. When Belmont won a key victory, Dagampat's sixty-eight-yard run proved crucial in leading his team to an eventual touchdown.[40]

After World War II, California's Central Valley hosted several Asian American high school gridders. Guard Jim Sasaki was a second team all-Northern California selection from Lodi High School in 1946. Modoc High School's coach praised Hank Yamagata as "the best open field runner I ever coached" in 1950. In California's capital, Harry Kuwabara stood out for Sacramento JC as a guard. Around the same time, Kat Komoto was an all-league center for Edison High. Near Sacramento, Courtland High suited up backfield aces, Aki Fukujima and Goro Kawamura after World War II. In a losing effort against El Dorado, the 1949 school yearbook testified, Fukujima proved a "sparkplug" for the offense, while Kawamura enjoyed a "field day" as a quarterback. Courtland High in 1957 could boast of Ron Ogawa, a formidable running back who carried the ball for 202 yards in sixteen carries against Clarksburg. The *Sacramento Bee* applauded him as "one of the outstanding backs in the league" after he scored two touchdowns, one of twenty-nine yards, against Winters. In Fresno, Fowler High suited up Hiro Tsukimura in the fall of 1951. The *Fresno Bee* claimed of Tsukimura that the star guard "us[ed] his 5 foot 4 inch and 143 pound frame to good advantage."[41]

Chinese American Sam Hom found a home in Davis High's backfield in the mid-1950s. When Davis High humbled an opponent, 53–19, in 1957, Sam Hom collected one of his team's many touchdowns. In another game against Rio Vista, Hom scored two touchdown runs of seven and twenty yards. Against Dixon, Hom performed well on defense and tossed a thirty-yard touchdown pass against Lincoln. The Davis High Yearbook also acclaimed Hom's "bang up job" against Folsom. He carried the ball seventeen times for 137 yards. After the season ended, Hom was honored as an all-league halfback.[42]

Placer High engaged the skills of several Japanese American athletes after the war. Jim Yokota, who also starred in basketball, stood out as a gridder in 1949. In a game against Nevada City, he scored one touchdown and passed for two more. Yokota also played for Placer Junior College in the early 1950s. In 1950, he scored a ten-yard touchdown against Santa Maria Junior College. Placer Junior College was also home to Harry Harimaki, a 125-pound halfback. The *Pacific Citizen* speculated that Harimaki was "probably the smallest player playing college football last year."[43]

San Francisco proffered opportunities for Asian American prep and junior college football players after World War II. In the fall of 1945, Poly High featured a sterling end named Bill Kang. Against St. Ignatius, Kang not only caught a touchdown pass but made a key recovery of a fumble. When San Francisco City College downed Los Angeles City College in the fall of 1946, Marshall Leong proved "the big gun" for the Rams as he scored two touchdowns in the 40–25 victory. The *San Francisco Examiner* maintained that San Francisco City College depended upon Leong's "ground power." Reflecting what Ellen D. Wu describes as postwar America's tepid embrace of racial liberalism, The *San Mateo Times* reported that the "Chinese fullback" was one of the two leaders of the Rams' offense. The other was "Sidney Webster, Negro quarterback." In 1950, Stan Ozaki stood out as a halfback for San Francisco's Poly High. Early in the 1950 season, he carried the ball for a thirty-three-yard touchdown against Mission. Subsequently, he nabbed a touchdown pass against Washington. Three newspapers in the city named him second team all-league.[44]

Asian Americans showed up on postwar Alameda and Contra Costa county high school and junior college gridirons. Pete Domoto excelled as a fullback for Berkeley High in the mid-1950s. He was also popular, winning election as junior class president. In 1956, Stan Nomura stood out for Oakland High. The next year, Hiro Kurotori quarterbacked for a Washington High team coached by the youthful Bill Walsh. When Washington High beat Mountain View, 11–0, Kurotori not only threw a thirty-eight-yard touchdown pass but kicked the conversion. In 1950, according to the *Pacific Citizen*, Ben Sugiyama was a good guard for El Cerrito High in Contra Costa County.[45]

Chang Tsang was an all-league halfback for Oakland Tech High School in the early 1950s. When Sacramento High School downed Oakland Tech in 1950, the *Sacramento Bee* called Tsang "almost the whole show for the visitors," scoring on thirty-seven and fifty-five-yard touchdowns. The *Bee* described the 138-pound running back as "a constant threat." Historian Roberta Park reported that Tsang led his eleven to its first league championship in a decade and was selected "Mr. Football" by the student body. Moreover, he was honored as an all-leaguer. Yet in an autobiography, teammate and future University of California and NFL tackle Proverb Jacobs maintained that Oakland Tech's coach referred to Tsang as his "Number One Boy" and Doug Chan, another Chinese American gridder, as his "Number Two Boy," clearly referencing the popular Charlie Chan movies which reinforced the exoticization of Chinese in mid-twentieth-century America. After serving in the military, Tsang subsequently starred at Oakland Junior College. In late October, 1955, Oakland JC lost to San Mateo JC, but the "elusive" Chang Tsang put on a great performance for the vanquished, carrying the ball for two touchdowns of twenty-nine and fifty-five yards.[46]

Another Chinese American, Bing Leong, quarterbacked San Lorenzo's eleven regularly in 1955, tossing a key thirty-yard touchdown pass in a league title game against Alameda. Leong also stood out on defense. In promoting a game between East and West Bay high school all-stars, the *Oakland Tribune* published a photo of the East Bay All-Star team's defensive lineup in August 1956, Leong was set to start at in the backfield. His coach at San Lorenzo was John Ralston, who later gained fame coaching at Stanford and then the Denver Broncos.[47]

San Mateo High School could boast of several Asian American varsity gridders during the postwar years. George Kitagawa was a second team all-leaguer for San Mateo High in 1953 and teammate Kent Ikeda performed outstandingly for San Mateo High School in 1954. Oliver Semba was an all-league guard for San Mateo High in 1955. Dick Takaki made the second team all-league and appeared in a postseason prep all-star game in the Bay Area. Moreover, he made second team all-Northern California. Takaki would later move on to Stanford, where he would play frosh football and varsity rugby. During the next decade, Ralph Ichimaru was an all-league back for San Mateo High. In the late 1960s, co-captain Ron Saito received all-league honors as a running back.[48]

A respectable number of prep and junior college Asian American gridders appeared in Santa Clara County in the late 1940s and 1950s. In the northern part of the county, high schools in Palo Alto suited up formidable Asian American football players. When Palo Alto beat Menlo-Atherton, 21–0, in 1956, the *San Jose Mercury* hailed the "brilliant running" of Ko Abe, who carried the ball eleven times for 144 yards. In the mid- and late 1950s, Cubberly High in Palo Alto suited up the Tana brothers. Shibun Tana helped Cubberly humble Sunnyvale, 34–6, by intercepting a pass and running the ball eighty-seven yards for a touchdown. Cubberly downed Sequoia High, 12–6, thanks in part to Yas Tana's seven-yard run to pay dirt. To the south, Shinji Ito made second team all-county while performing for Sunnyvale's Fremont High in 1950. In 1951, Fremont High suited up co-captains tackle Hiroshi Nakamura, and guard Tom Hashimoto. When Fremont beat James Lick in October 1951, the *San Jose Mercury* praised Nishimura and Hashimoto's outstanding performances. In the county's largest city, San Jose High called upon the services of gridders such as Hash Taketa who was an all-league guard in the late 1940s and early 1950s. In nearby Santa Clara, Herb Yamasaki was a fine lineman for Santa Clara High in the mid-1950s.[49]

Dick Kishimoto was one of the more outstanding Santa Clara Valley gridders in the late 1940s. In 1949, he surfaced as an exciting running back for Santa Clara. Indeed, the *Pacific Citizen* alerted readers in October 1949, to the "speedy halfback." The next month the weekly told readers that Kishimoto proved vital in Santa Clara's victory over Bellarmine. He scored one touchdown and averaged a good 5.7 yards per carry in thirteen carries. The *San Jose Mercury* asserted that an overflow crowd of 3,500 attended the Bellarmine game at Santa Clara's Townsend Field. Much of that crowd, according to the *San Jose Mercury*, uttered "the rhythmical name of Kishimoto." The daily added, "[T]he diminutive Japanese right half proved to be one of the most elusive and yard-eating runners on the field last night." Also in 1949, Kishimoto scored three touchdowns as Santa Clara pounded Los Gatos, 31–13. Kishimoto, moreover, ran for a seventy-yard jaunt against Washington High and a seven-ty-five-yard touchdown against Mountain View. At the end of the season, Kishimoto made second team all-league, prompting the question as to how good the first team backs had to have been.[50]

A pioneering, two-year postsecondary school in Santa Clara County, San Jose City College attracted Asian American football players in the 1950s. In 1957, the *San Jose Mercury* reported that quarterback Bing Leong transferred to City College from Cal after standing out at San Lorenzo High. The *San Jose Mercury* described Leong as "a clever play calling quarterback." Early in the 1957 season, Leong and Tom Koshiyama both helped in a 38–25 victory over Coalinga. The former tossed a touchdown pass, while the latter scored on a two-yard run. A week later, Leong contributed to a City College victory. He intercepted a pass and returned the ball for thirty yards. On offense, Leong threw a forty-yard pass and run. As a backfield performer, Koshiyama eventually developed into one of the better players on the squad, leading the Jaguars to victories over Ventura Junior College and other opponents.[51]

Asian American varsity football players could be found throughout the West in the postwar years. To California's north, Jimmy Tsugawa starred for Beaverton High School's squad in Oregon. Standing five-foot-four and weighing 140 pounds, Tsugawa captained the team in 1950. Early in the 1950 season, the *Pacific Citizen* reported, Tsugawa ran for three touchdowns in one game. After the 1950 season, Tsugawa earned a spot on the all-state all-star contingent. Before the all-star game in August 1951, a photo of Tsugawa appeared in the *Portland Oregonian*. The caption proclaimed him "probably the smallest player on either squad." In Idaho, Dick Matsumoto starred as a halfback for Middleton High in 1950 and Sam Goto stood out as a guard for Nampa High. Meanwhile, in the southwest, Ray Mitokawa was a stalwart lineman for Glendale High in Arizona in the late 1940s. And in the early 1950s, Ken Fujii carved out a fine high school career as a quarterback and defensive back at Reno High in Nevada. In 1952, he made all-state as a safety.[52]

Asian Americans surfaced on varsity elevens east of the Mississippi during the early Cold War years. In 1946, Ohio's *Canton Repository* told readers about Gene Sue. According to sportswriter, Bob Ries, Sue was a "plucky Chinese" trying out for Lehman High School's varsity. Previously, he had quarterbacked the reserve team. The son of a restaurant owner father, Sue was described as well liked and full of school spirit. In the 1947 school yearbook, Sue is pictured with the rest of the varsity. Reflective of the movement of some Japanese Americans to Chicago in the wake of West Coast internment, the *Pacific Citizen* reported in 1949 that George Morita and George Nakawatase starred on the Hyde Park High School football team in Chicago, while "Fred Yamashita" captained the Hyde Park eleven. The latter was probably the same young man the Hyde Park High Yearbook described as Fred Yamashiro, who had not only captained the team in 1948 but was honored as the squad's "lineman of the year" in both 1947 and 1948. Indeed, the yearbook declared that Yamashiro contributed from all positions on the line. The next year, George Morita was declared Hyde Park's "lineman of the year" and made all-league honorable mention, along with George Nakawatase. The *Pacific Citizen* counted eight Nisei in all on the 1949 edition of the Hyde Park varsity. In the mid-1950s, Bill Chung was an all-league fullback and captain of the Green River High School team in Wisconsin, while also serving as vice-president of the school's Lettermen's Club. The 1940 census data reveals that the Korean American Chung's working-class father was an immigrant who labored as a coal miner but his mother was born in California.[53]

LATE TWENTIETH- AND EARLY TWENTY-FIRST-CENTURY EXPERIENCES

During the last decades of the twentieth century and early years of the twenty-first century, Asian Americans, from increasingly varied ethnic backgrounds, surfaced on varsity high school squads. The diversity of these young athletes stemmed in part from liberalization of U.S. immigration laws in the 1960s but also the movement of significant numbers of Southeast Asian refugees to American shores from war-torn Vietnam, Laos, and Cambodia.

By the latter decades of the twentieth century, Santa Clara Valley had become Silicon Valley. By the latter twentieth century, it could claim a comparatively large, diverse population of Asian and Pacific Islander people. Wes Okamura emerged as a fine defensive back for Andrew Hill High School in San Jose in the mid-1970s. In the 1990s, West San Jose's Lynbrook High suited up fine gridders such as Jason Chiang and Vik Rajagopal. Kevin Kumagai starred at Cupertino's Homestead High. At Fremont High, Manvir Sandhu and Dennis Truong performed well, as did John Ho at Cupertino High. During the first decade of the twenty-first century, Kevin Pham was a fine quarterback for Westmont High in Silicon Valley and then excelled at De Anza Community College in Cupertino.[54]

Elsewhere in California, Asian American and Pacific Islander gridders donned shoulder pads for varsity squads. In the East Bay, Andrew Cho starred on Berkeley High's varsity team in the mid-1970s. In the late 1970s, Allan Tagami was a standout end for Watsonville High. In the Central Valley, Keith Yamamoto starred as a linebacker for Modesto Community College in 2009, winning the league's defensive most valuable player award. In 1990, senior running back, Quoc Pham run amuck for Costa Mesa High School in Orange County in a victory over Laguna Beach. He accumulated 199 yards and two touchdowns before an injury sidelined him in the third quarter. Standing out for Sherman Oaks' Notre Dame High School was Daniel Khan in the early 2010s. In 2011, Alex Yoon toted the ball twenty-eight times for a hefty 285 yards for Glendale against Hoover High. A son of a Mexican American father and a Japanese American mother, Thomas Duarte starred at Mater Dei High School in the early 2010s. In San Diego County, Dan Minamide stood out at quarterback for San Pascual High during the first decade of the twenty-first century. Indeed, he was honored as the Offensive Player of the Year in the San Diego Valley League.[55]

The Pacific Northwest fostered some quality gridders of Asian descent in recent years. In Oregon in the early 1990s, fullback Kailee Wong starred at North Eugene High, receiving plenty of attention from Division I football programs. Wong, who would star at Stanford and do well in the NFL as a linebacker, possesses Chinese ancestry. During the next decade, Joey Wong led Sprague High to a championship, completing eleven of sixteen passes in the championship game. Running back brothers and Vietnamese Americans David, Peter, and John Nguyen stood out at Washington's Bellvue High in the 2000s. In 2009, David Nguyen scored two touchdowns in Bellvue's victorious state title game.[56]

In the late 1980s, pass receiver Mike Nguyen gained national press attention while excelling for Portland's Franklin High. Bruce Newman chronicled Nguyen's career for *Sports Illustrated* readers. He told them that Nguyen came from a relatively privileged family that fled South Vietnam after the communist takeover. The high school hero informed Newman that he had no memory of the Mekong Delta village in which he was born. Considering that he was seen as larger than most Vietnamese, possessed a dark complexion, and was very good at football, many gossiped that Nguyen must have been of mixed black and Vietnamese background. Aware of the rumors, Nguyen told Newman, "I don't take it as an insult, if that's how they mean it, ... I didn't do anything wrong. And I don't consider being part black a bad thing. Even if I am part black, it wouldn't mean I had to work any less hard to accomplish the things I have."

According to Nguyen's coach at Franklin, he had "the most concentration I've ever seen . . . and he's got that motivation that just burns." Nguyen was so good that he attracted recruiters from Stanford and UCLA. Eventually, Nguyen settled on transporting his talents down to Los Angeles.[57]

After the war in Southeast Asia, the U.S. government aided Vietnamese, Cambodian, and Laotian refugees but channeled them to homes in locations often quite distant from what had become traditional Asian American communities on the East and West Coasts. Moreover, Asian Americans' quest for educational and economic opportunities often took them to places relatively unknown to Asian Americans earlier in the twentieth century. The South, for example, could boast of talented Asian

American players in the late twentieth and early twenty-first century. In 1996, the *Sarasota Herald-Tribune* told readers that Tuan Nguyen made a key tackle that helped Venice High defeat Belen. In Georgia, Hmong American Erick Yang made national news in 2009 because of his ability to place kick with both feet. A soccer player as well, Yang eventually wound up on Creighton University's soccer team. In 2014, Justin Pham starred as a pass receiver for Greater Atlantic Christian High. In Arkansas, the J.D. Leftwich High eleven achieved an undefeated state 2A championship in recent years—a feat significantly powered by gridders of Laotian Hmong descent.[58]

The Leftwich High team inspired Charles Pierce, a *Sports Illustrated* blogger. In 2011, Pierce informed readers that many of the Hmong gridders stood little over five feet tall and weighed no more than 120 or 130 pounds. Still, "their speed and power is so apparent that coaches have been forced to radically rethink the physical configuration of a football player." Quarterback Charley Moua was quoted as declaring, "I don't really know why I play. I like to run, and everybody wants to be on the team, you know? There's a tradition now here with the Asian kids, and the parents are really behind us, because of all they went through." Indeed, scholar Chia Youyee Vang points out that football has helped to develop a Hmong ethnic identity in the United States. which has challenged the assumptions underlying the model minority stereotype of Asian Americans.[59]

Excellent Asian American prep gridders have displayed their skills in the Midwest and Northeast. Winona High School in Minnesota featured in 2013 an explosive running back named Vincent Pham. When Winona easily beat Albert Lea, 60–21, Pham scored an astonishing six touchdowns while carrying ball for 192 yards. Tuan Pham was a linebacker for Nativity High in Pennsylvania in the early 1980s. Joey Pham stood out as a running back for Marple Newtown High School in southeastern Pennsylvania in the 2010s and Thuc Phan earned all-New England honors as a running back for Deerfield Academy in New England. Near Philadelphia, Haverford Prep School suited up a fine running back and pass receiver, John Kim in 2014.[60]

NONVARSITY GRIDDERS IN MID-TWENTIETH-CENTURY CALIFORNIA

In mid-twentieth-century California, as most elsewhere in the United States, elite high school athletes tended to be found in varsity sports. When it came to football, these athletes were male, usually upper third- or fourth-year students, larger than the typical high school male, and presumably possessing a requisite amount of skill. While rarely receiving the acclaim of varsity gridders, lightweight and other nonvarsity teams called upon participants' passion and talent. Indeed, lightweight gridders often displayed more agility and quickness than their varsity counterparts. In the 1930s and 1940s, Asian Americans excelled in nonvarsity football in San Benito, Santa Cruz, and Monterey Counties. Ted Hisatomi captained Watsonville's lightweight team in 1934. In 1936, his brother, Toyo Hisatomi, stood out as an all-league halfback and co-captain of Watsonville High's lightweight eleven. The next year, Hardy Tsuda and Shig Morimune co-captained Watsonville's lightweight team. The school yearbook hailed the former as the best blocker in the league, while the latter was extolled as the best end. After the war, Mits Hashimoto performed as an all-league fullback for Watsonville High's lightweight team in 1948. Also in Monterey County, Toshio Tokiwa served as honorary co-captain and star guard for Salinas High School lightweight squad in the fall of 1941.[61]

In Southern California, nonvarsity Asian American gridders go back at least to the 1920s. In 1926, future San Diego State standout Paul Yamamoto appeared as a guard for San Diego High's B squad. Kiyoshi Shigegawa starred as a "line plunger" for Anaheim High's B team in the late 1920s. A decade later, Jack Fuji captained the same squad. At rival Santa Ana High, another future San Diego State standout, Hideo Higashi, competed on the B squad in 1929. In the late 1930s, Tosh Asano played four years of B football for Monrovia-Arcadia-Duarte High School. During that time, he scored on a ninety-nine-yard rumble against Covina. Tak Mukaihita played stellar football for Belmont High's B team in the years before the war. Called by the *Los Angeles Times* the "versatile Belmont High School B gridder," he kicked a field goal to down Fairfax in October, 1939. The next year, he was still on the B team, which was captained by Eddie Urata and Yosai Sakamoto. Early in October 1940, Mukaihita ran the ball for a thirty-yard touchdown. In the fall of 1941, Mukaihita was elected student body president. Around the same time, John Yoshida captained Anaheim's C football squad. In the fall of 1941, Manual Arts B team suited up Mas Uchima, Eddie Nakazawa, and Sob Karatsu, elected captain for the 1942 season. All three were praised by the school yearbook, which also pointed out that Karatsu had made a "brilliant" eighty-yard run before getting hurt for the rest of the season. Manual Arts also fielded a C team, on which Sats Nakasone, Pete Ota, Mako Oi, and "Mousie" Shitsane played. Oi was elected captain for the 1942 season. Unsurprisingly, because of internment neither Karatsu or Oi fulfilled their captain duties.[62]

Non-varsity elevens in Southern California continued to suit up Asian Americans after World War II. Carl Honda excelled as a tackle for Huntington Beach High's C team in 1948. In 1949, San Pedro High's C team included captain and star Bob Miyakawa, as well as other standouts, Masaru Murata and Mike Nigashi. In 1950, Robert Koyamatsu co-captained Los Angeles's B squad. Two years later, end Jim Abe co-captained Belmont High's B team. During the 1953 season, Henry Yamata was named the best player on Pasadena's John Muir High's B eleven.[63]

COACHES

Asian American high school football coaches have been rare on the mainland compared to Hawai'i. Joe Nagata was a fine football player for LSU in the 1940s. After graduating from the university, he returned to his high school alma mater in Eunice, Louisiana, as a teacher and coach. According to historian Greg Robinson, Nagata coached for twenty-three years at Eunice High and St. Edmunds High. His squads got into state finals twice. In 1954, the *Pacific Citizen* pointed out that former Arizona lineman Ray Mitokawa had been working as an assistant coach at Peoria High School in Arizona. The "beefy" assistant concentrated on mentoring linemen and forging a good defense. He subsequently became a successful head coach in Arizona. Meanwhile, Fibber Hirayama, a star athlete from Fresno, took over the reins of Sanger High's lightweight squad in the early 1950s. In Southern California, Bob Sugino coached junior varsity football at Gardena High School, while Dale Hiramoto served as his assistant in the mid-1970s. Gardena High School's 1984 yearbook praised the work of varsity head coach Mike Sakurai and one of his assistants Sei Miyano. In the 2000s, Louis Wong achieved success at Timpview High in Utah. His teams won four state championships, but he resigned under pressure when state audits revealed that he and the school had processed booster money. Nevertheless, Mountain View High School in Utah hired Wong in 2014 after he had been reinstated. Elliot Vang has gained some national notoriety as St. Paul's only Hmong American football coach. After doing volunteer work a few years at his alma mater Highland High, he was eventually hired as a paid coach and promoted to defensive coordinator.[64]

CONCLUSION

Despite the relatively small numbers of Asian Americans living on the U.S. mainland for much of the twentieth century, Asian American participation in high school and other varieties of noncollegiate, nonprofessional football seems impressive. Some, such as Ralph Kubota, clearly starred on their teams. Others played a great deal as relatively anonymous 160-pound linemen. Others, of course, languished on the bench or because they were too small, too unskilled, or too Asian never rose above the nonvarsity level. In any event, even if they were not teenage football heroes, Asian American gridders on the mainland subverted prevailing orientalist narratives by showing a passion and talent for a highly physical, competitive sport. By traversing racial and ethnic frontiers and establishing a sense of gridiron spatial entitlement, they proved that sport could be experienced relatively equitably across racial and ethnic lines at a time when institutionalized racism and nativism persisted throughout the United States.

NOTES

1. *Oakland Tribune*, December 13, 1903; Mae Ngai, *The Lucky Ones: One Family and The Extraordinary Invention of Chinese America* (New York: Houghton Mifflin Harcourt, 2010).

2. *Seattle Times*, October 1, 1941; *Pacific Citizen*, November 25, 1950; November 28, 1952; *San Jose Mercury*, October 4, 1947; October 9, 1950; November 4, 1951; October 7, 1956; October 8, 1956; October 26, 1964; October 21, 1968; *San Rafael Daily Independent Journal*, November 6, 1961.

3. *Seattle Times*, October 6, 1936; November 1, 1936; November 14, 1937; December 16, 1937; November 12, 1938; *Japanese American Courier*, September 24, 1938; October 8, 1938; October 15, 1938; http://www.blackpast.org/aaw/ubangi-blackhawks (June 3, 2016).

4. *Chinese Digest*, March 27, 1936.

5. *San Jose Mercury*, November 16, 1902; *San Francisco Chronicle*, September 26, 1903; *Anaconda Standard*, November 11, 1902.

6. *Portland Oregonian*, November 21, 1912; October 12, 1916; December 7, 1919; *Seattle Times*, September 9, 1973; John J. Reddin, "'14 Teammates Meet by Chance," January 7, 1963; *Kalamazoo Gazette*, November 23, 1904; *Philadelphia Public Ledger*, November 11, 1915.

7. *Los Angeles Times*, December 1, 1920; December 11, 1920; December 15, 1929; Franks, *Crossing*, 142; *San Jose Mercury*, November 6, 1921; Commerce High School Yearbook, 1924, 1925, 1928, 1929, www.ancestry.com (March 27, 2015); *Chinese Digest*, October 23, 1936; San Jose High School Yearbook, 1930, www.ancestry.com (May 31, 2014); U.S. Census Bureau, Census Manuscript Schedules, 1920, City of San Jose and County of Santa Clara, www.ancestry.com (March 3, 2009); U.S. Census Bureau, Census Manuscript Schedules, City of Marysville and County of Yuba, 1930, 1940, www.ancestry.com (July 3, 2015); Mountain View High School Yearbook, 1929, www.ancestry.com (June 10, 2014); Marysville High School Yearbook, 1928, 1930, www.ancestry.com (June 19, 2015); Lodi High School Yearbook, 1930, www.classmates.com (June 3, 2015); Anaheim High School Yearbook, 1928, www.ancestry.com (February 20, 2015).

8. *Sacramento Bee*, October 4, 1930; October 12, 1930; October 17, 1930; October 20, 1930; October 15, 1937; Tom Kane, "Local Irish Score in Closing Minutes with Long Passes Clicking," October 16, 1937; *Chinese Digest*, October 23, 1936; Gayland Miller, "Edison Eleven and Wolves Play to 6 to 6 Tie," Fresno Bee, October 9, 1937; U.S. Census Bureau, Manuscript Census Schedules, 1930, City of Red Bluff and County of Tehama, www.ancestry.com (June 15, 2015); *Red Bluff Daily News*, February 6, 1970; Franks, *Crossing*, 143; Stockton High School Yearbook, 1935, www.ancestry.com (January 25, 2015); Courtland High School Yearbook, 1935, www.ancestry.com (April 29, 2015); Lodi High School Yearbook, 1937, www.ancestry.com (June 3, 2015); C.K. McClatchy High School Yearbook, 1941, www.ancestry.com (December 13, 2015).

9. *Sacramento Bee*, October 5, 1937; September 19, 1939; September 20, 1939; September 21, 1939; *Poston Chronicle*, May 23, 1943; Sacramento High School Yearbook, 1939, www.ancestry.com (June 25, 2015); Sacramento Junior College Yearbook, 1941, www.ancestry.com (December 13, 2014).

10. *Chinese Digest*, September 11, 1936; June 5, 1936; September 25, 1936; February, 1938; October, 1938; *San Francisco Chronicle*, October 1, 1937; John E. Spalding, "San Francisco vs. East Bay High School All-Star Football, 1932–1938, http://

www.weebly.com/uploads/3/0/9/7/30972031/football-aaa-oalall-starhisto-ry1931–38.pdf (December 26, 2014); U.S. Census Bureau, Manuscript Census Sched-ules, 1930, 1940, City and County of San Francisco, www.ancestry.com (April 29, 2015); Mission High School Yearbook, 1937, 1938, www.ancestry.com (April 30, 2016).

11. *San Francisco Chronicle*, October 12, 1940; October 1, 1941; Bob Stevens, "Irish Battle Poly Today," October 9, 1941; Bob Stevens, "Champion Poly Rolls over Mis-sion," October 16, 1941; Dick Toner, "Bulldogs Backs Ok, But Line Is Light," *San Francisco Examiner*, September 3, 1940; Dick Toner, "Eagles Have Lots of Color," Sep-tember 4, 1940; September 10, 1940; Dick Toner, "Parrots Have Big Power Play Edge," September 11, 1940; September 25, 1940; Dick Toner, "Poly Encounters Irish Today," November 6, 1940; Commerce High School Yearbook, 1941, www.ancestry.com (Au-gust 25, 2015).

12. Bill Hogan, "Castle Ready for Hornets," *Oakland Tribune*, September 7, 1932; *Chinese Digest*, November 15, 1935; November 29, 1935; February 21, 1936; October 9, 1936; *Hayward Review*, December 16, 1936; *Sacramento Bee*, September 23, 1937; Septem-ber 30, 1937; *San Jose Mercury*, November 12, 1938; Alameda High School Yearbook, 1942, www.ancestry.com(June 24, 2015); Douglas Guy, "Burlingame Scores Only Vic-tory, *San Francisco Chronicle*, October 2, 1937; Dick Kelly, "Japanese Lads on USF Frosh Team," October 4, 1940;. U.S. Census Bureau, Manuscript Census Schedules, City of Vallejo and County of Solano, 1930, www.ancestry.com (July 28, 2015); Mountain View High School Yearbook, 1933, 1936, www.ancestry.com (March 31, 2016).

13. *San Francisco Chronicle*, November 21, 1937; *Poston Chronicle*, June 20, 1943; Wat-sonville High School Yearbook, 1938, 1940, www.ancestry.com (June 24, 2015).

14. Santa Ana Register, September 5, 1930; December 12, 1930; October 28, 1936; November 27, 1936; February 26, 1937; January 31, 1940; *Los Angeles Times*, October 22, 1938; Anaheim High School Yearbook, 1935, 1936, 1939, 1940, www.ancestry.com (June 17, 2016).

15. *Los Angeles Times*, October 19, 1935; October 26, 1935; November 9, 1935; Octo-ber 13, 1936; September 25, 1937; Carl Blume, "Domencio Tops Prep Scoring," October 17, 1938; October 22, 1938; Carl Blume, "Chinese Gridder Leads Lincoln Varsity," October 9, 1939; October 10, 1939; October 5, 1940; October 11, 1940; Franks, *Crossing*, 143; *Poston Chronicle*, November 26, 1943; Belmont High School Yearbook, 1937, 1938, 1939, 1941, www.ancestry.com (May 5, 2012); San Fernando High School Yearbook, 1939, www.ancestry.com (September 14, 2015); Lincoln High School Yearbook, 1939, www.ancestry.com (May 14, 2016); Manual Arts High School, 1942, www.ancestry.com (July 16, 2015); http://articles.ivpressonline.com/2004–03–06/golden-bull-dogs_24190567/2 (November 14, 2014); http://search.ancestry.com/cgi-bin/sse.dll?_phsrc=fSR19&_phstart=successSource&usePUBJs=true&gss=angs-g&new=1&rank=1&msT=1&gsfn=Richard%20&gsfn_x=0&gsln=Ung&gsln_x=0&msypn__ftp=Los%20Angeles,%20Los%20Angeles,%20California,%20USA&msypn=68337&msypn_PInfo=8-%7C0%7C1652393%7C0%7C2%7C0%7C7%7C0%7C1813%7C68337%7C0%7C&MSAV=1&cp=0&catbucket=rstp&uidh=qc9&pcat=ROOT_CATEGORY&h=1977524&recoff=7%209&db=WWIIenlist&indiv=1&ml_rpos=12 (June 4, 2016); U.S. Census Bu-reau, Manuscript Census Schedules, 1930, 1940, City and County of Los Angeles (June 4, 2016).

16. Tim Asamen, "Nisei Greatness on the Imperial Valley Gridiron," http://www.discovernikkei.org/en/journal/2016/3/7/nisei-greatness/ (May 28, 2016).

17. Ibid.

18. Ibid; Martha Nakagawa, "Japanese with Ties to the Valley Take Imperial Tour," http://www.thedesertreview.com/japanese-with-ties-to-the-valley-take-imperial-tour/ (June 6, 2016).

19. *Baton Rouge Advocate*, November 10, 1933; Brawley High School Yearbook, 1934, www.ancestry.com (June 4, 2016).

20. *San Diego Union*, December 28, 1934; *San Bernardino County Sun*, October 3, 1937; U.S. Census Bureau, Manuscript Census Schedules, City of Brawley and County of

Imperial, 1940, www.ancestry.com (June 4, 2016); Martha Nakagawa, "Imperial Valley Reunion's Elder Statespeople," http://www.rafu.com/2014/11/imperial-valley-reunions-elder-statespeople/ (June 3, 2016).

21. http://articles.ivpressonline.com/2004–03–06/golden-bulldogs_24190567/2 (November 10, 2014); Asamen, "Nisei Greatness."

22. *Los Angeles Times*, November 8, 1935; October 13, 1936; October 7, 1939; October 14, 1939; October 4, 1940; September 20, 1941; October 18, 1941; January 22, 1942; Long Beach Junior College Yearbook, 1934, www.mocavo.com (December 4, 2014); Los Angeles Junior College Yearbook, 1936, www.ancestry.com (April 20, 2015); U.S. Census Bureau, Manuscript Census Schedules, City and County of Los Angeles,1940, www.ancestry.com (April 20, 2015); Pasadena Junior College Yearbook, 1938, www.ancestry.com (July 1, 2015); Franks, *Crossing*, 143; http://library.la84.org/SportsLibrary/HELMS/Football/CIFFOOTBALL1940.pdf (March 21, 2013).

23. Santa Ana Register, November 8, 1938; *Los Angeles Times*, September 20, 1941; Chaffey Junior College Yearbook, 1939, www.ancestry.com (July 18, 2016); U.S. Census Bureau, Manuscript Census Schedules, City of Upland and County of San Bernardino, 1940, www.ancestry.com (July 19, 2016); http://www.chaffey.edu/ath-pe/hof.shtml (July 19, 2016); http://www.rafu.com/2014/10/a-degree-of-justice/ (July 20, 2016).

24. *Japanese American Courier*, September 28, 1938; October 1, 1938; Broadway High School Yearbook, 1926, www.classmates.com (July 21, 2015); Broadway High School Yearbook, 1934 www.ancestry.com (October 22, 2016); Broadway High School Yearbook, 1938, 1940, 1941; Garfield High School Yearbook, 1933, 1935, 1940, www.ancestry.com (August 27, 2014); *Seattle Times*, December 1, 1933; September 15, 1935; October 31, 1937.

25. *Seattle Times*, November 11, 1938; December 24, 1939; September 9, 1973; Broadway High School Yearbook, 1938, 1940, www.ancestry.com (June 13, 2016); Bill Hosokawa, *The Two Worlds of Jim Yoshida* (New York: William Morrow & Company, 1972); On the in-betweeness of Asian American experiences, see Lisa Lowe, *Immigrant Acts: On Asian American Cultural Politics* (Durham, NC: Duke University Press, 1996).

26. *Arizona Republic*, October 10, 1930; November 11, 1930; January 26, 1940; Welky, "Viking Girls."

27. Mount Carmel Item, November 13, 1923; *Jamestown Evening Journal*, October 8, 1931; *Binghamton Press*, October 8, 1934; Dyreson, Making the American Team, 54.

28. *New London Day*, July 20, 1937; Audubon High School Yearbook, 1935, www.ancestry.com (November 14, 2014); *Sporting News*, November 5, 1947; *Lumberton Robesonian*, November 7, 1976.

29. John De La Vega, "Venice Team Dominates All-Western League," *Los Angeles Times*, December 16, 1942; December 17, 1943; http://library.la84.org/SportsLibrary/HELMS/Football/CIFFOOTBALL1943.pdf (October 17, 2015); http://library.la84.org/SportsLibrary/HELMS/Football/CIFFOOTBALL1946.pdf (October 17, 2015).

30. *Salt Lake Tribune*, October 1, 1942; *Pacific Citizen*, November 19, 1942; November 26, 1942; *Heart Mountain Sentinel*, September 25, 1943; May 26, 1945; *San Francisco Examiner*, September 21, 1945; Lewis and Clark High School Yearbook, 1945, www.ancestry.com (November 24, 2014); North Central High School Yearbook, 1944, 1945, www.ancestry.com (November 24, 2014); Franks, *Crossing*, 143.

31. U.S. Census Bureau, Manuscript Census Schedules, City and County of Alameda, 1940, www.ancestry.com (May 14, 2015); http://collinsvillepress.com/files/2014/09/14-CT-Football-Rec-Book.pdf (June 6, 2014); Hillview High School Yearbook, 1945, www.ancestry.com (May 14, 2015); 1948, www.ancestry.com (June 11, 2015).

32. John De La Vega, "Wilson Choice to Take North Prep Crown," *Los Angeles Times*, September 24, 1945; John De La Vega, "Canoga Park Figures on Abdicating Title," October 1, 1945; November 2, 1945; November 3, 1945; November 21, 1945; *Pacific Citizen*, January 7, 1950; Belmont High School Yearbook, 1947, www.ancestry.com (July 6, 2015); San Fernando High School Yearbook, 1946, www.ancestry.com (May 26, 2015); Franks, *Crossing*, 143; Pasadena Junior College

Yearbook, 1948, www.ancestry.com (July 1, 2015); Gardena High School Yearbook, 1949, www.classmates.com (August 13, 2015).

33. *Los Angeles Times*, October 5, 1951; John De La Vega, "CIF All-Stars Topple City, 19–6," September 1, 1951; *Los Angeles Sentinel*, October 25, 1951; *Nevada State-Journal*, December 20, 1951; Compton High School Yearbook, 1950; 1951, www.ancestry.com (May 28, 2015); *Pacific Citizen*, December 30, 1950.

34. *Los Angeles Times*, October 5, 1951; Don Snyder, "Tartars and Bulldogs Meet in Rose Bowl," November 2, 1951; October 14, 1951; *San Jose Mercury*, October 20, 1951.

35. U.S. Census Bureau, Manuscript Census Schedules, City of Torrance and County of Los Angeles, 1940, www.ancestry.com (May 2, 2015); Long Beach High School Yearbook, 1949, www.ancestry.com.,(May 29, 2015).

36. *Los Angeles Times*, October 6, 1951; October 13, 1951; Don Snyder, "Aoki Leads JC Scorers," October 17, 1951; October 20, 1951; Don Snyder, "Allen, Aoki Sharing Scoring Lead," November 8, 1951; *Torrance Herald*, November 8, 1951; Corsair, November 21, 1951; December 5, 1951.

37. *Pacific Citizen*, November 28, 1952; January 1, 1954; *Los Angeles Times*, October 6, 1952; http://library.la84.org/SportsLibrary/HELMS/Football/CIFFOOTBALL1952.pdf (June 7, 2012); Banning High School Yearbook, 1954, www.ancestry.com (August 13, 2016); http://library.la84.org/SportsLibrary/HELMS/Football/CIFFOOTBALL1955.pdf (July 21, 2016); http://library.la84.org/SportsLibrary/HELMS/Football/CIFFOOTBALL1957.pdf (July 21, 2016); *San Bernardino County Sun*, November 25, 1957.

38. Hal Totten, "Jackets Lose First Game, Tie for Title," *Oxnard Press-Courier*, November 16, 1957; December 27, 1957.

39. Bob Speck, "Chaffey's JV Smash Cards," *San Bernardino County Sun*, November 2, 1951; Jerry Boyd, "Chaffey Clobbers Alhambra, 20 to 7," September 26, 1953; Jerry Boyd, "Colton High Nips Chaffey 20 to 19," October 17, 1953; March 11, 1954; U.S. Census Bureau, Manuscript Census Schedules, City of Upland and County of San Bernardino, 1940, www.ancestry.com (June 14, 2016).

40. http://library.la84.org/SportsLibrary/HELMS/Football/CIFFOOTBALL1952.pdf (June 7, 2012); U.S. Census Bureau, Manuscript Census Schedules, City and County of Los Angeles, 1940, www.ancestry.com (July 3, 2015); Belmont High School Yearbook, 1953, www.ancestry.com (January 30, 2016); Hawaii Passenger and Crew Lists, 1900–1959, www.ancestry.com (October 20, 2017).

41. *San Francisco Examiner*, November 26, 1946; *Lodi News-Sentinel*, December 2, 1948; November 28, 1952; October 13, 1954; October 25, 1955, September 17, 1958; October 15, 1959; *Sacramento Bee*, September 17, 1955; October 22, 1955; November 22, 1955; November 2, 1957; November 3, 1957; November 9, 1957; Paul Zimmerman, "Lucero Scored 3 Times as Woodland Routs El Camino, 38–7, in Metro Game," October 31, 1959; Courtland High School Yearbook, 1949, www.ancestry.com (September 28, 2016); Lodi High School Yearbook, 1950, www.classmates.com (June 3, 2015); *Pacific Citizen*, November 12, 1949; September 16, 1950; September 23, 1950, September 30, 1950; October 7, 1950; November 25, 1950; December 9, 1950; Livingston High School Yearbook, 1951, www.ancestry.com (January 17, 2014); Sacramento Junior College Yearbook, 1949, www.ancestry.com (December 13, 2014); *Fresno Bee*, November 20, 1951; November 24, 1951; December 1, 1951; Stockton High School Yearbook, 1957, www.ancestry.com (April 20, 2012).

42. Davis High School Yearbook, 1958, www.ancestry.com (October 8, 2016).

43. *Pacific Citizen*, November 12, 1949; February 18, 1950; October 17, 1950; January 13, 1951.

44. Polytechnic High School Yearbook (San Francisco), 1946, www.ancestry.com (October 22, 2016); *Corsair*, November 6, 1946; *San Francisco Examiner*, November 22, 1946; *San Mateo Times*, November 28, 1946; *San Francisco Chronicle*, October 15, 1947; October 6, 1950; October 7, 1950; October 21, 1951; Al Moss, "Rede Counts on Handful of Vets," September 15, 1958; Al Moss, "Poly Rated Weaker This Year," September 16, 1958; *Pacific Citizen*, December 9, 1950; Franks, Crossing, 143, 144; Commerce High

School Yearbook, 1948, www.ancestry.com (December 6, 2014); *Pacific Citizen*, October 7, 1950; October 17, 1952; Galileo High School Yearbook, 1959, www.ancestry.com (May 30, 2011); http://www.cifsf.org/uploads/3/2/0/9/32099267/football-all-stars1922–1999.pdf (March 29, 2016); Wu, *Color of Success*.

45. *Oakland Tribune*, October 12, 1946; *Pacific Citizen*, September 16, 1950; November 25, 1950; *San Jose Mercury*, September 19, 1954; September 15, 1957; September 28, 1957; Oakland High School Yearbook, 1957, www.ancestry.com (August 5, 2011); Berkeley High School Yearbook,1954, www.ancestry.com (June 16, 2016).

46. Franks, "Crossing," 144; *Sacramento Bee*, October 2, 1950; Roberta J. Park, "Sports and Recreation Among Chinese American Communities of the Pacific Coast from Time of Arrival to 'The Quiet Decade of the 1950's," *Journal of Sport History*, 27, (2000), 466; *Oakland Tribune*, November 28, 1950; Ben Giuliano, "Ex Tech Cage Stars to Play for Oakland J.C.," October 13, 1955; October 17, 1956; *San Mateo Times*, October 29, 1955; Proverb. B. Jacobs, Jr., *The Autobiography of an Unknown Football Player* (Blooming-ton, Indiana: Author House, LLC, 2014), 134.

47. *Hayward Daily Review*, September 17, 1953; http://www.highbeam.com/doc/1P2–7051776.html (June 3, 2015); *Oakland Tribune*, August 23, 1956; San Lorenzo High School Yearbook, 1956, www.ancestry.com (June 17, 2015).

48. San Mateo High School Yearbook, 1954, 1956, 1958, 1959, 1968, www.ancestry.com., (November 29, 2014); Franks, *Crossing*, 144; *San Jose Mercury*, October 10, 1947; September 9, 1954; *Pacific Citizen*, January 7, 1956; *San Mateo Times*, October 29, 1955; March 27, 1956; October 31, 1959; *San Francisco Chronicle*, September 17, 1964; Sequoia High School Yearbook, 1967, www.classmates.com (April 24, 2015).

49. George Chrisman, Jr., "San Jose Tech Coach Has High Hopes of Good Season, in Second Year," *San Jose Mercury*, September 23, 1947; November 13, 1947; November 20, 1947; October 8, 1949; George Chrisman, Jr., "Light Eagle Team Counts on Its Speed," September 28, 1950; October 14, 1950; Dan Hruby, "Mt. View Grid Team Seeks Title," September 23, 1951; October 6, 1951; October 12, 1951; October 20, 1951; November 3, 1951; September 19, 1954; September 19, 1954; October 9, 1954; October 5, 1956; October 6, 1956; October 13, 1956; September 15, 1957; September 28, 1957; October 5, 1957; Santa Clara High School Yearbook, 1954, www.ancestry.com (July 24, 2014); *Pacific Citizen*, December 9, 1950; November 3, 1951.

50. *Pacific Citizen*, October 22, 1949; November 12, 1949; November 19, 1949; December 6, 1949. October 17, 1952; *San Jose Mercury*, October 8, 1949; October 15, 1949; November 5, 1949; October 19, 1951; October 20, 1951; November 17, 1951; November 20, 1951.

51. *San Jose Mercury*, October 12, 1956; September 17, 1957; September 20, 1957; September 21, 1957; September 28, 1957; September 8, 1960; *Oxnard Press-Courier*, October 11, 1958; San Jose City College Yearbook, 1960, www.ancestry.com (July 24, 2015).

52. *Pacific Citizen*, November 15, 1947; November 12, 1949; March 11, 1950; September 16, 1950; September 23, 1950; December 9, 1950; November 28, 1952; November 5, 1954; *Seattle Times*, November 26, 1949; *Portland Oregonian*, August 19, 1951; *Oregon Statesmen*, September 16, 1961; Beaverton High School Yearbook, 1951, www.ancestry.com., (July 7, 2016); http://www.beasport.com/assets/South_49_89.pdf (July 7, 2016); Reno High School Yearbook, 1953, www.classmates.com (August 10, 2016); Garfield High School Yearbook, 1958 www.ancestry.com (June 28, 2016).

53. Bob Ries, "Gene Sue is City's First Chinese Hopeful," *Canton Repository*, March 31, 1946; Lehman High School Yearbook, 1946, www.ancestry.com (June 1, 2015); Leh-man High School Yearbook, 1947, www.ancestry.com (June 1, 2015); Hyde Park High School Yearbook, 1949, 1950, www.ancestry.com (July 4, 2016); *Pacific Citizen*, January 7, 1950; Green River High School Yearbook, 1956, www.ancestry.com (June 9, 2016); U.S. Census Bureau, City of Green River and County of Sweetwater, 1940, www.ancestry.com (June 9, 2016); Wu, *Color of Success*.

54. Franks, *Crossing*, 144; San Jose High School Yearbook, 1979, www.classmates.com., (July 8, 2015); Dick Sparrer, "Tradition Continues in All-Star

Game, *Cupertino Courier*, July 24, 2015; http://www.deanza.edu/athletics/football/roster06.html (August 17, 2015).

55. Berkeley High School Yearbook, 1975, www.classmates.com (April 10, 2015); C.K. McClatchy High School Yearbook, 1987, www.ancestry.com (March 6, 2015); Lodi High School Yearbook, 1989, www.classmates.com., (June 3, 2015); Hollywood High School Yearbook, 1974, www.ancestry.com (October 10, 2011); *Los Angeles Times*, September 17, 1976; Len Hall, "Pham's Running Leads Costa Mesa Passed Laguna Beach," http://articles.latimes.com/1990–10–27/sports/sp-2740_1_laguna-beach (August 17, 2015); Belmont High School Yearbook, 1979, www.ancestry.com (July 6, 2015); Marina High School Yearbook, 1985, www.ancestry.com (May 6, 2015); Gardena High School Yearbook, 1984, www.ancestry.com (August 25, 2015); http://www.dailynews.com/sports/20140206/daniel-khan-signs-with-air-force-academy-football, (July 10, 2015); Jack Wang, "UCLA Receiver Thomas Duarte Proud of Biracial Heritage," http://www.dailynews.com/sports/20131125/ucla-receiver-thomas-duarte-proud-of-biracial-heritage, (June 22, 2015); http://www.glendalehigh.com/big-game-records-glendale-only-legends.pdf (July 13, 2015); http://www.rafu.com/2012/07/tackling-harvard-football (March 3, 2016); http://www.mjc.edu/athletics/football/awards.php (August 8, 2016).

56. Dave Kayes, "Wong is Back on Track and So Is North Eugene," *Eugene Register-Guard*, October 28, 1993; Ron Bellamy, "Little Kid Comes Up Big For Champions," December 12, 2004; Jason Cruz, "Top Asian Athletes to Watch for 2010," *Northwest Asian Weekly*, December 30, 2009; May 25-May 31, 2013; Jason Cruz, "Top API Athletes of 2014," January 15, 2015; http://www.heraldnet.com/article/20140905/SPORTS01/140909418 (July 15, 2015).

57. Bruce Newman, "The Class of '90 American Dreamers Fifteen Years after his Family Fled Saigon, Mike Nguyen Is Off to UCLA to Play Football," http://www.si.com/vault/1990/06/04/122097/the-class-of-90-american-dreamers-fifteen-years-after-his-family-fled-saigon-mike-nguyen-is-off-to-ucla-to-play-football (October 10, 2015).

58. Alan Dell, "New Look Indians Will Do 'Whatever It Takes," *Sarasota Herald-Tribune*, September 3, 1996; October 8, 2003; Cameron Smith, "Two-Footed Georgia Placekicker Creating quite a Stir," rivals.yahoo.com/highschool/blog/prep_rally/post/Two-footed-Georgia-placekicker-creating-quite-a-?urn=highschool-278339 (March 2, 2011); Vang, "Hmong Youth," 207; http://www.gocreighton.com/ViewArticle.dbml?DB_OEM_ID=1000&ATCLID=208888161 (March 2, 2011); http://www.yalebulldogs.com/sports/m-footbl/2014–15/bios/chang_jeho_qqxg (July 7, 2015); http://www.gettyimages.com/detail/news-photo/hmong-athletes-j-d-leftwich-high-senior-lineman-bobby-moua-news-photo/136061653 (July 7, 2015); http://www.gwinnettdailypost.com/news/2014/dec/10/diminutive-phan-casts-large-shadow-in-gac/Diminutive Phan casts large shadow in GAC's offense (November 7, 2015).

59. https://sigroup.wordpress.com/20 11/12/08/also-in-this-weeks-sports-illustrated-the-patriots-no-name-defense-a-first-of-its-kind-study-on-footballs-long-term-effects-on-an-entire-nfl-roster-and-comparing-the-bcs-to-las-vegas/#more-1888 (November 17, 2015); Vang, "Hmong Youth."

60. http://www.nguoi-viet.com/absolutenm2/templates/viewarticlesNV2.aspx?articleid=175463&zoneid=37 (August 17, 2015); http://www.marplenewtownfootball.com/wp/2013/08/27/joey-pham-making-strides-millersville/ (August 4, 2014); Doyle Dietz, "The Region Scene," *Reading Eagle*, January 8, 1983; http://www.elonphoenix.com/roster.aspx?rp_id=2910 (July 10, 2015); Terry Toohey, "Football: Kim Does It All to Spark Haverford in Winthrop," www.gametimepa.com/ci_26751896/football-kim-does-it-all-spark-haverford-win (August 12, 2015).

61. Watsonville High School Yearbook, 1935, 1937, 1938, www.classmates.com (July 8, 2015); 1949, www.ancestry.com (February 19, 2014); Poston Chronicle, November 26, 1943; Salinas High School Yearbook, 1942, www.ancestry.com (January 2, 2015);

San Jose Mercury, October 8, 1949; Santa Cruz High School Yearbook, 1958, www.classmates.com (July 7, 2011).

62. *Los Angeles Times,* October 13, 1939; October 4, 1940; October 17, 1941; San Diego High School Yearbook, 1927, www.ancestry.com (August 13, 2016); Anaheim High School Yearbook, 1928, 1929, 1940, 1941, www.ancestry.com (February 20, 2015); Santa Ana High School Yearbook, 1930, www.classmates.com (October 4, 2014); Garden Grove High School Yearbook, 1935, www.ancestry.com (October 19, 2012); Belmont High School Yearbook, 1941, 1942, www.ancestry.com (June 14, 2016); Manual Arts High School Yearbook, 1942, www.classmates.com (March 16, 2015); Tosh Kinjo, "Asano, Athletic Extraordinaire," http://www.rafu.com/wp-content/uploads/2014/10/tosh-asano-clipping.png (September 2, 2016); *Los Angeles Times,* October 17, 1941.

63. Huntington Beach High School Yearbook, 1949, www.ancestry.com (May 6, 2015); San Pedro High School Yearbook, 1950, www.classmates.com (June 28, 2012); Belmont High School Yearbook, 1953, www.ancestry.com (July 21, 2016); *Pacific Citizen,* November 25, 1950; January 1, 1954; Crenshaw High School Yearbook, 1969, www.ancestry.com., www.ancestry.com (November 5, 2014); Gardena High School Yearbook, 1966, www.classmates.com (August 13, 2015); Edison High School Yearbook, 1981, www.ancestry.com (May 6, 2015).

64. Greg Robinson, "Be a Good Sport about It: Early Nikkei Athletes in Louisiana," http://www.discovernikkei.org/en/journal/2017/9/5/nikkei-athletes-louisiana; *Pacific Citizen,* November 5, 1954; *Fresno Bee,* October 24, 1952; Tiffany Louie, "Hill Physicians Asian Heritage Street Celebration of Bay Area Educators," *Asian Week,* May 9, 2014; http://www.paloaltoonline.com/news/2014/03/19/palo-alto-names-fung-as-its-new-athletic-director (May 18, 2015); Jim Riggio, "Phan Returns to Nitro Football," *Glendale News-Press;* http://www.deseretnews.com/article/865607667/High-school-football-Louis-Wong-Tony-McGeary-headline-crop-of-20-new-coaches-in-2014.html?pg=all (February 13, 2015); http://www.elliottelevang.com/release/ (May 18, 2015); Gardena High School Yearbook, 1975, www.classmates.com (August 13, 2015); Gardena High School Yearbook, 1984, www.ancestry.com (August 25, 2015).

FIVE

Asian American Mainlanders and College Football

It is hard to make, let alone, shine on college football teams, even those representing the University of Alabama or USC. Nevertheless, just as Hawaiians of Asian ancestry suited up for mainland college teams and occasionally excelled, mainlanders of Asian ancestry rode the bench, started, and achieved honors as college football players. Indeed, while people of Asian ancestry encountered formal and informal patterns of racial exclusion in the United States, particularly during the first half of the twentieth century, Asian American football players claimed spatial entitlement and cultural citizenship on college gridirons. Yet some, in the process, could not escape the shadow of racial nativism as they crossed hazardous cultural borderlands. Michael Oriard tells us that American Indian football players had to weave their way through competing yet often ultimately demeaning popular narratives. Because of the varied ways Orientalism has worked its way into American popular culture, Asian American gridders undertook similar treks.[1]

Non-Hawaiian Asians began to appear on various four-year, post-secondary football fields in the early twentieth century. In 1905, readers of the *Salt Lake Tribune* learned that a Chinese student at West Point, Tai Ching Chen, stunned the campus with his football skills. Still, a sports-writer grumbled in a wire story in 1911 that while there were eight hundred Chinese students, of unspecified citizenship status, attending U.S. college, only one displayed the proper "American spirit" by playing college football.[2]

Meanwhile, a Filipino gridder gained attention in the U.S. press. In 1905, a wire story pointed out that Jose Burgos, a Filipino student at the University of Cincinnati Technical School, was both a good student and football player for his class team. Proud of the role that U.S. colonialism was playing in the Philippines, the story's writer speculated that Burgos was the only Filipino competing in football in the United States. It all seemed to prove "how quickly the inhabitants of our Asiatic islands may become animated with the progressive spirit of American ways and institutions." Indeed, Burgos was most likely part of the *pensionado* program implemented in the early 1900s to show off U.S. benevolence in the Philippines as a bitter war between anti-imperialist Filipino forces and U.S. colonizers wound down. Thus, while some European American mainlanders may have felt threatened by Asian athletic accomplishments, others saw those accomplishments as positive reflections on a nation carrying the "white man's burden" abroad.[3]

In 1916, a wire story reported that Rensselaer Poly's frosh squad played a quarterback named Pao Shun Kwan, "formerly of Shanghai." Described as a "scrappy Chink," the athlete had done well enough to suggest that he would go on to play with the varsity: "The young Chinaman is fast on his feet, uses good judgment in running the team, and his 'celestial smile' always looms up somewhere in the thick of the scrap." The next year Kwan was indeed a varsity quarterback, inspiring one sportswriter to name him to an All-American team of players possessing foreign sounding names in addition to famed African American Paul Robeson and a Native American standout from Carlisle. The journalist insisted, "They're all playing formal football and mighty good football, and they're all Americans too." In any event, Kwan could not escape Orientalism as he was called a "clever little Chinese quarterback" by the *Albany Evening Journal* in May 1918.[4]

In Berkeley, Son Kai Kee joined the University of California squad during World War I. Kai Kee's appearance on Cal's frosh team inspired national attention. The *Seattle Times* reported that the Cal frosh team had beaten the University of Nevada and "Kaikee, California's left end and, said to be the only Chinese football player in America, was the star of the game." Readers of the *Des Moines Daily News*, furthermore, learned "[t]he yellow peril bobbed up again. There's a Chinese player on the California university football team." The wire story pointed out that Son Kai Kee's performance on Cal's freshman squad convinced observers that he was a "comer" and had transformed him into a "new idol" on campus. Portraying Kai Kee as "an American Chinese student," the wire story asserted he won the starting quarterback position by combining intelligence and athleticism. Seemingly, he had a future with the Cal varsity.[5]

As he ventured into varsity football, press coverage of Kai Kee blended a heavy dose of Orientalism with concerns over whether academic problems would keep him off the gridiron. Showing up for the travails of varsity football in August 1917, "Kai Kee, the Chinese player" impressed the *Oakland Tribune*. The daily purported that "the little fellow" could be valuable for Cal if he got through his studies. A couple of months later, a wire story reported that "Kai Kee, the Chinese football player, has failed to make the team because of poor studies." It added, "He should worry, think of the money he can make in the laundry business." In January 1918, the *Oakland Tribune* proclaimed, "[g]ood news for the Chinese colony." Son Kai Kee, "the slippery little pigskin warrior" would be eligible for football in the fall since he had negotiated a deal with the faculty that if his grades improved after considerable slippage he could rejoin the Cal team. The *Tribune* asserted that the Bay Area Chinese community supported Kai Kee and that "young China will get out and root" for Cal.[6]

In the fall of 1918, Kai Kee joined the varsity, although it is not clear how much he really played. Early in the season, the *San Francisco Chronicle*'s Ed Hughes noted, "Ki-Kee [sic] . . . is rather light, but he is fast, and will be given every chance to show what he can do." Herbert Hawes of the *Oakland Tribune* reported that Kai Kee "is as fast as lightning and not very easy to tackle." When Cal beat St. Mary's, Kai Kee was listed as a Bear sub but did not get into the game even though his team won easily, 40–14. In early December 1918, the *Washington Times* published two adjacent photos of Kai Kee. One showed him standing in his uniform and described as "husky on gridiron." However, a close-up of the smiling Californian depicted him as "childlike and bland." After the 1918 football season, the *Grand Rapids Tribune* printed an Orientalist-tinged story purporting that even though China was weak internationally, at least Son Kai Kee held up his end for Cal: "The only celestial who has ever played on a big college team, Sammy Kee has added some ways that are dark and tricks that are vain to pigskin lore—to the glory of his varsity and the delight of the bleachers."[7]

College football in the 1920s witnessed the emergence of a couple of very good Nikkei gridders. Taro Kishi and Art Matsu, moreover, played in regions of the United States not known for historically possessing an abundance of Asian Americans. In so doing, they excelled; Kishi for Texas A&M and Matsu for William and Mary in Virginia. While Kishi did not seemingly provoke much more than insulting language from the press, Matsu apparently aroused some racial anxiety.

In 1965, the *Dallas Morning News*' Francis Tolbert introduced Taro Kishi to his readers as a sixty-two-year-old rice farmer and son of a man who founded a "Japanese colony" in Texas's Orange County in the eastern part of the state. Dubbed "Terrible Togo" in the story's title, Kishi reportedly possessed a paternal grandfather who was a large landowner in northern Japan. As a child, he was scalded by boiling water and the doctor treating him prescribed a "vitamin- and protein-rich" diet that turned him from an undersized boy to a 160-pound halfback. Journalist Joe Michael Feist maintains that it was a miracle that Kishi wound up as a college gridder.[8]

Kishi was a productive, although often injured, running back for Texas A&M. After his frosh year in 1922, a reporter for a local newspaper proclaimed Kishi the first person of his ethnic background to play in the Southwestern Conference. The reporter described him as the star of the frosh squad, adding that the halfback was "an artful dodger and exceptionally fast." When a junior on the varsity, Kishi's A&M squad tied Southern Methodist University (SMU) in 1924. The Nisei, according to sportswriter William R. Ruggles, displayed "offensive flashes." Also in 1924, Kishi, christened the "Terrible Jap" in the press, caught a touchdown pass against Baylor and returned a punt for a touchdown against Texas Christian (TCU). The next season Kishi was hurt early in A&M's football campaign. One small town Texas newspaper bemoaned the loss of the "brilliant Jap" to A&M. However, in late October, the *Dallas Morning News* exulted in the "Jap Star"'s return. The daily published a photo of Kishi and pronounced A&M supporters happy they would see him on the gridiron again. Referring to Kishi as a "star halfback" and "fast little Jap star," the *Morning News* called him A&M's most brilliant offensive weapon before his injury, adding that he was the "only Jap" to play college football in the Southwest. Kishi did manage to perform well in a game against TCU. In mid-November, Kishi, recovering after reinjuring himself, ran for two touchdowns, one of thirty-nine yards as A&M shut down Rice, 17–0. A Texan sportswriter praised Kishi's "gameness," while the A&M student newspaper claimed he was playing "purely on guts."[9]

That same student publication, called *The Battalion*, sought to honor Kishi as he left varsity college football behind in 1925: "The Southwest Conference will see the passing of the only Jap star that ever donned a uniform in the circuit and also one of the most consistent ground gainers that the Aggies have ever known." Perhaps granting Kishi honorary whiteness, *The Battalion* asserted, "He has made himself one of the fellows, and a truer friend and comrade we have ever known."[10]

Kishi got a degree in agriculture and tried to help his family out during the depression. But after the family lost their farm as many other Texans lost their farms at the time, Kishi got a job in New York City with a Japanese shipping firm. At the outset of U.S. entry in the war, Kishi's father was arrested and detained in Camp Kennedy in Texas. Kishi himself was interrogated at Ellis Island but remained free. After the war, Kishi returned to Texas and took up farming.[11]

Called the "top Nisei star" by the *Pacific Citizen* in 1947, Art Matsu was the son of a Nikkei father and a white mother. Historian Greg Robinson tells us that Matsu was born in Scotland, the native land of his mother, but came to America as a toddler. At Cleveland 's East High School, Benny Friedman, one of the famous college stars of the 1920s, played behind Matsu at quarterback. Unfortunately, the Nikkei seemed to have gotten involved in something of a high school football scandal during his senior year. Described in the *Massillon Evening Independent* as the team's "star quarterback and captain," Matsu was one of five players suspected of breaking training rules.[12]

The scandal did not significantly tarnish Matsu's reputation as he moved on from high school to Virginia's William and Mary University. Playing quarterback in William and Mary's single wing formation, Matsu earned the plaudits of the sporting press. Greg Robinson depicts Matsu as short, even for the 1920s. Still, Matsu was widely recognized as an accurate passer and skilled kicker. He booted eighteen points after touchdowns during his career, as well as three fifty-yard-plus field goals. [13]

During Matsu's first varsity year at William and Mary, his quarterbacking earned praise. In 1924, the *Washington Post* hailed Matsu as the "William and Mary General" and maintained that "fans say [he] has been displaying genius in his field marshaling." In October 1924, the *Post* described Matsu inaccurately as an "American born Japanese." Nevertheless, the quarterback "played a star game" against Syracuse. Remembering Matsu as "the only Japanese ever to be prominent in American football," the *Washington Post* recalled that Matsu's field goal provided the only points scored against a powerful Syracuse eleven. When William and Mary trampled Kings College, 37–0, in November 1924, the *Post* declared that Matsu "outgeneraled" the opposition. [14]

In 1925, Matsu's achievements continued to win him applause. Before the season began, a wire story, entitled "Jap Triple Threat Man," asserted that football observers considered Matsu the best field general in the South Atlantic region. It added that opponents such as the Naval Academy had not been able to figure out Matsu's play calling. Late in the year, a wire story told readers in a headline, "Freak Feat, Jap Scores on Every Major Eleven He Plays Against." Indeed, Matsu, called "the Japanese quarterback" in a November 1925 wire story, earned that distinction when scoring a touchdown against Harvard. The 1926 Syracuse University Yearbook observed that while the school's eleven beat William and Mary the previous fall, it had to grapple with the ability of the "little Jap-Scot" to "play real football." [15]

In his senior year, Matsu continued to corral praise, albeit somewhat tainted by racialism. Before the season began, the *Washington Post* observed that Matsu, now captain of the William and Mary eleven, was a "Japanese star," who arrived at preseason workouts "tanned and hardened from a summer's work as lifeguard at Virginia Beach." Matsu's arrival was motivated, the *Post* declared, by a desire to aid William and Mary's younger gridders. In November 1926, readers of the *Gastonia Daily Gazette* discovered the following headline: "Matsu the Jap Quarter for W.M. a Good Student." The accompanying story offered biographical tidbits. Matsu's Japanese father was a prosperous businessperson, while his mother was "a girl of Scottish descent." The "wiry son of the Orient" grew up in Cleveland, where he not only thrived in football but in swimming and diving as well. At William and Mary, Matsu was "liked from the start" and enjoyed a versatile athletic career, competing in basketball, baseball, and the pole vault for the track and field team. While attending to academics, Matsu reportedly worked as a lifeguard at a Norfolk beach. The five-foot-eleven and 160-pound Matsu was portrayed as a "triple threat," who could pass, run, and kick, as well as a fine field general. While people of Matsu's ancestry had not flourished in American football, Washington and Mary expressed pride that their "Jap captain" was the first person of Japanese descent to gain fame in the sport. At the end of the 1926–1927 academic year, Matsu was chosen the school's football player of the year by William and Mary's yearbook.[16]

Beyond athletics, Matsu seemed relatively well integrated into William and Mary culture. For example, he was a member of both the Cotillion Club and the "13" Club. Nevertheless, Greg Robinson writes that while Matsu was seemingly popular at William and Mary, his presence at the Virginia university sparked fears of interracial fraternization. Consequently, the state legislature passed the Racial Purity Act, which extended Virginia's antimiscegenation law by explicitly forbidding marriages between Asians and whites. It was this act, Robinson points out, which was overturned, with some help from the Japanese American Citizens League, in the famed *Loving v. Virginia* case (1967).[17]

Journalist Jack Powers reinforces the sense of irony Robinson introduced to Matsu's story. Powers asserts, "While interracial marriage was being banned in Virginia, an interracial Art Matsu was being celebrated as a football player. While Matsu's importance to the team was evident, his relatively reassuring biracial appearance may have contributed to the student body's tolerance." Powers, furthermore, cites Professor Francis Tanglao-Aquas, director of Africana Studies at William and Mary as someone intrigued by Matsu's acceptance at the college in the 1920s. Tanglao-Aquas tells Powers:

> In a way, his excellence in sports coupled with good looks prefaced the notion of the model minority syndrome that many Asian Americans (and possibly other people of color) face today. . . . To be precise, yet without taking any of his achievements from him, Art Matsu may have been able to successfully navigate the racist period of American history because he presented an image closer to the likeness of the pervading identity coupled with his extraordinary athletic abilities in sports clearly deemed as 'American.'"[18]

San Diego State accommodated fine Nikkei gridders between the wars. John Yamamoto lettered in varsity football from 1928 through 1930, and younger brother, Paul, did so in 1931 and 1932. The 1930 census data reveals that their Issei father ran a fruit stand in San Diego in 1930. In 1927, John Yamamoto started at quarterback for San Diego State's frosh team. Upon moving up to the varsity, Yamamoto clearly had a future, the *San Diego Evening Tribune* contended. Informing readers that he had performed well on the frosh team, the *Tribune* celebrated Yamamoto's "pair of tricky legs and . . . disconcerting loping motion." Later in 1928, the

Evening Tribune showcased John Yamamoto's speed by calling him the "Yokohama Express." It added that Yamamoto was "one of the greatest halfbacks ever to wear the colors of San Diego State." The "Japanese lad," the *Tribune* explained, proved tough for Whittier to stop in a 1928 game. Unfortunately, the San Diego State yearbook explained, "the flashy ball toter" got hurt during the Whittier game while making a magnificent run and was shelved for the rest of the season. Coincidentally, the yearbook noted, Johnny's brother, Paul, incurred a season-ending injury a week later while a "star guard" for the frosh squad. By the 1930 season, the elder Yamamato had been switched from the backfield to a starting end on the San Diego State team.[19]

Joining the varsity in 1931, Paul Yamamoto switched from guard to quarterback. In November 1931, the *San Diego Evening Tribune* described him as "a diminutive Japanese speedster" and a smart signal caller from his quarterback position. The 1933 San Diego State yearbook tells us that Paul Yamamoto performed well against La Verne in the fall of 1932. Even though San Diego State could only manage a 0–0 tie against Occidental, the yearbook asserted that the "flashy little quarterback guided the team faultlessly." Against Redlands, he suffered an injury but before that, the yearbook asserted, Yamamoto stood out. As had many mainland Nisei, Paul Yamamoto found out that a college education did not translate into a white-collar job. With the help of the 1940 census data, we can find Paul Yamamoto several years later working as a receiving clerk for a wholesale company and living with parents and siblings.[20]

Another pair of Nikkei brothers, George and Lyman Domoto shined for Fresno State. George Domoto played tackle for Fresno State in the late 1920s and early 1930s. After his frosh year in 1928, the Fresno State Yearbook praised his work as a lineman. The 1932 Fresno State yearbook extolled Domoto's performance for the varsity against Chico State and lamented that he had been injured for much of the 1931 season. A decade after George Domoto ceased playing for Fresno State, he made news again when it became known that his white wife had chosen to relocate with him to a concentration camp. Five years earlier Domoto and his fiancée Rebecca Christiansen had defied California's antimiscegenation laws by getting married in Tijuana, Mexico. They had originally met as students at Fresno State, and the *Fresno Bee* reported that friends and relatives were generally supportive of their marriage. The *Bee* further reported that the couple intended to go to Hawai'i and work as teachers. In the meantime, Domoto was working as a "nurseryman." In the mid-1930s, brother Lyman competed for Fresno State as a 168-pound guard. Like his older brother, Lyman was good. In 1936, the Hardin-Simmons football team named him on its second team all-opponents squad. After the 1937 season, Domoto made second team all-conference.[21]

Few mainland Asian American athletes, indeed, few American athletes in general, could match Bill Kajikawa's accomplishments in Arizona during the 1930s and beyond. Born in Oxnard, California, he spent much of his youth in the Golden State. In the 1920s, Kajikawa's family moved to Phoenix, where he worked in agriculture while excelling as a true scholar-athlete in high school. His Phoenix High School yearbook described him as a member of the Lettermen's Club in 1933, as well as Vice-President of the Boys' Federation and Home Room President who lettered in football, basketball, and baseball. Moreover, he made all-state twice in football. Kajikawa remembered, "Sports was a great vehicle for me because I could meet people and fit in. . . . I was the first Japanese-American to play sports at Phoenix Union, and I enjoyed it."[22]

In the mid-1930s, he played superbly for Arizona State Teacher's College, which eventuated into Arizona State University. When Arizona State ventured into San Diego for a game in 1934, the *San Diego Union* published a photograph of Kajikawa and hailed him as the "speediest" back on the squad and as "shifty as they come." The Spanish language *Continental* in Texas proclaimed in October 1935 that "Bill Kajikawa japonese del collegio de Tempe" starred against New Mexico Agriculture. In November 1935, the *Albuquerque Journal* called Kajikawa "the highly publicized Japanese backfield star." Later in November, Kajikawa's team beat Texas Mines, 14–10. According to a published account of the game, "Kajikawa, diminutive Japanese quarterback" went on a thirty-seven-yard jaunt for a touchdown. At the end of the 1935 season, Kajikawa was honorable mention all-conference. The following season, Kajikawa threw a fifty-yard touchdown pass in a losing effort against New Mexico. The next week, the *Arizona Republic* praised Kajikawa as the "brilliant Japanese back" as he starred in a winning game against Texas Mines. By the time Kajikawa's college football career had ended, George Moore of the *Arizona Republic* summed him up as "the outstanding Japanese footballer in the United States." Moore added, "Lacking in size—his peak weight was 145 pounds—he relied upon shiftiness and skill to roll up substantial yardage. He has powerful legs and could punch a line as much as heavier men." As we will explore later, Kajikawa enjoyed a successful coaching career at his alma mater.[23]

A standout from Santa Ana Junior College, Hideo Higashi played for San Diego State in the mid-1930s. The 1920 U.S. census data tell us that Higashi's parents were Issei and his father ran a pool hall in Santa Ana. In 1935, Higashi shined in a victory over La Verne. "The Japanese halfback," the *Los Angeles Times* reported, plunged for a one-yard touchdown after catching a pass to set up his own score. Moreover, he kicked conversions for San Diego State. After starring for San Diego State in 1935, Higashi dropped out of school. *The Los Angeles Times'* Charles Curtis reported that San Diego State mourned Higashi's loss as "the Japanese veteran was the most versatile" on the team. On top of that, he had broken up a well-publicized "United Nations" backfield of "Mexican" Frank Galindo, "Indian" Allen Locke, and "German" Art Metzgar. Happily, Higashi returned to the school and its varsity football team for the 1937 season. He proved key in San Diego State's crusade for a conference championship in 1937. Against Whittier, Higashi tossed a fifty-yard touchdown pass. He scored a touchdown against New Mexico and stood out as a ball carrier and punter against Santa Barbara State, a game which prompted the school yearbook to laud his punts averaging forty yards. Acclaimed as "the Japanese jackrabbit" by the 1938 yearbook, Higashi made second team all-conference.[24]

In Orange County Dick Kunishima was a quarterback at Whittier College. Called "a Los Angeles boy" by the *Los Angeles Times*, the newspaper displayed a photo of Kunishima doing barefoot kicking for Whittier in 1935. The caption described him as a "clever Japanese quarterback." Kunishima kicked three field goals when Whittier lost to Fullerton Junior College, 13–9, in 1935. In 1937, the *Times* hailed "the 140-pound Japanese quarterback" as integral to the Poets offense. While raised in Southern California, Kunishima was, according to the U.S. census data of 1940, born in Hawai'i. In 1940 he was driving a truck for a produce company in Los Angeles.[25]

The former Brawley High School great, Hank Sasaki joined USC's frosh squad as a quarterback in 1936. The school's yearbook dubbed him the "oriental flash." Indeed, his performance as a frosh elevated him above future Trojan great Doyle Nave as starting quarterback. Consequently, the *Oakland Tribune* labeled Sasaki the "160-pound Japanese star." Before the 1937 season started, the *Los Angeles Times'* Braven Dyer asserted, "the little Japanese flash Sasaki" was competing for a quarterback job for the Trojans' varsity team. Subsequently, Dyer informed readers that Sasaki was a very accurate kicker, claiming he "kicks the ball as straight as most chaps can throw it." When USC took on Cal, the *Oakland Tribune* listed him as a varsity member, wearing jersey number 55 and playing quarterback, but he did not seemingly play much, if at all. He got more action on the junior varsity squad called the Spartans. The *Fresno Bee* noted in September 1937 that the "Nipponese" quarterbacked the Spartans and was the fastest player on the squad. The *Santa Ana Register* reported during August 1938 that like many Trojan varsity players, he was working hard during the summer. In Sasaki's case, he was laboring in a packing house in the Imperial Valley. In any event, Sasaki's did not appear again in a Trojan uniform nor would he ever.[26]

Perhaps Sasaki's college football life would have been more enduring had he entered nearby San Diego State rather than trek up to Los Angeles and USC. Indeed, Nikkei George Kita enjoyed a good football career at San Diego State before EO 9066, Franklin D. Roosevelt's executive order which set the stage for Japanese American internment. In the fall of 1938, Kita was named the frosh MVP. In 1939, the San Diego State's 1940 yearbook pointed out, Kita played an inspired game as a running guard against Santa Barbara State, as well as starring against Whittier. When

San Diego State took on San Jose State in the fall of 1940, Kita was listed as the starting quarterback. Some days later, Kita performed well in a triumphant game against Redlands, carrying the ball for twenty yards in one play. After Pearl Harbor was attacked, Kita's parents, who owned a market in Calexico, were arrested for breaking curfew. Kita had to make a long hard drive of over one hundred miles from San Diego to take care of his siblings.[27]

During the war, Kita could leave camp to enroll at Drake University in Iowa. There, he continued to excel on the gridiron. The *Poston Chronicle* reported that former inmate Kita was doing well at Drake. Scot Rawley, a newly hired project director at Poston, had taught pre-law to Kita at Drake. Rawley stressed that Kita was an excellent student and was liked and respected by other students. He also maintained that another teacher at Drake claimed he hated Japanese until he met Kita. As for football, Rawley asserted that Kita's coach considered him one of the hardest blockers he had ever seen. Kita's versatility on offense and defense proved handy to Drake. Kita was used as a 165-pound starting guard during the fall of 1943. In October 1944, the *Manzanar Free Press* reported to inmates that Kita had been moved to fullback by Drake because of his blocking ability and that it was widely believed he was the lightest full-back in college football. It not only praised the San Diegan as a "heavy-duty blocking ace" but also his defensive work as a linebacker. Kita, moreover, did more than block on offense. When Drake edged Wichita 13–12 in November 1944, he plunged over the goal line for a touchdown. Indeed, Kita proved good enough at Drake to get drafted in 1945 by the New York Giants of the NFL. A wire story speculated that he would become one of the lightest players in the NFL. Kita never made a career as an NFL player. Instead, he became an attorney in Chicago after the war. In the early 2000s, Kita was named to the Imperial Valley Football Hall of Fame.[28]

In Northern California, Mits Nitta captained the Cal Aggies football team out of Davis in the late 1930s. More than that, he made the all-conference team as an end. In 1939, Nitta stunned the crowd at Cal Berkeley's Memorial Stadium when he led the Davis contingent to a brief 14–12 lead over the heavily favorite Bears. Nitta accounted for both touch-downs for the Aggies by blocking two Bear punts and running the loose ball into the end zone not once but twice. Nitta was not the first Japanese American Cal Aggie to take on the Cal Bears. In 1932, Norman Oda played for the Davis eleven when it visited Berkeley. As a boy, Oda grew up watching Cal Bear football. He later remembered "I used to dream that, boy, if I could only be, you know, when I get big, I was dreaming that one of these days I hope I could come through that tunnel." When he appeared in Memorial Stadium as a member of the Cal Aggie squad on September 17, 1932, Oda recalled "tears were coming out of my eyes" as he entered the stadium. Yoshio Oda donned a Cal Aggie varsity uniform from 1931 through 1933.[29]

To the north, a couple of Japanese Americans played at least first year football for the University of Washington in 1935—Ray Nakagawa and Harry Yanagamichi. Syndicated sports columnist Dick Ramey reported early in 1936 that "a Japanese player"—Harry Yanagamichi—was expected to perform as a center for the Husky varsity. Yanagamichi did not make the varsity. Subsequently, journalist Bill Hokosawa expressed astonishment, hinting that more than size and skill was the determining factor. To Hosokawa, the former Garfield standout was big enough and good enough to help the Husky line. Ray Nakagawa later remembered that he and Harry Yanagamichi were cut because they could not make the "first team." He subsequently left school to work on a sawmill, but decided to give college and college football another try by attending Washington State. He claimed that Washington State's coach assured him of a varsity position, but he quit college when his father died and he felt he needed to support his family.[30]

Not all Asian American gridders were Nikkei in the decade before World War II. In the mid-1930s, Ed Yee performed for San Francisco State as an end. The school's 1935 yearbook pointed out that "Ed Yee, flashy Gator half, pulls off most spectacular play of the season" by running back an interception for a ninety-seven-yard touchdown. A few years later, Dick Chin emerged as the "Chinese sensation" according to the *San Francisco Chronicle* in the fall of 1941. After playing on the Gator varsity in 1940, Chin was, the *San Francisco Examiner* explained, a "package of dynamite, a 130-pound Chinese firecracker" extolled by his coach as "one of the best passers to ever throw a ball for the Gators." Even though his team did not score against the Mather Air Field team in a 0–0 tie, Chin's play was lauded by the *Chronicle.* When San Francisco State took on San Francisco Junior College in 1941, Chin hurled a touchdown pass.[31]

During the 1939 season, "a Chinese lad Marshall Leong is sparkling at fullback" for the St. Mary's freshman team, according to sports columnist Eddie Breitz. The next year, a wire story notified readers that the former Commerce High star had bypassed varsity football to get a job. Noted *San Francisco Examiner* sports columnist Prescott Sullivan observed in early September 1940 that "Leong, giant Chinese fullback, who was to have been [coach] Slip Madigan's ace ballyhooed medium for the Fordham game . . . has asked for credentials needed to transfer to San Francisco Junior College." A few years later, Leong was playing for the Coast Guard Sea Lions.[32]

NISEI GRIDDERS AND WORLD WAR II

Jack Yoshihara played big-time college football for Oregon State in 1941 as the Corvallis eleven journeyed toward a Pacific Coast Conference championship and a Rose Bowl appearance. Yoshihara claimed later in his life that his mother was a picture bride who came to the United States to live with an abusive husband. Pregnant, she went back to Japan, where Jack was born, but returned to the United States just before American immigration laws made it nearly impossible for Nikkei to enter the country after the mid-1920s. In the United States, she remarried, and the couple ran a restaurant in Portland.[33]

An end for Oregon State, Yoshihara recalled that he lingered on the "scout team" rather than getting much action in real games. One of his teammates, George Zellick, remembered things differently. "Jack was a really good athlete. . . . He was fast and tough. He's just being modest." In mid-December, Oregon State was preparing for the Rose Bowl, which was to take place in Durham, North Carolina because its customary venue in Pasadena was deemed too dangerous due to wartime conditions. Zellick recollected, "It was late afternoon. It was drizzling. We noticed two men coming onto the field. They were very well-dressed, wearing overcoats and hats. You could tell they were different people. They met with the coach and, the next thing we knew, Jack left with them. It was the first indication that Jack had a problem." Yoshihara would, accordingly, not make the trek to Durham with the rest of his team. Teammate James Busch testified in the early 2000s, "Nobody felt that Jack was a subversive threat. He was an American. My heritage was German. Nobody discriminated against me."[34]

After Executive Order 9066 was issued, Yoshihara was taken to an assembly center and then the Minidoka camp, where the *Minidoka Irrigator* described him as a "place kicking artist." In an interview with a *Los Angeles Times* reporter, Yoshihara remembered the conditions he and other Japanese Americans experienced at the assembly centers and the camps. At the former, "The wood floors were really dirty and the big mistake we made was hosing them down. All the animal manure underneath came though the floors." Subsequently, Yoshihara and his family were interned at Minidoka, where the temperature ranged from 21 degrees below zero to 104 degrees. He recalled, "They just had barracks, with wood siding and a tar roof," Yoshihara said. "We could see the dust come through the walls when the wind blew. And it always blew."[35]

Yoshihara was fortunately released from Minidoka so that he could attend Utah University. Before the 1943 season began, Utah's coach praised the Oregonian as one of the most promising players on the team. A key member of Utah's backfield, Yoshihara did not disappoint. In a month, the *Salt Lake Tribune* called him one of Utah's "chief backfield threats." The *Tribune* also published a photo of Yoshihara carrying the ball against the University of Nevada. Although Utah lost the game, 27–9, the *Tribune* commended Yoshihara as "one of the backfield standouts in the Utah defeat." After World War II, Yoshihara returned to Oregon and worked as a lab technician at Multnomah Junior College. Before he died, he and other Japanese Americans who attended Oregon State before their education was interrupted were given honorary degrees by the school.[36]

While Yoshihara was at Oregon State, Los Angeles–born and –raised Chet Maeda was fortunately attending Colorado State, outside the impact of Executive Order 9066. In 1941, the *Helena Independent* described Maeda as a six-foot Hawaiian. Perhaps Colorado State promoted their fine back as Hawaiian to avoid any concerns about him as anti-Japanese fears mounted in the few months before Pearl Harbor was attacked. And perhaps the people in charge of athletic publicity at the school did not know any better. In any event, the *Independent* informed readers that Maeda had led the Rams to an upset victory over Colorado Mines in late September 1941. A couple of months later, Maeda guided Colorado State to a key victory over Brigham Young University (BYU). The *Salt Lake Tribune's* Bill Coltrin enthused, "Chet Maeda . . . gave about as flashy a performance as ever seen at the 'Y' Stadium. [Maeda] ran and passed the Cougars dizzy, dancing through holes in the forward wall and hitting his receivers right on the button with his passing."[37]

The 1920 U.S. census data discloses that Maeda came from a racially mixed background. His father was a Japanese immigrant, who owned a florist shop in Los Angeles, and his mother was white. Since interracial marriages were banned in California, the couple probably married out of state. Ten years later, Maeda's mother operated the florist shop on her own.[38]

Maeda would have a fine 1942 season. It was perhaps little for Maeda to boast about, but before the 1942 season, Red Grange, who became a broadcast and print analyst after a legendary football career in the 1920s and 1930s, branded Maeda as "more than adequate." As it turned out, he proved much "more than adequate." When Utah downed Colorado State easily, 33–14, Maeda's passing was credited for keeping his team from suffering even further. Early in November, Maeda led Colorado State to a 25–0 whitewashing of Utah State. The *Pacific Citizen* boasted that Maeda was an "Irish-Japanese halfback," who earned all-conference honors at the end of the 1942 season. The school's 1943 yearbook praised Maeda, calling the all-conference back a "serious student" and "very much the gentleman." Described as "one of the most popular men on campus," Maeda apparently evaded American society's fears of interracial romance as he also was "known as a charmer of ladies."[39]

A couple of New Years after Yoshihara failed to show up at the Rose Bowl, Joe Nagata was starting quarterback for Louisiana State (LSU) as it took on Texas A&M in Miami's Orange Bowl. Evidence of the intriguing, liminal experiences of people of Asian ancestry in the South, Nagata was a son of a Japanese immigrant father and an Irish American mother. After living in Alabama, Nagata's parents settled amid "Cajun Country"—Eunice, Louisiana, where they operated a fruit stand. After Pearl Harbor was attacked, Joseph's father was briefly held by the FBI before released. A football star at Eunice High in 1941, Nagata was recruited by LSU.[40]

Nagata had some outstanding moments for LSU while apparently accepted as a student-athlete at the Baton Rouge school. In 1942, he was called one of the better frosh gridders in the nation at a time when wartime conditions permitted college teams to field first-year students while upperclass gridders disappeared into the service. When LSU downed Fordham at New York City's famed Polo Grounds in the fall of 1942, Nagata nabbed a thirty-nine-yard touchdown pass. The next football season, readers of the *Dallas Morning News* learned that Nagata was a 165-pound "letterman wingman" for LSU. The *Morning News* also called Nagata a "talented" athlete who had done some "brilliant" ball carrying for the Tigers.[41]

The *Poston Chronicle* expressed pride in the "handsome" gridder's accomplishments. In October 1943, the camp newspaper told readers that Nagata was the only Japanese American to hold down a regular starting job in the South. The *Chronicle* paid tribute to his performance against Georgia, claiming that LSU fans cheered him on by yelling, "Come on you little Jap. . . . We've got money on you." It reported that he returned a punt sixty yards, ran the ball three times, gaining 5.3 yards per carry, and punted for a forty-one-yard average. On defense, Nagata was responsible for one quarter of LSU's tackles. He made a key interception to stifle a Georgia rally and was eventually carried off the field in triumph.[42]

After helping LSU get into the Orange Bowl, Nagata discovered himself shadowed by the suspicions raised by World War II. Veteran Southern sportswriter, Furman Bisher, recalled that the "Japanese quarterback" named "Nogato" needed Secret Service operatives to protect him at the game. Yet despite what must have been a humiliating experience, Nagata left LSU and served in the 442nd. After winning the Bronze Star and seven other medals, Nagata returned to LSU but in an apparently diminished role in the years after V-J day.[43]

Because he lived out of the war zone established by E.O. 9066, Nagata did not have to worry that much about internment. Likewise, Jim Yagi was a guard for Utah University, and Jim Kishi performed as a tackle for the University of Texas in 1943. According to one wire story, Kishi had previously played for Texas A&M. Moreover, while West Coast Japanese Americans faced internment, some young people, like Jack Yoshihara and George Kita, were afforded the opportunity to live, work, and attend school elsewhere on the mainland. Accordingly, Albert Nakazawa suited up for Valparaiso College of Indiana, while Bright Onodo, hailing from Washington, played football for little Hillsdale College in Michigan. Min Sano, a former Berkeley resident interned at Topaz, played for the University of Denver. The school's 1944 yearbook showed him on the bench with teammates, wearing number 4 on his jersey. Meanwhile, a Korean American from Southern California, Sam Kim, suited up as a lineman for the University of San Francisco. [44]

THE POST-WAR YEARS

Cal's George Fong put together a respectable college grid career in the years right after World War II. Fong entered Cal in 1942. At that time, he started at quarterback for the frosh squad. After a couple of years in the service, Fong returned to the Cal campus and a three-year hitch on the Bear varsity. In the fall of 1945, Braven Dyer of the *Los Angeles Times* noted that Cal's coach, Buck Shaw, had "two Chinese players" — cousins Dick and George Fong. Attempting humor, Dyer added, "When all the tongs of the Fong crowd Berkeley Stadium Buck expects the place to be sold out." Dick wound up playing for the Ramblers, the junior varsity squad; but George proved instrumental to the Cal's varsity success over the next three seasons. In 1945, he often started as a sophomore at half-back for Shaw, who would depart Cal for the then novice professional San Francisco 49ers team in 1946. When Cal downed Washington in early October 1945, George Varnell of the *Seattle Times* called him the "fine Chinese halfback" as he helped lead the Bears to victory. In early November, readers of a small-town Pennsylvania newspaper discovered a wire photo of George Fong in action. Captioned "California Chinese Football Star," the text explained that Fong gave Cal an "asiatic touch" but had scored his share of touchdowns. [45]

In subsequent years, Fong lost time out on the field to the great Jackie Jensen and other, perhaps more talented, Bear backs, but he usually played quite a bit for Shaw's successors, Frank Winkhorst and Lynn "Pappy" Waldorf. The *Oakland Tribune* praised Fong's work on defense against UCLA in October 1946. In mid-November 1946, the Bears lost to Oregon State, but Winkhorst hailed Fong's play during the game. Indeed, Winkhorst named Fong to Cal's starting lineup as the Bears took on Stanford in the venerable Big Game, thus making him the first Chinese American to start in the rivalry. A critic of Cal's coach, the *San Francisco Examiner*'s Prescott Sullivan was not impressed with Cal's losing effort against Stanford. He told his readers that Winkhorst promised fans something new in the Big Game, but nothing novel happened to deter Cal from defeat "unless you count the appearance of George Fong in California's starting backfield as 'new.' It was an innovation of sorts. During World War I, California had a Chinese-American back named Sam Kai-Kee. But until last Saturday none had started the Big Game." At season's end, Fong was honored as "the most courageous and inspirational member of the [1946] squad." [46]

Fong's 1947 season proved memorable. When Cal beat Santa Clara in 1947, the respected *Washington Post* sports columnist, Shirley Povich, observed that "it was the sweep running of George Fong, Chinese halfback" that helped the Bears beat their South Bay neighbors. More locally, the *San Jose Mercury*'s Fred Merrick pointed out the stirring performance of Fong, scoring on a forty-yard touchdown and making two twenty-two yard jaunts against Santa Clara. Fong, Merrick reminded readers, was "the only Chinese player in major college football." The next month, Fong scored on a two-yard touchdown against Wisconsin. In mid-November 1947, Robert Prescott of the *San Jose Mercury* wrote that the "big Chinese-American back" made a thirteen-yard touchdown run against Montana. Writing for the *Sporting News* in 1947, Rube Samuelson reported that Cal could boast of "George Fong, a Chinese who is very remarkable." Cal's 1948 yearbook declared that Fong "can only be described as a player and teammate as terrific."[47]

World War II and the emerging Cold War encouraged tributes to racial democracy as a way of displaying social progress and race-free meritocracy under American capitalism. Decades of over anti-Asian politics were often, in the process, conveniently downplayed by the mainstream media. Thus, *San Francisco Chronicle* sportswriters linked Fong to San Francisco's Chinese community and the city's presumed transcendence of racial bias. The occasion was Pappy Waldorf's intention of naming Fong captain for the Bears' intersectional contest with the Naval Academy. Columnist Will Connolly alluded to Fong's high school and San Francisco's Chinatown primary street, when he asserted, "Poly High and Grant Avenue should be proud of Fong." In celebrating Waldorf's decision to honor Fong, Connolly ignored the Bay Area's anti-Chinese history and wrote that Fong's captaincy "could only happen in this cosmopolitan community." As far as Connolly was concerned: "The rest of the country considers a Chinese an exotic creature, but in this town and environs U.S. citizens of Chinese ancestry are accepted as one of the boys." Connolly's *Chronicle* colleague, Bill Leiser, also congratulated his readers for their unique lack of bigotry and maintained that "it's a given fact that this is the first-time Midshipmen have ever played against a team captained by a real Chinese."[48]

After his Cal days ceased, at least one Bay Area newspaper speculated that Fong might take on pro football. In 1948, readers of the *San Francisco Examiner* learned that the San Francisco 49ers were mulling over making an offer for Fong. If the 49ers did so, the *Examiner* added, "they'll have the only Chinese and Japanese twosome in pro football: Wally Yonamine is the Nipponese scooter." We will examine Yonamine's stint with the 49ers in a future chapter.[49]

Five-feet-eight and 153 pounds, the versatile Frank Miyaki played for Washington State in the months after Hiroshima and Nagasaki were devastated. Before the 1945 season began, Sandy McDonald of the *Seattle*

Times described Miyaki as a "scooter back," who would be used in spot situations. Early in the 1945 season, Miyaki scored on an eleven-yard touchdown run against Idaho. In October 1945, Miyaki came off the bench in a game against Oregon State to make a key interception, running the ball back for forty-five yards before getting tackled near the goal line. A year later, Miyaki was in the military. While serving in Europe, Miyaki made a touchdown as his Army General Headquarters humbled the Ninth Corps, 48–0. Indeed, in the spring of 1950, Miyaki was still serving in the military, and, in the process, earned the plaudits of the *Pacific Citizen*, which lauded him as the best all-around athlete among U.S. military personnel in the Far East. Miyaki apparently stood out not only in football, but in basketball and baseball as well.[50]

Playing with his brother, Tad, Babe Nomura began to attract press attention as a "lightweight" star at Hollywood High School in 1940. The 1940 U.S. Census manuscripts tell us that Babe Nomura's Issei father was a gardener, while his Issei wife kept a lodging house with the help of her older, Nisei children. After leaving Wyoming's Heart Mountain camp, Babe Nomura returned home to Los Angeles, where he not only played for Los Angeles City College but threw fifteen touchdown passes in 1945. Against Pasadena Junior College, Nomura chucked three touchdown passes, while also returning a punt for a forty-five-yard touchdown.[51]

Although only a junior college star, the national press spotlighted Nomura shortly after the war ended. In a wire story written by Bill Becker, Tomatsu 'Babe' Nomura was lauded as a "terrific halfback" for Los Angeles City College. Becker informed readers that the former Heart Mountain inmate was the most popular player on his team and had led his eleven as co-captain. Described as personable but shy, Nomura declared he was glad to be back in Los Angeles where his parents now ran a hotel. Prior to coming back to California, according to Becker, he had done a stint in Chicago as a defense worker since a slight knee injury had caused the military to tag him as 4-F. Upon his reappearance in Southern California gridiron battles, Nomura asserted he stood out as a "marked man" in every game. His coach, meanwhile, called him the most deliberate passer he had ever seen. Nomura, apparently, would not get rid of the ball unless he knew a receiver was in the open.[52]

The next fall Nomura headed up the coast to San Jose State College. Nearby, the *San Francisco Chronicle*'s Bill Leiser expected him to stand out. Like Leiser, the *San Jose Mercury*'s Louis Duino was impressed with Nomura's potential contribution to San Jose State's football fortunes, writing that the Angeleno was a "shifty runner and a good defensive man." Nomura generally played up to expectations. Late in September 1946, San Jose State clobbered Willamette, 44–6, and Nomura scored a touchdown. In early October, Hardin-Simmons thrashed the Spartans, but Nomura managed to make the only touchdown for the losers. In the first half of the San Jose State's game against the Hawaiian All-Stars

Nomura was "a whirling dervish." A few weeks later, Nomura's coach Bob Bronzan said the Japanese American "stole the show" when the Spartans beat Idaho. Harry Borba, a *San Francisco Examiner* sportswriter, labeled Nomura as a "tricky Japanese-American back." In mid-November, Clark Mallory, who did public relations for the Spartans, extolled "San Jose's Japanese-American halfback," declaring he could star on any team on the Coast. A week later, Nomura did well against Fresno State. The "Japanese American back" returned a punt for fifty-five yards and then lateraled the ball to another Spartan who carried it further into Fresno State territory, setting San Jose State up for its first touchdown. Indeed, as the 1946 campaign drew to a close, Nomura was named to the all-conference team. On January 1, 1947, Nomura starred for San Jose State when it shutout Utah State in the Raisin Bowl.[53]

The 1947 season proved something of a down year for Nomura. Before it started, the *Pacific Citizen* reported that San Jose State's new coach Bill Hubbard was tailoring plays for Nomura to better take advantage of his passing skills. The previous year "the Nisei" had concentrated on ball carrying. To the *San Francisco Chronicle*, Nomura was "a very fast and shifty runner," but also "a good passer." The *San Francisco Examiner*, depicted him as an "elusive Japanese pass throwing left half." The *San Jose News"* Frank Bonnano extolled Nomura as "the best all-around Spartan back." As the season began, Nomura played good defense and got off some good gains as a ball carrier in San Jose State's defeat by USF. In October, Nomura scored a touchdown against Puget Sound. A week later, he had a good game against Santa Barbara State. But for reasons that remain a mystery Hubbard did not seem to use Nomura as much as other backs during the 1947 season.[54]

Fibber Hirayama was a versatile athlete who starred in both football and baseball for Fresno State in the late 1940s and early 1950s. After the 1949 season, the Fresno State yearbook showed a photograph of Hirayama as he "scoots through the [Pepperdine] Wave line." In 1950, Fresno State scored only one touchdown against San Jose State—a pass thrown by Hirayama to receiver Chuck Toy. Against UH, Hirayama ran the ball for an eighteen-yard touchdown. A year later, he caught the eye of a *Dallas Morning News* reporter who described Hirayama as a "145 pound scatback" and a "break-away threat" for Fresno State before a game against North Texas State. At the end of the 1951 season, Hirayama, dubbed "Fresno's brilliant 140-pound scatback" by the *Fresno Bee*, earned Honorable Mention all-league honors. Moreover, Duke Jacobs, Hirayama's Fresno State coach, made an unsuccessful pitch for him to be named to the West All-Stars set to compete in the East-West Shrine game. Jacobs asserted, "For his height and poundage, Hirayama is one of the greatest athletes I've ever coached." He would, Jacobs insisted, give fans a thrill even if he only returned punts. However, the West team was loaded with future Hall of Famer backfield luminaries such as Hugh McElhenny, Ollie Matson, and Frank Gifford. So, there was not much room for Hiraya-ma on the squad.[55]

Other Japanese Americans played relatively big-time football after the war. Ray Mitokawa was a lineman for the University of Arizona. Born in California, Mitokawa's father, according to the U.S. 1940 census sched-ules, was a farmer in Maricopa, Arizona. Playing with Nomura on the Spartans in 1947 was Jake Kikuchi. The *San Jose Mercury* described Kiku-chi as a 190-pound "Japanese American guard" from Los Angeles. When San Jose State beat the Hawaiian All-Stars in 1947, Kikuchi intercepted a pass. The *Mercury*'s Louis Duino bemoaned Kikuchi's loss through an injury to the Spartans. Kikuchi may have been a second stringer but "the stocky Japanese boy is both a good defensive and offensive guard."[56]

Indeed, San Jose State's football program seemed notably willing to recruit talented gridders of Asian and Pacific Islander ancestry during the post-World War II era. In 1951, tackle Jim Kajioka joined the varsity after transferring from Modesto Junior College. Tipping the scale at 250 pounds, San Jose State did not have a uniform big enough for him when he reported. The next year, the *Pacific Citizen* displayed a photograph of Kajioka with another large, but European American, San Jose State tackle. The caption described Kajioka as a 250-pounder from Turlock, California. The 1952 squad included Kajioka, guard Hash Taketa, and center Tom Yagi, a son of a Japanese immigrant father and Tulare, California, truck farmer, according to the 1940 U.S. Census manuscripts. In mid-October 1952, the *San Francisco Chronicle* complemented Yagi's work at defensive linebacker. Playing with Yagi on the 1954 squad was James Nakagawa. In addition, Lincoln Kimura was team trainer in 1954. Kimura, by the way, not only was the Spartan's team trainer for many years but subsequently worked for the San Francisco 49ers in the same capacity. The 1940 U.S. census data tells us that the sixteen-year-old Kimura was the son of Issei parents. His father worked in San Jose as a life insurance agent. In 1954, San Jose State upset neighboring Stanford, beating the Palo Alto squad for the first time in school history. On that team were linemen James Nabeta, Jim Kajioka, James Nakagawa, and Tom Yagi. In 1956, the Spar-tans lost to a John Brodie–led Stanford team, but on the roster was half-back Ken Matsuda. The former did not get a great deal of action for the Spartans, at least on offense. In 1957, Matsuda carried the ball eight times for twenty-seven yards. During the late 1950s and early 1960s, Herb Yamasaki was a fine lineman for San Jose State.[57]

Ken Fujii excelled as a quarterback for the University of Nevada in the mid-1950s. After the 1955 season ended, Sacramento State named him to its All-Opponents contingent. In 1957, Fujii ranked ninth in passing and twentieth in total offense among small college gridders. In early October, Fujii completed eight of fourteen passes and tossed one pass for a touch-down against the Cal Aggies. Nevertheless, he had an off-day against Sacramento State in early November 1957, connecting on only seven of twenty-seven passes as Nevada was shutout 7–0. Despite this off day, Fujii managed to earn honorable mention for the small college All-American squad. [58]

A Filipino American from Southern California, Dick Dagampat proved a solid performer for the Naval Academy in the mid- to late 1950s after a post-high school stint in the marines. The U.S. Census records of 1940 show that the five-year-old Dagampat's father, a barber in Los Angeles, was born in the Philippines and racially categorized as "Polynesian." His mother was born in Hawai'i and was likewise designated as Polynesian. When Navy decisively beat William and Mary in 1956, the sportswriters in attendance named Dagampat the game's outstanding player. Dagampat, among other feats, scored a touchdown in Navy's victory. That same year, he also distinguished himself by scoring Navy's only touchdown in the classic Army/Navy game after toting the ball five times during his team's scoring drive. In October 1957, North Carolina's *Daily Tar Heel* displayed a photo of Dagampat. It referred to him as Navy's "little fullback" and the smallest fullback in the academy's football history. Called the "little Filipino-Hawaiian fullback" by a wire story in January 1958, Dagampat suffered a season-impairing injury in 1957. In 1958, Dagampat captained the Navy team and against William and Mary, he and all-time Navy great Joe Bellino proved instrumental in the victory. [59]

Interestingly, before the 1958 season, a wire story appeared that revealed controversy over Dagampat's ethnic background. During the 1956 season, the print media referred to the fullback as a Hawaiian, which led the Mayor of Los Angeles to complain that Dagampat came from California. Moreover, the Philippines' embassy added that the captain of Navy's football team was actually Filipino. Consequently, the Naval team's press book listed "Dagampat as a Hawaiian—Californian-Filipino." The wire story reported that indeed Dagampat's mother was Hawaiian, while his father, still a barber, was Filipino. [60]

It is hard to say what was going on here. Given Los Angeles's and California's long embrace of boosterism, it is not surprising that the Mayor of Los Angeles would claim a college football stalwart as a home town hero, especially since Dagampat lived and attended school in Los Angeles. Nor is it stunning that the Philippines' government would want bragging rights over a relatively celebrated Filipino descendant, because that is what nations do, developing or developed, brag about accomplished people they claim as their own. However, the Naval Academy's part in all this strikes a curious note. By the time Dagampat entered the school, it, as did the Navy, in general consigned Filipinos to service related occupations. Thus, it might have been reluctant to publicize Dagampat's Filipino heritage and when it agreed to do so, perhaps legitimately identified him as also Californian and Hawaiian. [61]

Statistics do not seem to tell all there is to know about Dagampat's football career at Navy. In 1956, he carried the ball sixty-four times for 296 yards and six touchdowns. In 1957, he carried the ball forty-four times for 168 yards and three touchdowns. And, in his senior year, he gained 182 yards on thirty-nine carries and scored one touchdown. Meanwhile, he was given a berth on *Boys Life* All American team. After graduating, Dagampat served twenty years in the military as a regular Navy officer and then as a Marine. In civilian life, he worked in management for several Southern California corporations. [62]

At 198 pounds and standing six feet, Pete Domoto contributed to Cal's success in the late 1950s. Born in Alameda, Domoto's parents, according to the U.S. census manuscripts of 1940, were living in Berkeley. His father worked as a clerk. After leaving Berkeley High, Domoto captained Cal's frosh team and then played fullback as a sophomore for the Bears, moving in and out of the starting lineup. But he was eventually shifted to guard by coach Pete Elliot. When the switch was made during the spring practice sessions of 1958, assistant coach Dee Andros said Domoto had the "speed, agility, and toughness" to do the job at guard. Andros seemed to have been right. When Cal's great quarterback, Joe Kapp, was named player of the week in college football in 1958, he credited Domoto's line work as a crucial help. The university's yearbook of 1959 praised Domoto's play against the University of Washington the previous fall, calling him a "mainstay for the Bears." Against USC, Domoto set up the Bears' only touchdown with a thirty-three-yard interception. Following the 1958 season, Domoto was named to the second team all-Pacific Coast as a guard and won the Brick Muller Award as the team's most valuable lineman. Entering his last year of eligibility in 1959, the major in physiology was named co-captain. Praised as "an excellent linebacker and a very speedy lineman," by the school's 1960 yearbook, Domoto was named to the 1960 West all-star squad in Honolulu's Hula Bowl, where he made an interception that set up his team's only touchdown. [63]

Fresno State suited up star halfback, Larry Iwasaki in the late 1950s and early 1960s. In 1960, Iwasaki scored a touchdown in the school's upset of COP, 32–7. Consequently, Fresno State awarded Iwasaki a watch "emblematic of the most deserving . . . back." He also won a first team berth on the all-conference team. Iwasaki, subsequently, coached and taught at his high school alma mater. [64]

Tony Yim was an effective running back for Occidental in the late 1950s and early 1960s. In 1958, Yim made second team all-league. In 1959, the *Pasadena Independent* reported that "Yim runs wild" in Occidental's humiliation of Cal Tech, 75–14. He tallied four touchdowns with a "couple of redwood stumps for legs." One touchdown was a twenty-six-yard ramble and the other went for twenty-seven yards. In 1960, his thirty-five-yard run for Occidental cost Redlands a claim to a conference title. After leaving Occidental, Yim was given a tryout by the Los Angeles

Rams. And while he was ultimately cut, the *Redlands Daily Facts* seemed surprised he lingered with the professional team as long as he did. [65]

Other Asian American mainland gridders experienced college football firsthand in the early postwar years. One-time Chaffey Junior College great, Kobe Shoji joined the Pomona College backfield in 1946 after serving in the 442nd Regiment during the war. After graduating, Shoji joined academia, eventually moving to Hawai'i, where he taught botany at UH. His son Dave has been a revered women's volleyball coach at UH and one of his grandchildren, a prominent male volleyball player for Stanford and the U.S. national team. Former Beaverton High School great Jimmy Tsugawa was a halfback for Lewis and Clark in the early 1950s. Playing quarterback and place kicking for Rutgers in the mid-1950s was Japanese American Toshismasha Hosoda. Serving as an assistant coach for Rutgers at the time was another athlete of Japanese ancestry, Art Matsu. A wire story in October 1955, hailed Hosoda's "perfect placements," allowing Rutgers to edge Brown, 14–12. In Southern California, Joe Agapay competed for USC in 1956, carrying the ball four times for twelve yards. On a lower level, former junior college standout Benny Aoki played for Cal Poly. When Cal Poly lost to Redlands in 1956, the *San Fernando County Sun* reported that "[l]ittle Benny Aoki" returned a punt for a sixty-yard touchdown and added the extra point for Cal Poly's only scoring." [66]

Roman Gabriel was the most notable gridder of Asian ancestry to emerge in the middle of the twentieth century. Like many Filipino immigrants in the early twentieth century, Gabriel's father performed itinerant labor throughout the U.S. empire. After working in an Alaskan cannery, he found a job as a railroad company cook in North Carolina where he met Gabriel's white mother. Gabriel was subsequently born in Wilmington, North Carolina. Growing into a young man well over six feet, Gabriel enrolled at North Carolina State. [67]

Roman Gabriel was clearly one of the best quarterbacks in big-time college football during the late 1950s and early 1960s. In his first year of varsity eligibility in 1959, Gabriel gained recognition as a "sophomore sensation," turning into the NCAA's most accurate passer by completing over 60 percent of his 134 attempts. Gabriel's 1959 season earned him an All American honorable mention from noted sportscaster Mel Allen, previewing the 1960 season for *Sport*. Indeed, the junior, according to a *Washington Post* sportswriter, was "a professional prospect who has the talent scouts agog." [68]

Even in losing efforts, Gabriel's passing won plaudits. After North Carolina State fell to Duke, the media raved that Gabriel completed sixteen of thirty passes for 182 yards. Later in 1960, Gabriel and North Carolina State arrived in Los Angeles to take on UCLA. The *Los Angeles Times'* Jamie Curran portrayed Gabriel as "the most publicized backfield star in college football." This may have been an exaggeration, but Gabriel no doubt impressed those choosing year-end All-American teams. He was named a second team All-American by the UPI and a third team All American by the AP.[69]

Gabriel's senior year proved no disappointment. Before it began, sportswriter Fred Russell noted in the *Saturday Evening Post* that Gabriel was the heart and soul of North Carolina State's team. Calling Gabriel "a superb passer," Russell lauded his "instinctive, split second reactions" which, the journalist believed, would render him a first round choice of the pros. In November 1961, the Associated Press named Gabriel its college back of the week. The reason was that against South Carolina State, Gabriel completed seventeen passes in twenty-two attempts for 215 yards. After Gabriel broke two Atlantic Coast Conference records against him, the South Carolina State coach called him the best quarterback he had ever seen. At the end of the 1961 season, Gabriel was the Los Angeles Rams' first draft choice. His statistics, while meager by today's standards, stood out over fifty years ago. He connected on 99 of 186 passes for 937 yards and eight touchdowns. Gabriel also rushed for 196 yards and four touchdowns. In the process, he set Atlantic Coast Conference records for most pass completions and passing accuracy. Thus, Gabriel was unsurprisingly chosen the ACC's player of the year.[70]

In the meantime, the print media occasionally shined a light on Gabriel's ethnic background. Frank Gianelli, sports editor of the *Arizona Republic*, noted Gabriel's toughness and that "Big Gabe is an unusual racial combination of Filipino and German and is one of those 'natural' athletes." Al Abrams, who edited sports for the *Pittsburgh Post-Gazette*, described Gabriel as shy, adding that "[h]e is of Filipino descent."[71]

Much less acclaimed than Gabriel, Seichi Miyano was one of the best passers in small college football while quarterbacking for Whittier College in the early 1960s. Standing only five feet seven, Miyano was hailed by the *Los Angeles Times* as a superb small-college quarterback. Indeed, Miyano ranked eleventh among small college National Association of Intercollegiate Athletics (NAIA) passers in 1961. In mid-October 1961, Miyano tossed two touchdown passes in a 46–10 rout of Cal Western. Against Redlands, Miyano heaved two touchdown passes. Praised in the Whittier yearbook as demonstrating "poise and confidence," Miyano threw a touchdown pass and led his team to an easy victory over Occidental. Nicknamed "the Japanese bandit" by the Whittier yearbook, Miyano proved crucial as Whittier carved out an undefeated season and a league championship. In November 1961, a UPI story publicized Miyano's season. The UPI declared that "[l]ittle Sei Miyano" was the chief reason for Whittier's success, while describing the quarterback as "unique in that he is one of the few American college football players of Japanese ancestry." Miyano, the story maintained, had previously played quarterback in high school and at East Los Angeles Junior College, where he had to suffer through insults about his size. When he got to Whittier, the coach tried to switch him to a defensive back. He told the press he did not mind playing in the defensive backfield, but always wanted to prove he could play quarterback in college. Accordingly, he bulked himself up to throw longer passes and used rollouts so that he would evade taller defensive linemen.[72]

Other western colleges suited up Asian Americans in the 1960s. In the early years of the decade, Eddie Kawano, a halfback from Powell, Wyoming, suited up for Utah. "Little Eddie," as a Salt Lake City sportswriter called him, had once been a high school sprint champ in Wyoming. Described as a "senior sprinter" in 1961, Kawano set up a touchdown with a twenty-five-yard run which help Utah win a game. He also carried the ball for a forty-five-yard jaunt. Hailing from San Bruno, California, John Browne was, according to *Seattle Times'* Georg Meyers in 1963, the only Filipino playing college football. Meyers described Browne as a "stocky halfback" for Washington State. Browne subsequently coached at Santa Maria High in Southern California.[73]

On the East Coast, Stockton's Danny Wong played fullback for the Naval Academy in the mid-1960s. Only five feet six, but a sturdy 196 pounds, Wong was inaccurately described as Navy's "first Chinese football player." In 1964, sports columnist Bob Inghram told readers that Wong was the "only Chinese football player among nation's colleges." Wong proved one of the few bright spots in Navy's lost to Maryland in 1964, lugging the ball nine times for thirty-six yards and catching five passes for forty-eight yards and a touchdown. A wire story in late October 1965, asserted that Wong had lost and then won back his starting position for a game against Notre Dame. Accompanying the wire story was a photo of Wong entitled "Wong is right again." Sports columnist Dick Kelly confided that Maryland assistant Lee Corso believed Wong ran the draw play as well as anyone Maryland's coaching staff had seen. To be sure, Wong was no superstar, but one sportswriter likened him to another great Navy running back, Joe Bellino. Loy Holman declared that "the 194-pound Chinese American [possessed] quick reactions and the ability to make the most of a small hole." The Naval Academy's 1967 yearbook extolled "The Wonger." It claimed, "His ability to think fast on his feet and turn his butterball frame into maximum power soon reserved him a spot on the Varsity football team as fullback." The yearbook also praised Wong's academic record and sense of humor. Wong subsequently served with distinction aboard a nuclear submarine. In 2016, he was named to Stockton's Athletic Hall of Fame.[74]

LATE TWENTIETH- AND EARLY TWENTY-FIRST-CENTURY EXPERIENCES

In the late 1970s, Napoleon Carbonnel started at linebacker for the University of Kansas. What struck Georg Myers of the *Seattle Times* about

Carbonnel was that he possessed Filipino ancestry. Myers asserted that he doubted that Filipinos would succeed Samoans as the next big wave of Asian and Pacific Islanders to hit mainland football teams. Carbonnel agreed, conceding that there were "not many of us" playing college football in the United States. Born on Mindanao, the six-foot two-inch, 225-pounder moved with his family to Illinois as a child.[75]

Around the same time, biracial Bruce Harrell stood out as a linebacker for the University of Washington. Harrell also excelled in the classroom. Part Nikkei, he earned the National Football Foundation Scholar-Athlete award and was honored as a first team Academic All-American. Yet he was also named defensive player of the year for the University of Washington. Rather than chase after an NFL career, Harrell took up law and civic service. He became a Seattle City Council member, running unsuccessfully to become the city's mayor. In 2013, Harrell was named to the Pacific Northwest Football Hall of Fame.[76]

During the late 1970s and early 1980s, a couple of gridders surnamed Wong distinguished themselves on the gridiron. In small-college football, David Wong excelled for Willamette. Also a fine baseball player, who would eventually coach his alma mater's nine, Wong made all-conference and all-NAIA district teams twice as a defensive end. In 1979, he was a NAIA All-American choice. In the early 1980s, San Franciscan Daryl Wong emerged as a quarterback for Dartmouth University. Before heading east, Wong was a three-sport star at Lowell High School. Stanford tried to recruit him, but he chose the Ivy League instead. Dartmouth did not prove a completely happy experience for the Chinese American quarterback. He confided to *East/West* reporter Mark Jue that racial prejudice confined him to the bench for too much of his Dartmouth career. Wong, indeed, only threw five passes in 1980, completing two of them. Still, Wong attracted the attention of the 49ers legendary coach Bill Walsh. Wong signed with the 49ers in 1983, but was subsequently cut. Walsh then recommended Wong to the San Diego Chargers. But he did not make that team either. Still, Wong was a source of pride to the Bay Area's Chinese American community. When Jue asked him why so few Asian Americans played football, Wong asserted, "I think it's the stereotype of football being brute force and fear of injury that dissuades Asians from playing. Nobody likes to get hurt . . . football requires quickness and thinking. I wish more Asians would play." Now known as Daryl Kan, he not only has been an orthopedic surgeon in Honolulu but coached Punahou's offense.[77]

In the 1980s, various universities recruited and played at least a few Asian Americans. Don Ting, Andy Hsu, and Tuan Van Le played for Stanford. The latter was a pioneering Vietnamese American football player. As a defensive back, he had his moments for Stanford. In 1988, he blocked a Cal field goal to preserve a 19–19 tie in the Big Game. Korean American John Lee was a fine placekicker for UCLA, gaining All-

American distinction for the Bruins in 1984 and 1985. Across the country, the University of Georgia recruited the Taiwanese-born William Tang. A tackle, Tang's services had been sought by other Southeastern Conference teams as his high school career wound down. In the mid-1980s, Sanjay Beach, possessing East Indian and Jamaican descent, performed well as a pass receiver for Colorado State. His best season was his second year in 1985. He caught thirty-seven passes for 381 yards and three touchdowns.[78]

Mike Nguyen proved a capable wide receiver for UCLA in the early 1990s. As a high school standout, Nguyen was avidly recruited by Stanford. The Palo Alto school dispatched Tuan Van Lee, whom *SI*'s Bruce Newman dismissed as "Amerasian" to "blatantly" persuade Nguyen to become a Cardinal. However, the two, according to Newman, had little in common, and Nguyen wound up in Westwood.[79]

Very skilled bi- and multiracial athletes showed up in college football stadiums in the 1990s. During the middle of the decade, Kailee Wong joined Bill Walsh's Stanford team. Possessing mixed ancestry, Wong garnered numerous honors while playing linebacker for the Cardinal. He also garnered plenty of attention from NFL scouts. Wong wound up as a high draft choice of the Minnesota Vikings. Around the same time, linebacker Tedy Bruschi, possessing Filipino ancestry, made a splash with the University of Arizona, ending up a draft choice of the New England Patriots. Meanwhile, part-Japanese Johnnie Morton stood out at the University of Southern California in the early 1990s. A consensus All-American in 1993, Johnnie Morton snagged eighty-eight passes for 1,520 yards and fourteen touchdowns that year, inspiring the Detroit Lions to draft him in the first round. Johnnie's younger brother Chad put on a USC uniform, but later in the 1990s. Chad Morton played mainly as a fine running back. In 1999, he wound up as a fifth-round draft choice of the New Orleans Saints. A son of an African American father and a Korean mother, Hines Ward played superbly at Georgia. At one time or another Ward performed as a quarterback, running back, and wide receiver for the Bulldogs. In 1996 and 1997, he caught more than fifty passes each season and was consequently drafted in the third round by the Pittsburgh Steelers. In the Ivy League, Korean American Lloyd Lee stood out as a defensive back for Dartmouth in the mid- to late 1990s. Possessing Japanese ancestry, Joey Getherall was an exciting, albeit small, receiver for Notre Dame in the late 1990s and early 2000s. In 1999, Getherall caught thirty-five passes for 436 yards and three touchdowns. In 2000, he achieved an impressive punt return average of sixteen yards per return, scoring two touchdowns.[80]

In the late 1990s, Dat Nguyen gained honors as an All-American linebacker for Texas A&M. A son of Vietnamese refugees, Nguyen was born in a refugee camp near Little Rock, Arkansas. The Nguyens then moved to Rockport, Texas, where his father took up shrimping—an occupation which witnessed bitter conflict between whites and Vietnamese in the 1980s. Dat Nguyen's parents later operated a Chinese-Vietnamese restaurant. Not exactly a child of privilege, Nguyen's youth threatened to be devoured by the street until he tried football in the eighth grade. He and his brother Hung became gridders in high school. Initially, Dat Nguyen might have been considered too small for college recruiters, but, according to journalist Jim Hodges, "American food, eaten at the house of a friend helped. . . . So did time in the weight room. As his body grew in South Texas, recruiters began to call."[81]

UCLA earnestly sought Nguyen's services. Former Bruin receiver Mike Nguyen tried to persuade Dat Nguyen to head to Southern California. The future professional linebacker admitted he was almost swayed. Mike Nguyen told him that he could become the Vietnamese American Jackie Robinson in Westwood, emphasizing that Robinson was a onetime Bruin. However, Nguyen decided to stick it out in Texas and joined the Texas A&M program.[82]

At Texas A&M, Nguyen led the team in tackles three years in a row. In 1998, he was awarded with All-American honors. Adding icing on the cake, Nguyen earned the Lombardi Award for the best defensive player in college football and the Chuck Bednarik award for the best linebacker in college football. Interestingly, one of Nguyen's greatest games was a 1998 Cotton Bowl contest against UCLA. In that game, he made an astounding twenty tackles. After the 1998 Cotton Bowl, unconventional Texas journalist Molly Ivins asserted, "Well, we've all read about Vietnamese-Americans graduating as valedictorians of their high schools, but there's something wonderfully Texan about Dat Nguyen's triumph." Meanwhile, reporters often asked his teammates whether he spoke English, underscoring scholar Mia Tuan's reference to Asian Americans as "forever foreigners." Nguyen, moreover, remembered as his college career wound down the racism he encountered as a youth in Texas, adding that he still ran into bigots, but apparently not among those who knew about his football accomplishments. Apparently, they were willing to grant him what Tuan has called "honorary whiteness." In 2017, Nguyen was inducted into the College Football Hall of Fame along with luminaries such as Peyton Manning, Marshall Faulk, and Adrian Peterson.[83]

As the twenty-first century ensued, more players of Asian descent filled roster spots on college teams. In the early 2000s, Asian Indian American Brandon Chillar stood out as a linebacker for UCLA. The son of a Pakistani mother and a Filipino father, Jamil Soriano grew into a six-foot-four, 300-pound offensive lineman for Harvard and became good enough to be a "practice team" player for the New England Patriots' Super Bowl team of 2004. Playing defensive back for the University of Texas in the early 2000s, Tren Van Nguyen earned a place on the Academic All-Big 12 squad. At Rutgers, Jeremy Ito marshalled an outstanding career as a kicker in the early 2000s. In 2006, his twenty-eight-yard field goal allowed Rutgers to upset third-ranked Louisville, 28–25. Hailing from San Jose, Louis Sakoda was an even more successful kicker. Performing for the University of Utah, Sakoda became the school's only consensus All-American in 2008.[84]

Running backs Scott Phaydavong, Ki-Cheng Ho, and Brian Kariya deserve mention. Possessing Laotian ancestry, Phaydavong put up prodigious rushing numbers at Drake University from 2004 through 2007. His first year, he ran the ball for 1,539 yards in 234 carries. In 2006, he made over 1,600 yards in 277 attempts. Ho was one of the better running backs in the Ivy League during the first decade of the twenty-first century. An immigrant from Taiwan, Ho's Harvard coach called him "the Tasmanian devil." In 2007, Ho was named to the Ivy League's second team. Kariya played for BYU from 2008 to 2011. Generally a backup, he still carried the ball for more than 1,000 yards in his career and over the goal line fifteen times.[85]

Lineman Ed Wang was born in Fairfax, Virginia. Both of his immigrant parents were track and field athletes who represented China internationally. Wang claimed that he heard racial taunts while playing football as a youth. Still, he persisted in the sport and was named Virginia's high school player of the year in 2005. Recruited as a tight end by Virginia Tech, Wang switched to offensive line, where he stood out, although confused and perhaps insensitive teammates referred to him as Godzilla. Big and athletic, Wang became second league all-ACC player in his senior year, starred in the Senior Bowl, and was drafted fifth by the Buffalo Bills. Moreover, he impressed Virginia Tech administrators and students as he emerged as a student leader in the aftermath of the tragic shootings on campus in 2009. His brother, David, subsequently played for Virginia Tech as a 300-plus-pound center. In 2013, he earned Honorable Mention recognition for the all-conference team.[86]

Possessing Vietnamese ancestry, Neal Huynh was an imposing defensive tackle for Ohio University from 2009 to 2012. A graduate of Altoona High School in Pennsylvania, the 315-pound Huynh started consistently during his last two years of eligibility at Ohio and earned a spot on the third team all-conference contingent. Huynh also made the all-conference academic team. Moreover, he attracted attention from the pros. The Atlanta Falcons signed him as a free agent, but he was not able to stick with the NFL.[87]

Also on the Pacific Coast, Patrick Chung, Doug Baldwin, and Thomas Duarte stood out for Oregon, Stanford, and UCLA respectively. Possessing Chinese and Jamaican ancestry, Patrick Chung was an All-American defensive back for Oregon in 2008. Around the same time, part-Filipino Doug Baldwin emerged as a fine receiver for Stanford. In 2013, Thomas Duarte, the previously mentioned biracial star for Mater Dei, showed up at UCLA. There, he demonstrated a great deal of talent as a pass receiver. He was honorable mention all-conference in both his first and second seasons at Westwood. As a junior, in 2015, he earned second team all-conference. Meanwhile, the Fullerton native told the press that he was proud of his biracial heritage. Journalist Jack Wang wrote in 2013:

> Thomas has embraced the position of role model. True, he knows he doesn't have much of a choice in the matter, If he wants to become a star athlete, the spotlight will only continue to grow. It never feels like a burden, however. He likes that he can stand for something larger than the game. . . . "Little Asian boys looking up at the screen, and there I am," he said. "I'm playing football. I'm being successful out there. I feel like I have to carry myself a certain way. . . . I love it. I love going out there and seeing other kids try hard because of me."[88]

Hailing from Seattle, the Nguyen brothers have been fine running backs for the University of Montana. The older brother, Peter, put together a career rushing total of 1,985 yards that was sixth in the school's long history of football—a career which earned him a tryout with the Seattle Seahawks. The five-foot-seven and 180-pound John surfaced as a "quality halfback" in the mid-2010s. In 2015, he gained 881 yards in 184 attempts. The next year stats were down a bit—679 yards but a fine 4.6 rushing average. Meanwhile, David Nguyen played defensive back for Montana Western.[89]

A couple of Korean American place kickers did well in the mid-2010s. A son of Korean immigrants, Younghoe Koo went to high school in New Jersey. From there, he journeyed south to Georgia Southern. There, he primarily took on the role of a kickoff specialist and placekicker. In 2015, he nailed seven of nine field goal attempts. The next year, he did even better, making nineteen of twenty field goal attempts. Furthermore, he became the first Georgia Southern football player to receive All-American mention when he made a third team squad. Justin Yoon was considered by many the top placekicker to come out of high school in the spring of 2015. He subsequently wound up at Notre Dame and had a fine first year for the Irish, hitting on fifteen of seventeen field goal attempts and scoring ninety-five points in all. The next year, he made thirteen of seventeen field goal attempts.[90]

MAINLAND COACHES

Asian American mainlanders have joined the ranks of college football coaching. None, yet, could boast of becoming a head coach of a major college team, although Art Matsu came somewhat close. Once his playing career ended, Art Matsu headed into coaching. Possessing a varied athletic background, Matsu coached swimming and golf at his alma mater, William and Mary, in 1927. In 1929, readers of the *Washington Post* learned that a "Jap Coaches Football." It seems that Matsu had become the "first Japanese football coach," when he took over the Asheville High

School team in North Carolina. Meanwhile, the *Post* still remembered Matsu as a "tricky Jap quarterback." In 1930, Matsu moved on to run a small college football program at Benedictine College in Virginia.[91]

Matsu joined Rutgers as a backfield coach during the early 1930s. In 1931, Matsu's former William and Mary coach took over Rutgers football program and hired him as an assistant. The *New York Times'* Allison Danzig credited Matsu for helping Rutgers improve. However, Greg Robinson reports mixed reviews of Matsu's coaching performance at Rutgers. Quarterback Frank Burns, who would subsequently become a head coach at Rutgers, hailed Matsu as "[a] master of offensive football, a true innovator." Another Rutgers' gridder, Leonard Weissburg, recalled that Matsu was a very serious man but a very good coach. Arthur Victor Mann complained that while Matsu was a great coach, he insisted upon calling all the plays, thereby stultifying his players' creativity. Toshima Hosoda was a Japanese American quarterback for Rutgers in the 1950s. He remembered that Matsu showed no favoritism toward him and dealt with him just as sternly as he did other players.[92]

Toward the end of the 1930s, sportswriter, Eddie Brietz reported a rumor that William and Mary alumni wanted Matsu to head the school's football program—a rumor which failed to eventuate. During World War II, Matsu taught physical education at Rutgers and ran Rutger's physical fitness program for its Army Specialized Training Corps. In 1955, Matsu left Rutgers and headed west to Arizona. There he sold real estate and did some scouting for Arizona State, which had a Nisei assistant, Bill Kajikawa. Living near Phoenix, Matsu died in 1987.[93]

After graduating from Arizona State, Bill Kajikawa was named by the school's athletic director to head the freshman football squad, a decision that rankled some because of Kajikawa's race and ethnicity. Kajikawa also coached the varsity backfield. During World War II, Kajikawa served in the military. Upon his induction, he maintained, "This war is an international football game we cannot lose." After V-J Day, Kajikawa returned to Arizona State to concentrate on serving as head baseball and basketball coach at Arizona State. However, he also helped coach the football squad. In 1951, the Arizona State Yearbook described him as an assistant coach, who focused on scouting the opposition. In 1959, Kajikawa served the grid program as a head freshman coach at a time when first-year students were ineligible for varsity play. Six years later, Kajikawa was still heading the frosh team, according to the school's yearbook. Arizona State's long-time coach Frank Kush declared, "He was great around young people because he really cared." Kajikawa also took over Hawai'i as his recruiting area for the Tempe school. After Kajikawa left coaching, the ASU football program continued to honor Kajikawa, naming an award for Arizona State's top first-year player after him, as well as a practice field.[94]

Sam Nakaso actually ran a small-college program in mid-twentieth century America. A former football player for Trinity University in Connecticut, the California native attained a master's in physical education at Columbia University. Then, he became head coach of Missouri's Central College football team in the late 1950s. His teams were not big winners. In 1958, Central College went one and six. The school's yearbook explained that injuries and "bad breaks" contributed to the team's poor record. However, it added that "Nakaso's multiple offense made the team more interesting to watch." Subsequently, Nakaso would return to California to coach, teach physical education, and serve as a trainer for San Jose City College from 1961 to 1991. Thanks substantially to the efforts of young Japanese American legal and political activists, Nakaso, like many Nisei, became eligible in the late 1980s for remuneration from the federal government for having been unjustly sent to a concentration camp. Nakaso, however, announced he would not accept money from the U.S. government "because you can't pay for liberty."[95]

CONCLUSION

Considering the relatively small number of Asian Americans living on the U.S. mainland for much of the twentieth century, it seems impressive that as many of them performed on college football teams as they did. Accordingly, in the face of racialized immigration laws, at least some Asian American mainlanders mastered the athletic skills needed to play football at a relatively high level. Moreover, they did not just fill roster spots. Taro Kishi, Art Matsu, Roman Gabriel, Kailee Wong, and Dat Nguyen were legitimate college football stars.

Thanks to the liberalized 1965 Immigration Act and the willingness of the United States to accept refugees from the Southeast Asian war zones, the diversity of Asian American college football players in the late twentieth and early twenty-first century is striking. Globalization's impact has also been felt on the gridiron. Many of these gridders have possessed mixed racial ancestry, thus reflecting globalization's blurring of national and cultural boundaries as American football voyaged to the millennium and beyond.

To be sure, football propelled some Asian American young men across racial and ethnic frontiers and allowed them to claim spatial entitlement and assert a sense of cultural citizenship on mainland college gridirons. Yet their liminal experiences seem evident. They found themselves as honorary white enough to make teams and even star on them but forever foreign enough to wind up the target of often condescending media Orientalism or worse in World War II concentration camps. If they took up coaching, they might be perceived as honorary white enough to get hired as assistants but forever foreign enough to bar them from head coaching.

NOTES

1. Oriard, *Reading Football*, 238.

2. *Salt Lake Tribune*, September 24, 1905; *Coalville Times*, November 17, 1911.

3. *Jonesboro Evening Sun*, November 29, 1905; Paul A. Kramer, *The Blood of Government*, 204–205.

4. *Fort Wayne News*, December 9, 1916; *Washington Post*, December 2, 1917; *Albany Evening Journal*, May 24, 1918.

5. *Seattle Times*, October 22, 1916; *Grand Rapids Press*, October 24, 1916; *Des Moines News*, October 26, 1916.

6. *Oakland Tribune*, August 23, 1917; January 19, 1918; *Rockford Republic*, October 14, 1917.

7. *San Francisco Chronicle*, October 3, 1918; *Oakland Tribune*, November 1, 1918; November 8, 1918; *Washington Times*, December 23, 1918; *Grand Rapid Tribune*, March 20, 1919.

8. Francis Tolbert, "Terrible Togo from Texas A&M," *Dallas Morning News*, December 18, 1965; Joe Michael Feist, "Japanese Player Relied on Heart," http://hirasaki.net/Family_Stories/Taro_Kishi/A_M.htm (August 10, 2015).

9. Ibid; William R. Ruggles, "Texas Aggies and Mustangs Battle to 7–7 Tie," *Dallas Morning News*, October 26, 1924; October 29, 1925; *Bryan Eagle*, September 30, 1925; Marvin Stephens, "Plowing Farmer Four Will Start Game against Texas," November 25, 1925; *Waco News-Tribune*, November 15, 1925.

10. Feist, "Japanese Player."

11. Ibid.

12. *Pacific Citizen*, September 30, 1947; Greg Robinson, "Gridiron Pioneer: Art Matsu, a Multi-racial Nikkei, Broke Ground," *Nichi Bei Times Weekly*, April 5, 2007; *Massillon Evening Independent*, November 15, 1922.

13. Robinson, "Gridiron Pioneer."

14. *Washington Post*, October 12, 1924; November 2, 1924; November 6, 1924; March 12, 1931.

15. *St. Petersburg Independent*, September 2, 1925; *Lima News*, December 6, 1925; *Havre Daily Promoter*, November 14, 1925; Syracuse University Yearbook, 1926, www.ancestry.com (January 13, 2011).

16. *Washington Post*, August 18, 1926; *Gastonia Daily Gazette*, November 12, 1926; College of William and Mary Yearbook, 1927, 1928, www.ancestry.com (January 13, 2011); Robinson, "Gridiron Pioneer."

17. Robinson, "Gridiron Pioneer"; College of William and Mary Yearbook, 1928, www.ancestry.com (January 13, 2011).

18. Jack Powers, "Art Matsu: Hero amidst Hatred," http://flathatnews.com/2014/10/02/art-matsu/ (July 13, 2015).

19. *San Diego Evening Tribune*, October 21, 1927; September 27, 1928; October 31, 1928; *San Diego Union*, October 14, 1930; *Granada Pioneer*, December 5, 1942; https://issuu.com/sdsuathletics/docs/2014-sdsu-fb-media-guide/171 (August 16, 2016); U.S. Census Bureau, Manuscript Census Schedules, City and County of San Diego, 1930, www.ancestry.com (August 13, 2016); San Diego State College Yearbook, 1929, https://library.sdsu.edu/pdf/scua/yearbooks/1929.pdf (August 16, 2016).

20. *San Diego Evening Tribune*, November 10, 1931; San Diego State College Yearbook, 1933, www.ancestry.com (August 13, 2016); U.S. Census Bureau, Manuscript Census Schedules, City and County of San Diego, 1940, www.ancestry.com (August 13, 2016).

21. *Fresno Bee*, December 12, 1936; December 16, 1937; August 5, 1937; December 2, 1937; August 7, 1942; http://grfx.cstv.com/photos/schools/fres/sports/m-footbl/auto_pdf/06-mg-part5.pdf (June 9, 2016); Fresno State College Yearbook, 1929, 1932, www.ancestry.com (August 6, 2015).

22. *Pacific Citizen*, July 31, 1943; Phoenix High School Yearbook, 1933, www.ancestry.com (May 27, 2006); *Pacific Citizen*, July 31, 1943; Bob Jacobsen, "A Man For All Seasons," www.asu.edu/alumnivision.com (October 21, 2002).

23. *San Diego Union*, November 29, 1934; *Continental*, October 21, 1935; *Albuquerque Journal*, November 2, 1935; December 9, 1935; *Dallas Morning News*, November 12, 1935; *Arizona Republic*, November 8, 1936; November 15, 1936; January 26, 1940.

24. *Los Angeles Times*, October 20, 1935; November 8, 1935; Charles Curtis, "Aztecs Lose Japanese Star," September 12, 1936; September 11, 1937; San Diego State College Yearbook, 1938, www.mocavo.com (January 24, 2015); U.S. Census Bureau, Manuscript Census Schedules, City and County of Los Angeles, 1920 (July 5, 2016).

25. *Los Angeles Times*, November 5, 1935; November 16, 1935; Charles Curtis, "Poets Crush Oxy, 18–0, October 18, 1936; October 3, 1937; U.S. Census Bureau, Manuscript Census Schedules, City and County of Los Angeles, 1940, www.ancestry.com (June 16, 2016).

26. *Oakland Tribune*, October 16, 1936; October 22, 1937; Braven Dyer, "Very Strong Trojan Team," *Los Angeles Times*, September 10, 1937; Dyer, "Trojan Horses to Have Kickers," September 12, 1937; *Fresno Bee*, September 23, 1937; University of Southern California Yearbook, 1937, 1938 www.ancestry.com (June 7, 2016); *Santa Ana Register*, August 24, 1938.

27. *San Francisco Examiner*, October 11, 1940; *San Diego Union*, October 20, 1940; San Diego State College Yearbook, 1940, www.mocavo.com (September 15, 2014); http://articles.ivpressonline.com/2004–03–06/golden-bulldogs_24190567/2 (November 14, 2014).

28. *Council Bluffs Nonpareil*, November 13, 1943; November 24, 1944; *Poston Chronicle*, January 14, 1944; *Manzanar Free Press*, October 28, 1944; *Colorado Times*, September 25, 1945; *Pacific Citizen*, October 26, 1946; http://articles.ivpressonline.com/2004–03–06/golden-bulldogs_24190567/2 (November 10, 2014).

29. *Sacramento Bee*, September 8, 1939; Dave Jones, "14–12," http://ucdavismagazine.ucdavis.edu/issues/sp10/sports.html (June 21, 2016); https://issuu.com/ucdavisaggies/docs/2011fbmediaguide/115 (June 21, 2016).

30. *Rockford Register-Republic*, July 3, 1936; *Japanese American Courier*, October 22, 1938; University of Washington Yearbook, 1936, www.ancestry.com (July 7, 2016); http://archive.densho.org/main.aspx (October 3, 2016).

31. San Francisco State College Yearbook, 1935, 1942, www.ancestry.com (August 25, 2015); *Chinese Digest* November 15, 1935; November, 1938; *San Francisco Examiner*, October 11, 1940; *San Francisco Chronicle*, October 4, 1941; October 5, 1941, October 10, 1941; *Jamestown Evening Journal*, October 8, 1931; Charles Curtis, "Poets Crush Oxy, 18–0," *Los Angeles Times*, October 18, 1936; September 14, 1937; *Japanese American Courier*, October 22, 1938; *San Francisco Examiner*, September 19, 1940; October 6, 1940; October 8, 1940; *East Liverpool Evening News,* November 1, 1940; *San Francisco Examiner*, October 10,1942; Santa Barbara State College Yearbook, 1933, www.ancestry.com (October 20, 2015); *Chinese Digest*, April, 1937; *Chinese Digest*, November, 1938; *Nevada State Journal*, October 18, 1929; U.S. Census Bureau, Manuscript Census Schedules, City and County of Fresno, 1940, www.ancestry.com (November 29, 2014); *Poston Chronicle*, September 9, 1944; *Huron Huronite*, December 12, 1941.

32. *Lockport Union Sun and Journal*, April 20, 1940; *San Francisco Examiner*, September 9, 1940; October 10, 1942; St. Mary's College Yearbook, 1940, www.ancestry.com (June 24, 2015).

33. Chris Foster, "War and Roses," http://articles.latimes.com/2008/nov/22/sports/sp-beavers22, (March 3, 2015).

34. Ibid., *Minidoka Irrigator*, October 14, 1942.

35. *Minidoka Irrigator*, October 14, 1942; *Pacific Citizen*, October 5, 1946; http://archeologygroup9.blogspot.com/2009/12/jack-yoshihara-osu-football-player.html (February 13, 2015).

36. *Ogden Standard-Examiner*, September 16, 1943; *Salt Lake Tribune*, October 16, 1943; October 17, 1943 *Portland Oregonian*, August 3, 1948. http://oregonstate.edu/ad-

missions/blog/2009/05/14/honorary-degree-recepient-jack-yoshihara-passes-away/
(February 15, 2015).

37. *Helena Independent,* September 28, 1941; Bill Coltrin, "Cougar Loss Gives Title to Redskins," *Salt Lake Tribune,* November 23, 1941.

38. U.S. Census Bureau, Manuscript Census Schedules, City and County of Los Angeles, 1920, 1930, www.ancestry.com (April 25, 2016).

39. Red Grange, "Neglect Big 7 Grid Circuit," *Ironwood Daily Globe,* September 1, 1942; *Helena Independent,* November 8, 1942; *Pacific Citizen,* December 10, 1942; Colorado State College Yearbook, 1943, www.ancestry.com (April 11, 2016).

40. Greg Robinson, "Be a Good Sport."

41. *Pacific Citizen,* November 19, 1942; February 18, 1950; *Jefferson City Daily Capital News,* December 12, 1942; *Dallas Morning News,* October 2, 1943; October 5, 1943; October 9, 1943; http://content.cdlib.org/ark:/13030/ft0g5002v1/?brand=calisphere (June 1, 2009).

42. *Poston Chronicle,* October 15, 1943.

43. *Dallas Morning News,* December 19, 1943; *San Antonio Express,* October 23, 1962; Louisiana State University Yearbook, 1948, 1949, www.ancestry.com (May 29, 2015); Robinson, "Be a Good Sport."

44. Harold V. Ratcliff, "17-Year Old Lad to Lead Texas Squad," *Niagara Falls Gazette,* September 15, 1943; *Dallas Morning News,* October 10, 1943; *Salt Lake Tribune,* November 6, 1943; Gary Y. Okihiro, *Storied Lives: Japanese American Students and World War II* (Seattle: University of Washington Press, 1999), 90, 92; *Topaz Times,* September 21, 1943; Denver University Yearbook, 1944, www.ancestry.com (March 25, 2015); Franks, *Crossing,* 131; *San Francisco Examiner,* October 22, 1943; October 31, 1943.

45. *San Francisco Examiner,* October 24, 1942; *Los Angeles Times,* September 12, 1945; *Daily Californian,* October 5, 1945; George M. Varnell, "Huskies Bow to Bears," *Seattle Times,* October 7, 1945; *McKean County Democrat,* November 1, 1945.

46. *Oakland Tribune,* October 20, 1946; November 17, 1946; *San Francisco Examiner,* November 23, 1946; November 25, 1946; *San Francisco Chronicle,* September 27, 1947.

47. *Washington Post,* September 27, 1947; Fred Merrick, "Cal Impressive in Waldorf's Western Debut," *San Jose Mercury,* September 21, 1947; October 12, 1947; Robert Prescott, "Bears Strong on Ground, Rip Montana, 60–14," November 16, 1947; Rube Samuelson, "Eight Contests," *Sporting News,* October 22, 1947; University of California Yearbook, 1948, www.ancestry.com (November 29, 2014).

48. *San Francisco Chronicle,* September 27, 1947; September 29, 1947; Wu, *Color of Success;* Cheng, *Citizens of Asian America.*

49. *San Francisco Examiner,* February 19, 1948.

50. Franks, *Crossing,* 131; *Seattle Times,* September 20, 1945; October 7, 1945; November 12, 1946; *Portland Oregonian,* September 30, 1945; *Pacific Citizen,* April 1, 1950.

51. *Los Angeles Times,* October 25, 1940; October 26, 1945; November 10, 1945; November 11, 1945; U.S. Census Bureau, Manuscript Census Schedules, 1940, City and County of Los Angeles, www.ancestry.com., (March 3, 2008); *Corsair,* December 5, 1945.

52. Bill Becker, "Jap-American Stars in West Coast Football," *Lead Daily Call,* December 19, 1945.

53. Leiser, "The Coast," p. 54; *Los Angeles Times,* October 4, 1946; *San Jose Mercury,* September 5, 1946; October 11, 1946; *Seattle Times,* September 28, 1946; *Dallas Morning News,* October 6, 1946; *Nevada State-Journal,* October 22, 1946; January 2, 1947; *San Francisco Examiner,* November 8, 1946; November 23, 1946; *San Diego Union,* November 16, 1946; December 2, 1946.

54. *Pacific Citizen,* September 13, 1947; *San Francisco Chronicle,* September 18,1947; October 12, 1947; *San Francisco Examiner,* September 6, 1947; Frank Bonnano, "Nomura Impresses," *San Jose News,* September 13, 1947; Frank Bonnano, "Spartans Prove Disappointment before 15,500," September 20, 1947; Louis Duino, "Spartans Overwhelm Santa Barbara in 39–0 Win," *San Jose Mercury,* October 18, 1947; *Bakersfield Californian,* January 8, 1948; *El Mustang,* September 24, 1948.

55. *Pacific Citizen*, October 14, 1950; *Portland Oregonian*, November 4, 1950; *Dallas Morning News*, November 15, 1951; *Fresno Bee*, November 24, 1951; November 30, 1951; Fresno State College Yearbook, 1950, www.ancestry.com (August 6, 2015).

56. University of Arizona Yearbook, 1950, www.ancestry.com (November 29, 2014); U.S. Census Bureau, Manuscript Census Schedules, City of Maricopa and County of Pinal, 1940, www.ancestry.com (March 16, 2015); *Pacific Citizen*, September 13, 1947; *San Jose Mercury*, October 3, 1946; September 27, 1947; Louis Duino, "Kikuchi Main Loss from CPS Tilt," October 18, 1947.

57. *San Jose Mercury*, September 1, 1951; September 6, 1951; *Pacific Citizen*, October 17, 1952; U.S. Census Bureau, Manuscript Census Schedules, City of Tulare and County of Exeter, 1940, www.ancestry.com (April 20, 2015); City of San Jose and County of Santa Clara, 1940, www.ancestry.com (July 16, 2015); *San Francisco Chronicle*, October 18, 1952; San Jose State College Yearbook, 1955, 1957, www.ancestry.com (April 20, 2015); *Pacific Citizen*, October 26, 1946; September 24, 1954; San Jose State College vs. Stanford University Football Program, Stanford Stadium, Palo Alto, California, November 1, 1952; San Jose State College vs. Stanford University Football Program, Stanford Stadium, Palo Alto, California, October 13, 1956; *San Jose Mercury*, September 1, 1954, September 25, 1954; November 13, 1954; *Bend Bulletin*, September 10, 1960; *Spartan Daily*, October 11, 1957; http://www.sports-reference.com/cfb/schools/san-jose-state/1957.html (March 29, 2016).

58. *Sacramento Bee*, November 15, 1955; Marco Smolich, "Nevada Dulls Homecoming for Aggies, 21–13," October 14, 1957; November 1, 1957; November 4, 1957; December 4, 1957.

59. *Milwaukee Journal-Sentinel*, December 1, 1956; *Daily Tar Heel*, October 5, 1957; *Terre Haute Tribune*, January 19, 1958; U.S. Census Bureau, Manuscript Census Schedules, City and County of Los Angeles, 1940, www.ancestry.com (July 3, 2015); U.S. Naval Academy Yearbook, 1957, 1959, www.mocavo.com (June 30, 2015); http: // www.scout.com/college/army/story/109026-army-vs-navy-1956 (June 30, 2015).

60. *Springfield Union*, August 22, 1958.

61. Yen Le Espiritu, *Filipino Lives* (Philadelphia: Temple University Press, 1995).

62. http://www.sports-reference.com/cfb/players/dick-dagampat-1.html (June 30, 2015); http://queenofheaven.tributes.com/our_obituaries/Richard-Manuola-Dagampat--101149226 (June 30, 2015).

63. U.S. Census Bureau, Manuscript Census Schedules, City of Berkeley and County of Alameda, 1940, www.ancestry.com (June 17, 2015); *San Jose Mercury*, September 19, 1957; University of California Yearbook, 1957, 1959, 1960, www.ancestry.com (June 3, 2015); *Sports Illustrated*, September 22, 1958, p. 106; "California Birth Directory," www.ancestry.com (June 2, 2010); Ed Schoenfeld, "Cal Gridders Switched in Opening Drills," *Oakland Tribune*, April 22, 1958; *Sarasota Herald Tribune*, October 29, 1958; *Springfield Union*, January 11, 1960; *Portland Oregonian*, November 7, 1959; Franks, *Crossing*, 134.

64. Fresno State College Yearbook, 1959, 1962, www.ancestry.com (June 10, 2015); *Nichi Bei Times*, January 1, 1973.

65. *Pasadena Independent*, September 23, 1959; November 14, 1959; http://www.oxyathletics.com/sports/fball/awards/1958AllSCIAC (July 13, 2015); *Redlands Daily Facts*, July 25, 1961.

66. *Portland Oregonian*, November 4, 1951; October 5, 1952; *Bridgeport Telegram*, November 21, 1954; *New York Times*, September 19, 1955; *Petersburg Progress-Index*, October 16, 1955; *San Francisco Chronicle*, October 2, 1955; *Sacramento Bee*, September 15, 1956; http://www.hornetsports.com/sports/fball/alltimeroster (February 5, 2014); *Sacramento Bee*, October 22, 1955; *Nevada State-Journal*, October 28, 1959; *San Bernardino County Sun*, October 14, 1956; Denver University Yearbook, 1952, www.ancestry.com (July 24, 2015). University of Southern California Yearbook, 1957, www.ancestry.com (November 25, 2015); Pomona College Yearbook, 1947, www.ancestry.com (July 19, 2016); Ann Miller, "Kobe Shoji, father of Dave Shoji, Dead At 84," http://the.honoluluadvertiser.com/article/2004/Nov/15/sp/sp03p.html (July 19, 2016); http://

content.lib.utah.edu/utils/getfile/collection/uuath2/id/18/filename/115.pdf (August 7, 2016).

67. Franks, *Crossing*, 134.

68. Jamie Curran, "Wolfpack's Gabriel Coming to Town," *Los Angeles Times*, October 27, 1960; Mel Allen, "Mel Allen's All-American Football Preview," *Sport*, October, 1960, 19; Dick Herbert, "Experience Will Help Gabriel, N.C. State," *Washington Post*, September 11, 1960.

69. *Hendersonville Times-News*, October 19, 1960; Curran, "Wolfback's Gabriel"; *San Jose Mercury*, December 1, 1960; December 3, 1960.

70. Fred Russell, "Pigskin Review," *Saturday Evening Post*, September 9, 1961; *Schenectady Gazette*, November 23, 1961; *Los Angeles Times*, December 3, 1961; December 5, 1961; *Robesonian*, December 14, 1961.

71. *Arizona Republic*, November 11, 1960; *Pittsburgh Post-Gazette*, December 13, 1960.

72. Redlands University Yearbook, 1962, www.ancestry.com (July 16, 2015); *Los Angeles Times*, October 18, 1961; December 7, 1961; *San Diego Union*, October 16, 1961; *Bridgeport Herald*, November 12, 1961; Whittier College Yearbook, 1962, www.ancestry.com (June 6, 2015).

73. John Mooney, "Late Splurge Gives Utah, 28–26 Win," *Salt Lake Tribune*, October 8, 1961; http://content.lib.utah.edu/utils/getfile/collection/uuath2/id/100/filename/76.pdf (June 9, 2016); *Seattle Times*, September 10, 1963; February 14, 1966; *Eureka Time Standard*, October 14, 1966; January 18, 1968; http://www.sports-reference.com/cfb/players/john-browne-1.html (November 13, 2014).

74. *El Paso Herald-Post*, September 5, 1964; *Salisbury Daily-Times*, November 12, 1964; *Simpson Leader*, October 28, 1965; *Silver City Daily Press*, November 2, 1965; *Hagerstown Daily Mail*, November 4, 1965; Loy Holman, "Navy QB May Miss Academy," *Colorado Springs Telegram*, September 28, 1966; http://www.sports-reference.com/cfb/players/danny-wong-1.html (September 22, 2014); http://www.e-yearbook.com/yearbooks/United_States_Naval_Academy_Lucky_Bag_Yearbook/1967/Page_217.html (September 22, 2014); http://www.recordnet.com/article/20141119/sports/141119523, (April 1, 2016).

75. *Seattle Times*, September 14, 1978.

76. http://www.nwasianweekly.com/2013/05/bruce-harrell-inducted-to-pacific-northwest-football-hall-of-fame/ (April 29, 2015).

77. http://www.willamette.edu/athletics/hall_of_fame/members/1996/, (May 22, 2010); http://www.sports-reference.com/cfb/schools/dartmouth/1980.html (June 8, 2015); *East/West*, June 15, 1983; May 23, 1984; http://biggreenalertblog.blogspot.com/2006/09/former-qbs-son-starring-in-hawaii.html (June 8, 2015).

78. Franks, *Crossing*, 136–137; http://www.gostanford.com/ViewArticle.dbml?DB_OEM_ID=30600&ATCLID=208077543 (June 8, 2015); https://lvironpigs.wordpress.com/2014/08/18/establishing-uclas-all-time-placekicking-records/ (June 8, 2015); *Augusta Chronicle*, May 25, 1983; http://www.fanbase.com/william-tang/, (June 9, 2015); http://www.sports-reference.com/cfb/players/sanjay-beach-1.html (June 9, 2015).

79. Bruce Newman, "The Class of '90"; http://www.sports-reference.com/cfb/players/mike-nguyen-1.html (June 9, 2015).

80. Franks, *Crossing*, 137; http://www.pro-football-reference.com/players/B/BrusTe99.htm, (May 2, 2015); Cynthia De Castro, "NFL Hero Is Fil/Am," https://asianjournal.wordpress.com/2008/02/11/nfl-hero-is-filam/ (May 2, 2015); http://www.sports-reference.com/cfb/players/johnnie-morton-1.html (June 9, 2015); http://www.sports-reference.com/cfb/players/chad-morton-1.html (June 9, 2015); http://www.sports-reference.com/cfb/players/hines-ward-1.html (June 9, 2015); http://asian-players.com/football, (May 3, 2016).

81. Franks, *Crossing*, 140.

82. Ibid.

83. Franks, *Crossing*, 140; *Seguin Gazette-Enterprise*, January 1, 1999. Molly Ivins, "Texans, Old and New," *Wilmington Morning-Star*, January 8, 1998; Lakshmi Gandhi,

"Former Dallas Cowboy Dat Nguyen to Be Inducted into College Football Hall of Fame," http://www.nbcnews.com/news/asian-america/former-dallas-cowboy-dat-nguyen-be-inducted-college-football-hall-n705206 (January 10, 2017); Mia Tuan, *Forever Foreigners or Honorary Whites?: The Asian Ethnic Experience in Today* (New Brunswick, NJ: Rutgers University Press, 1998).

84. http://www.uclabruins.com/ViewArticle.dbml?DB_OEM_ID=30500&ATCLID=208195513 (March 3, 2014); Emil Guillermo, "Good and Plenty," *Asian Weekly*, November 29–December 5, 2002; www.gobears.com (February 10, 2003); www.mackbrown-Texas-football.com (January 20, 2004); Matt Stanmyre, "Six Years Later, Rutgers Grad Jeremy Ito is Just a Regular Guy," http://www.nj.com/rutgersfootball/index.ssf/2012/11/six_years_later_rutgers_grad_j.html (June 10, 2016); http://www.kickingworld.com/former-utah-utes-all-american-louie-sakoda-joins-kicking-world-as-kicking-coach (June 10, 2016); http://asianplayers.com/football/ (June 10, 2016).

85. espn.go.com/college-football/player/stats/_/id/158631/scott-phaydavong (September 23, 2015); Stephanie M. Woo, "15 Most Interesting Seniors, 2010," http://www.thecrimson.com/article/2009/12/11/15-most-interesting-seniors-ho// (September 23, 2015); http://www.ivyleaguesports.com/sports/fball/2007–08/releases/allivy_football__2007.htm (September 23, 2015); http://asianplayers.com/football/ (June 10, 2016).

86. John P. Lopez, "Getting to Know NFL Hopeful Ed Wang," http://sportsillustrated.cnn.com/2010/writers/john_lopez/04/21/wang/index.html (December 24, 2010); http://www.nfl.com/players/edwang/profile?id=WAN272761 (December 24, 2010); http://www.arenafootball.com/sports/a-footbl/aflrtl/mtt/david_wang_991559.html (June 11, 2016).

87. http://www.ohiobobcats.com/sports/m-footbl/mtt/neal_huynh_365746.html (June 11, 2016); http://asianplayers.com/football/ (June 10, 2016).

88. http://www.goducks.com/ViewArticle.dbml?ATCLID=175546 (June 7, 2013); http://www.sports-reference.com/cfb/players/doug-baldwin-1.html, (June 10, 2015); http://www.uclabruins.com/ViewArticle.dbml?ATCLID=208817184 (July 13, 2015); Jack Wang, "UCLA Receiver Thomas Duarte Proud of Biracial Heritage," http://www.dailynews.com/sports/20131125/ucla-receiver-thomas-duarte-proud-of-biracial-heritage (June 22, 2015).

89. *Northwest Asian Weekly*, May 25-May 31, 2013; http://www.gogriz.com/sports/m-footbl/mtt/john_nguyen_850833 (June 9, 2015); http://www.gogriz.com/sports/m-footbl/stats/2014–2015/teamcume.html (June 9, 2015); http://sports.yahoo.com/ncaa/football/players/198906 (July 15, 2015); http://www.foxsports.com/college-football/john-nguyen-player (January 25, 2017).

90. http://www.gseagles.com/roster.aspx?rp_id=560 (January 25, 2017); http://asianplayers.com/football/ (June 10, 2016); http://www.und.com/sports/m-footbl/mtt/justin_yoon_976665.html (January 25, 2017).

91. *Washington Post*, January 12, 1928; September 15, 1929; October 4, 1929; Robinson, "Gridiron Pioneer."

92. *New York Times*, September 15, 1931; Allison Danzig, "Rutgers Displays Much Improvement," October 4, 1932; *Pacific Citizen*, September 13, 1947.

93. *Charleston Daily Mail*, May 12, 1938; Robinson, "Gridiron Pioneer."

94. *Rohwer Outpost*, March 31, 1943; *El Paso Herald-Post*, September 10, 1937; *Pacific Citizen*, July 31, 1943; Arizona State University Yearbook, 1951, 1965, www.ancesry.com (November 7, 2012); Franks, *Crossing*, 124.

95. *Berkshire Evening Eagle*, October 3, 1949; Central College Yearbook, 1958, 1960, ancestry.com (June 11, 2015); San Jose City College Yearbook, 1962, www.ancestry.com (June 11, 2015); http://www.fa-aft6157.org/newsletters/0502_newsletter.pdf (December 26, 2014).

SIX

The Pros

Football players of Asian and Pacific Islander ancestry have played professionally in the United States and Canada, as well as Europe. In the process, they encountered daunting, often Orientalized, racial borderlands, while availing themselves of opportunities, however ephemeral at times, to compete at the game's heights, achieving a measure of fame and even relative fortune. This chapter will focus on professionals of Asian ancestry as well as Pacific Islander gridders performing before the late twentieth century. The next chapter will more fully explore Pacific Islander experiences since the 1970s.

In 1927, Hawaiian Chinese Walter Achiu became probably the first professional gridder of Asian ancestry when he joined the Dayton Triangles. A charter member of the American Professional Football Association, which later morphed into the NFL, the Triangles competed professionally throughout the 1920s. In July, the Triangles prepared to play the then youthful franchise known as the Green Bay Packers. At that time, a Michigan newspaper in trying to compliment Achiu wound up demeaning people of Chinese ancestry. It described Achiu, who started at left half, as "Chinese." Even so, the article went on, he was good enough to perform effectively against the vaunted Packers. Wisconsin's *Appleton Post-Crescent* noted Achiu's presence on the Triangles, hailing him as "a first-class player," skilled as a ball carrier, receiver, and passer.[1]

Achiu also played professionally for Portsmouth in Ohio. An independent franchise, Portsmouth assembled a team capable of holding its own against elevens such as the Green Bay Packers. In a game against Columbus in mid-September 1928 Achiu's passing and ball carrying stood out. Dick Young of the *Portsmouth Daily Times* praised him as a "fine halfback." In September 1929, Achiu subbed at fullback as the Green Bay Packers blanked Portsmouth, 14–0. A couple of months later, Achiu started at right half and punted for Portsmouth as it blanked Middletown Armco, 23–0.[2]

Achiu left professional football to become a well-traveled professional wrestler. Interestingly, in the initial stages of Achiu's professional wrestling career, the *Oregon Statesmen,* publishing out of Salem, Oregon, confided that Achiu was getting consideration for a college head football coaching job. Albany College, now Lewis and Clark, had been suffering through too many losing seasons, and Achiu, according to the *Statesmen,* believed he was the man who could turn things around. Recognizing the marketability of Orientalism, the Hawaiian Chinese added that because of his ethnicity he would lure needed publicity to the campus. Mulling over the possibility, the *Statesmen,* which called the adult Achiu a "China boy," joked the team's nickname could be changed to the "Chinese Pirates." Achiu, as it turned out, never coached Albany.[3]

Art Matsu, after leaving William and Mary, played one year for Dayton's NFL team in 1928. The Dayton Triangles were not a good team, winning only one game in 1926 and 1927. Matsu, for some reason, played fullback for the Triangles despite his college reputation as a quarterback. Matsu did not shine in the pros. He took part in only two games for a team that failed to win a single game in 1928. Matsu managed to catch two passes for fifteen yards, returned a pair of kickoffs for insignificant yardage, and completed one pass out of eight attempts. Worse, he threw two interceptions.[4]

Hawaiians Henry Hughes and Harold Field played elite professional football in the 1930s. After leaving Oregon State, Hughes suited up for the Boston Braves of the NFL in 1932. He appeared in ten games for the Braves, a team that eventuated into the Washington franchise in today's NFL. In 1935, Harry Field joined the Chicago Cardinals. Arch Ward of the *Chicago Tribune* insisted that the toughest job the Cardinal coach had was keeping shoes on Field, who Ward wrote, was a "huge Hawaiian tackle" who learned to play football barefooted and had worked barefooted at a Hawaiian pineapple cannery the previous summer. Field appeared in thirty-four games for the Cardinals, the ancestor of today's Arizona Cardinals. According to the *Honolulu Star-Bulletin,* Field made all-league with the Cardinals in 1936. The next year, he was with the American Football League's Los Angeles Bulldogs, for whom he also made all-league as a tackle. After his sojourn with the Bulldogs, Field was set to return to the NFL, when he decided to head back to Hawai'i.[5]

A decade later, Hawaiian Al Lolotai became the first gridder of Samoan ancestry to play professional football when he joined the NFL's Washington franchise in 1945. The 1940 U.S. census manuscripts tell us that in 1940, he lived with his Samoan-born stepfather and biological mother on Oahu. At the time, the twenty-year-old future professional gridder labored on a sugar plantation. Lolotai did well in his first season in the NFL. His coach, Dudley Degroot, told the press that he "was one of the finest first year men in the league," a sentiment echoed by the *Ogden Standard Examiner's* Al Warden. After World War II, Lolotai departed the NFL for the All-American Football Conference's Los Angeles Dons. When the Dons defeated the Brooklyn Dodgers in 1946, the *Brooklyn Daily Eagle* lamented Al Lolotai's role. During the game, the "Hawaiian guard" rushed Dodger passer Glen Dobbs so hard that he forced a fumble recovered by the Dons; a fumble which led to a key Don touchdown. In 1947, Lolotai was named to the second team all AAFC. When the Dons beat the Brooklyn Dodgers in September 1948, Dick Hyland of the *Los Angeles Times* exulted in "the big Samoan guard's" work on defense. In 1949, the *Long Beach Independent* reported that the Dons had re-signed Lolotai for the coming season, adding that he was "the only Samoan in football."[6]

After leaving professional football, Lolotai wrestled professionally. But after retiring from wrestling, Lolotai became active in Samoan American affairs. In 1962, columnist Victor Reisel described Lolotai as "prominent in Hawaii's Samoan community." In 1965, the *Los Angeles Times* identified the former Don as "head of the United Samoan Community Association," as well as director of the Hawaii-Kai Recreation Center. Informing the press that he had come to Hawai'i as a child, Lolotai expressed concern about the liminal experiences of Samoans migrating to the United States: "[Y]ou find yourself hung in the middle between western culture and your own. You just don't have a footing to stand on."[7]

The second Nikkei to play major league football in the United States was biracial Chet Maeda who appeared briefly with the NFL's Chicago Cardinals in 1945. Maeda's biggest impact as a pro seems to have taken place when he reportedly collided with another Cardinal during a preseason practice session and knocked himself out. Maeda subsequently devoted his life to a lengthy career as a veterinarian in Southern California.[8]

HAWAIIAN HALFBACKS

The 1930 U.S. Census Manuscripts state that Kaname Yonamine was four and a half years old when the census was taken. His parents, siblings, and he lived in Olowalu Village on Maui. His father was a Japanese immigrant, while his mother reportedly was born in Hawai'i. In any event, both parents were defined as racially Japanese and "aliens." His father worked on a sugar plantation.[9]

Yonamine emerged from the Hawaiian working class to stand out as a prep star in football on Maui and then Oahu, where he competed for Farrington High School. In 1944, Farrington achieved an undefeated season and a league championship, thanks in no small part to Yonamine's football wizardry. One rival coach declared that Yonamine was "like a man among boys" when Farrington beat his team. Yonamine joined the military toward the end of World War II. He, fortunately, saw more action on the gridiron than the battlefield, playing for a service team coached by the well-respected Jock Sutherland. Readers of the *Stars and Stripes* learned that Yonamine was "a flashy ex-Honolulu semi-professional." [10]

Once Yonamine left the service, word reached the mainland that he might be just as good as the celebrated Herman Wedemeyer, if not better. In February 1946, the *San Francisco Chronicle* quoted Edwin Noonan, described as "a noted athletic trainer in Hawaii." Noonan insisted that the "Hawaiian Japanese" was "better than Wedemeyer." Yonamine also surfaced as a star on the touring Hawaiian All-Star eleven, mentioned in an earlier chapter. When his squad visited Portland, the *Portland Oregonian* called Yonamine a "triple-threat halfback." It also informed readers that Hawaiian football fans rated Yonamine as Wedemeyer's equal. A few months earlier, Honolulu sportswriter Loui Leong Hop arrived in Portland and sought to prepare the city's football fans for Yonamine's coming. Al Stump interviewed Hop, describing the Honolulan as "hep" and the only Chinese sports editor of a metropolitan newspaper. Hop stressed that Yonamine was every bit as talented as Wedemeyer. In addition, the Japanese Hawaiian "weighs 175, hits'em in the head [punts] up to 60 yards, and is just a blur with the ball." Stump found it hard to believe that Yonamine could match Wedemeyer, declaring that he had seen the latter in action and swore that the "Hula Kid" was the best all-around gridder he had ever encountered. Hop, however, insisted that Yonamine was talented enough to entice interest from USC and that he was better than Wedemeyer as a passer and punter. When the Hawaiians reached San Jose, their coach, Chin Do Kim, speculated that Yonamine had "a brilliant grid future," while the *San Jose Mercury* described him as a "powerhouse runner." Chuck Mallory, San Jose State's athletic publicity director, asserted that Yonamine was as talented as Wedemeyer and that "[g]ood players must be a dime a dozen in the islands." [11]

Because of Yonamine's exploits for the Hawaiian traveling grid squad, Ohio State, as well as the New York Yankees and the San Francisco 49ers of the All-American Football Conference, sought his services. Engaged in an ultimately losing battle with the NFL for professional football supremacy, AAFC teams like the Yankees and 49ers may have thought someone like Yonamine would provide a needed jolt of fan excitement for the upstart league. In May 1947, the press announced that the 49ers had inked the Japanese Hawaiian described as a "175 pound Japanese halfback." Yonamine recalled that the contract was for two years and $14,000. The 49ers, the *San Francisco Chronicle* asserted, were acting on the recommendation of former Stanford great Bob Grayson, who had seen the halfback in action in Portland. [12]

After the 49ers signed him for the 1947 season, Yonamine found himself the focus of generally hospitable media attention. Of course, the *Pacific Citizen* was pleased, calling him the "hula-hipping Nisei halfback from Hawaii." A wire story in the *Nevada State-Journal* maintained that "Wally Yonamine sensational halfback from Hawaii's Barefoot Leagues lived up to advanced notices" at the 49ers' training camp. Coach Buck Shaw was quoted as expressing admiration for the "Japanese-Hawaiian's passing and insisted that Yonamine would play a key role on the ream.[13]

Yonamine arrived in the 49ers' training camp with Henry Hosea, another Japanese Hawaiian, who had shown talent as a center on the traveling all-star squad on which Yonamine starred in 1946. Bay Area newspapers subsequently enjoyed exoticizing the halfback. The *San Francisco Chronicle* informed readers of an apparent conversation between 49ers' coach Buck Shaw and a pidgin speaking Yonamine. Yonamine supposedly complained to Shaw, "I don't eat. I lose 12 pounds." Shaw asked if Yonamine was eating enough, and the "Hawaiian HB" responded "No, No. That's not it. But coach we get no rice." As Yonamine was considered an exciting newcomer, the 49ers, according to the *Chronicle*, furnished him with all the rice he needed.[14]

The Bay Area press generally praised the 49ers' acquisition of the Hawaiian Japanese. To the *San Francisco Chronicle*'s Will Connolly, Wally Yonamine was not large, but he was a "sturdy right halfback of 175 pounds with a compact chassis." The *Chronicle* also reported on Yonamine's football virtuosity. Soon after arriving in camp, Yonamine participated in a punting contest. The 49ers' star quarterback, Frankie Albert, won the competition by booting an average of 70.5 yards per punt. Yonamine took third, but the "Hawaiian ace" averaged a respectable 60.5 yards. The *San Francisco Call-Bulletin* described Yonamine as the 49ers' "new Japanese QB." It told readers of Buck Shaw's praise for the Hawaiian newcomer. Yonamine, Shaw claimed, "throws a sharp, accurate ball. He's a terrific cutter as a runner. I'd like to clock him with a stopwatch. Might be the fastest runner in the league." Louis Duino, a sportswriter for the *San Jose Mercury*, extolled "Wally Yonamine, the Japanese-Hawaiian" as capable of becoming as "big a name in professional football as Herman Wedemeyer is in college circles." To Duino, Yonamine "has what it takes—speed, finesse, and brains." Duino, moreover, advised the 49ers to draft Wedemeyer after the 1947 season, adding "what a combination Yonamine and Wedemeyer would make a year from now."[15]

Perhaps to diminish his Nikkei identity in the eyes of his readers, the *San Francisco Examiner's* Curley Grieve depicted Yonamine as a "happy Hawaiian." His article, entitled "Wally Eats Rice. Can He Run?" pointed out that Yonamine's toughness had won the admiration of the 49ers leader, Frankie Albert. Grieve also testified that after Yonamine whirled through tacklers for a twenty-yard run in a practice scrimmage, "the dark-skinned Hawaiian" allegedly joked to teammates on the sidelines,

"You think too much hula." The gridders laughed at Yonamine, who reportedly loved to walk about barefooted. The *Examiner* asserted that Yonamine confidently looked forward to making the 49ers, telling the press, "I not worried. . . . All my pals in Honolulu send me letters saying I getting lots of newspaper stuff." [16]

Appreciating full well his Nikkei background, Japanese Americans were pleased with Yonamine's signing. In a fine biography of the Hawaiian, Robert Fitts argues, "Many Japanese Americans wanted to assimilate to demonstrate they were loyal Americans. Perhaps nothing was more American at that time in California than football. By signing with the 49ers, Yonamine became a symbol that Japanese Americans could make it in mainstream American society." Moreover, an informant told Fitts that San Francisco's Japantown rejoiced that Yonamine was headed to the city's only big-league franchise. This resulted in Yonamine attending picnics, sponsored by Bay Area Nikkei at Golden Gate Park as well as invitations for home-cooked meals at Japanese American homes. Indeed, Yonamine wound up living with a Japanese American family in San Francisco. Fitts speculates that Yonamine may have added pressure on himself because he knew his football career was watched closely by Nikkei in the Bay Area and California in general. [17]

On August 9, 1947, the *Pacific Citizen* reported that Yonamine had probably clinched a spot on the 49ers. The weekly asserted that Shaw was trying to come up with plays that would take advantage of Yonamine's abilities. It conjectured that the Hawaiian might even kick for the team that finished second to the Cleveland Browns in the AAFC in 1946. In any event, Yonamine had lost twelve pounds while in camp. The "Nisei star" needed rice to keep up his strength, the *Pacific Citizen* pointed out. [18]

More focused on Yonamine as a Nikkei than Grieve. UPI sportswriter Hal Wood had a great deal to say about the 49er recruit. One story he wrote was headlined in the *Oxnard Press-Courier*, "Jap Gridder Fears No Pro Behemoths." Wood predicted, "This year the San Francisco Forty-Niners will introduce to the fans across the nation one Wally Yonamine (pronounced Yon-a-mean-e), a full blooded Japanese who never set foot on the U.S. mainland until 1946, as one of its backfield stars." To Wood, "Wally . . . is real American despite his ancestors . . . and has absorbed the game of football just as the average U.S. mainland boy does in his school days." Yonamine, Wood conceded, was a smallish 170 pounds, but big for a "Japanese." In any event, he can hit as hard as a 200-pounder and was not "afraid of any man on the gridiron." Shaw, according to Wood, believed that Yonamine would become "one of the sensations" of the AAFC—a sensation who would excel on both sides of the ball. Revealingly, Shaw conceded that Yonamine was "tied up a bit" but no more than "you or I would be if we were playing as the only white man on a Japanese team." A week later, Wood quoted Shaw again on Yonamine. The coach said the Hawaiian provided a key to the 49ers success. The franchise needed a "scat back," and Yonamine would hopefully offer the speed and elusiveness the 49ers needed. [19]

An intrasquad game in Salinas presented Yonamine with his first public exposure as a 49er. The *Pacific Citizen* avowed, "The Hawaiian Nisei who is the most highly touted rookie in the All-American Football Conference proved himself to be a press agent's dream." Yonamine, indeed, returned a punt for an eighty-nine-yard touchdown and scored another touchdown on a twenty-six-yard pass from Frankie Albert. On defense, the Hawaiian pulled down an interception. In addition, the weekly reported that among the 3,500 who watched the game were 400 Nisei, about half of whom were GIs enrolled at the Military Intelligence School in nearby Monterey. The next week the *Citizen* explained that while the 49ers signed Yonamine because of his ability, the team's front office, engaging in niche marketing, saw dollar signs since so many Nisei showed up for the Salinas game and another intrasquad contest at San Jose, where Yonamine also shined. [20]

While Yonamine made the 49ers, Hosea did not. Even so, the Hawaiian halfback became a steady denizen of the 49ers' bench. After the 49ers beat the Brooklyn Dodgers in the 1947 season opener, the "Japanese American halfback from Hawaii" saw little action. In late September, a wire story in the *Nevada State-Journal* revealed that Yonamine would probably get plenty of work against the New York Yankees by spelling starting halfback John Stryskalski. "The young Hawaiian-Japanese star" had seemingly been very much involved in the 49ers workouts leading up to the game. [21]

But the Hawaiian remained little used. The *San Francisco Chronicle* maintained: "Wallace Yonamine, Hawaii-born Japanese, gets all tied up on the San Francisco 49er bench and can't do his best work when sent in at halfback. . . . Yonamine is afraid the big crowds at Kezar—biggest he's ever seen in his life—won't accept him as a U.S. citizen, because of his ancestry. In Honolulu, yes; on the mainland, no. That's what he thinks, though he's an ex-GI." Buck Shaw elaborated, asserting that Yonamine's effectiveness had been impacted by the gridder's apprehensiveness over whether he would gain acceptance. Shaw insisted that Yonamine was "extremely conscious of being a Japanese. I try to tell him everything is okeh, but he is worried anyhow." [22]

Seemingly to discredit Yonamine's concerns, the *Chronicle* interviewed Babe Nomura competing down the peninsula from Yonamine in San Jose. Nomura responded that he had not encountered racism, adding, "I don't know what you're talking about. Everybody treated me fine. At home and on the road." Spartan coach, Bill Hubbard, stressed that Nomura was well liked by teammates and welcomed by fans at home and away. In other words, if Yonamine feared anti-Nikkei bigotry, it was all in his head. This will hardly be the last time a member of a racial minority group will be told this. [23]

As it turned out, Yonamine got his first and last taste of significant action against the Chicago Rockets. Before the game, the *Chronicle*'s Bruce Lee speculated that the Rockets' weak defense was vulnerable to a "breakaway" back like Yonamine, who apparently had been improving. The "Nisei scatback" carried the ball eight times, averaging a competent 4.7 yards per carry. His longest run was seventeen yards. In addition, Yonamine caught two passes, while intercepting another.[24]

Yonamine told Robert Fitts that his experiences with his 49er teammates were pleasant enough. He especially got along with his roommate, halfback Ed Carr. Yet Yonamine believed that he was targeted by the opposition in that rival players, he believed, proved quite willing to use excessive violence against him. Despite charges that he could not put up with the pressure of playing big-time football in San Francisco and fumbled too often, Yonamine thought things went reasonably well in 1947 and that he had a good chance to stick around for another season with the 49ers. Indeed, Yonamine's statistics were not shabby. He got into twelve games and started three. He rushed nineteen times for seventy-four yards, caught three passes for forty yards, and did a little kick returning for the 49ers, as well as intercepting a pass for twenty yards. Moreover, despite his reputation as a fumbler, he apparently lost no fumbles.[25]

So Yonamine did not give up on football after 1947 season. He tried out for the 49ers again in 1948, but a hand injury suffered while playing baseball in Hawai'i, made it hard for the versatile athlete to make the team that now boasted of an exciting, swift rookie running back from Los Angeles, Joe Perry, who would ultimately put together a Hall of Fame career with the 49ers. Yonamine therefore headed home to play for the Hawaiian Warriors, a powerhouse in the Pacific Coast Football League. The *Honolulu Record* cheered Yonamine's homecoming to Hawaiian football. At the very least, he did well with the Warriors. He added more punch to an already effective contingent of backfield standouts such as Wally Lam Ho, Richard Asato, and Joe Corn as well as extend the Warriors' gate appeal.[26]

The *Pacific Citizen* reported to Nikkei readers that Yonamine had proven a "sensation" with the Warriors. Consequently, the 49ers promised him another chance. But the *Citizen* cautioned readers that the Bay Area franchise was loaded with backfield talent. In any event, Yonamine might turn up on another AAFC team, the *Pacific Citizen* guessed, having the Los Angeles Dons in mind.[27]

In 1949, Yonamine gave big league pro football one more shot, but once again the 49ers cut him. Arriving in camp with another Hawaiian, a colorful placekicker of Portuguese and Spanish descent, Bill Pacheco, Yonamine did well in an intrasquad game held in Kezar Stadium, nabbing a touchdown pass from Frankie Albert. But it was not enough as both he and Pacheco were released and would, according to the *Chronicle*, "pay . . . their own fares back to the islands."[28]

Thus, Yonamine was back in Hawai'i and with the Warriors in the fall of 1949. In September 1949, the Warriors traveled to North Carolina to down the Wilmington Clippers of the American Professional League. Yonamine scored on a seventy-two-yard pass and run. Eventually, he gave up on professional football and embarked on a pioneering baseball career on the U.S. mainland and Japan. Yonamine later explained, "I thought I could make it in football, but I didn't realize the other players were giants." Moreover, he noted that professional baseball paid better than professional football.[29]

When Herman Wedemeyer's college career ended, he was drafted by the AAFC's Los Angeles Dons for the 1948 season. Wedemeyer was so embraced by Bay Area football fans that rumors circulated that the San Francisco 49ers, like the Dons a charter member of the short-lived AAFC, were willing to trade star quarterback Frankie Albert for Wedemeyer. This was no small matter as Albert was not only one of the best quarterbacks in pro football at the time but a former Stanford hero.[30]

Much was expected of Wedemeyer as a professional. Southern California sportswriter, Rube Samuelson, lauded Wedemeyer as "a money player if there was one" before the 1948 season officially began. The *San Francisco Chronicle*'s Bill Leiser, clearly one of Wedemeyer's most fervent supporters, opined that the Hawaiian was the "best all purpose backfield football player we ever saw," while predicting he would adjust to the pros adequately. The *Los Angeles Times* added that Wedemeyer was "one of the shiftiest, trickiest runners in the game."[31]

Yet Wedemeyer did not live up to the bloated expectations of him as a Don, although he was far from bad. The fact that his former St. Mary's coach, Jimmy Phelan, was named head coach of the Dons probably perhaps added pressure on Wedemeyer. Still, when the Los Angeles Dons beat the Brooklyn Dodgers in early September 1948, "Squirmin" Herman Wedemeyer was credited for helping teammates Glenn Dobbs and Len Ford attain the victory. During the game, he made a key twenty-seven-yard run and twenty-six-yard pass reception. In October, the Dons beat the Chicago Rockets, thanks, in part, to Wedemeyer's sixty-one-yard run which set up a touchdown pass thrown to him by star tailback, Glen Dobbs. Against the powerful Cleveland Browns, Wedemeyer caught a twenty-five-yard pass, representing one of the few offensive highlights for the Dons. But despite showing some prowess on defense, Wedemeyer's season with the Dons was seen widely as a disappointment. One wire story claimed that the "little Hawaiian struggled" to gain 249 yards in seventy-nine carries. The 49ers, in any event, sought to trade for Wedemeyer's services, although Phelan preferred to send him across the country to the Baltimore Colts, which caused one wire report to compare the ballyhoo attending the Dons' signing of Wedemeyer and the reclusive way they sold him to the Colts.[32]

Many wondered why Wedemeyer did not take the AAFC by storm. Some asserted that the Dons' single wing formation did not effectively take advantage of Wedemeyer's skills, although the Hawaiian had played in the single wing while at St. Mary's. Still, Jimmy Phelan himself speculated that Wedemeyer's skill set was a better fit for the Colts' T-Formation. But Baltimore proved not so welcoming either, inspiring others to speculate that injuries hampered Wedemeyer's development in the AAFC. Others believed that Wedemeyer just did not take it seriously enough to excel as a pro.[33]

Discouraged by his AAFC experiences, Wedemeyer sought a career in professional baseball in the spring of 1950. However versatile an athlete, Wedemeyer's dalliance with professional baseball proved brief. The San Francisco Seals gave him a tryout, and after they shipped him down the minor-league ladder, Wedemeyer drifted from one "bush league" team to another.[34]

Still optimistic about their one-time hero, the prayers of some Bay Area football fans were no doubt answered when the San Francisco 49ers signed Wedemeyer for the 1950 season. It was hoped that Wedemeyer would finally get the opportunity to shine that he failed to attain with the Dons or the Colts. Moreover, he would perhaps raise attendance at Kezar Stadium, where the 49ers played their home games. Some, albeit unfairly, expected that Wedemeyer would prove once and for all whether he had been overrated or not as a collegiate. Nevertheless, Bay Area sportswriters doubted Wedemeyer could break into the roster of the 49ers, a team with a plethora of offensive talent. To be sure, Wedemeyer showed flashes of preseason promise for the youthful San Francisco franchise, but the 49ers, facing their first year in the NFL, decided to cut Wedemeyer.[35]

A closer look at Wedemeyer's professional career indicates that he was hardly a failure, if perhaps a disappointment. As a Don, in 1948, he was sixth in the AAFC in all-purpose yards through passing, rushing, receiving, and kick returning with 1,187 yards. The next year with Baltimore, he placed third with 1,226 yards, tying him, by the way, with 49er great, Joe Perry. What is more, his 1949 performance garnered him first team International News Service all-NFL/AAFC team as a defensive back.[36]

After Wedemeyer's pro career ended, he took up a variety of occupations on the islands. In the mid-1950s, a wire story reported that he worked as a representative for Hawaiian Airlines, while informing the press that he quit football because it was no longer enjoyable, and he wanted to return to Hawai'i. Aside from working for Hawaiian Airlines, Wedemeyer also served on the Honolulu city council and Hawaiian state legislature. However, Wedemeyer was most visible as an actor, mainly in the original *Hawaii Five-0* television show.[37]

Yonamine and Wedemeyer were not the only Hawaiian running backs getting a look-see from the pros in the late 1940s. In 1948, John

Naumu joined the same Los Angeles Dons that also employed Wedemeyer. His career with the Dons was even more brief. Naumu came off the bench in nine games. In the process, he returned six kickoffs for 121 yards. John and his brother, Sal, who would play for USC, were, according to the U.S. Census manuscripts in 1940, sons of a racially Hawaiian father who operated a pineapple farm on Molokai and a "Caucasian Hawaiian" mother.[38]

The son of a Hawaiian mother, Joe Corn came from a Honolulu working-class background to eventually play for the Los Angeles Rams. The five-foot six-inch Corn had starred for Farrington High School in Honolulu. In 1947, he competed for the semi-professional Moiliili Bears in Hawai'i's Senior Football League and was called the league's "best climax runner." In 1948, Corn impressed the Los Angeles Rams when the NFL squad visited the islands before the onset of the NFL season to play the Warriors. The *Los Angeles Times'* Braven Dyer described the Hawaiian halfback as "one of the fastest men in captivity." Surely, Dyer claimed, a major-league pro franchise should avail themselves of Corn's services.[39]

Taking Dyer's hint, the Rams picked up Corn, although the Los Angeles team was well supplied with offensive backfield talent. As of October 31, Corn played little for the Rams, which disappointed columnist Frank Finch of the *Los Angeles Times*. The next game, however, Corn was given the opportunity to return two kickoffs—for nineteen and thirty-two yards. Finch seemed somewhat mollified. Still, Finch argued that "ukulele Ike" should play more. As it turned out, Corn got little action in his only NFL season. He managed to carry the ball eleven times for twenty-seven yards and returned four punts for forty-nine yards.[40]

HAWAIIAN PROS OF THE 1950S AND EARLY 1960S

Hawaiian linemen succeeded in putting together longer careers in the pros in the 1950s. Jim and Herman Clark began their pro careers early in the decade. Jim played a couple of years as a lineman for the NFL's Washington franchise. However, Herman starred for the Chicago Bears. In the mid-1950s, Irv Goodman claimed that Herman Clark's line work aided the Chicago Bears as the "Monsters of the Midway" powered their way to an NFL championship in 1956. Herman made the *Sporting News'* All-NFL team in 1955. The next year, the Associated Press and the *New York Daily News* named him to their second string All-NFL team.[41]

While Herman Clark strengthened the Bears, Charlie Ane did likewise for their conference rival, the Detroit Lions, from 1953 through 1959. As in college, Ane could not escape exoticization in the pros. During his first training camp, according to *Philadelphia Inquirer* writer Hal Freeman, the Hawaiian became known as "'Pineapple' Ane." Drafted in the fourth round, Ane stood out as a versatile lineman, mastering both tackle and center for the Lions. During his seven years in Detroit, Ane was named to the Pro Bowl game twice, 1956 and 1958. In 1956, the Associated Press tabbed Ane for its second team, all-NFL. However, the Newspaper Enterprise Associates (NEA) and the UPI chose him for the first team that same year. The next year the NEA named him on its second team, all-NFL.[42]

In 1960, the NFL expanded to Dallas, in part to confront the newborn American Football League (AFL), which installed a franchise in the Texas city. To stock the Dallas franchise's roster, the new team, then called the Rangers, could draft players from other NFL franchises — players seen as expendable by those franchises. Ane had previously announced his retirement from the Lions, who, in turn, saw no problem with the Rangers trying to sign him but warned the new franchise that Ane was determined to leave professional football. The Rangers' general manager, Tex Schramm, hoped to persuade "the colorful Hawaiian" to reconsider. Nevertheless, Ane declared he would rather stay in Honolulu and coach high school football than report to the team that would eventually be called the Cowboys.[43]

A few years after Ane's retirement, Lion teammate Bobby Layne told the press that the Hawaiian had a bad temper. A tempestuous sort himself, the Hall of Fame quarterback said he had a tough time controlling Ane. He feared that if the lineman got out of line Ane would be thrown out of the game. Indeed, Ane was tossed from an NFL championship game with the Cleveland Browns in 1954 after tangling with the latter's Carlton Massey. The AP account of the game gave no reason for the fracas.[44]

Unlike the Clark brothers and Ane, Joe Francis was an NFL quarterback. In the late 1950s, Joe Francis left the single wing Oregon State football program to move under center and try his hand as a T-formation quarterback for the Green Bay Packers, but after a couple of years was moved aside by the great Bart Starr. Francis returned to the islands, where he coached and taught at Pearl City High School. One of his sons later played football and basketball at the University of Hawai'i and then a few years in the pros.[45]

Transitioning from a single wing tailback to T-formation quarterback might have proven too difficult for Francis, although he showed glimpses of competence to his Green Bay bosses. The Packers drafted Francis in the fifth round after the 1957 season. In February 1958, Francis signed a Packers contract. According to the *Milwaukee Journal*, the "native of Hawaii" provoked coach Ray McLean into boasting that the gridder was talented enough to excel at quarterback, halfback, or defensive back. West Coast scouts, McLean testified, had hung a "can't miss" label on Francis.[46]

At the end of the 1958 season, Chuck Johnson of the *Milwaukee Journal* expressed disappointment in all three of the Packer quarterbacks. Starr needed more experience, and veteran Babe Parilli was inconsistent. As for Francis, his inexperience with the T-formation had exiled him to the bench more than Starr and Parilli. Still, Packers coach Ray McLean averred that Francis had potential. Mclean had apparently thought about switching Francis into a defensive back, but the Hawaiian was too slow. Meanwhile, he was also thinking about using Francis in some kind of spread formation to take advantage of Francis's running and throwing ability.[47]

Because Starr and Parilli were proving unsatisfactory and the Packers' season was doomed in any event, McLean started Francis against the San Francisco 49ers and Los Angeles Rams late in 1958. The Rams beat the Packers, but Francis earned praise for keeping Green Bay in the game with his talent for running and passing. The Hawaiian threw for one touchdown and rushed for another. Francis finished the 1958 season completing fifteen of thirty-one passes. More impressively, he carried the ball twenty-four times for over six yards per rush.[48]

Before the 1959 season, new coach Vince Lombardi gave Francis a chance to quarterback the Packers in an exhibition game against the Philadelphia Eagles. According to former Packer end, Gary Knafelc, Lombardi liked "Pineapple Joe"'s potential. Francis seemingly responded well to the challenge. The Packers won, and Francis was accorded a great deal of credit for the victory. Indeed, Francis threw key pass completions of forty-four and fifty-three yards. However, during the regular season, Francis stayed mostly on the bench, throwing but eighteen passes for five completions. During training camp in 1960, Francis broke a leg, and Lombardi subsequently pinned the Packers' hopes on Bart Starr. Francis then departed from the NFL for a stint in the Canadian Football League before returning to the islands to a career as a teacher and coach. Some decades later, Joe Francis's son Ikaika Alama-Francis would suit up for the Detroit Lions during the 2007 and 2008 seasons.[49]

ROMAN GABRIEL AND LATE TWENTIETH-CENTURY PROS

Fortunately finding himself the object of a bidding war between the AFL's Oakland Raiders and the NFL's Los Angeles Rams, Roman Gabriel signed with the latter, claiming he got more money than he expected from the older franchise. As it turned out, Gabriel did not really become a full-time starter for the Rams until the 1966 season. However, he periodically commanded the Rams' offense before then. For example, after the Rams' 1963 season soured, Gabriel was given a chance to start a game against the Minnesota Vikings. Gabriel's turn as a starting quarterback worked out fine as he led the Rams to a surprising victory. The next week Gabriel passed for one touchdown and scored another as the Rams beat the rival San Francisco 49ers, 28–21. Apparently, Gabriel was not an overnight sensation as a starter in his early years as he frequently found others quarterbacking the Rams in his stead. Nevertheless, in 1964, his head coach, Harland Svare, insisted, "He stays in the cup as well as any quarterback in the league."[50]

Gabriel's career proved durable and productive, while occasionally evoking commentary about his ethnic ancestry. In 1967, Sam Blair of the *Dallas Morning News* asserted that Gabriel was "known as the world's tallest Filipino." He was also becoming one of the elite quarterbacks in the NFL. In December 1967, Gabriel was named NFL player of the week for heaving three touchdown passes and leading the Rams to an easy 34–10 victory over the Baltimore Colts. In September 1969, a piece in the *Trenton Evening Times* depicted Gabriel as the "biggest Filipino alive." The daily added that as quarterback and team leader, Gabriel was not "ultra-animated. But then nobody shoves him around either. He's an imperturbable field general, not terribly emotional, with a strong arm." After the 1969 season, Gabriel won the prestigious Jim Thorpe Award, bestowed on the NFL's most valuable player of the year. In a wire story announcing the quarterback's honor, he was described as "a big guy with dark moody features reflecting his Filipino ancestry. Gabriel's success led the *Seattle Times* to call him a "Pinoy hero." Meanwhile, Gabriel acknowledged his Filipino ancestry by jokingly referring to himself as a member of the "all-Filipino team."[51]

Gabriel maintained an elevated level of success over the next few years. Sam Blair told readers in 1971 that in a poll of NFL head coaches Gabriel and Joe Namath were considered the two most wanted quarterbacks in the league. Nevertheless, at a time when elite quarterbacks were not multimillionaires, Gabriel partnered with fellow Ram Merlin Olson to run a travel agency in 1968, while eschewing many endorsements because advertisers demanded he advocate liquor and tobacco products.[52]

Meanwhile, Gabriel, as did some other prominent professional athletes in Los Angeles, got a taste of Hollywood. In 1969, Gabriel and Merlin Olson were acting on the set of *The Undefeated*, a Western starring John Wayne and Rock Hudson. Gabriel, surprisingly, had more than a bit part. He played "a full blooded Cherokee" and Wayne's character's adopted son. That Gabriel played an American Indian did not seem so surprising at the time, given that his appearance led teammates to call him "Indian."[53]

In all, Gabriel lasted sixteen years battling off NFL linebackers and defensive linemen. For twelve years, he quarterbacked the Rams, while his last four years were with the Philadelphia Eagles. He was named to the Pro Bowl four times, led the NFL in touchdown passes in 1969 and 1973 and the NFL in pass completions and yardage in 1973. After Gabriel's playing career ceased, he headed into coaching. He coached college ball at Cal Poly, quitting the school when he feared it would dump football. He subsequently became an assistant for the Boston Breakers of the United States Football League.[54]

In the late 1960s and early 1970s, Hawaiian Mel Tom was a fine defensive end in the NFL. After his rookie year with the Philadelphia Eagles, Tom was named to the all-Rookies' defensive team. In 1971, the NFL fined him for excessive aggressiveness in blocking Roger Staubach after the great Cowboy quarterback tossed an interception. Headline to the wire story reporting the fine declared "Mel Tom Fined 1,000 Pineapples." Tom's stint with the Eagles abruptly ended amid the 1973 season. Apparently, Tom got into a dispute with an Eagle assistant coach. "The reserved Hawaiian" testified that the coach had made degrading comments about him and that he would just as soon retire to tend to his business interests on the West Coast if the Eagles did not trade him. The Eagles, indeed, moved Tom to the Chicago Bears for a future draft choice. After sticking it out with the Bears for a couple of years, in November 1975 Tom was put on waivers, and his NFL career had ended. Notably, his daughter Logan was a star volleyball player at Stanford and performed for the U.S. Olympic team.[55]

Three Hawaiians not only showed up on NFL rosters in the 1970s but demonstrated that they could excel beyond the gridiron. Hawaiian Rockne Freitas played several years as a tackle in the NFL for the Detroit Lions. In 1970, Freitas was named by *Pro Football Weekly* to the all-NFC's first team. In 1972, the UPI honored him as an all-NFL second team pick. After leaving professional football, Freitas put together a distinguished career in higher education. A holder of a Ph.D. in education from UH, Freitas became Vice-Chancellor of UH, West O'ahu in 2013. A couple of Hawaiians by way of Michigan State wound up with the Kansas City Chiefs in the 1970s. In the mid- to late 1970s, Jim Nicholson started at offensive tackle for the Chiefs, while also playing a bit for the San Diego Chargers and then the 49ers. Nicholson subsequently became a lawyer, serving recently as a head of Hawai'i's labor relations board. Arnold Morgado eventually joined him in Kansas City after leaving East Lansing via UH. Playing four years with the Chiefs, Morgado generally came off the bench. Upon returning to the islands, Morgado did many things such as chair the Honolulu city council and coach football at UH.[56]

The 1980s witnessed Asian and Pacific Islander Americans competing in the NFL. One of them possessed South Central Asian ancestry. Former Colorado University standout Sanjay Beach headed to the NFL in the late 1980s. The pass receiver played four years as a nonregular for teams such as San Francisco 49ers, Green Bay Packers, and New York Jets. In 1992, he caught seventeen passes for the Packers for 122 yards and one touchdown. Beach moved on to eventually become a financial advisor for Merrill Lynch after getting an MBA at Colorado State.[57]

Offensive lineman Eugene Chung was the first Asian American drafted in the first round by an NFL team. Taken by the New England Patriots, the Korean American offensive lineman from Virginia Tech started several games his first two years in the NFL in 1992 and 1993. The last three years of his career he was a nonstarter for the Patriots, Jacksonville Jaguars, and then the Indianapolis Colts. Chung remained in football as a coach. Most recently, he has been an assistant offensive line coach for the Philadelphia Eagles and the Kansas City Chiefs.[58]

A couple of mixed racial linebackers stood out in the NFL in the late 1990s. Possessing Filipino ancestry, Tedy Bruschi starred as a linebacker for the New England Patriots from 1996 through 2008. The former Arizona University standout was named to the 2004 Pro Bowl. After a severe illness laid him low for the 2004 season, he returned to the Patriots and won the AP's NFL Comeback Player of the Year in 2005. Bruschi has since become an analyst for ESPN. Meanwhile, an interviewer asked him about his Filipino heritage, telling the former linebacker he was "an inspiration to Filipino-Americans." Bruschi said he had never been to the Philippines but was proud of his Filipino heritage, adding "My mother taught my wife to make lumpia." Stanford All-American Kailee Wong carved out a durable NFL career. Starting in 1998, the linebacker performed for nine years, four with the Minnesota Viking and five with the Houston Texans. Armed with a degree in Economics from Stanford, Kailee Wong was most recently a derivatives broker in Houston.[59]

Possessing Korean heritage, Hines Ward came into the NFL in 1998 as a Pittsburgh Steeler. The durable Ward helped spark the Steelers to a Super Bowl victory over the Seattle Seahawks in 2004, winning the Super Bowl's MVP award. He remained a feared receiver for the Steelers until he retired in 2011. Among postseason honors he earned were trips to the Pro Bowl from 2001 to 2004. Moreover, the AP selected him as second team all-NFL from 2002 through 2004. Since retirement, Ward has worked as a television football analyst, but also engaged in a wide variety of charitable activities.[60]

NFL players with Vietnamese ancestry begin and end thus far with Dat Nguyen. In 1999, the Dallas Cowboys drafted Nguyen, making him the first Vietnamese American picked by an NFL franchise. While excited, Nguyen expressed some concern to the press. He wondered "if I will go through the kind of racism that African American players went through when they first came into the league." He also hoped that he could be a role model for budding Asian American athletes. Known as a hard-hitting tackler, albeit a bit undersized for his position, Nguyen retired from the NFL in 2005 after several years of starting as a linebacker for the Cowboys. Painful injuries seemed to have cut short his career. Meanwhile, the AP named him to second team all-NFL in 2003. Subsequently, Nguyen took up coaching for the Dallas Cowboys and Texas A& M. More recently, he became a sports talk show host for a San Antonio radio station while becoming a committed spokesperson for Roman Catholicism.[61]

Before Nguyen's playing days with the Cowboys were done, Irwin Tang wrote a piece about him for *Asian Week*. Tang called Nguyen the "quarterback" of the Cowboys defense and proclaimed him well liked by Cowboy fans. "America's Team" as the Cowboys were branded by the team's front office, adoring fans, and sometimes sycophantic press, had fallen on troubled times in the late 1990s. However, Tang proclaimed, "The one bright spot over the last three years has been the Nguyen-led Dallas defense. His ability to identify plays and blast to the ball, often in the offense's backfield, has changed the course of many games. Of course, he's also known for laying some 'licks,' as they say in Texas."[62]

Nguyen told Tang that he experienced racism growing up in Texas. His family handled it by looking inward. His parents told him to "hang out" with Vietnamese American friends, as well as his family, because they could not trust whites. The linebacker remembered that as a youth he and his Vietnamese friends were segregated on one team in a local soccer league. His team did not lose a game in its last season, but, Nguyen remembered, won no applause from the white people attending the awards ceremony.[63]

His relative uniqueness as an Asian American professional football player exerted pressure on Nguyen. He feared that if he failed, people would say, "Oh, he's Asian. He can't play. . . . The things I do, not just on the field, but off the field, I know I'm representing the Asian culture, my family, my community. I'm representing all the Southeast Asians." To which, Tang responded, "He proved himself 172 times in his second season as a starter. His 172 tackles that year placed him as the second all-time single season tackler in Cowboys history."[64]

Other football players possessing Asian ancestry joined the NFL in the late 1990s and early 2000s. Korean American Lloyd Lee became a San Diego Charger in 1998 after playing with Dartmouth. He saw very little action, but after his playing days in the NFL, he took up coaching. He served as an assistant coach for the Chicago Bears in the 2000s. More recently, he has worked as Vice-President for Football Operations @ USA Football. Joe Wong was an offensive lineman who had more than a taste of the NFL. A Hawaiian, Wong originally competed for the University of Hawai'i before transferring to BYU. The Miami Dolphins drafted Wong for the 1999 season. Wong subsequently played for the Philadelphia Eagles and the Oakland Raiders. Returning to Hawai'i after his playing days ended, Wong became a high school coach at his alma mater, Kailua High. The sons of an African American father and a Japanese mother, Johnnie and Chad Morton achieved more than a few fine moments in the NFL. The former had some good years as a pass receiver and kick returner, particularly for the Detroit Lions from 1994 through 2005. He later got involved in mixed martial arts but also with the law for lying under oath. In 2000, brother Chad joined the NFL, where he remained through the 2006 season as mostly a kick returner for teams such as the New Orleans Saints and New York Giants. He since has served as an assistant coach for the Green Bay Packers and, more recently, the Seattle Seahawks.[65]

TWENTY-FIRST-CENTURY PROS

The NFL in the early twenty-first century was sprinkled with players of Asian ancestry who reflected the demographic changes brought on by liberalization of America's immigration laws and the growing presence of mixed race people in the United States. A Californian who played for little Augustiana College in South Dakota, part-Thai, Kevin Kaesviharn roamed the defensive backfields of NFL squads from 2001 to 2009. Will Demps, a son of an African American father and Korean mother, left San Diego State to often perform well as a defensive back in the early 2000s. After leaving the NFL, Demps told a reporter, "I've always embraced my Korean side throughout my life. I never felt like I had to choose myself." In 2004, Brandon Chillar, a 253-pound linebacker and Indo-American, began a seven-year career in the NFL. Possessing Filipino ancestry, Chris Gocong and Eugene Amano played NFL football for much of the twenty-first century's first decade. A defensive back from Cal Poly, Gocong started many games for the Philadelphia Eagles and Cleveland Browns. For nine years, Eugene Amano was an offensive lineman for the Tennessee Titans in the early 2000s.[66]

Before entering the NFL, Ed Wang expressed immense pride in the possibility of becoming the first Chinese American drafted in the NFL. He said, "It's going to mean the world to me. . . . It will make my parents happy, too. I am doing it for them." A *Sports Illustrated* reporter, John Lopez, maintained that his parents sent videos of him in action for Virginia Tech to their relatives in Beijing. In response, the relatives communicated confusion over what exactly they were seeing. Lopez stressed that if drafted Wang would achieve a pioneering status as the first of his ethnicity taken in the NFL draft: "It will be a significant barrier-breaking moment for Chinese-Americans, a proud moment for the parents who always convinced him to ignore perceptions. It also will be a potential marketing plum for the team that drafts him. But beyond the cultural significance, Wang is a humble, high-quality player who overcame stereotypes and could open a lot of doors for Asian-Americans." Wang responded, "I've embraced it. . . . I definitely take pride that I could be the first Chinese-American to play in the NFL. . . . My mom always told me to live a low-key life. You don't have to brag or talk about yourself a lot. Just do the right things and you'll be noticed." After being drafted in the fifth round, Wang, as it turned out, enjoyed only a brief career in the NFL, getting into six games for the Bills in 2010, although he tried to hook on to the Oakland Raiders and Philadelphia Eagles in subsequent years.[67]

Part-Japanese Haruki Nakamura was an effective defensive back during a five-year stint in the NFL. Drafted by the Baltimore Ravens in 2008 out of Cincinnati University, he got into two Super Bowls. Then, he moved on to the Carolina Panthers where he started all thirteen of the games he was in during the 2012 season. A concussion, however, apparently put an end to his career. While with the Ravens, Nakamura claimed a responsibility as a role model for athletically inclined Asian Americans. He told the *Rafu Shimpo*'s Jordan Ikeda:

> I think it's our responsibility to kind of show those kids who think that they can't play in a professional sport. I think it's our responsibility to show that it is very possible. It's a very possible thing to do in life. I'm getting ready to do a camp next summer, and I'm going to try and focus it more towards the Asian population. One of our goals is to obviously incorporate football, but the one background that I had in my life was judo. It was a very, very important background for me. My father was an eighth degree black belt and an Olympic coach and world team coach here in the United States. It's one of those things that I want to make sure that the Asian population is included. I mean, that's where I came from, that's my background. It's mostly to show that we can make it to the NFL. [68]

While undrafted by the NFL, Doug Baldwin emerged as a fine receiver for the Seattle Seahawks. He became the first person of Filipino ancestry to catch a touchdown pass in a Super Bowl game when the Seahawks subdued the Denver Broncos in 2014. Baldwin's grandmother was born and raised in the Philippines, where she met his grandfather who was then in the U.S. military. Moreover, she has kept Filipino traditions and customs alive for the succeeding generations. Baldwin, indeed, claims he has learned about heart from his maternal grandmother, takes pride in his Filipino heritage, and eats lumpia. Moreover, in 2014 he was anxious to show his support for the survivors of the devastating typhoon Haiyan, which demolished much of the region of the Philippines where his grandmother originated. Indeed, journalist Filipino Elton Lugay has written that Baldwin tried to raise consciousness about the devastation caused by Haiyan: "Remember that November photo where he came running down Century Link Field before their game with the Minnesota Vikings carrying a Filipino flag? Sure, the flag was carried wrong—red side up—but Filipinos were more enthused to learn that Baldwin is Filipino-American inspiring the people of Leyte to keep fighting, rather than the flag signifying a state of war." [69]

BEYOND THE NFL

In the mid-1950s, *Sports Illustrated* reader Robert Mariucci wrote *SI* that while traveling through the upstate New York, he caught a few semi-pro games. In so doing, "I noticed a very fast right halfback, who ran full speed every minute of the game. He blocked viciously, hit the middle of the line and ran the ends like fury. He ran 85 yards for a touchdown against Batavia and set up two more on runs of 20 and 30 yards. In the game against Fredonia, he gained almost 200 yards, including runs of 70 and 55 yards." Mariucci discovered eventually that he was watching a thoracic surgeon who, at the time, was assistant director of the Niagara Chest Hospital and a Fellow of the American College of Chest Physicians. "When I met Dr. Tashiro," Mariucci concluded, "I asked him if the other ballplayers called him "Pappy." He smiled, shook his head and said, 'No, they call me 'Grandpappy.'"[70]

In 1963, the *Rome Daily Sentinel*, published out of Rome, New York, declared Kiyoshi Tashiro its Man of the Year in sports. The honor derived from his still playing semi-professionally at forty-seven as a member of the Mohawk Valley Falcons of the Atlantic Coast League. *Sentinel* columnist Fran Regan informed readers that Tashiro was recruited by the NFL after leaving Harvard, where the surgeon claimed he played intercollegiate football with Joe Kennedy, Jr. Rather than bother with the NFL, Tashiro decided to pursue a medical career while playing minor league and semi-professional football on the side. Among the teams he claimed to have competed for were the Akron Bears, Brooklyn Bushwicks, Duluth Eskimos, and Buffalo Bills. Tashiro later clarified that he had played frosh football at Harvard, but was declared ineligible for the varsity because had earned money as a judo instructor, thus making him a professional athlete.[71]

In 2009, Jason Cruz of the *Northwestern Asian Weekly* told readers about Rich Lee-Kim who played semi-professional football for the Snohomish Vikings of the Northwest Football League. The six-foot-one, 278-pound Lee-Kim came from Minnesota but played high school football at Lake Washington. Wearing a bandana of the South Korean flag on his helmet, Lee-Kim told Cruz he experienced a great deal of racism growing up and stares and insults while playing football. But Cruz writes, "Despite derogatory remarks, there are many positive aspects. After a game, a young Japanese kid wanted to meet Lee-Kim because he recognized that Lee-Kim was Asian. Lee-Kim remembers the parents of the child saying, 'He wanted to meet you right away. They haven't seen a full Asian [football player].'"[72]

The Pacific Coast Football League (PCFL) offered relatively elevated level professional football in the 1940s. One of the league's biggest stars in the early 1940s was Kenny Washington, whose racial identity kept him from joining the NFL until after World War II. Around the time that Washington joined the NFL's Los Angeles Rams, the Hawaiian Warriors entered the PCFL. In the Pacific Coast Football League, Joe Kaulukukui did an excellent job of quarterbacking the Hawaii Warriors. Many other Warriors possessed Asian Pacific ancestry. The 1947 and 1948 editions of the Warriors were colorful and talented and included former Redlands star Al Chang, as well as exciting halfbacks, Wally Yonamine and Joe Corn.[73]

Playing for the PCFL's Sacramento Nuggets were Hawaiian John Kalemiano and Japanese American Paul Kuwabara. Kalemiano, according to the U.S. census data of 1930, lived with a Honolulu family headed by Alfred Wong, a clerk, and his Hawaiian wife, Abigail. The ten-year-old future gridder was described as Hawaiian. Prior to suiting up for the Nuggets, Kalemiano had played for the semi-pro Richmond Boilermakers in 1943. At the time, the *San Francisco Examiner* dubbed him the "Kanaka wingman from Honolulu." Reportedly he had come to the mainland on a college scholarship but wound up, the *Examiner* maintained, working for Kaiser Shipyards in the East Bay. Kalemiano also played for the San Jose Mustangs of the PCFL. As for Kuwabara, he had previously proven a stellar lineman at Sacramento High School and Sacramento Junior College.[74]

In the 1970s, the short-lived World Football League installed a franchise in Honolulu. Called the Honolulu Hawaiians, the team proved effective at recruiting NFL standouts such as former Dallas Cowboy backs, Calvin Hill and Duane Thomas. Among the Hawaiians playing for the franchise were running back Glenn Hookano, defensive tackle Levi Stanley, linebacker Jim Kalili, and quarterback Milt Holt.[75]

In Canada, professional football became not only more Americanized by the mid-twentieth century, but capable of attracting talented Americans and nurturing very capable Canadians. Among the latter was Chinese Canadian Norm Kwong. Indeed, few matched Norm Kwong's accomplishments in Canadian football during the postwar era. Hailed as the "China Clipper," Kwong played for both Calgary and Edmonton. Alberta's *Lethbridge Herald* described him as not only a "chunky fullback" but "one of the best Canadians playing Canadian football" at a time when the latter was becoming increasingly dominated by gridders from south of the border. Kwong was not only an exceptional, record-breaking ball carrier in Canada but known as a blocker who could quite capably knock defenders to the ground and then graciously help them to their feet. While Kwong surfaced as a ball-carrying legend in Canada, Hawaiian and former Denver University standout Tom Hugo turned into a perennial all-league lineman in the 1950s as a member of the Montreal Alouettes.[76]

In more recent years, Asian American kickers have made their way into the CFL. After a stint as an All-American placekicker and punter at Utah, Louis Sakoda performed for the Saskatchewan Rough Riders and Edmonton Eskimos. Unfortunately, injuries seemingly limited his professional career. Rutgers grad Jeremy Ito kicked briefly for the Hamilton Tiger-Cats after failing to make the Minnesota Vikings. Ito then turned to the more solid life of investment banking.[77]

The NFL Europe proved an interesting gambit on the part of the NFL to internationalize its brand. Further, it employed some athletes of Asian and Pacific Islander ancestry. Pacific Islander Neo Aoga was a 300-pound-plus quarterback for Azusa Pacific in the late 1990s and early 2000s. He was also good enough to get a shot at playing for Frankfurt in

2001. Since then the NFL pulled out of Europe officially, but professional football, American style, is still played. Former Drake star Scott Phayda-vong decided to give American football in Europe a try, playing for a professional team in Germany. While he claimed he enjoyed his Euro-pean sojourn, Phaydavong returned to the states and pursued a career as an educator. Meanwhile, Timmy Chang never made it in the NFL, al-though he did play professionally in Canada, as well as for NFL Europe. In Canada, he toiled for the Hamilton Tiger-Cats and Winnipeg Blue Bombers, while in Europe he appeared as a quarterback for the Rhein Fire.[78]

Either to exploit female athletes or encourage their agency, some pro-moters have attempted to organize women's professional football leagues. It may not have been their intention, but they opened a social space for at least a couple of Asian American women to cross racialized and genderized borders. One such endeavor placed a team in Hawai'i in the 1990s. Called the Hawaiian Wave, it included pediatrician Debbie Nojima, a five foot, 130-pound fullback. Previously, Nojima had taken up rugby at the University of Colorado and was a big American football fan. In explaining her desire to play professional football, Nojima maintained, "I didn't do it to make a statement. . . . If it does, maybe that's a happy side benefit. I think it's neat to get dirty and mix it up, and then be able to put on a dress and go to a meeting. Being female is just being a person." On the mainland, Alice Wong appeared as a five-foot-one, 130-pound defensive back for the New York Sharks between 2004 and 2007.[79]

PROFESSIONAL COACHES, FRONT OFFICE PERSONNEL, AND OWNERS

As yet, there has been no head coach of an NFL team possessing either Asian or Pacific Islander ancestry. Still, assistant coaches of Asian or Pa-cific Islander ancestry have popped up in recent years. For example, Indo-American Sanjay Lal coached several years as an NFL assistant. The former UCLA and University of Washington wide receiver began his coaching stint at his high school alma mater, Miramonte in Los Angeles in 1996. In the early 2000s, he moved on to college coaching, most con-spicuously for Cal. His work with the Bears must have attracted the nearby Oakland Raiders, which hired him as a wide receiver coach in 2007. Since then he coached wide receivers for the New York Jets, Buffalo Bills, and, more recently, Indianapolis Colts. After playing for USC's "scout team" in the mid-1990s, Rocky Seto joined the Trojan coaching staff as a volunteer assistant. He remained with head coach Pete Carroll when he left Los Angeles for the Seattle Seahawks in 2010. With the Seahawks, he served as a defensive coach until he quit to become a Chris-tian pastor.[80]

There have been a few Pacific Islanders involved in professional coaching. Born in Pago Pago, Kennedy Pola served as running back coach for the Tennessee Titans while Norm Chow was offensive coordinator. A graduate of the prestigious Mater Dei High School program in Santa Ana, California, Pola played linebacker and fullback for USC in the mid-1980s. The history major then headed into coaching—serving as an assistant coach for UCLA, San Diego State, Colorado, USC, and the NFL's Cleveland Browns and Jacksonville Jaguars before journeying with Chow to the Titans. He then returned to USC as an offensive coordinator. Subsequently, USC stirred some controversy by firing him, but he landed on his feet as running backs coach for rival UCLA. Pola's nephew is Troy Polamalu, and he could claim about five other relatives who played big-time college football, including running back Nicky Sualua.[81]

Joe Paopao has been a venerable and peripatetic coach in the Canadian Football League. He also has been the one Pacific Islander to head coach an elite professional squad in North America. Born in Hawai'i but raised in Oceanside, California, the Samoan American quarterbacked at Long Beach State in the mid-1970s. Paopao subsequently took his talents northward to the CFL, where his career began with the British Columbia Lions. In a game against the Toronto Argonauts, Paopao set a CFL record by throwing eighteen consecutive completions. Like Jack Thompson, whom we will discuss more in the next chapter, he was known as the "Throwin' Samoan."[82]

Paopao began his long coaching stint tenure after taking the shoulder pads off for good. First, he was named the British Columbia Lions quarterback coach—a position from which he mentored the legendary Doug Flutie toward CFL greatness. In 1994, he became the Lions' offensive coordinator. Two years later, he was the team's head coach. Paopao resigned his head coaching position after a change in ownership, but he subsequently became Winnipeg's offensive coordinator. In 1999, he returned to British Columbia, where he served as assistant head coach and offensive coordinator. Two years later, Paopao left Canada for a job as offensive coordinator for the San Francisco Demons of the XFL. After the XFL's mourned-by-few demise, he returned to the CFL to work as the Ottawa Renegades' offensive coordinator in 2002 and when the Renegades ceased operations in 2005, he moved on to the Hamilton Tiger-Cats and the BC Lions.[83]

Americans of Asian ancestry have shown up in professional football front offices. War hero and physician Katsumi Kometani served as a board member of the Hawaiian Warriors back in the late 1940s. More significantly, Asian Indian American Parag Marathe worked in the 49ers front office in many positions until named team president in 2014. The man Marathe replaced was Gideon Yu, a Korean American businessperson and part owner of the 49ers. *San Jose Mercury* sportswriter Tim Kawakami declared that the recently constructed Silicon Valley venue for 49er football would not have been built without Yu's guidance. Omar Khan, the son of an Indian father and a Honduran mother, moved up from a student volunteer for the Tulane University football team to a front office position for the Pittsburgh Steelers. As of this writing, he serves as the Director of Football Administration for the Steelers with the hope of eventually becoming an NFL general manager.[84]

Shahid Khan owns the Jacksonville Jaguars as of 2017. A naturalized citizen originally from Pakistan, Khan became a wealthy auto parts magnate. In college, he grew to love football while watching it with his fraternity brothers. Possessing deep pockets, Khan also owns Fulham, a London-based soccer club. His son, Tony, serves as the Jaguars senior vice-president in charge of football technology and analytics.[85]

While undoubtedly successful in many ways, Khan has not been able to escape the racist Islamophobia shadowing the culturally diverse people possessing Middle Eastern and Southern Asian ancestry. A 2012 interview with CBS reveals that not everyone in the Jacksonville area accepted Khan's ownership of the team. Crawling out of social media at the time were comments condemning Khan as a "terrorist from Pakistan" and a "sand monkey." The question was even raised that if someone bought a Jaguar season ticket, would a prayer rug come with it? Echoing the Model Minority stereotype, the CBS report on Khan maintained that he had been "living the American dream for 45 years." Nevertheless, that very same report maintained that Khan, a citizen since 1991, was subject to considerable harassment after 9/11. He was even detained and imprisoned briefly while trying to cross the bridge connecting Detroit to Canada.[86]

Khan is not the only present-day Asian American owner of an NFL franchise. Korean orphan Kim Pegula, as of this writing, is co-owner with her husband of the Buffalo Bills. She has been called "one of the most powerful women in sports." Not satisfied with one Buffalo franchise, Pegula and her husband also own the National Hockey League's Buffalo Sabres. Pegula seems to recognize male privilege in elite professional sports, but she also suggests it does not need to pose an overwhelming obstacle. In doing so, Pegula calls upon the kind of meritocratic rhetoric admonishing women and minority group members down through the years to work hard and be quiet about institutional inequities—a rhetoric undercut, in this case, by the fact that not all that many women and minority group members, however smart and diligent, have the luxury of marrying a wealthy white spouse. She declares:

> Like any industry, it's about networking and who you know and putting yourself into situations where you can create an opportunity. The more women can do to build experience and a skill set in a particular area, the better their chances. I don't think it does anyone any good just to hire someone because they are a female. They have to have the

qualifications and skill set to substantiate the hire, and make the gender a non-factor — that's the best thing women can do.[87]

CONCLUSION

Americans of Asian and Pacific Islander ancestry played a role in the early development of professional football in the United States. To be clear, none were all-time greats, but Walter Achiu and Harry Field seemed to have held their own. While some might consider the professional careers of Wally Yonamine and especially Herman Wedemeyer as disappointing, they had their moments. Indeed, it is hard to remember Wedemeyer as a professional failure when, after all, he was an all-pro his second and last year in 1949. Moreover, shadowing their professional careers is the sense that racialized exoticism may have opened doors for Yonamine and Wedemeyer, but it also ushered them out of those same doors quicker than they deserved.

The 1950s and 1960s witnessed the advent of Asian and Pacific Islander stars. In the 1950s, Charlie Ane and Herman Clark ranked among the best of NFL linemen. During the next decade, there were few professional quarterbacks better than Roman Gabriel. A contemporary of Gabriel's, Mel Tom was a solid, if not dominant, defender.

In more recent decades, we will find a growing number of Pacific Islander gridders; a phenomenon to be addressed in the next chapter. But we will also find gridders of diverse Asian origins. The first and only Vietnamese American professional, Dat Nguyen, performed well and courageously for "America's Team" — the Dallas Cowboys — in the early 2000s. The first "full-blooded" Filipino professional gridder, Eugene Amano, was a good offensive lineman for the Tennessee Titans around the same time. Meanwhile, in the last decade, biracial athletes such as Hines Ward and Tedy Bruschi put together potential Hall of Fame careers for the Pittsburgh Steelers and New England Patriots respectively.

The NFL has yet to see a head coach of either Asian or Pacific Islander ancestry. Still, a few Asian Americans can be found in the management and ownership of NFL franchises. That would seem to be progress, but seeing an Asian American or Pacific Islander running an NFL team from the sidelines would probably make a more conspicuous stereotype-breaking statement.

NOTES

1. *Escanaba Daily Press*, July 20, 1927; *Appleton Post-Crescent*, September 14, 1927.

2. C. Robert Barnett, "The Portsmouth Spartans," http://profootballresearchers.com/coffin-corner80s/02–10–044.pdf (June 20, 2015); *Appleton Post-Crescent*, September 16, 1929; *Stevens Point Daily Journal*, September 14, 1929; Dick Young, "Spar-

tans, Despite Intense Heat, Defeat Columbus, Eleven," *Portsmouth Daily Times*, September 17, 1928; November 18, 1929.

3. *Oregon Statesmen*, March 4, 1935.

4. Franks, *Crossing*, 125; http://www.jt-sw.com/football/pro/stats.nsf/Annual/1928-day (October 26, 2015); Robinson, "Gridiron Pioneer."

5. *Los Angeles Times*, November 18, 1932; http://www.databasefootball.com/players/playerpage.htm?ilkid=HUGHEHAN01, (July 28, 2010); *Chicago Tribune*, September 16, 1935; http://www.databasefootball.com/players/playerpage.htm?ilkid=FIELDHAR01, (July 28, 2010); *Honolulu Star-Bulletin*, October 2, 1940.

6. David K. Choo, "The Polynesian Powerhouse: University of Hawaii Football Counts On Its Samoan Connection," *Pacific Magazine and Islands Business*, July 2003; U.S. Census Bureau, Manuscript Census Schedules, City of Laie and Island of Oahu, 1940, www.ancestry.com (April 29, 2015); *Deseret News*, December 19, 1945; *Ogden Standard Examiner*, December 12, 1945; Tommy Holmes, "Dons Make Flock Forget Gridiron Aspirations," *Brooklyn Daily Eagle*, November 18, 1946; *Nevada State-Journal*, November 22, 1947; *Los Angeles Times*, September 11, 1948; *Long Beach Independent*, June 28, 1949.

7. *Oakland Tribune*, August 31, 1962; *Los Angeles Times*, December 10, 1965.

8. www.nfl.com/player/chetmaeda/2519956/profile (April 11, 2016); *Ironwood Daily Globe*, September 21, 1945; *San Bernardino County Sun*, November 15, 1984.

9. U.S. Census Bureau, Manuscript Census Schedules, Olowalu Village and Island of Maui, 1930, www.ancestry.com., (June 3, 2005).

10. Franks, *Hawaiian Sports*, 78; Frank Ardolino, "Wally Yonamine: In Japan's Hall of Fame," *The National Pastime*, no. 19 (1999): 10; *New York Times*, January 28, 1946; *Stars and Stripes*, January 28, 1946.

11. *San Francisco Chronicle*, February 19, 1946; *Portland Oregonian*, July 16, 1946; September 29, 1946; *San Jose Mercury*, October 10, 1946; Franks, *Crossing*, 116.

12. Ohio State's attraction to Yonamine probably stemmed from the school's ability to recruit world class Hawaiian swimmers to its campus (*Pacific Citizen*, July 26, 1947); *Los Angeles Times*, May 15, 1947; Arthur Suehiro, *Honolulu Stadium; Where Hawaii Played* (Honolulu: Watermark Publishing, 1995), 34; *San Francisco Chronicle*, July 20, 1947.

13. *Pacific Citizen* July 12, 1947; *Nevada State-Journal*, July 23, 1947.

14. Franks, *Crossing*, 128; *San Francisco Chronicle*, August 1, 1947.

15. *San Francisco Chronicle*, July 20, 1947; July 22, 1947; July 25, 1947; *San Francisco Call-Bulletin*, July 24, 1947; *San Jose Mercury*, August 14, 1947; August 16, 1947.

16. Curley Grieve, "Wally Easts Rice. Can He Run?" *San Francisco Examiner*, August 5, 1947; August 10, 1947.

17. Fitts, *Yonamine*, 36–37, 41,

18. *Pacific Citizen*, August 9, 1947.

19. Hal Wood, "Jap Gridder Fears No Pro Behemoths," *Oxnard Press-Courier*, August 6, 1947; August 13, 1947.

20. *Pacific Citizen*, August 16, 1947; August 23, 1947; Louis Duino, "Yonamine the Star of Reds Win, 33–23," *San Jose Mercury*, August 16, 1947.

21. *Nevada State-Journal*, September 20, 1947.

22. *San Francisco Chronicle*, September 27, 1947.

23. *Pacific Citizen*, September 13, 1947.

24. Bruce Lee, "TD Crazy Rockets Face Rough 49ers in Kezar Today," *San Francisco Chronicle*, October 12, 1947; *Pacific Citizen*, October 18, 1947.

25. Fitts, *Yonamine*, 45–47; http://www.pro-football-reference.com/players/Y/YonaWa20.html (October 28, 2015).

26. Franks, *Crossing*, 130; *Honolulu Record*, August 26, 1948; *Honolulu Star-Bulletin*, September 11, 1948; *Los Angeles Times*, November 29, 1948.

27. *Pacific Citizen*, November 13, 1948.

28. *San Francisco Chronicle*, July 23, 1949.

29. In 1951, the San Francisco Seals of the Pacific Coast League, then managed by Lefty O'Doul, a longtime friend of Nikkei ballplayers, offered Yonamine a try out. The Hawaiian did not make the Seals, but showed enough promise that O'Doul moved him down to a Seal farm team in Ogden, Utah. Even though Yonamine hit well over .300 and played well enough to earn a spot on the Seal roster and consideration from a major league ball club, O'Doul advised him to head to sign a contract with the Tokyo Giants, Japan's leading major league franchise. The veteran manager reasoned that Yonamine would have a better shot at a living playing professionally in Japan than United States. Despite being perceived as a gaijin, a foreigner, by many Japanese fans, the Hawaiian crisscrossed the cultural borderlands between Japan and Hawai'i and put together a stellar career as a player, coach, and manager in Japan before returning permanently to his Hawaiian home. *San Jose Mercury*, September 2, 1949; Fitts, *Yonamine*; Suehiro, Honolulu Stadium, 33–34.

30. *Helena Independent Record*, December 30, 1947.

31. Los Angeles Dons v. San Francisco 49ers Football Program, Kezar Stadium, San Francisco, CA., September 19, 1948; *Los Angeles Times*, October 27, 1948; *San Francisco Chronicle*, August 3, 1948.

32. *Oxnard Press-Courier*, September 11, 1948; *Belvedere Daily Republican*, September 11, 1948; *Brooklyn Daily Eagle*, October 9, 1948; Dave Lewis, "Unbeaten Browns Nail Down 12th in Row Before 60,031," *Long Beach Independent*, November 26, 1948; *Klamath Falls Herald*, September 1, 1949; *Los Angeles Times*, July 16, 1949; *Ironwood Daily Globe*, September 1, 1949.

33. *Los Angeles Times*, September 1, 1949; July 19, 1950.

34. *Spokane Daily Chronicle*, January 10, 1948; Franks, *Asia Pacific Americans*, 151–152.

35. *Los Angeles Times*, July 19, 1950.

36. http://www.pro-football-reference.com/players/W/WedeHe20.htm (July 13, 2014).

37. *Dallas Morning News*, March 7, 1936; *Los Angeles Times*, December 22, 1978.

38. *Los Angeles Times*, September 11, 1948; http://www.pro-football-reference.com/players/N/NaumJo20.htm (March 7, 2015); U.S. Census Bureau, Manuscript Census Schedules, Island of Molokai, 1930, www.ancestry.com (May 21, 2015).

39. U.S. Census Bureau, Manuscript Census Schedules, City and County of Honolulu, 1930, www.ancestry.com (March 3, 2008); *Los Angeles Times*, December 25, 1947; September 11, 1948; September 12, 1948.

40. *Los Angeles Times*, October 11, 1948; October 31, 1948; November 1, 1948; November 3, 1948; Official National League Football Pro Record and Rule Book, 1949 (St. Louis: CC. Spink and Son, 1949), 127, 139.

41. Irv Goodman, "Pro Football Preview," *Sport*, September 1956; http://www.pro-football-reference.com/players/C/ClarHe20.htm (August 30, 2014).

42. Hal Freeman, "Ane, Lions' Hawaiian Rookie, Really Handles a Pineapple," *Philadelphia Inquirer*, August 26, 1953; *Ironwood Daily Globe*, July 29, 1958; *Sporting News*, September 23, 1959; http://www.pro-football-reference.com/players/A/AnexCh00.htm (August 30, 2014).

43. Charles Burton, "Rangers Buy Ane, 5 Others," *Dallas Morning News*, March 17, 1960; Charles Burton, "5 Cowboy Vets Still Unsigned," July 15, 1960.

44. Gary Cartwright, "A Sort of Superior Feeling," *Dallas Morning News*, August 28, 1963; December 27, 1954.

45. Dave Reardon, "Alama Francis Born for Football," *Honolulu Advertiser*, July 22, 2006.

46. *Milwaukee Journal*, January 28, 1958; February 20, 1958.

47. Chuck Johnson, "Quarterback Is Heart of Team and That Explains Packer Ills," *Milwaukee Journal*, November 13, 1958.

48. *Bend Bulletin*, December 13, 1958; *Daytona Beach Journal*, December 15, 1958; http://www.pro-football-reference.com/players/F/FranJo20.htm (October 30, 2015).

49. Cliff Christi, "An Oral History—Gary Knafelc," http://www.packers.com/news-and-events/article-1/An-Oral-History----Gary-Knafelc/ff9ce7a5-bf28–4d0a-a18a-

f86643ef5ddc, November 17, 2017; John Eisenberg, *That First Season: How Vince Lombardi Took the Worst Team in the NFL and Set it on the Path to Glory* (Boston and New York: Harcourt Mifflin Harcourt, 2009), 126, 270; *Eugene Register-Guard*, August 30, 1959; http://www.pro-football-reference.com/players/F/FranJo20.htm, (October 30, 2015); http://www.detroitlions.com/team/history/all-time-roster.html (June 21, 2016).

50. *Robesonian*, December 14, 1961; *Richmond County Journal*, October 22, 1963; *Youngstown Vindicator*, October 28, 1963; *San Jose Mercury*, October 18, 1964.

51. *Dallas Morning News*, November 19, 1967; December 20, 1967; Hank Hollingsworth, "Gabriel Shows His Class," *Long Beach Independent*, September 19, 1968; *Trenton Evening Times*, September 3, 1969; *Springfield Union*, December 25, 1969; *Seattle Times*, July 5, 1970.

52. *Dallas Morning News*, June 24, 1971; Phil Estrada, "LA's Powerful Quarterback," *Soul City Times*, December 14, 1968.

53. *Rockford Morning Star*, February 9, 1969.

54. Franks, *Crossing*, 135; http://www.pro-football-reference.com/players/G/GabrRo00.htm (April 13, 2013); *Cleveland Plain Dealer*, November 27, 1982; *Frederick Post*, February 7, 1983.

55. Bob St. John, "Cheap Shot by an Eagle," *Dallas Morning News*, December 15, 1967; September 29, 1971; November 12, 1971; *Shenandoah Evening Herald*, November 12, 1971.

56. *New Orleans Times-Picayune*, October 12, 1973; *Aberdeen News*, October 17, 1973; *Cleveland Plain Dealer*, November 12, 1975; Franks, *Crossing*, 135; http://www.pro-football-reference.com/players/F/FreiRo00.htm (September 12, 2014); https://www.hawaii.edu/admin/chancellors/westoahu.html (June 11, 2015); http://www.hawaiitourismauthority.org/default/assets/File/13–2%20NFL%20and%20HTA%20to%20Honor%20Inaugural%20Hawaii%20NFL%20Greats%20NR.pdf (June 11, 2015); http://www.profootballarchives.com/nich03800.html (June 11, 2015); http://www.pro-football-reference.com/players/M/MorgAr00.htm (June 11, 2015).

57. http://www.nfl.com/player/blanegaison/2514552/profile (June 11, 2015); http://www.hawaiitourismauthority.org/default/assets/File/13–2%20NFL%20and%20HTA%20to%20Honor%20Inaugural%20Hawaii%20NFL%20Greats%20NR.pdf (June 11, 2015); http://www.pro-football-reference.com/players/P/ParkKa20.htm (March 17, 2009); Franks, *Crossing*, 136–137; https://www.pidf.org/about/board_of_directors/kaulana_park, (June 11, 2015); http://sepiamutiny.com/blog/2006/02/05/desis_in_the_nf/ (June 11, 2015); http://www.pro-football-reference.com/players/B/BeacSa00.htm (June 11, 2015); Martin Hendrics, "Sanjay Beach Was Catching Ball From Elite QB," http://www.jsonline.com/sports/packers/sanjay-beach-was-catching-balls-from-elite-qbs-b99260168z1–258342141.html (June 11, 2015).

58. http://www.pro-football-reference.com/players/C/ChunEu20.htm (May 13, 2012); http://www.kcchiefs.com/team/coaches/eugene-chung/697bc44e-1126–4955-a601–9a956f50e1ed (June 11, 2015).

59. http://www.pro-football-reference.com/players/B/BrusTe99.htm (June 12, 2015); http://espn.go.com/video/clip?id=12848278 (June 12, 2015); http://espn.go.com/sportsnation/boston/chat/_/id/40436 (May 2, 2015); http://www.pro-football-reference.com/players/W/WongKa20.htm (June 7, 2015); https://www.linkedin.com/pub/kaileewong/10/149/5b4 (June 11, 2015).

60. Franks, *Crossing*, 138; http://www.pro-football-reference.com/players/W/WardHi00.html (June 7, 2015); http://www.hinesward.com/hines-ward-biography.php (June 12, 2015).

61. http://www.pro-football-reference.com/players/N/NguyDa20.htm (August 7, 2014); http://espn.go.com/blog/dallas/cowboys/post/_/id/4711414/sean-lee-soaks-updat-nguyens-wisdom (June 7, 2014); http://www.12thman.com/ViewArticle.dbml?ATCLID=205236164 (June 12, 2015); http://www.mysanantonio.com/news/local_news/article/Refugee-football-star-practices-his-faith-4045087.php (June 12, 2015).

62. Irwin Tang, "Nguyen Blitzes the NFL," *Asian Week*, September 5, 2003.

63. Ibid.

64. Ibid.

65. http://asianplayers.com/football/ (May 9, 2016); http://biggreenalertblog. blogspot.com/2008/01/lloyd-lee-moves-up.html (June 9, 2016); https:// www.linkedin.com/in/lloydslee (June 9, 2016). Franks, *Crossing*, 138; Kalani Takase, "Wong Eager to Assume Reins at Kailua," http://scoringlive.com/story.php?storyid=11249, (June 12, 2015); http://www.pro-football-reference.com/players/M/MortJo00.htm (June 12, 2015); http://www.nfl.com/news/story/09000d5d82a495da/article/johnnie-morton-given-two-years-probation-for-lying-under-oath (June 12, 2015); http://www.pro-football-reference.com/players/M/MortCh00.htm (June 12, 2015); http://profootballtalk.nbcsports.com/2014/05/02/chad-morton-lands-in-seattle-as-assistant-special-teams-coach/ (June 12, 2015).

66. http://www.nfl.com/player/kevinkaesviharn/2504426/profile (June 10, 2016); http://asianplayers.com/football/ (June 10, 2016); http://bengals.enquirer.com/2002/01/05/ben_math_teacher_adding.html (June 10, 2016); http://koreanamericanstory.org/the-will-to-win/, November 22, 2017; Abbie Alford, "Former NFL Player Involved in Rare Tree Crash at Balboa Park," http://www.cbs8.com/story/26851862/former-nfl-player-involved-in-rare-tree-crash-at-balboa-park (June 21, 2015); http://www.nfl.com/player/chrisgocong/2495837/profile (June 10, 2016); http://asianplayers.com/football/, (June 10, 2016); http://www.pro-football-reference.com/players/A/AmanEu20.htm (June 25, 2015).

67. Alvin Lin, "Watch for Ed Wang in Tomorrow's NFL Draft," http://www.hyphenmagazine.com/blog/2010/04/watch-ed-wang-tomorrows-nfl-draft (December 24, 2010); John P. Lopez, "Getting to Know NFL Hopeful Ed Wang" http://sportsillustrated.cnn.com/2010/writers/john_lopez/04/21/wang/index.html (December 24, 2010); http://www.pro-football-reference.com/players/W/WangEd20.htm (December 24, 2010).

68. Jordan Ikeda, "Drawing Raven Reviews," http://www.rafu.com/2009/07/drawing-raven-reviews (June 17, 2016); http://www.pro-football-reference.com/players/N/NakaHa99.htm (June 15, 2015).

69. Steve Kelley, "Doug Baldwin: Pinoy Heart," http://www.seahawks.com/news/articles/article-1/Doug-Baldwin-Pinoy-heart/3ffc0c21–4521–4d24-a19c-035c0f058924 (November 22, 2013); Elton Lugay, "Fil-Am NFL Star Doug Baldwin on Lumpia, Football and Beast Mode's Cavities," http://www.gmanetwork.com/news/story/346383/pinoyabroad/news/fil-am-nfl-star-doug-baldwin-on-lumpia-football-and-beast-mode-s-cavities (May 27, 2015); http://www.pro-football-reference.com/players/B/BaldDo00.htm (January 31, 2017); Gel Santos Relos, "Triple Victory for Pinoys in Superbowl," http://asianjournal.com/editorial/triple-victory-for-pinoys-in-the-superbowl (May 27, 2015).

70. http://www.si.com/vault/1956/12/24/668638/19th-hole-the-readers-take-over (July 16, 2015); *Honolulu Record*, December 27, 1956.

71. I have had a challenging time pinning down some of Tashiro's claims in terms of football experience. He was raised in Cincinnati and a Tashiro did play football for Hughes High School in that city in early 1930s. Moreover, the *Shreveport Times* in 1934 published a photo of him as he was trying out for Harvard's frosh squad (*Cincinnati Enquirer*, November 25, 1933; *Shreveport Times*, October 22, 1934; *Rome Daily Sentinel*, December 12, 1963; *Appleton Post-Crescent*, November 12, 1964; *New York Times*, August 7, 1973).

72. Jason Cruz, Semi-Pro: Korean American Keeps Football Dream Alive," http://www.nwasianweekly.com/2010/09/semi-pro-korean-american-keeps-football-dream-alive/ (March 25, 2015).

73. Bob Gill, *Best in the West: The Rise and Fall of the Pacific Coast Football League, 1940–1948* (n.p.: Professional Football Research Association, 1988), 127, 248–263; Franks, *Crossing*, 118, 119; *Honolulu Star-Bulletin*, August 31, 1948; September 1, 1948; October 1, 1948.

74. *San Francisco Examiner*, October 2, 1943; http://www.profootballarchives.com/ 1943pcflric.html (December 13, 2014); Franks, *Crossing*, 133; Gill, *Best in the West*, 195, 237; United States Census Bureau, Manuscript Census Schedules, City and County of Honolulu, 1930, www.ancestry.com (July 28, 2015).

75. Dan Cisco, *Hawai'i Sports*, 178–179; http://www.nasljerseys.com/WFL/Players/ H/Holt.Milt.htm (March 8, 2005).

76. *Bridgeport Telegram*, November 12, 1955; *Lethbridge Herald*, January 7, 1955; *Ottawa Citizen*, August 31, 1957; *Montreal Gazette*, November 29, 1954; http://en. montrealalouettes.com/all-time-all-stars/ (August 11, 2016). http://slam.canoe.com/ Slam/Wrestling/2010/12/05/16435751.html (July 20, 2015).

77. http://www.kickingworld.com/former-utah-utes-all-american-louie-sakoda-joins-kicking-world-as-kicking-coach (June 10, 2016); http://asianplayers.com/football/ (May 9, 2016); Stanmyre, "Six Years Later."

78. Franks, *Crossing*, 137; http://www.footballdb.com/players/neo-aoga-aogane01 (September 14, 2010); http://www.jsutigers.com/ViewArticle.dbml?DB_OEM_ID=29000&ATCLID=209390204 (September 14, 2010); http://www. godrakebulldogs.com/ViewArticle.dbml?DB_OEM_ID=15700&ATCLID=209788397/ (March 3, 2015).

79. Dave Reardon, "Pigskin Pediatrician," www.islandscene.com, January 5, 2000; http://nysharksfootball.com/team/player.cfm/player=183/all=1 (June 7, 2014).

80. http://www.buffalobills.com/team/coaches/lal_sanjay/5c6a8125–0a99–46bb-8e26-f0e5da3d8a0b (June 13, 2015); http://bleacherreport.com/articles/2689429-seahawks-assistant-head-coach-rocky-seto-leaves-team-to-enter-the-ministry (November 25, 2016).

81. http://www.usctrojans.com/sports/m-footbl/mtt/pola_kennedy00.html (May 24, 2013).

82. http://cfl-scrapbook.no-ip.org/Paopao.Joe.php (March 2, 2011).

83. Ibid.; http://bclions.com/page/staff-joe-paopao (March 2, 2011).

84. *Pacific Citizen*, June 8, 1946; http://www.100thbattalion.org/history/veterans/ officers/katsumi-doc-kometani/ November 27, 2017; http://www.sepiamutiny.com/ sepia/archives/001905.html (March 18, 2007); http://www.49ers.com/news/article-2/ Paraag-Marathe-Named-Team-President/8f12e082-f0d4–4f40-aeba-911d553f4bec (September 11, 2014); http://blogs.mercurynews.com/kawakami/2014/01/21/gideon-yu-steps-down-as-49ers-president-paraag-marathe-steps-in-its-jed-yorks-whole-show-now/ (September 11, 2014); http://espn.go.com/espn/hispanicheritage2013/story/_/ page/onenationsteelers131008/hispanic-heritage-month-omar-khan-pittsburgh-steelers-front-office-dreams-big (May 18, 2015).

85. http://www.jaguars.com/team/management/shad-khan.html (May 9, 2015).

86. Erik Love, *Islamophobia and Racism in America* (New York: New York University Press, 2017); http://www.cbsnews.com/news/shahid-khan-from-pakistan-to-pro-football/3/ (May 9, 2015).

87. Sal Mahoran, "From Orphan to NFL Owner," http:// www.democratandchronicle.com/story/sports/2015/08/23/kim-pegula-making-difference-adopted-hometown/32166573/ (September 5, 2015); http://www.espn.com/ espnw/voices/article/17316264/buffalo-bills-co-owner-kim-pegula-talks-women-nfl (August 19, 2016).

SEVEN

Pacific Islanders

Since the last decades of the twentieth century, Pacific Islanders have become prominent on all levels of American football. This has not, however, generally mainstreamed Pacific Islanders into American society. To be sure, Pacific Islander gridders have acquired some respect as well as fame and fortune in the National Football League. Yet they have continued to be racialized and exoticized, while Pacific Islanders commonly continue to face colonization in the lands of their births and a whole host of social problems on the U.S. mainland and Hawai'i. Indeed, whether successful NFL football players or not, Pacific Islanders remain a colonized people in the American empire.[1]

ROOTING FOOTBALL IN THE PACIFIC

American football has been played on U.S.-controlled Pacific Islands since before World War II. Still, despite the experiences of Al Lolotai and Al Harrington, football across the Pacific largely went unnoticed on the U.S. mainland until Pacific Islanders made their way on to elite college programs, as well as NFL rosters, in the 1970s and 1980s. In 1985, an AP report on high school football in Samoa stressed that it was played a long way out of the comfort zone for college scouts, while also suffering from comparative underfunding and, therefore, lack of proper equipment. This was all a shame because, the report insisted, Samoans were naturally gifted in football. Tu'ufuli Uperesa, a former NFL lineman and coach at Fagaitua High School, served as the report's chief informant. A former Hawaiian prep star who went to Montana University to play college football, Uperesa maintained he saw plenty of potentially elite football players in Samoa. But if they were going to gain notice from college scouts, he said, they should move to Hawai'i and compete in prep football.[2]

Tengan and Markham trace the origins of American football on Samoa to the intervention of U.S. Navy personnel before the 1950s. Sailors played football with Samoans while stationed at Pago Pago. Meanwhile, Samoans were recruited into a naval reserve unit called the Fitafita Guard. However, when the Navy was replaced by the Interior Department as the administrator of American Samoa, many of the recruited Samoans were allowed to journey to the United States free of charge. Called "The Great Migration of 1952," Samoans moved first to Honolulu and then, in the case of many, to the American mainland's Pacific Coast. Significantly, a Samoan Hawaiian population had existed since the 1920s as Mormon missionaries enticed them to La'ie on Oahu, where a Mormon temple had been built. While in Hawai'i and cities such as Seattle, Los Angeles, Long Beach, and San Diego, Samoans gained familiarity with American football. Their communities in Hawai'i and the U.S. Pacific Coast grew because of Samoan recruitment into the military or Samoans seeking educational opportunities. Among the latter were young men heading to USC or the University of Washington with football scholarships in hand. Moreover, the "Mormon Polynesian enclave" at La'ie emerged as a nurturer of talented football players.[3]

Tengan and Markham assert that Vaughn Hawks, a teacher at the Mormon-run Mapusaga High School, helped solidify American football on Samoa by organizing a game between Mapusaga and the government-run Samoan school in 1963. They also credit the role of Al Lolotai. The ex-football star arrived in American Samoa to launch football camps before becoming Samoa's athletic director for the colony's Department of Education. Lolotai's return to Samoa represented, according to Tengan and Markham, a significant element of the Samoan diaspora: "[I]t is rarely one-way. Indeed, Samoans continue to circulate between American Samoa, (independent) Samoa, the United States, New Zealand, Australia, Hawai'i and Guam in temporary, repetitive movements known as malaga, a traditional practice of inter-village and inter-island visiting and sharing of resources."[4]

Scholar Vicente Diaz has explored the world of youth American football on Guam. Diaz grew up playing for the Tamuning Eagles, a boys' team that won 125 consecutive games against squads throughout the Pacific Basin—including predominantly European American elevens. The Eagles, according to Diaz, were founded by men raised in Hawai'i. They possessed Filipino, Japanese, Chinese, Portuguese, and European ancestry and made their way to Guam to seek employment with the U.S. military occupying the island. These men had typically played football on Hawai'i before World War II, and many of them had sons on the Eagles.[5]

Thus, Diaz maintains, Guamian football owed a great deal to American imperialism in the Pacific, but also to the Hawaiian "warrior's tradition." He remembers that his team's battle cry was *imua*. Translated into "forward," *imua* furnished a key theme of Hawai'i's Kamehameha School's fight song. For Diaz, his team performed gender; in this case, masculinity. However, it was a complex masculinity, comprised of an American masculinity of hypercompetitive, gridiron physicality, and a "Pacific Islander masculinity," encompassing "music-making and merriment" and treating the opposing team to show up for a postgame pot luck. For Diaz, Guamian football meant something different than American football does for all the pseudo-Vince Lombardis who have infested the game for so many years. Among his best memories were "of the *aloha* that the Eagle *ohana* gave me that I have in return." And echoing C. L. R. James's *Beyond a Boundary*, Diaz adds, "That, and the rarest experience that colonized islanders can ever have: knowing what it means to be a winner at the colonizer's own game."[6]

PACIFIC ISLANDER FOOTBALL GETS NOTICED IN THE 1970S

Because of gridders such as Al Lolotai, Charlie Ane, Packard Harrington, and Al Harrington, the mainland American football world was aware that people of Pacific Islander descent could play football quite competently by the 1960s. However, the decade of the 1970s seems to represent a time when mainland media started to focus substantial attention on Pacific Islander football. This was especially the case in Southern California where various journalists commented on the emerging presence of Samoans on the region's football fields. The *Sporting News'* Jim Scott wrote in 1971 that a San Diego State "redshirt" named Tuffy Avii was a Samoan. Before each home game, this young man reportedly ran out with the team, carrying a spear and making a "blood-curdling yell."[7]

In 1974, the *Los Angeles Times'* Early Gutskey observed that gridders of Samoan ancestry were contributing to USC's impressive football program. Focusing on Junior Epati, Gutskey wrote that the lineman bore a fierce demeanor on the field, but carried himself with good humor off the field. The Oceanside High School grad reportedly persuaded a gullible teammate that Samoans "still eat people."[8]

Santa Monica Community College's *Corsair* introduced students to defensive lineman Joel Tauleva. Correspondent Andy Bernstein wrote that Tauleva was born on Tonga, but moved with his family to Hawai'i when he was eleven. He attended Kahuku High School, for which he played not only football but rugby. After leaving high school, he was recruited by UH and East Arizona. Bernstein described Tauleva as a hard worker on and off the football field, earning money as a Polynesian dancer at a place called the Tiki in Monterey Park.[9]

In the mid-1970s, a wire story about Samoans in Southern California stressed that in such places as Torrance, in south Los Angeles County, they were confronted with assimilation problems and generational tensions, much like other immigrant groups. When it came to football, "[t]he Samoans who tend to have massive shoulders and strong arms and legs are making it big." Racializing its subjects, the article also observed that Samoans were even tempered when not aroused to aggression. However, it assured readers, football channeled that aggression. [10]

In 1976, Mal Florence of the *Los Angeles Times* noted the proliferation of athletes of Samoan ancestry on Southern California teams. UCLA, for example, suited up future professionals as well as lesser-known Samoan gridders. In 1975, UCLA's coach, Dick Vermeil, bragged to the press that he had "the two best Samoans in college football" in Terry Tautolo and Manu Tuiasosopo. Also playing for the Bruins in the mid-1970s were Pete Pele and Anthony Pao. [11]

A few years later, the *Times'* Scot Ostler reported that Carson High School in southern Los Angeles County included twenty gridders of Samoan ancestry on its varsity roster. Ostler asserted that these athletes might have experienced some discrimination on the U.S. mainland, but through football they could forge a path to the American Dream. Delving into sociology, Ostler claimed that Samoans liked football because they valued teamwork and were deeply committed to community pride. One Carson High School gridder told Ostler that "Samoans" go to America to get educated and return to Samoa in order "to teach our people." In other words, "We just want to bring our race up." Ostler added that many of the Samoan players were "professional dancers," thus reinforcing the aura of exoticism enveloping Pacific Islanders in the United States. Apparently, Ostler asserted, the "low squatting" in their dances helped them in terms of agility and leg strength. [12]

In the meantime, *Sports Illustrated* cast an eye on the developing cadre of Pacific Islander gridders competing in elite mainland football. In an article unfortunately entitled "Shake'em Out of the Coconut Trees," Journalist Richard W. Johnson told *SI* readers to be on the lookout because the football world was changing. He wrote, "What is coming on is a swarm of Polynesian warriors—not your run-of-the-reef, gin mill flamethrowers, but strong, fierce men, six to seven feet tall, who seem to have stepped into the 20th century from some secret museum of oceanic antiquities." Indeed, according to Johnson, these "warriors" came from a "museum"—American Samoa. Relatively unknown to Americans, Johnson asserted, "but, together with Western Samoa, it also is the only island group where the Polynesian culture—and the Polynesian race—has survived virtually intact." [13]

Samoan football players, Johnson insisted, considered themselves missionaries for "fa'a Samoa, the Samoan way of life." Their coaches, he also insisted, understood the Samoan allegiance to football's mission.

That is, "if you ask a Samoan to run five miles, he'll run 10; if you ask him to take out an opponent, he is apt to clear him out of the stadium."[14]

The racialization of Pacific Islanders proved a strong subtext of Johnson's piece. Al Harrington appeared as one of his key sources. Johnson identified Harrington as a onetime history major at Stanford, who taught at Punahou and the University of Hawai'i. Then, according to Johnson, the former Stanford star decided to take advantage of "his warrior body, chiefly mien, and dramatic skills" and turn to acting. Unlike Native Hawaiians, Harrington revealed to Johnson, "Samoans have not been watered down . . . by Boston missionaries. . . . So we not only tend to be bigger, but we retain a fierce sectional, cultural, and family pride. The soul of Samoa still is competitiveness." The advent of Pacific Islanders as football's Model Minority had clearly gotten underway.[15]

PACIFIC ISLANDERS AND AMERICAN FOOTBALL IN THE LATE TWENTIETH AND EARLY TWENTY-FIRST CENTURIES

Jackie Thompson was the most famed of Samoan American football players in the 1970s. He was a cousin to notable and talented Samoan gridders Mosi Tatupu and Manu Tuiasosopo, as well as Washington State teammate and starting quarterback successor Samoa. Thompson's fraternal grandfather was, however, English. Unhappy with his nickname of "Throwin' Samoan," Thompson was born in Samoa but raised since five in Seattle. His father had migrated to Seattle in the hopes of furthering his children's education, but did not send for his family until he was sure of economic stability. Thompson told the press in 1978 that one reason why Samoans excelled in football was that they both respected themselves and authority. His Washington State coach, Jim Walden, concurred, "They're the finest people I know in terms of having their heads screwed on right."[16]

Interestingly, Thompson was not heavily recruited while quarterbacking for Seattle's Evergreen High School. Washington State, nevertheless, gave Thompson an opportunity to show what he could do, and he rewarded Washington State by becoming one of the finest quarterbacks in college ball in the late 1970s. The *Sporting News* columnist Tom Siler declared him a legitimate Heisman Trophy candidate in 1977, while *Sporting News* correspondent, Nick Peters, acclaimed him an excellent pro prospect.[17]

Meanwhile, AP sportswriter Mel Reisner purported that Thompson had "become the darling of American Samoa." Reisner uncovered an individual proclaiming himself the "Prince of Samoa," who insisted the Cougar quarterback had won the admiration of "the Polynesian people." Thompson, according to Reisner, expected to play in the pros but hoped to open a Polynesian restaurant in Seattle once his playing career was done. Since Thompson had redshirted a season, he was eligible for the professional draft after his junior year. However, while the quarterback considered going pro, Thompson's working-class parents told him that they really did not need the money. Thus, he remained at WSU another year.[18]

When his Washington State days ended, Thompson achieved a moderately successful NFL career. He was drafted by the Cincinnati Bengals and played for them for four years. He generally rode the bench for the Bengals, but got into enough games in 1980 to attempt over two hundred passes. In 1983, he joined the Tampa Bay Buccaneers for whom he became a regular quarterback that season, completing 59 percent of 423 passes. However, after 1984, he was out of the league. Still, *Sports Illustrated* in 2000 named Thompson as the thirty-third best athlete in Washington's history. Meanwhile, Jackie's brother Gene suited up as a defensive tackle for New Mexico State.[19]

After retirement, Thompson settled in his hometown of Seattle. He kept his hand in football by helping coach quarterbacks at Seattle's Ballard High. He was even mentioned as a possible candidate for head coach of Washington State's football team before Mike Leach took over the program in 2012. Thompson, moreover, worked as a mortgage banker, while his son eventually joined Washington State as a tight end.[20]

Aside from the Thompsons, Washington State suited up other Pacific Islanders in the 1970s and 1980s. Succeeding Thompson as starting quarterback for Washington State, Samoa performed well even if he was not Thompson's equal. However, the *Sporting News'* Bob McCoy took the occasion to call Samoa Samoa "the player of the year" in his discussion of "all-name" teams. Samoa, McCory told readers, was ambidextrous, "wears 11 and his nickname is Repeat." A left-handed passer, Samoa had transferred to Pullman after a stint at Long Beach City College. Once Samoa's Washington State eligibility was up, the Cincinnati Bengals drafted him, but he never made it in the NFL. He did, however, show up along with former NFL player Tu'ufuli Uperesa as a high school coach in Samoa in the mid-1980s.[21]

Washington State continued to recruit Samoan Americans into the 1980s. Coach Walden was especially high on Junior Tupola, claiming that "[h]e could be the most dominating player on the field." Early in the 1980s, sportswriter Hy Zimmerman wrote a piece in the *Seattle Times* in response to the influence of Thompson and other Samoan Americans on Washington State's football fortunes, Acknowledging the growing number of Samoans throughout American football, Zimmerman quoted Manu Tuiasosopo, an All-American at UCLA who turned professional: "The reason so many fellows are coming over from American Samoa is education. In Samoa, right now, you can't go farther than the community-college level. So the fellows come over here." Indeed, according to the former Bruin, there were just more opportunities on the U.S. mainland. Jackie Thompson added, "Kids in Samoa grow up big and strong. So they are naturals at football." To Zimmerman, "Samoans . . . contribute a warm and welcome stripe in our ethnic spectrum and are an enrichment of many a football program."[22]

Washington State's rival, the University of Washington, had started recruiting Samoans in a concerted fashion in the 1970s. For example, Willy Galoia was a fine linebacker for the Huskies in the later 1970s after competing for Farrington High School in Honolulu. When interviewed by sports columnist Georg Myers, Galoia mentioned that his father was a pastor and village judge in Pago Pago. The elder Galoia did not understand why colleges handed out scholarships for football, but was glad that they did. Galoia insisted that, like other Samoan Americans, he played football not for himself but for his family and people.[23]

Other schools recruited Pacific Islanders in the Pacific Northwest. Alofa Lue Tauvaga competed for the University of Idaho in the early 1970s. In the fall of 1972, sportswriter Bruce Brown maintained, Tauvaga found himself a "little homesick." He told the press, "I'd sure like to have a Samoan guy on the team so I could rap with him in my native language." Tauvaga's coach said he understood the problem. That is, he added, Hawaiians and Samoans were very clannish but also "very proud" in that they hated to make mistakes, but they also hated to be told how to do something more than once. Born in a Samoan village, Tauvaga spent his adolescence in Hawai'i. Cherishing his Samoan home, the young Tauvaga apparently had a hard time adjusting to Hawaiian life. Making matters worse, he could not initially speak English. However, while delivering newspapers in Honolulu, he would ride by UH's football practices and learned to love the sport. After standing out in high school, Tauvaga went to Columbian Basin Community College before heading to Idaho.[24]

In Northern California, San Jose State recruited immensely talented Samoan American athletes. Defensive lineman Wilson Faumuina was so good as a Spartan that he was drafted in the first round by the Atlanta Falcons. This prompted sportswriter Bob Oates to remark in the *Sporting News*, "The Samoan invasion of the United States which began on the Coast reached Georgia." Sadly, Faumuina died at thirty-two of a heart attack. At that time, he was seeking an opportunity to renew a pro career, damaged, the *Sporting News* reported, because he never fulfilled his potential as a pass rusher. For sportswriter Scot Ostler, Frank Manumaleuga disproved the stereotype of Samoans as "unambitious" and "lazy." Manumaleuga was turned away from UCLA because of a congenital heart defect. Undeterred, he headed north to San Jose State, where he was called the "mowin' Samoan" and earned All-American recognition. Manumaleuga subsequently suited up for the Kansas City Chiefs for three years.[25]

In Southern California, Pacific Islander athletes proved vital to the region's college football programs in the late 1970s and early 1980s. In 1976, Long Beach State had Joe Paopao at quarterback in addition to other Pacific Islanders. Readers of the *San Bernardino County Sun* learned that "Long Beach seems to have cornered the market on Samoan football players." In a presumably humorous vein, Ray Ripton of the *Los Angeles Times* noted that Santa Monica Junior College suited up a running back named Ulukita Ulukita. Ripton wrote, "Ulukita Ulukita is not the name of an exotic car that looks the same whether it goes backwards or forwards," but a running back born in American Samoa.[26]

Southern California college standouts like Mosi Tatupu and Manu Tuiasosopo, according to writer David K. Choo, helped pave the way for Samoan Americans to reach the highest rungs of elite college and professional football. Mal Florence extolled Tatupu in the mid-1970s as "one of the best blocking backs in USC history." Calling Tatupu a "squat Samoan," Florence stressed that "Mosi Tatupu is a man." Born in Pago Pago, Tatupu was raised on the Hawaiian Islands, where he went to "Punahoe [sic]" High School. Florence quoted Tatupu remarking, "I consider myself a pure Samoan. . . . I just happened to have been brought up in Hawaii, which I love." Drafted by the New England Patriots, Tatupu drew attention while a rookie at the Patriot's training camp. The *Sporting News* reported that the former Trojan craved "raw fish" and was disappointed at its absence at the Patriot camp. The team trainer responded that the fullback would get plenty of tuna once he made the team. Tatupu made the team. Indeed, he played thirteen years in the NFL, winning a spot on the 1986 Pro Bowl team.[27]

Tatupu died in 2010 of a heart attack. Only fifty-four at the time, it was subsequently discovered that he also suffered from chronic traumatic encephalopathy (CTE), which has afflicted too many other NFL players. According to an ESPN report, "Depression, dementia, erratic behavior, financial instability and substance abuse are common symptoms associated with the CTE. In the most extreme cases, some former NFL players linked to CTE have committed suicide . . . " In Tatupu's case, a genial young man in the 1980s became increasingly morose, temperamental, and abusive of alcohol. Tatupu's former wife and mother of his son, Lofa, who would join the NFL's player ranks in the 2000s proclaimed, "If I knew then what I know now, would I have encouraged Mosi's dream? Would I have encouraged Lofa's dream? . . . I wouldn't have. The risk is not worth the reward."[28]

As a defensive lineman, Manu Tuiasosopo stood out for UCLA. *Sports Illustrated* remarked that he came from "far off Samoa." Subsequently, Tuiasosopo joined the Seattle Seahawks. After five years in the Pacific Northwest, Tuiasosopo headed south where he became a nose tackle for Bill Walsh's estimable 49er teams of the mid-1980s. Upon retirement from the NFL, Tuiasosopo remained active in Samoan American affairs from his home in the Seattle area. He also got involved in youth and high school football coaching.[29]

USC clearly remained vigilant for skilled Pacific Islander football players. None were more talented than Junior Seau, who could not speak English until he was seven. Recruited by USC out of Oceanside, California, he then earned All-American honors for USC in the late 1980s before moving on to an all-pro career with the San Diego Chargers. During the 1990s and early 2000s few, if any, NFL linebackers were better than Junior Seau. *Sports Illustrated* football writer Michael Silver praised Seau as the NFL's most intense player in the mid-1990s. After several years with the Chargers, Seau finished his long career with the New England Patriots. In all, Seau put in twenty seasons in the NFL. He made all-pro six times and was picked for twelve Pro Bowls. Furthermore, in 1994 Seau won the NFL's Walter Payton Award for community service. Sadly, he ended his life in 2012, leaving many to wonder about NFL policy regarding concussions and their long-term consequences for professional football players.[30]

Several gridders of Samoan descent made their way to southwestern college football programs. A Hawaiian of Samoan ancestry, Junior Ah You won plaudits on the U.S. mainland as a star linebacker for Arizona State in the late 1960s and early 1970s and then earned money and honors in the Canadian Football League. Playing for the Montreal Alouettes, Ah You became the only gridder from Hawai'i to earn a place in Canada's Football Hall of Fame. He was named to the All-Canadian All-Star team twice, participating in five Grey Cup Championships. In 1984 and 1985 Ah You headed south of the border to play football for franchises in Chicago, New Orleans, and Arizona belonging to the ill-conceived United States Football League.[31]

In 1976, *SI* readers discovered in Richard Johnson's article that Ah You was a "6' 2", 218-pound holy Mormon terror," plucked from Honolulu Kahuku High School by Arizona State. Johnson proclaimed, "Nobody looks more like a Polynesian warrior than Junior—he has a body-builder's physique, smoky eyes flanking a hawk-nose in a high cheek-boned face, a Fu Manchu moustache embracing a mouth full of flashing white teeth." At the same time, Johnson testified, "nobody's name sounds less like" that of a "holy Mormon terror." "Ah You?," he queried, "Junior Ah You?" Such a name, Johnson insisted, more likely belonged to "a waiter, or a busboy, maybe, helping out in his father's Chinese restaurant." Ah You conceded that his father was "half-Chinese," adding that his mother was "pure Samoan." But, according to Ah You, he was not a quarter Chinese but "all Samoan!" Thus, Johnson maintained that Ah You proved his actual racial heritage by starring in football at Arizona State and then Canada. In other words, Chinese people were racially less fit for football stardom than Samoans.[32]

In other parts of the West, Samoans showed up on college football rosters. Paul Nunu was a fine linebacker for the University of Wyoming in the mid-1970s. Sportswriter Corky Simpson insisted that the Samoan native had supposedly never heard of football until his family moved to Hawai'i. At high school, he starred at Kahuku High on Oahu. However, two college programs that had been recruiting Samoans, Arizona State and BYU, passed on him—the latter even though he was a Mormon. A Physical Education major at Wyoming, Nunu declared he had little problem adjusting to the frigid climate embracing Wyoming in late fall and winter.[33]

Tongan Vai Sikahema helped BYU become a national champion in 1984. An exciting punt and kickoff return specialist, who also rushed from scrimmage, Sikahema became the first person of Tongan ancestry to join the NFL. He played several years with the St. Louis and then Arizona Cardinals as well as the Green Bay Packers and Philadelphia Eagles. Like many Tongans who made their way to the United States, Sikahema has been a devout Mormon. After leaving the gridiron, he become a popular television sports journalist in the Philadelphia area.[34]

Great Pacific Islander gridders helped keep UH respectable in Division I competition in the late twentieth century. Born in California but raised in Hawai'i, Mark Tuinei played two years at UCLA before transferring to UH, where he played as an offensive lineman for two more seasons. He would then go on to fifteen years as a stalwart blocker for the Dallas Cowboys and gain two invitations to the Pro Bowl in the 1990s. Illuminating the dark side of professional football success, Tuinei died of a drug overdose in 1999. UH must have had a magnificent offensive line in the mid-1980s. A teammate of Tuinei's at UH, Jesse Sapolu was born in Samoa and raised in Hawai'i. A versatile offensive lineman, Sapolu played both center and guard. Beginning in 1983, he carved out a distinguished thirteen-year career with the San Francisco 49ers after leaving UH. Like Tuinei, Sapolu would be invited to the Pro Bowl two times. The Noga brothers performed well for UH in the 1980s before heading to the pros. Linebacker Falinka Noga won a place on the West all-star team in the 1984 Shrine game in San Francisco. He then spent eight years as a linebacker for the St. Louis Rams, Phoenix Cardinals, and Detroit Lions. A defensive lineman, Al Noga was named the Western Athletic Conference (WAC) defensive player of the year in 1986 before playing several years for the Minnesota Vikings, Indianapolis Colts, and Washington. Pete Noga, a linebacker, left UH for a year in the NFL as a linebacker for St. Louis.[35]

In the late twentieth and early twenty-first century, many Pacific Islanders gained recognition in elite college and professional football—too many to mention in all.

Playing linebacker for the Seattle Seahawks when they got into their first Super Bowl in 2006 was former USC standout Lofa Tatupu. Mosi's son, Lofa Tatupu claimed he never gave much thought to his heritage while growing up. He said the only Samoan football player he followed was his dad, who played for the New England Patriots. Otherwise, his favorite pro football player was running back Thurman Thomas. Tatupu admitted, "I'm a Massachusetts suburban kid. . . . I didn't put too much thought to it." Tatupu played several years for the Seahawks as a starting linebacker. He particularly excelled in his early years, when he was invited to the Pro Bowl his first three season—2005 through 2007. In the latter year, as well, he was honored as first-team All-Pro. Subsequently, Tatupu was dogged by injuries, and he never played NFL football beyond the 2010 season.[36]

Despite the accomplishments of Jack Thompson and others in the "skilled positions," many of us picture Pacific Islander gridders as aggressive defenders or offensive linemen perhaps because those in charge of elite college football programs and NFL teams have not been able to see beyond the stereotype. The son of Manu Tuiasosopo, quarterback Marques Tuiasosopo was to the University of Washington from 1998 to 2000 what Jack Thompson was to rival Washington State several years earlier. Interestingly, he was recruited by the Huskies to play safety. Eventually, however, he would become the first player in college football history to run for more than 200 yards and pass for more than 300 in a game against Stanford. In the process, he was named PAC-10 player of the year in 2000. Tuiasosopo's grandfather was reportedly a village chief in American Samoa. His siblings were accomplished athletes. Sister Leslie played volleyball, and one brother, Zach, played linebacker for the Huskies and a bit for the Philadelphia Eagles, while another, Matt, took some swings in major league baseball. Tuiasosopo, regrettably, never quite worked out as a NFL quarterback. He played backup for the Oakland Raiders in the early 2000s. In 2003, he was given one start and managed to complete twenty-five of forty-five passes during the year. After his quarterbacking days ended, Tuiasosopo took up coaching. In 2013, he was named interim head coach of the University of Washington. After he was passed over as permanent head coach of the Huskies, he moved on to USC's coaching staff.[37]

Troy Polamalu emerged in the 2000s as one of the NFL's most feared defensive backs. Before then, Polamalu was an All-American safety for USC. From the beginning of his NFL career, Polamalu expressed pride in his Samoan ancestry. During the 2006 Super Bowl's media day, Polamalu, according to the *Seattle Times'* Greg Bishop, talked about how "the family atmosphere Samoans are raised in translates to their love of football. . . . He even gave a dissertation on Samoan life in America. . . . Samoans have had a problem assimilating in American society. . . . Because they're very different. American society is a rat race. Samoa is really open and really laid back. In that sense, we've had a tough time assimilating."[38]

Polamalu's family initially migrated to Southern California. But when he was eight, they moved him to Tennile, Oregon, to escape the criminal environment they found in the Golden State. Polamalu lived with an aunt and uncle in Oregon. He remembered he belonged to the only "minority household" in town and was nurtured in a lifestyle about which he joked "the FBI has some public files on." More seriously, Polamalu recalled the collective care of his family—that he was really "raised by a village."[39]

Polamalu joined the Pittsburgh Steelers in 2003. The strong safety subsequently garnered many postseason honors. In 2010, the Associated Press named him the league's Defensive Player of the Year. Moreover, the Pro Football Hall of Fame placed him on its second team all-2000s Team. In addition, he was chosen all-pro four times and invited to the Pro Bowl eight times. After establishing himself as an NFL star, Polamalu has used the off season not to luxuriate in his celebrityhood but, along with his wife, heads to American Samoa with a retinue of physical and academic educators as well as physicians and nurses. He hopes that his initiative will, historian Rob Ruck writes, "build social capital by imparting life skills to help in the classroom and workplace as much as on the ball field."[40]

In 2012, Notre Dame's linebacker Manti Te'o emerged as a Heisman Trophy candidate even though the Heisman typically has gone to an offensive backfield star. A one-time star for Punahou, Te'o wound up second in the vote to Texas A&M sensation Johnny Manziel. The Samoan American, nevertheless, managed to win plenty of awards, including the Maxwell Award, usually considered second to the Heisman in prestige. He did find himself, moreover, in the middle of a ridiculous, well-publicized, but relatively minor, scandal, as college football scandals have gone in recent years. Te'o was accused of making up an online romance with the aid of a member of the Tuiasosopo family. In reality, Te'o was "catfished." His online romance, that is, was with someone whose identity was false; indeed a male. Accordingly, scholar David Leonard maintains, Te'o's identity as a hypermasculine Polynesian football player was undercut. Indeed, Te'o was suspected in the world of American football as being guilty of something worse than possibly a less than stellar linebacker—he was suspected of being gay. Nevertheless, as of this writing, Te'o is a linebacker for the New Orleans Saints.[41]

In 2015, Marcus Mariota joined the Tennessee Titans, who made him the first college player chosen in the NFL draft that year. Mariota, as his Heisman Trophy speech would suggest, seems to value his Hawaiian identity as much as, if not more, than his Samoan roots. Thus, it is not surprising that even before Mariota threw footballs for the Titans in their Nashville home stadium, it was announced that an L&L restaurant would be established in Franklin, Tennessee, twenty-two miles from Nashville. Claiming to offer patrons authentic Hawaiian barbeque, the L&L chain had yet to venture into Tennessee. L&L's chief operating officer admitted leeriness about opening a restaurant in Tennessee where the "demographics" seemed doubtful. However, due to the Titans drafting of Mariota "we are moving full-speed ahead." Erwin Corpuz and Fred Amano, who ran L&L restaurants in San Diego, were publicized as spearheading the venture. Amano's brother, Eugene, who had played with the Titans, would chip in financially. Although probably not an elite NFL quarterback, Mariota, as it turned out, has performed well in his first few years with the Titans.[42]

A COLONIZED FOOTBALL MODEL MINORITY

As the twentieth century ended, the presence of Samoan Americans and other Pacific Islanders on numerous college rosters provoked all sorts of commentary, often well-intentioned but often not always thought out. Tom Holmoe, then head coach of Cal, emphasized in 1999: "It's the simple fact that Hawaii and other Polynesian Islands has some really good football. A lot of players from the islands are fantastic players . . . there's no reason why they shouldn't succeed."

In 2003, journalist David Choo reported that two hundred gridders of Samoan descent played Division 1 college football. Focusing on UH, Choo told readers that by 2000 the school's football program had fallen on hard times, but turned around when its coaching staff began to make concerted recruiting inroads among talented gridders nurtured on American Samoa. David Choo estimated that in 2002, 60 percent of the UH squad possessed Samoan ancestry.[43]

Media attention on the Pacific Islander impact on American football and vice versa has blended stereotyping and thoughtful analyses. A good example is a 2009 National Public Radio piece produced by Tom Goldman, who racialized "Polynesians" as "distinguish[ing] themselves at football's elite levels for many reasons, including their traditional body types: broad shoulders, wide hips, thick legs. These football players' love of hard physical contact and fierce competition has its roots in Polynesian culture as well."[44]

Goldman pointed out that several high school football squads in Utah were powered by Pacific Islanders. He explained that Mormon missionaries made significant incursions among the indigenous island populations of the Pacific. Accordingly, Utah become a major destination for Pacific Islanders migrating to the U.S. mainland and Utah grid teams a major destination for Pacific Islanders inclined toward and skilled in football. Goldman claimed that of the twenty-eight Division I football scholarships given to Utah high school gridders, eighteen went to Pacific Islanders.[45]

Not interested in a mindless cheering of Pacific Islander football prowess, Goldman's key theme was that football has allowed young Pacific Islander males to both reflect and transcend their cultures. He quoted a Utah-based Samoan American assistant coach who remembered that football back home in American Samoa represented a proclivity toward collective violence among male Samoans to protect their village and family. Goldman also, however, cited Fotu Katoa, Utah's director of Pacific Islander affairs at the time. Katoa told Goldman that the transition for many from the Pacific to Utah had been difficult. Pacific Islander migrants to Utah hoped to achieve a Mormon version of the American Dream. Some succeeded, but more did not as they "struggled with low-paying jobs with little English skills." Yet Pacific Islanders continued to lean on a culture which stressed family and community, but that culture clashed with a mainstream American culture that worshipped individualism.[46]

Katoa hoped, according to Goldman, that football would allow at least Pacific Islander young men to straddle the cultural divide. That is, football success could inspire an individual to connect to the collective, Pacific Islander culture. At the same time, the Pacific Islander gridder could revel in American individualism. As Katoa explained, "Football has been really good to us in a sense of publicity and getting our kids out there and some going on to the NFL arena. . . . It's that we just want to be known for more."[47]

Not only public radio, but also the most prestigious newspaper in the United States appraised the impact of Pacific Islanders on early twenty-first century American football. Writing for the *New York Times* in 2008, Jerre Longman discussed the "Polynesian Pipeline" that delivered football talent from Tonga to the football crazy town of Euliss, Texas. Thanks to "[p]layers of Tongan descent, Trinity High School could boast of state championships in 2005 and 2007." As for the young men involved, Longman wrote, they "have brought imposing size, strength, and toughness to the [local high school eleven]—and the need for a roster with phonetic spelling for the announcers."[48]

Close to Dallas, Euliss seemed notably diverse. Students at Trinity spoke fifty-three languages and the flags of thirty-one nations flew at the school's entrance. More to the point, Longman stressed, thirteen of the twenty-four Trinity gridders to make all-state since the 1980s possessed Tongan ancestry. As for the 2008 squad, sixteen of the Euliss varsity football roster were of Tongan descent. A father of two of those players told Longman, "When you think of Texas high school football, you don't expect to see players from the South Pacific."[49]

Longman talked to football players and faculty on the Trinity campus. Uatakini Cocker was one of the players Longman interviewed. Whenever the nearly 300-pound offensive tackle knocked an opponent to the ground, he yelled, "Mate ma'a Tonga," or "I will die for Tonga." Described by Longman as playful, Cocker reported that opposing players and fans often asked, "Are you Mexican?" A women's volleyball coach at

Trinity declared that the Tongan athletes at Trinity "set the tone for the whole school." She described them as "self-confident," honoring a "culture . . . taught to respect authority." She added that they valued family and regarded the team as an extension of their families.[50]

Like Goldman, Longman interviewed Katoa, who was the first Tongan football player at Trinity before heading for Utah. Further, Katoa's younger brother, Sammy, starred as an all-state linebacker at Trinity. Longman wrote that the brothers' ethnic heritage may have been novel to the residents of Euliss at the time, but there was nothing strange about their gridiron skills. Ofa Fiale-Sale, a one-time Tongan classmate of the Katoas and at that time an official in Euliss's Parks and Community Services Department, insisted to Longman that "their athletic success helped engender the general acceptance of Tongans.[51]

Katoa told Longman that for the families of the Tongan gridders, Euliss proved a sanctuary from the violent streets they found in California and even Utah. Euliss gridder Sione Moeakiola remembered growing up in Long Beach, California, contrasting his childhood with Euliss, where his family could experience "simple freedoms . . . like being able to place a television near a window without risking gunshots fired into the living room."[52]

Meanwhile, Fiale-Sale explained to Longman that Euliss had taken care to acclimate Tongan newcomers, adding:

> Compromises have been reached to accommodate large family gatherings at funeral rituals that last for days. And the city has promoted alternatives to the slaughtering of pigs at home for open-pit cooking. A mobile health unit helps to provide free flu shots and medical check-ups. . . . [City officials] have been very understanding of the huge adjustment it takes for many people.

Indeed, the city offered "police escorts for Trinity's football team and signs for fans to wave at games." Yet it is far to wonder if Euliss would have been so openhanded had Tongans not contributed to the success of the local high school football team.[53]

Like many observers of Pacific Islanders football players, Longman seemed fascinated with the *haka* dance, introduced largely to the sports world by the New Zealand All Blacks rugby team, possessing a significant contingent of players possessing Maori ancestry. Subsequently, football and rugby squads composed in large measure of Pacific Islanders have performed the haka before games. The UH football team offers one example. Elikenna Fiello, a star linebacker for Trinity, explained to Longman that the "haka was meant to 'ignite the breath of competition.'" Opponents, Longman observed, did not always welcome the haka. He averred that an opposing school band struck up the national anthem while Trinity gridders performed the haka. Opposing players ridiculed the dance, but, Longman insisted, "at their own peril."[54]

Early in 2011, a piece in *USA Today* focused on Kyle Gouveia, a member of a famed Hawaiian football family. His uncle Kurt, for example, soldiered for several years as a linebacker in the NFL. Young Gouveia hoped to play college football after his high school days were over. Author Jim Halley noted that the percentage of Pacific Islanders on college football squads was significantly higher than the proportion of Pacific Islanders in the U.S. population. That is, Native Hawaiian or Pacific Islanders comprised just under 0.2 percent of the U.S. population in 2009, but made up nearly 2 percent college football players. Like other discussions of Pacific Islander football, this article stressed the collective/familial mentality of Pacific Islander gridders. Halley quoted George Malamalu, a former University of Arizona quarterback and then president of the AIGA foundation, an organization bent on aiding Pacific Islander student-athletes. Malamalu told Halley that Pacific Islanders "are family-oriented" and thus out of synch with U.S. culture's embrace of individualism. Moreover, Halley's article spoke to the physicality of Pacific Islander gridders. He maintained that Kyle Gouveia was small for college recruiters, standing at six feet two and weighing slightly over two hundred pounds. Yet the gridder "shares an affinity with many Polynesian players in that he enjoys hitting." [55]

Significantly, some journalists and academics from Pacific Islander and Asian American communities have expressed concerns about the generally positive, but often racialized, media reports on Pacific Islander football. In 2010, ESPN added its voice to those acclaiming the interaction between Pacific Islanders and football. Yet a 2010 editorial in the *Northwest Asian Weekly* countered:

> Though the ESPN story is a good story, it does have a few troubling spots. Between statistics and good quotes, the story also perpetuates stereotypes—probably unwittingly. Part of it says, "Samoans once were known as fierce warriors who practiced cannibalism. Now they take their aggressions out on the football field, and they do so with uncanny power and skill due to a potent brew of genetics and culture. Their bodies are naturally big-boned." [56]

In the same edition as the editorial, journalist Jason Cruz questioned the way in which Pacific Islanders were depicted as football's "model minority." He quoted UH professor Ty Kāwika Tengan who told him in an email, "I find depictions of Polynesians as 'naturally fit' for football to be racist stereotypes that draw on a longer colonial history of misrepresentations not only of Polynesians, but also of other indigenous and negatively racialized peoples." A cultural anthropologist at the University of Washington, Rochelle Fonoti echoed Tengan's analysis. She told Cruz that "Samoan male bodies have been commodified." That is, Samoan and other Pacific Islander gridders have been represented as "savage warriors" to enrich the NCAA and the NFL. "It's all good for football," Fonoti claimed, "but oftentimes, there is no career to fall back on."[57]

Hawaiian scholars Tengan and Jesse Makani Markham have sought to undermine the dominant narrative celebrating Pacific Islander football. They asserted little opposition to young men playing college football. But they clearly believed that UH commodified and exploited Polynesians while claiming to celebrate them. In a 2009 article in the *International Journal of the History of Sport*, they likened the conventional storyline of Polynesian football players to that of the way media has often handled African American athletes. They wrote, "Though a common story bearing resemblance to the 'hoop dreams' narrative, we find this to be a very partial and limiting view of factors contributing to the prevalence of Polynesian football players." Tengan and Markham lament that Pacific Islanders, too, have bought into the "partial and limiting view" of Polynesian football. This has especially been the case for Polynesian males who "make claims to an 'authentic' pre-colonial and pre-modern masculinity" to counteract the presumably emasculating consequences of colonization and diaspora.[58]

Tengan and Markham stressed that the representation of Pacific Islander males as football "warriors . . . becomes a commodity image to be sold to big business." They argued that the commodification of Pacific Islander gridders has helped to market big-time football to white middle-class men who fear the feminization of modernity and crave identification with hyper masculine linebackers and defensive lineman. Tengan and Markham explore the pertinent case of the branding of UH football in the early twenty-first century. During the late 1990s, the nickname for UH athletic teams came under fire, especially among players, coaches, and fans of the football team. At the time, UH male teams were called "Rainbows" or "Rainbow Warriors," and a rainbow design adorned UH football helmets. Some in the UH community, as well as supporters of the football team, bridled at a nickname and a logo which they associated with the struggle for gay and lesbian rights. UH's administration surrendered to the critics. UH's football team hitherto became known as the Warriors and in 2000 a new logo was introduced—a logo which Tengan and Markham described as "a stylized green and white letter 'H' with a pattern of geometrical shapes meant to replicate Hawaiian motifs . . . and bands of triangles were printed around the upper arm and thigh in a fashion similar to the tattoos worn by many local and Polynesian men."[59]

Former UH student body president Pi'ilani Smith spoke out against the rebranding of UH football. She and others in the Hawaiian nationalist movement had previously condemned the university for residing on lands illegally taken from the Hawaiian people. Smith accused the university of trying to marginalize the Native Hawaiian critique by claiming a superficial alliance with indigenous Pacific people. Smith, according to Tengan and Markham, asserted to the press, "My issue is about institutionalized racism. Not so much the marketing, but its misappropriation of the Hawaiian image. . . . They're using what will sell, but it doesn't belong to them."[60]

For Tengan and Markham, a long history of "colonization, particularly through militarism and tourism," shadowed the marketing of UH football. The rebranding of UH football, they emphasized, eventuated largely because "[s]uch an assertion of hyper masculinity was needed precisely because the processes of colonization . . . had configured Hawai'i as a feminine space, the 'hula girl' waiting to be taken." Tengan and Markham also maintained that the rebranding allowed "multiple parties to (re)make and perform Polynesian masculinity." They equated the process to what scholar Philip Deloria has described in his book *Playing Indian*, which, among other things, examined how whites in America appropriated Indian imagery for commercial and cultural reasons. Tengan and Markham also perceived an echo in Hawai'i of what occurred "in the settler state of Aotearoa/New Zealand." There Maori male athletes "are represented in the sport-media complex and in the national imaginary as the embodiment of primal, savage warriorhood. The usurpation of the Maori as a sport symbol is rooted in the desires, envies, anxieties and fears of male colonizers whose own masculinity is defined, in part, with and against the colonized man's."[61]

The appropriation of the haka from what the Maori call Aotearoa, Tengan and Markham asserted, encouraged UH football players, coaches, and fans to "play Polynesian." The haka has come to represent the masculinity of Maori and Pacific Islander males. Perceived incorrectly as a traditional "war dance," the haka has been seen as both a way to motivate the rugby- and football-playing dancers, while intimidating their opponents.[62]

Analysts such as Tengan, Markham, and Margaret Jolly have observed similarities in the way Maori and Hawaiian people were colonized, but what Jolly calls "the predominant colonial discourse" differed. Maori men were represented as threatening, hypermasculine while Hawaiian men were more feminized or, as in the case, of "Waikiki Beach Boys" rendered unmanly because they were ostensibly "lazy, unduly sexual, and rebellious." Hawaiian males, Tengan and Markham argued, have used the haka to overcome the feminized representations of them.[63]

Like rituals in general, the haka performances at UH football games have attempted to plaster over very real differences and tensions among Pacific Islanders in Hawai'i. These people have varied in terms of ethnicity, class status, politics, and religion. These differences and tensions were replicated on UH's football teams and their supporters. Through the haka, participants could, if but briefly, minimize social distinctions among Polynesian people.[64]

Eventually, the university's football players took up a revised haka from that performed in New Zealand. University officials and the football program justified the change because of the need for "cultural respect and authenticity." The unveiling of a new haka, however, provoked a rehashing of old stereotypes. ESPN commentator Chris Spielman hoped that the new haka would not resemble a hula dance, quipping, "I can't see 500 lb. linemen doing the hula with a grass skirt. That would give me confidence if I was the opponent."[65]

Tengan and Markham articulated a graver concern when it came to UH's treatment of its largely Polynesian football players. They quoted UH ethnic studies professor Marion Kelley who described the university as Hawai'i's "last plantation." In graduating its student athletes, UH clearly underperformed. Its forty-two percent rate in 2008 was next to last in the NCAA. Pointing out the example of Levi Stanley, Tengan and Markham lamented that UH had served Pacific Islander football players relatively well in the past but the school's commitment to educate an important segment of its student-athletes dissipated in the hopes of attaining Division I glory. As mentioned earlier, under Norm Chow's tenure, the classroom performances of UH players was taken seriously, but unfortunately for Chow gridiron performances did not impress school authorities or supporters.[66]

Other critical analysts point out that social and economic inequality has hovered over Polynesian participation in American football. Poverty, for example, still haunts American Samoa, and even if Samoans are greatly overrepresented in the NFL and college football, upward social mobility through football remains at best an illusion for all but the very few. Sadly, perhaps, this illusion has been reinforced by well-meaning players such as Troy Polamalu, who make annual trips to Samoa representing the promise of NFL careers. Indeed, the attraction of football to young Pacific Islanders has been alluring. In a 2011 paper, scholar Adam Beissel maintained that one out of eight Samoans playing high school football on Samoa attain college scholarships from schools on the mainland and Hawai'i. Meanwhile, the unemployment rate on American Samoa has lingered around the 30 percent mark. Facing a future of dead-end jobs or unemployment, young Samoan men understandably seek brief and even dangerous football careers if it can mean a scholarship to USC, BYU, or UH, and an NFL career or, more realistically, a college degree leading to potentially significant upward mobility.[67]

A 2014 article by Fa'anofo Lisaclaire Uperesa reinforces the argument that football has encouraged the racialization of Pacific Islanders. Like Blacks, "Polynesian players have been racialized in ways that help them" gain access to elite college and professional football ranks but exclude them from other pursuits. That is, Black and Pacific Islanders possess the body type and innate athletic skills that should pave their way to gridiron success. However, what seems to distinguish Pacific Islanders as a football model minority has been that they also possess the discipline and respect for authority that presumably too many African Americans lack.[68]

Recently, historian Rob Ruck has also taken on the prevalent notion that all is right in a world where Pacific Islanders play football. While seemingly advancing the notion of Pacific Islanders as football's model minority, Ruck nevertheless argues that Pacific Islander gridders are "athletic outliers" who have "pa[id] a steep price for their commitment to the game." Those qualities that have made many of them effective football players—"their extraordinary internalization of discipline and warrior self-image that drives them to play with no fefe (no fear)—have often proven hazardous to their mental and physical health":

> Samoan boys, who train year-round on fields blistered with volcanic pebbles and use helmets that should have been discarded long ago, incur far too much neurological damage. Any studies to support this assertion at the high school level? They have a difficult time adjusting to college and maximizing the benefit of an athletic scholarship. More important, this micro-culture of football excellence coexists with a public health crisis. Samoans and Tongans are among the most diabetic and obese people on the planet, the consequence of forsaking a traditional diet for cheap and fast food.[69]

CONCLUSION

However famous and relatively wealthy, individual Pacific Islander football players have been, it remains important to keep in mind that they represent only a small portion of historically colonized peoples. Colonization, as in any form of political domination, has not required unrelenting, brutal exploitation and oppression to thrive. Colonizers have long enjoyed patting themselves on the back whenever a colonized person seems to make it in the colonizer's world. That is, such "success stories" prove that colonization has never been about power but about uplift. Such narratives of uplift can serve to divert attention from to those Indians unable to gain entrance to Oxford and those Samoans unable to get football scholarships to USC. Moreover, if the colonized demonstrate a facility to learn the white colonizer's lessons too well, they undermine the need for uplift in the first place and the racial supremacy often justifying colonization.[70]

Football's contradictions play themselves out powerfully in how they influence disadvantaged young men of color. The sport promises fulfillment of the American Dream and masculine fantasies. It has shown the capacity to satisfy those promises, but perhaps, as the all too brief lives of Mark Tuinei and more recently Junior Seau suggest, at too dear a price for themselves, for their loved ones, and society. Critical scholars and journalists have sought with some success to point out the ramifications of all this for Pacific Islander communities. We need to pay attention to these critiques and hope that they will help break down the model minority narrative of Pacific Islander football without diminishing the very real joy and success achieved by Polynesian gridders.

NOTES

1. https://cdn.americanprogress.org/wp-content/uploads/2014/08/AAPI-IncomePoverty.pdf (July 9, 2016).

2. *Greenwood Index-Journal*, March 3, 1985.

3. Tengan and Markham, "Performing," 2416.

4. Ibid.

5. Vicente M. Diaz, "Fight Boys, 'til the Last . . . ": Islandstyle Football and the Remasculation of Indigeneity in the Militarized American Pacific Islands," in Paul Spickard, Joanne L. Rondilla, and Debbie Hippolite Wright (eds.), *Pacific Diaspora: Island Peoples in the United States and across the Pacific* (Honolulu: University of Hawai'i Press, 2002), 172.

6. Ibid., 187–188.

7. *Sporting News*, September 25, 1971.

8. Early Gutskey, "Smile When You Call Him Junior," *Los Angeles Times*, November 1, 1974.

9. Andy Bernstein, "Polynesian, 'Bigger, Stronger, Quicker,'" *Corsair*, October 15, 1975.

10. *San Bernardino County Sun*, January 2, 1975.

11. *Long Beach Independent-Press*, July 13, 1975; *Los Angeles Times*, December 25, 1976.

12. Scot Ostler, "Carson's Samoan Connection," *Los Angeles Times*, December 16, 1978.

13. Richard W. Johnson, "Shake-em Out of the Coconut Trees" *SI*, http://www.si.com/vault/1976/08/16/613329/shake-em-out-of-the-coconut-trees (August 16, 2016).

14. Ibid.

15. Ibid.

16. Nick Peters, "Thompson's Dream Has Rosy Glow for Cougars," *Sporting News*, October 8, 1977; Terry Shepherd," From Samoa with Talent," *Los Angeles Times*, October 13, 1978.

17. *Sporting News*, October 1, 1977; Peters, "Thompson's Dream"; Peters, "Thompson Prime Pro Prospect," November 18, 1978.

18. Mel Reisner, "Cougs 'Throwin Samoan' Rather Win Than Throw Passes," *Seattle Times*, October 26, 1977; *Nevada Herald*, August 6, 1978.

19. *Sports Illustrated*, December 27, 1999-January 3, 2000; Franks, *Crossing*, 135; http://www.pro-football-reference.com/players/T/ThomJa00.htm (June 3, 2007); Nick Peters, "Prime Pro Prospect."

20. http://www.historyguy.com/sportshistory/jack_thompson_quarterback.htm, (June 16, 2015).

21. Chuck Ashman, "Samoa Samoa Shows up at W.S.U W.S.U," *Seattle Times*, February 14, 1978; June 12, 1979; *Sporting News*, November 1, 1980; *Aberdeen News*, June 9, 1981; *Greenwood Index-Journal*, March 3, 1985.

22. Washington State University vs. Stanford University, Football Program, Stanford Stadium, Palo Alto, California, October 20, 1984; Hy Zimmerman, "Sports Fans Glad to 'See Samoa of Samoa,'" *Seattle Times*, November 3, 1981.

23. *Seattle Times*, October 8, 1976.

24. Johnson, "Shake'em Out" Bruce Brown, "Samoan Lonely, but Loves Football," *Spokane Daily Chronicle*, October 12, 1972.

25. *Sporting News*, August 27, 1977; October 13, 1986; Ostler, "Carson's Samoan Connection."

26. *San Bernardino County Sun*, September 16, 1976; Ray Ripton, "SMC Power Runner," *Los Angeles Times*, October 2, 1980.

27. David K. Choo, "The Polynesian Powerhouse"; Mal Florence, "Tatupu Top Rated Blocker," *Los Angeles Times*, December 25, 1976; *Sporting News*, September 2, 1978; http://www.pro-football-reference.com/players/T/TatuMo00.html (July 7, 2007).

28. http://espn.go.com/boston/nfl/story/_/id/12237694/former-new-england-patriots-fan-favorite-mosi-tatupu-suffered-chronic-traumatic-encephalopathy-cte, (June 17, 2015).

29. *Sports Illustrated*, September 11, 1978; http://www.pro-football-reference.com/players/T/TuiaMa20.htm (May 14, 2009); http://www.asianhalloffame.org/portfolio/manu-tuiasosopo/ (June 17, 2015).

30. Michael Silver, "The Last Best Word," *Sports Illustrated*, January 23, 1995; Franks, *Crossing*, 136; http://www.pro-football-reference.com/players/S/SeauJu00.htm (March 24, 2015); http:// espn.go.com/espn/otl/story/_/id/8830344/study-junior-seau-brain-shows-chronic-brain-damage-found-other-nfl-football-players (June 17, 2015).

31. *Sporting News*, October 3, 1970; http://hawaiisportshalloffame.com/xahyo.htm (June 17, 2015).

32. Johnson, "Shake'em Out."

33. Corky Simpson, "Wyoming's Nunu a Hit," *Tucson Daily Citizen*, November 4, 1976.

34. http://byucougars.com/athlete/m-football/vai-sikahema (June 7, 2016); Rob Ruck, "Football's Polynesian Movement: Samoa's Athletic Outliers Are Paying a Steep Price for Their Committment to the Game," http://www.salon.com/2016/02/05/footballs_polynesian_moment_samoas_athletic_outliers_are_paying_a_steep_price_for_their_commitment_to_the_game/ (April 4, 2016).

35. Franks, *Crossing*, 192; http://www.pro-football-reference.com/players/S/SapoJe00.htm (June 4, 2010); East-West Shrine Football Program, Stanford Stadium, Palo Alto, CA, January 4, 1984; http://www.pro-football-reference.com/players/N/Noga-Ni20.htm (August 17, 2010); http://www.sports-reference.com/cfb/players/al-noga-1.html (August 17, 2010).

36. Greg Bishop, "Tatupu, Polamalu Take Different Paths to Same Place," *Seattle Times*, February 2, 2006; http://www.pro-football-reference.com/players/T/Tatu-Lo99.htm (July 18, 2015); http://profootballtalk.nbcsports.com/2014/03/04/broncos-working-out-lofa-tatupu-today-after-long-layoff/ (July 18, 2015).

37. Gail Wood, "Tuiasosopo not Pretty, but He just Wins," *Gannett News Service*, December 19, 2000; http://www.pro-football-reference.com/players/T/TuiaMa00.htm (March 7, 2014); http://www.usctrojans.com/sports/m-footbl/mtt/marques_tuiasosopo_880407.html (October 23, 2015).

38. *Sports Illustrated*, August 12, 2002; Bishop, "Tatupu, Polamalu."

39. Bishop, "Tatupu, Polamalu."

40. http://www.pro-football-reference.com/players/P/PolaTr99.htm (April 14, 2015); Ruck, "Football's Polynesian Moment."

41. David Leonard, "Lin, Te'o, and Asian American Masculinities in Sporting Flux," in Stanley I. Thangaraj, Constancio R. Arnoldo, Jr., and Christine B. Chin (eds.), *Asian American Sporting Cultures* (New York: New York University Press, 2016); *Northwest Asian Weekly*, June 6, 2015; Shanahan, "Kale Ane."

42. Darin Moriki, "L&L Hawaiian Grill to Follow Hawaii Native Marcus Mariota to Nashville," *Pacific Business News*, http://www.bizjournals.com/pacific/blog/2015/05/l-l-hawaiian-grill-to-follow-hawaii-native-marcus.html (July 23, 2015); http://www.nfl.com/player/marcusmariota/2552466/profile (January 24, 2017).

43. Brian Liou, "The API Lineup," *Asian Week*, October 14, 1999; Choo, "The Polynesian Powerhouse."

44. Tom Goldman, "Young Polynesians Make a Life Out of Football," http://www.npr.org/templates/story/story.php?storyId=112970742 (September 22, 2014).

45. Ibid.

46. Ibid.

47. Ibid.

48. Jere Longman, "Polynesian Pipeline Feeds a Texas Football Titan," *New York Times*, October 8, 2008.

49. Ibid.

50. Ibid.

51. Ibid.

52. Ibid.

53. Ibid.

54. Ibid.

55. Jim Halley, "Young Gouveia Hopes He's a Hit in All-Star Game," *USA Today*, January 13, 2011.

56. "Polynesians, Not Just Football Players," *Northwest Asian Weekly*, April 3, 2010-April 9, 2010.

57. Jason Cruz, " Island Ball, Pacific Islands Are Good at Producing Pro Football Players—Reality or Stereotype," in *Northwest Asian Weekly*.

58. Tengan and Markham, "Performing Polynesian," 2413–2414

59. Ibid., 2414, 2419.

60. *Ibid*. 2419.

61. Ibid., 2421.

62. Ibid., 2421–2422.

63. Tengan and Markham, "Performing Polynesian," 2421–2422; Margaret Jolly, "Moving Masculinities: Memories and Bodies Across Oceania," *The Contemporary Pacific*, 20, no. 1 (2008): 6–7. See also Isaiah Helekulunihi Walker, *Waves of Resistance: Surfing and History in Twentieth-Century Hawai'i* (Honolulu: University of Hawai'i Press, 2011) for an examination of how Pacific Islander males have been gendered thanks to racialized colonization.

64. Tengan and Markham, "Performing Polynesian," 2422.

65. Ibid., 2423.

66. Ibid., 2424.

67. Adam Beissel, "Reducing the Samoan Body: Articulating Scientific Racism and Neoliberal Sport," ISSA Conference, Havana, Cuba, July 14, 2011. Thanks to Gerald Gems for drawing my attention to this source.

68. Fa'anofo Lisaclaire Uperesa, "Fabled Futures: Migration and Mobility for Samoans in American Football," *Contemporary Pacific* 26, no. 2 (2014): 281–301.

69. Ruck, "Polynesian Movement."

70. C. L. R. James, *Beyond a Boundary*.

Conclusion

Football's relationship to Americans of Asian and Pacific ancestry has not always been easy, partly because it's relationship to Americans in general has not always been easy. If it has served as a "cosmopolitan canopy," under which people of diverse ethnic descent have encountered one another with a certain amount of equitability, it has also occasioned attempts to marginalize Asian and Pacific Islander people as, if not inferior, at least different, exotic, or strange. Through football, individuals of Asian and Pacific ancestry have faced subtle and not so subtle forms of discrimination. Moreover, the cult of football in America, while fostering admirable displays of courage, endurance, and selfless teamwork, has also fostered destructive violence, excessive worship of masculinity, and, of course, rampant commercialism.[1]

Perhaps elite football in America should be applauded for its comparative inclusiveness, especially in recent years. Still, Asian and Pacific Islanders involved in football as competitors and coaches have found elite American football not so evenhanded as it presumably became more egalitarian. Samoan tackle and former Tennessee Titan Joe Salave'a insisted to the *Asian Weekly* in 1999 that Pacific Islanders experienced discrimination in the NFL. He tried to "let it all slide by" — tried not to "let it get to me." However, "I don't know, maybe you can call it ignorance, but I didn't care for it."[2]

The sluggishness in which American elite college and professional teams turned to coaches of Asian and Pacific Islanders infuriated commentators such as journalist Jon Chang in the early 2000s. Chang noted that many sportswriters were rightfully bothered by the leisurely effort Division I colleges and NFL teams made to hire African Americans as head coaches. Yet he noted that no Division I school team had placed an Asian or Pacific Islander American in command of its football program. Chang asked, "Did any of these sportswriters or activists mention that? Did any of them mention the lack of Latino and APA coaches in American sports at all? No! So, all of their laments and handwringing about 'diversity' ring a little hollow?" Hoping at the time that Norm Chow would break the barrier, Chang asserted that the hiring of an Asian or Pacific Islander American head football coach would make a difference: "First, a football coach is leader, educator and role model for the university and the community at large. An APA (Asian Pacific American) football coach adds yet another facet to the diamond called America.

Finally, with all the clamoring for diversity, the opportunity is here. The response has been dead silence. Where are the activists and sportswriters now?" However, Chow was apparently consigned to the realm of the model minority thesis—someone fit to serve, to assist, but not necessarily to lead. In the intervening years, moreover, less than a handful of major college programs have hired Asian or Pacific Islander head coaches. Despite the celebrated presence of Pacific Islanders in the NFL, no NFL team, as of this writing, has employed a head coach of either Polynesian or Asian ancestry.[3]

The experiences of Samoan Esera Tuaolo have brought into focus another key issue attending the American "Cult of Football." In the early 2000s, Esera Tuaolo made news not because he had been a consistently good NFL performer for nine years, but because he had outed himself as gay. Before turning pro, Tuaolo was an all-conference player for Oregon State. A gifted singer, Tuaolo had also performed the national anthem before several NFL games. Writer Brian Kluepfel disclosed, "The double-life he was forced to lead had him suicidal at times. . . . He said that he made sure teammates saw him kiss women in bars, to keep them from being suspicious. 'They didn't know who Esera Tuaolo is,' he said. 'What they saw was an actor.'"[4]

To Tengan and Markham, Tuaolo's "double life" exemplified a "homophobic masculinity . . . pervasive in college and professional football." Given how much Pacific Islander gridders have been hypermasculinized, the scholars added that it was "fitting" that Tuaolo emerged as one of the most "vocal opponents" of football's obsession with heterosexual masculinity. But the going has been tough. Sterling Sharpe, the talented tight end who played with Tuaolo at Green Bay, declared on an episode of HBO's *Real Sports* show focusing on Tuaolo's coming out that if Tuaolo had made his sexuality known while playing in the NFL, "he'd be eaten alive and he would have been hated for it."[5]

STRANGERS ON THE GRIDIRON

Several years ago, Ronald Takaki, then a historian affiliated with the Ethnic Studies Department at the University of California, Berkeley, wrote a pioneering survey of Asian American history called *Strangers from a Different Shore*. An eloquent testament to the ability of Asian Americans to tell their own stories, to make history, a central theme of Takaki's book is that Asian Americans in the late twentieth century had been and continued to be marginalized. For years, people of Asian ancestry were labeled as a "Yellow Peril" threatening Western civilization. The "Yellow Peril" stereotype has not disappeared, but it now shares the stage with softer, but ultimately no less deceptive, illusions. That is, as the twenty-first century neared, Asian Americans were more and more represented and perceived in American society as unobtrusive, courteous spectators to the grand sweep of U.S. history. They had become "model minority" members, happy to do their bit in shoring up the sagging faith in the American Dream, but, at the same time, not full-fledged Americans. Borrowing from pioneering sociologists such as Georges Simmel and Robert Park, Takaki employed the concept of stranger to depict the seemingly enduring foreignness of people of Asian ancestry in the United States. The real but often exaggerated cultural differences between the East and the West aside, Takaki claimed, Asian immigrants and third- and fourth-generation Asian Americans encountered a racialization process which has tried to exclude them from "We" in "We the People." While Takaki specifically referred to Asian Americans, we might be able to see the application of the concept of strangers to the experiences of Pacific Islanders as well.[6]

Takaki, as well as other past and present Asian American scholars, have stressed the perniciousness of the Model Minority stereotype in marginalizing Asian Americans. Among other things, the Model Minority stereotype demeans the historical struggles of working-class Asian Americans to attain decent livings in the United States. Many of the early and mid-twentieth-century Asian American gridders I have explored through census data and city directories could claim lower-class backgrounds. The parents of most were either wage workers or owned small businesses or farms. Accordingly, their willingness to engage in a physically demanding sport such as football could have expressed Bourdieu's concept of habitus. But while class might have encouraged their desire to play football, it could well have made football relatively inaccessible to them.[7]

On the American mainland, football, advocates such as Theodore Roosevelt hoped, would teach privileged young males to be just as tough as working-class males and tough enough to build and maintain an American empire abroad. Thus, schools nurtured organized football largely because economically privileged young men were more likely to attend and stay in schools than their more plebian counterparts even though football eventually put down roots in the hardscrabble working class communities of Pennsylvania and Ohio—communities which fostered professional football. Nevertheless, while many Asian American athletes emerged from the lower classes, their families seemed to have had enough income and what social scientists call "human capital" to permit them to go to high school and even two- and four-year colleges. But it could not always have been easy. Using a little historical imagination, we can envision struggling families wondering if they could spare Robert from working on the family farm or in the family restaurant so that he could play high school football. Furthermore, class conflict was not unknown to Asian American football players. That is, the Hawaiian barefoot participants were often plantation workers who found themselves mired in labor struggles with their employers in the mid-twentieth century. Barefoot football, moreover, was introduced on the islands, in part, by employers to blunt labor militancy. Indeed, the presence of barefoot football teams and leagues, as well as teams unattached to schools on the islands, suggests that Hawaiian football fostered participation across class lines more readily than on the mainland, at least through the mid-twentieth century.[8]

Interestingly, Pacific Islander gridders, because of their seemingly disproportionate impact on elite football in recent years, have been seen as football's "model minority." Beginning in the mid-1960s, Asian Americans have been labeled a model minority as an ideological weapon against Black, Chicano, and American Indian militancy. Why, model minority advocates proclaimed, could not African American, Latino/as, and American Indians follow the lead of Asian Americans who quietly advance themselves educationally and economically rather than bother with political protest? Ronald Takaki and other Asian American scholars and activists have powerfully contested the model minority stereotyping of Asian Americans and other racial groups.[9]

The shaping of Pacific Islanders as football's model minority worked differently. That is, like African Americans they were recognized as a racial minority. Like their African American teammates, Polynesian football players have been stereotyped as possessing an innate capacity to excel at the game. Yet during the 1970s, as black athletes were being regaled with accusations that they were insufficiently appreciative to white fans, coaches, and administrators for giving them opportunities to do much of the heavy lifting in making elite college and professional teams better, mainstream media noticed Pacific Islander football players. In contrast to ungrateful African Americans who believe they deserve more respect and financial security for entertaining white fans and enriching white owners and predominantly white universities, Pacific Islander football players have been perceived as uncommonly devoted to hard work in football's trenches and quietly respectful of their coaches' authority.[10]

However directed, the model minority arguments discussed here normalize Asian Americans as educational overachievers and Pacific Islanders as hypermasculine football overachievers. Connell's notion of hegemonic masculinity protrudes at this point. To be properly masculine in America has meant to maintain a balance between brains and brawn. By focusing so much on their SAT scores, Asian American males have demonstrated their lack of *appropriate* manliness (italics mine). By focusing so much on football, Pacific Islander males have also demonstrated a lack of appropriate manliness. Thus, football reinforces gender hierarchy not only because it largely marginalizes females, but also because it cages males as well.

Yet like Herman Wedemeyer eluding would-be tacklers, Asian and Pacific Islanders such as the Hmong American female flag football players have often wiggled free of would-be labelers inspired by orientalism and primitivism, traversed cultural frontiers, and enjoyed, however briefly, a sense of spatial entitlement. In the process, they have shown themselves able to construct admirable lives away from gridirons. John Wise proved willing to go to prison in the name of Hawaiian sovereignty. Gordon Chung-Hoon, Richard Dagampat, and Danny Wong served their country as officers in the U.S. Navy. Al Lolotai and more recently, Troy Polomalu committed themselves to aiding the diasporic Samoan community. Many, too numerous to list here, dedicated themselves to careers in education. They have asserted their cultural citizenship as well—their right to join other Americans on the football gridiron while remaining proud of their ethnic distinctiveness. In so doing, they have aided the cause of cultural democracy in America.

Given the popularity, indeed the gravity, of football in American culture, the participation of Asian and Pacific Islander people in the game might well have transformed them from the strange to the familiar. To be sure, a high school football practice in Hawai'i held any time throughout much of the twentieth and into the twenty-first century would reveal the possibility of such as transformation. Yet a Hawaiian high school football team mirrored class and racial dynamics historically distinctive from the U.S. mainland, which given the sad resonance of the birther movement, still struggles to concede that Hawai'i is part of the United States.

While butting heads with opponents, Asian and Pacific Islander gridders have long had to butt heads with enduring stereotypes that reinforced the marginalization of Asian and Pacific Islander ethnic groups in the United States. Walter Achiu's success on American gridirons did not eliminate the Chinese Exclusion Law. It took the World War II alliance between the United States and China to do that. Taro Kishi's similar success in Texas did not inspire the United States to seriously question the 1924 Johnson-Reed Act nor the wisdom of interning West Coast Japanese Americans during World War II.

In more recent years, the cult of football in America has found itself under attack. Critics have charge it breeds violence, corporate greed, sexism, racism, and, at the same time, overly indulges attacks on racism in the NFL and American society at large. Still, at least since the mid-twentieth century, elite American football has reigned supreme in popularity as a team sport in America. Therefore, it seems conceivable that presence of so many Pacific Islander football players might significantly change the lives of Pacific Islander people in the United States and its empire. However, as African Americans well know, sport heroism does not translate into racial equality. Samoans, while celebrated as proof of football's inclusiveness, remain ineligible for U.S. citizenship if born in American Samoa, and Pacific Islanders in the United States remain outsiders in

American society. While fewer Asian Americans have found their way into NFL and Division I NCAA stardom, some have at least shown an ability to break down long-venerated stereotypes. Yet despite all those young men and a few young women of Asian descent playing football for community, high school, college, and pro teams, they and their families remain strangers in American society.

NOTES

1. Anderson, *Cosmopolitan Canopy*.

2. Liou, "The API Lineup."

3. Jon Chang, "Where Are the APA Football Coaches," *Asian Week*, December 13–19, 2002; David J. Leonard, "Chow Can Coach: Against Model Minorities within College Sports," in C. Richard King (ed.), *Asian American Athletes in Sport and Society* (New York: Routledge, 2015).

4. Brian Kluepfel, "Tuaolo Emerges from the NFL Closet," *Asian Week*, November 1–7, 2002.

5. Tengan and Markham, "Performing Polynesian," 2424.

6. Takaki, *Strangers*.

7. Bourdieu, *Distinctions*.

8. Richard C. Crepeau, *NFL Football: A History of America's New National Pastime* (Champaign: University of Illinois Press, 2014).

9. Takaki, *Strangers*.

10. Amy Bass, *Not the Triumph but the Struggle: The 1968 Olympics and the Making of the Black Athlete* (Minneapolis: University of Minnesota Press, 2002), 291–349; William C. Rhoden, *40 Million Dollar Slaves: The Rise, Fall, and Redemption of the Black Athlete* (New York: Three Rivers Press, 2007).

Bibliography

PUBLISHED WORKS

Anderson, Benedict. *Imagined Communities: Reflections on the Origins and Spread of Nationalism*. London: Verso, 1983.

Anderson, Elijah, *The Cosmopolitan Canopy: Race and Civility in Everyday Life*. New York: W.W. Norton, 2012.

Anzaldua, Gloria. *Borderland/La Frontera; The New Mestiza*. San Francisco: Spinsters/ Aunt Lute, 1987.

Ardolino, Frank. "Wally Yonamine: In Japan's Hall of Fame." *The National Pastime*, no. 19 (1999): 10–11.

Bass, Amy. *Not the Triumph but the Struggle: The 1968 Olympics and the Making of the Black Athlete*. Minneapolis: University of Minnesota Press, 2002.

Bederman, Gail. *Manliness and Civilization: A Cultural History of Gender and Race in the United States, 1880–1917*. Chicago: University of Chicago Press, 1996.

Beissel, Adam. "Reducing the Samoan Body: Articulating Scientific Racism and Neoliberal Sport." ISSA Conference, Havana, Cuba. July 14, 2011.

Bourdieu, Pierre. *Distinction: A Social Critique of the Judgement of Taste*. Translated by Richard Nice. Cambridge, MA: Harvard University Press, 1984.

Bow, Leslie. *'Partly Colored': Asian Americans and Racial Anomaly in the Segregated South*, New York: New York University Press, 2010.

Brilliant, Mark. *The Color of America Has Changed: How Racial Diversity Shaped Civil Rights Reform in California 1941–1978*. New York: Oxford University Press, 2010.

Buck, Elizabeth. *Paradise Remade: Politics of Culture and History in Hawai'i*. Philadelphia: Temple University Press, 1993.

Burrows, Edward. *Hawaiian Americans: An Account of the Mingling of Japanese, Chinese, and Polynesian People*. New York: Archon Books, 1970.

Cavallo, Dominick. *Muscles and Morals: Organized Playgrounds and Urban Reform, 1880–1920*. Philadelphia: University of Pennsylvania Press, 1981.

Chan, Sucheng. *Asian Americans: An Interpretive History*. Boston: Twayne, 1991.

Chang, Roberta, and Wayne Patterson. *The Koreans in Hawai'i: A Pictorial History, 1903–2003*. Honolulu: University of Hawai'i Press, 2003.

Cheng, Cindy I-Fen. *Citizens of Asian America: Democracy and Race during the Cold War*. New York: New York University Press, 2013.

Chinn, Thomas. *Bridging the Pacific: San Francisco Chinatown and Its People*. San Francisco: Chinese Historical Society, 1989.

Cisco, Dan. *Hawai'i Sports: History, Facts, and Statistics*. Honolulu: University of Hawai'i Press, 1999.

Connell, R. W. *Gender and Power: Society, the Person, and Sexual Politics*. Palo Alto, CA: Stanford University Press, 1987.

Crepeau, Richard C. *NFL Football: A History of America's New National Pastime*. Champaign: University of Illinois Press, 2014.

Cumings, Bruce. *Dominion from Sea to Sea: Pacific Ascendancy and American Power*. New Haven and London: Yale University Press, 2009.

Des Jardins, Julie. *Walter Camp: Football and the Modern Man*. New York: Oxford University Press, 2015.

Diaz, Vicente M. "'Fight Boys, 'til the Last . . . ': Island-style Football and the Remasculation of Indigeneity in the Militarized American Pacific Islands." In Paul Spickard, Joanne L. Rondilla, and Debbie Hippolite Wright (eds). *Pacific Diaspora: Island Peoples in the United States and across the Pacific*. Honolulu: University of Hawai'i Press, 2002.

Dyreson, Mark. *Making the American Team: Sport, Culture, and the Olympic Experience*. Urbana: University of Illinois Press, 1997.

Elias, Robert. *The Empire Strikes Out: How Baseball Sold U.S. Foreign Policy and Promoted the American Way Abroad*. New York: New Press, 2010.

España-Maram, Linda. *Creating Masculinity in Los Angeles's Little Manila*. New York: Columbia University Press, 2006.

Espiritu, Yen Le. *Filipino Lives*. Philadelphia: Temple University Press, 1995.

Ethnic Studies Oral History Project. *Kalihi: Place of Transition*. Social Science Research Institute, University of Hawai'i, 1984.

Fainaru-Wada, Mark and Steve Fainaru. *League of Denial: The NFL, Concussions, and the Battle for Truth*. New York: Three Rivers Press, 2014.

Fitts, Robert K. *Wally Yonamine: The Man Who Changed Japanese Baseball*. Lincoln: University of Nebraska Press, 2008.

Flores, William V., and Rina Benmayor (eds). *Latino Cultural Citizenship: Claiming Identity, Space, and Rights*. Boston: Beacon Press, 1997.

Franks, Joel S. *Asian American Basketball: A Century of Sport, Community, and Culture*. Jefferson, NC, and London: McFarland & Company, Inc., 2016.

Franks, Joel S. *Asian Pacific Americans and Baseball: A History*. Jefferson, NC: McFarland & Company, 2008.

Franks, Joel S. *The Barnstorming Hawaiian Travelers: A Multiethnic Baseball Team Tours the Mainland*. Jefferson, NC: McFarland & Company, Inc., 2012.

Franks, Joel S. *Crossing Sidelines, Crossing Cultures: Sport and Asian Pacific American Cultural Citizenship*. Lanham, MD: University Press of America, 2009.

Franks, Joel S. *Hawaiian Sports in the Twentieth Century*. Lewiston, ME: The Edwin Mellen Press, 2002.

Gems, Gerald. *The Athletic Crusade: Sport and American Cultural Imperialism*. Lincoln: University of Nebraska Press, 2006.

Gems, Gerald. *Sport and the American Occupation of the Philippines: Bats, Balls, and Bayonets*. Lanham, MD: Lexington Books, 2016.

Gill, Bob. *Best in the West: The Rise and Fall of the Pacific Coast Football League, 1940–1948*. N.P.: Professional Football Research Association, 1988.

Goo, T. C. "Wonderful Athletes When They Want to Be." In *Chinese in Hawaii: A Historical Sketch*. Robert M. Lee (ed.), Honolulu: Advertising Publishing Company, 1961.

Hoganson, Kristin L. *Fighting for American Manhood: How Gender Politics Provoked the Spanish-American and Philippine-American Wars*. New Haven: Yale University Press, 2000.

Hosokawa, Bill. *The Two Worlds of Jim Yoshida*. New York: William Morrow & Company, 1972.

Imada, Adria L. *Aloha America: Hula Circuits through the U.S. Empire*. Durham, NC: Duke University Press, 2012.

Jacobs, Proverb. B., Jr. *The Autobiography of an Unknown Football Player*. Bloomington, IN: Author House, LLC, 2014.

James, C. L. R. *Beyond a Boundary*. Durham, NC: Duke University Press, 1993.

Jenkins, Sally. *The Real All-Americans: The Team That Changed a Game, a People, a Nation*. New York: Doubleday, 2007.

Jolly, Margaret. "Moving Masculinities: Memories and Bodies across Oceania." *The Contemporary Pacific* 20, no. 1 (Spring, 2008): 1–24.

Johnson, Gaye Theresa. *Spaces of Conflict, Sounds of Solidarity: Music, Race, and Spatial Entitlement in Los Angeles*. Berkeley: University of California Press, 2013.

Jung, Moon-Kie. *Reworking Race: The Making of Hawaii's Interracial Labor Movement.* New York: Columbia University Press, 2010.

Kauanui, J. Kēhaulani. *Hawaiian Blood: Colonialism and the Politics of Sovereignty and Indigeneity.* Durham, NC: Duke University Press, 2008.

Kramer, Paul A. *The Blood of Government: Race, Empire, the United States & the Philippines.* Chapel Hill: University of North Carolina Press, 2006.

Kurashige, Lon. *Two Faces of Exclusion: The Untold History of Anti-Asian Racism in the United States.* Chapel Hill: University of North Carolina Press, 2016.

Lee, Shelley Sang-Hee. *Claiming the Oriental Gateway: Prewar Seattle and Japanese America.* Philadelphia: Temple University Press, 2011.

Lee, Shelley Sang-Hee. *A New History of Asian America.* New York: Routledge, 2014.

Leonard, David J. "Chow Can Coach: Against Model Minorities Within in College Sports." In C. Richard King (ed.) *Asian American Athletes in Sport and Society.* New York: Routledge, 2015.

Leonard, David J. "Lin, Te'o, and Asian American Masculinities in Sporting Flux." In Stanley I. Thangaraj, Constancio R. Arnoldo, Jr., and Christine B. Chin (eds.) *Asian American Sporting Cultures.* New York: New York University Press, 2016.

Lim, Shirley Jennifer. *A Feeling of Belonging: Asian American Women's Public Culture, 1930–1960.* New York: New York University Press, 2006.

Lott, Juanita Tamayo. *Common Destiny: Filipino American Generations.* Lanham, MD: Rowman & Littlefield Publishers, 2006.

Love, Erik. *Islamophobia and Racism in America.* New York: New York University Press, 2017.

Lowe, Lisa. *Immigrant Acts: On Asian American Cultural Politics.* Durham, NC: Duke University Press, 1996.

Ma, Eve Armentrout and Jeung Hui Ma. *The Chinese of Oakland: Unsung Builders.* Oakland, CA: Chinese History Research Committee, 1982.

May, Elaine Tyler. *Homeward Bound: American Families in the Cold War Era.* New York: Basic Books, 1988.

McCarty, Bernie. "Squirmin' Herman and the Whiz Kids." *College Football Historical Society.* (November 1987): 3–6.

Merry, Sally Engle. *Colonizing Hawai'i: The Cultural Power of Law.* Princeton: Princeton University Press, 2000.

Nelson, Lyle E. "A Real Upset." *College Football Historical Society* (May 1996): 10–11.

Ngai, Mae. *The Lucky Ones: One Family and the Extraordinary Invention of Chinese America.* New York: Houghton Mifflin Harcourt, 2010.

Odo, Franklin S. *No Sword to Bury: Japanese Americans in Hawai'i During World War II.* Philadelphia: Temple University Press, 2003.

Official National League Football Pro Record and Rule Book, 1949. St. Louis: C. C. Spink and Son, 1949.

Okihiro, Gary Y. *American History Unbound: Asians and Pacific Islanders.* Berkeley and Los Angeles: University of California Press, 2015.

Okihiro, Gary Y. *Island World: A History of Hawai'i and the United States.* Berkeley and Los Angeles: University of California Press, 2008.

Okihiro, Gary Y. *Storied Lives: Japanese American Students and World War II.* Seattle: University of Washington Press, 1999.

Omi, Michael and Howard Winant. *Racial Formation in the United States: From the 1960s to the 1990s.* London: Routledge, 1994.

Oriard, Michael. *Reading Football: How the Popular Press Created an American Spectacle.* Chapel Hill, NC: University of North Carolina Press, 1998.

Oriard, Michael. *King Football: Sport and Spectacle in the Golden Age of Radio and Newsreels, Movies and Magazines, the Weekly and Daily Press.* Chapel Hill: University of North Carolina Press, 2001.

Park, Roberta J. "Sports and Recreation among Chinese American Communities of the Pacific Coast from Time of Arrival to 'The Quiet Decade of the 1950's.'" *Journal of Sport History.* 27 (Fall, 2000): 445–480.

Pfaelzer, Jean. *Driven Out: The Forgotten War against Chinese Americans*. Berkeley and
    Los Angeles: University of California Press, 2008.
Putney, Clifford. *Muscular Christianity: Manhood and Sports in Protestant America,
    1880–1920*. Cambridge: Harvard University Press, 2003.
Regalado, Samuel O. *Nikkei Baseball: Japanese American Players from Immigration and
    Internment to the Major Leagues*. Champaign: University of Illinois Press, 2013.
Rhoden, William C. *40 Million Dollar Slaves: The Rise, Fall, and Redemption of the Black
    Athlete*. New York: Three Rivers Press, 2007.
Riess, Steven. *City Games: The Evolution of American Urban Society and the Rise of Sport*.
    Champaign: University of Illinois Press, 1991.
Rosa, John P. *Local Story: The Massie Kahahawai Case and the Culture of History*. Honolu-
    lu: University of Hawai'i Press, 2014.
Rosaldo, Renato. *Culture and Truth: The Remaking of Social Analysis*. Boston: Beacon
    Press, 1989.
Said, Edward. *Orientalism*. New York: Vintage Books, 1979.
Sakamaki, George. "Japanese Athletes in Hawaii." *Bulletin of the Pan–Pacific Union*
    (August, 1931): 12–13.
Saxton, Alexander. *The Indispensable Enemy: Labor and the Anti-Chinese Movement*.
    Berkeley and Los Angeles: University of California Press, 1971.
Smith, Rogers M. *Civic Ideals: Conflicting Visions of Citizenship in US History*. New
    Haven, CT: Yale University Press, 1997.
Smith, Ronald S. *Sports and Freedom: The Rise of Big-Time College Athletics*. New York:
    Oxford University Press, 1988.
Smith, William Carlson. *Americans in Process: A Study of Our Citizens of Oriental Ances-
    try*. New York: Arno Press, 1970.
Stannard, David. *Honor Killing: Race, Rape, and Clarence Darrow's Spectacular Last Case*.
    New York: Penguin Books, 2006.
Suehiro, Arthur. *Honolulu Stadium: Where Hawaii Played*. Honolulu: Watermark Pub-
    lishing, 1995.
Takaki, Ronald. *A Different Mirror: A History of Multicultural America*. Boston: Back Bay
    Books, 2005.
Takaki, Ronald. *Pau Hana: Plantation Life and Labor in Hawaii, 1835–1920*. Honolulu:
    University of Hawai'i Press, 1984.
Takaki, Ronald. *Strangers from a Different Shore: A History of Asian Americans*. Boston:
    Little Brown, 1998.
Tengan, Ty P. Kāwika and Jesse Makani Markham. "Performing Polynesian Masculin-
    ities in American Football: From 'Rainbows to Warriors.'" *International Journal of the
    History of Sport* 26 (December 2009): 2412–2431.
Tuan, Mia. *Forever Foreigners or Honorary Whites?: The Asian Ethnic Experience in Today*.
    New Brunswick, NJ: Rutgers University Press, 1998.
Uperesa, Fa'anofo Lisaclaire. "Fabled Futures: Migration and Mobility for Samoans in
    American Football." *Contemporary Pacific* 26, vol. 2 (2014): 281–301.
Vang, Chia Youyee. "Hmong Youth, American Football, and the Cultural Politics of
    Ethnic Sports Tournaments." In Stanley I. Thangaraj, Constancio R. Arnaldo, Jr.,
    and Christina Chin (eds.) *Asian American Sporting Cultures*. New York: New York
    University Press, 2016.
Veblen, Thorstein. *Theories of the Leisure Class*. New York: Oxford University Press,
    2009.
Walker, Isaiah Helekulunihi. *Waves of Resistance: Surfing and History in Twentieth-Cen-
    tury Hawai'i*. Honolulu: University of Hawai'i Press, 2011.
Watterson, John Sayle. *College Football*. Baltimore, MD: Johns Hopkins University
    Press, 2000.
Welky, David B. "Viking Girls, Mermaids, and Little Brown Men: U.S. Journalism and
    the 1932 Olympics." *Journal of Sport History* 24 (Spring 1997): 24–49.
Wiebe, Robert H. *Self-Rule: A Cultural History of American Democracy*. Chicago: Univer-
    sity of Chicago Press, 1995.

Willard, Michael Nevin. "Duke Kahanomoku's Body: Biography of Hawai'i." In John
Bloom and Michael Nevin Willard (eds.) *Sports Matters: Race, Recreation and Culture.*
New York: New York University Press, 2002.

Williams, Raymond. *Keywords: A Vocabulary in Culture and Society.* New York: Oxford
University Press, 1983.

Wu, Ellen D. *Color of Success: Asian Americans and the Origins of the Model Minority.*
Princeton: Princeton University Press, 2015.

Yep, Kathleen S. *Outside the Paint: When Basketball Ruled at the Chinese Playground.*
Philadelphia: Temple University Press, 2009.

Zia, Helen. *Asian American Dreams: The Emergence of an American People.* New York:
Farrar, Straus & Giroux, 2001.

DISSERTATION

Morimoto, Lauren Shizuyo. "The Barefoot Leagues: An Oral (Hi)story of Football in
the Plantation Towns of Kaua'i." PhD dissertation. The Ohio State University, 2005.

NEWSPAPERS AND MAGAZINES

Aberdeen Daily News
Albany Evening Journal
Albuquerque Journal
Alton Evening Telegram
Altoona Tribune
Anaconda Standard
Appleton Post-Crescent
Arizona Republic
Asian Journal
Asian Week
Augusta Chronicle
Bakersfield Californian
Bangor News
Baton Rouge Advocate
Bellingham Herald
Belvedere Daily Republican
Bend Bulletin
Berkeley Daily-Gazette
Berkshire Eagle
Big Spring Daily Herald
Binghamton Press
Bradford Era
Bridgeport Herald
Bridgeport Post
Bridgeport Telegram
Brooklyn Daily Eagle
Bryan Eagle

Burlington Times-News
Canton Repository
Charleston Daily Mail
Charleston Gazette
Chicago Tribune
Chinese Digest
Chinese Press
China Champion
Comcommato Enquirer
Cleveland Plain Dealer
Coalville Times
Collier's
Colorado Springs Telegram
Colorado Times
Continental
Corsair
Corvallis Gazette-Times
Council Bluffs Nonpareil
Cupertino Courier
Daily Californian
Daily Tar Heel
Dallas Morning-News
Danville Bee
Daytona Beach Journal
Dayton Daily News
Decatur Review
Delta Democrat Times
Deseret News
Des Moines News
Eagle Valley Enterprise
East Liverpool Evening News
East/West
Ellensburg Daily Record
El Mustang
El Paso Herald-Post
Escanaba Daily Press
Eugene Register-Guard
Eureka Time Standard
Fort Wayne News
Fort Wayne Sentinel
Fort Worth Star-Telegram
Frederick Post
Fresno Bee
Gannett News Service
Garden Island

Gastonia Daily Gazette
Glendale News-Press
Granada Bulletin
Granada Pioneer
Grand Rapids Press
Grand Rapids Tribune
Greeley Daily Tribune
Greenwood Index Journal
Gwinnett Daily Post
Hagerstown Daily Mail
Hamilton Journal-News
Harvard Crimson
Hawaiian Gazette
Havre Daily Promoter
Hawaii Herald
Hawaii Mirror
Hawai'i News Now
Hayward Review
Hazleton Standard-Speaker
Heart Mountain Sentinel
Helena Independent Record
Hendersonville Times-News
Honolulu Advertiser
Honolulu Evening-Bulletin
Honolulu Record
Honolulu Star-Advertiser
Honolulu Star-Bulletin
Huron Huronite
Hyphen
Idaho State Journal
Illustrated Football
Ironwood Daily Globe
Island Scene
Jamestown Evening Journal
Japanese American Courier
Jefferson City Daily Capital
Jonesboro Evening Sun
Kalamazoo Gazette
Kansas City Times
Ka Leo O' Hawaii
Kingsport Times
Klamath Falls Herald and News
Kokomo Tribune
Lawrence Journal World
Lead Daily Call

Lethbridge Herald
Lima News
Lincoln Star
Lockport Union Sun and Journal
Lodi News Sentinel
Logan Daily News
Long Beach Independent
Long Beach Independent Press
Look
Los Angeles Daily News
Los Angeles Sentinel
Los Angeles Times
Ludington Daily News
Lumberton Robesonian
Mansfield News
Mansfield News-Journal
Manzanar Free Press
Marion Star
Massillon Evening Independent
Mason City Globe-Gazette
McKean County Democrat
Medford Mail Tribune
Milwaukee Journal
Milwaukee Journal-Sentinel
Minidoka Irrigator
Modesto Bee and Herald News
Montana Butte-Standard
Montreal Gazette
Mount Carmel Item
Nevada Herald
Nevada State-Journal
New London Day
New Orleans States
New Orleans Times-Picayune
Newport Daily News
New York Evening Post
New York Evening Telegram
New York Times
Niagara Falls Gazette
Nichi Bei Times
Northwest Arkansas Press
Northwest Asian Weekly
Oakland Tribune
Ogden Standard-Examiner
Olean Times Herald

Oneonta Star
Oregon Statesmen
Oshkosh Daily
Ottawa Citizen
Owosso Argus-Press
Oxnard Press-Courier
Pacific Business News
Pacific Citizen
Pacific Commercial Advertiser
Pacific Magazine and Islands Business
Palm Beach Post
Pasadena Independent
Pasadena Star-News
Petersburg Progress-Index
Philadelphia Inquirer
Philadelphia Public Ledger
Piqua Daily Call
Pittsburgh Post-Gazette
Pittsburgh Press
Pomona Progress Bulletin
Portland Oregonian
Portsmouth Daily Times
Poston Chronicle
Providence News
Provo Daily Herald
Rafu Shimpo
Reading Eagle
Red Bluff Daily News
Redlands Daily Facts
Reno Evening Gazette
Richmond County Journal
Riverside Daily Press
Robesonian
Rochester Democrat and Chronicle
Rockford Morning Star
Rockford Register-Republic
Rockford Republic
Rohwer Outpost
Rome Daily Sentinel
Roseburg News-Review
Sacramento Bee
Sacramento News
Salem Daily Capital Journal
Salem Statesman
Salisbury Daily-Times

Salt Lake Tribune
San Antonio Express
San Bernardino County Sun
San Diego Evening Tribune
San Diego Union
San Diego Union Tribune
San Francisco Call
San Francisco Call-Bulletin
San Francisco Chronicle
San Francisco Examiner
San Francisco News
San Jose Mercury
San Jose News
San Mateo Times
San Rafael Daily Independent
Santa Ana Register
Santa Cruz Sentinel
Sarasota Herald-Tribune
Saturday Evening Post
Sausalito News
Schenectady Gazette
Seattle Times
Seguin Gazette-Enterprise
Shamokin News-Dispatch
Shenandoah Evening Herald
Shreveport Times
Silver City Daily Press
Simpson Leader
Soul City Times
Spartanburg Herald Journal
Spartan Daily
Spokane Daily Chronicle
Sport
Sporting News
Sports Illustrated
Sports Review Football Annual, 1957
Springfield Republican
Springfield Union
Stanford Daily
Stars and Stripes
Stevens Point Daily Journal
St. Joseph Herald-Press
St. Petersburg Independent
St. Petersburg Times
Terre Haute Tribune

Toledo Blade
Topaz Times
Torrance Herald
Trenton Evening Times
Tri-City Herald
Trinity Tripod
Troy Times Record
Tucson Daily Citizen
UC Davis Magazine
USA Today
Utica Observer
Waco News-Tribune
Walla Walla Union-Bulletin
Washington Post
Washington Times
Waterloo Daily Courier
Wichita Beacon
Wilkes Barre Times Leader
Wilmington Morning-Star
Wilmington News-Journal
Youngstown Vindicator
Zanesville Signal

ARCHIVAL SOURCES

442nd Regimental Monthly Report, September 3, 1945; January 21, 1946; February 20, 1946.
Alameda High School Yearbook, 1942.
Anaheim High School Yearbook, 1928, 1929, 1935, 1936, 1939, 1940, 1941.
Arizona State University Yearbook, 1951, 1965.
Auburn High School Yearbook, 1932, 1934.
Audubon High School Yearbook, 1935.
Banning High School Yearbook, 1954.
Beaverton High School Yearbook, 1951.
Belmont High School Yearbook, 1937, 1938, 1939, 1941, 1942, 1947, 1953, 1979.
Berkeley High School Yearbook, 1954, 1975.
Brawley High School Yearbook, 1934.
Brigham Young University Yearbook, 1955, 1960.
Broadway High School Yearbook, 1926, 1934, 1938, 1940, 1941.
Central College Yearbook, 1958, 1960.
Central High School Yearbook, 1956.
Chaffey Junior College, 1939.
C.K. McClatchy High School Yearbook, 1941, 1987.
College of the Pacific Yearbook, 1941.
College of William and Mary Yearbook, 1927, 1928.
Colorado State College Yearbook, 1943.
Commerce High School Yearbook, 1924, 1925, 1928, 1929, 1941, 1948.
Compton High School Yearbook, 1950, 1951.
Compton Junior College Yearbook, 1949, 1950, 1951, 1953.

Courtland High School Yearbook, 1935, 1949.
Crenshaw High School Yearbook, 1969.
Davis High School Yearbook, 1958.
Dayton University Yearbook, 1926, 1927, 1949, 1950.
Dennison College Yearbook, 1946.
Denver University Yearbook, 1944, 1952.
East-West Shrine Football Program, Kezar Stadium, San Francisco, CA, December 19, 1951.
East-West Shrine Football Program, Stanford Stadium, Palo Alto, CA, January 4, 1984.
Edison High School Yearbook, 1981.
Farrington High School Yearbook, 1940.
Fife High School Yearbook, 1938.
Fresno State College Yearbook, 1929, 1932, 1950, 1959, 1962.
Galileo High School Yearbook, 1959.
Gardena High School Yearbook, 1949, 1955, 1966, 1975, 1984.
Garden Grove High School Yearbook, 1935.
Garfield High School Yearbook (Seattle), 1933, 1935, 1940, 1958.
Granite High School Yearbook, 1932.
Green River High School Yearbook, 1956.
Hillview High School Yearbook, 1945, 1948.
Hilo High School Yearbook, 1941, 1965.
Hollywood High School Yearbook, 1974.
Honolulu City Directory, 1958, 1973.
Huntington Beach High School Yearbook, 1949, 1958.
Hyde Park High School Yearbook, 1949, 1950.
Iolani High School Yearbook, 1949.
James Lick High School Yearbook, 1964.
John Carroll University vs. Dayton University Football Program, Luna Park Stadium, University Heights, Ohio, October 9, 1926.
Kahuku High School Yearbook, 1965.
Kaimuki High School Yearbook, 1946, 1959.
Kamehameha School Yearbook, 1945, 1956.
Kapa'a High School Yearbook, 1950.
Kaua'i High School Yearbook, 1950.
Lehman High School Yearbook, 1946, 1947.
Leilehua High School Yearbook, 1938.
Lewis and Clark High School Yearbook, 1945.
Lincoln High School Yearbook, 1939.
Linfield College Yearbook, 1963.
Livingston High School Yearbook, 1951.
Lodi High School Yearbook, 1930, 1937, 1950, 1989.
Long Beach High School Yearbook, 1949.
Long Beach Junior College Yearbook, 1934.
Los Angeles Dons v. San Francisco 49ers Football Program, Kezar Stadium, San Francisco, CA, September 19, 1948.
Los Angeles Junior College Yearbook, 1936.
Louisiana State University Yearbook, 1948, 1949.
Marina High School Yearbook, 1985.
Manual Arts High School Yearbook, 1942.
Marysville High School Yearbook, 1928, 1930.
McKinley High School Yearbook, 1934, 1936, 1956. 1959, 1965.
Miliani High School Yearbook, 1988.
Mission High School Yearbook, 1937, 1938.
Mountain View High School Yearbook, 1929, 1936, 1963.
Nampa High School Yearbook, 1939.
North Central High School Yearbook, 1944, 1945.

North Dakota State University Yearbook, 1937.
Oakland High School Yearbook, 1957.
Oberlin College Yearbook, 1892.
Occidental College Yearbook, 1951, 1952.
Oregon State University Yearbook, 1930, 1931.
Pasadena Junior College Yearbook, 1938, 1948, 1951, 1952, 1953.
Phoenix High School Yearbook, 1933.
Polytechnic High School Yearbook, 1946.
Pomona College Yearbook, 1947.
Portland State University Yearbook, 1949.
Punahou Yearbook, 1940, 1941, 1949.
Redlands University Yearbook, 1940, 1962.
Reno High School Yearbook, 1953.
Sacramento High School Yearbook, 1939.
Sacramento Junior College Yearbook, 1941, 1949.
Salinas High School Yearbook, 1942.
San Diego High School Yearbook, 1927.
San Diego Junior College Yearbook, 1953.
San Diego State College Yearbook, 1929, 1933, 1938, 1940.
San Fernando High School Yearbook, 1939, 1946.
San Francisco State College Yearbook, 1935, 1942, 1954.
San Jose City College Yearbook, 1960, 1962.
San Jose State College vs. Stanford University Football Program, Stanford Stadium, Palo Alto, California, November 1, 1952.
San Jose State College vs. Stanford University Football Program, Stanford Stadium, Palo Alto, California, October 29, 1955.
San Jose State College vs. Stanford University Football Program, Stanford Stadium, Palo Alto, California, October 13, 1956.
San Jose High School Yearbook, 1930, 1959, 1979.
San Jose State College Yearbook, 1955, 1957.
San Lorenzo High School Yearbook, 1956.
San Mateo High School Yearbook, 1954, 1956, 1958, 1959, 1968.
San Pedro High School Yearbook, 1950.
Santa Ana High School Yearbook, 1930.
Santa Barbara State College Yearbook, 1933.
Santa Clara University Yearbook, 1948, 1950, 1954.
Santa Cruz High School Yearbook, 1958.
Sequoia High School Yearbook, 1967.
Stanford University Yearbook, 1954.
St. Louis High School Yearbook, 1951, 1959.
St. Mary's College Yearbook, 1940.
Stockton High School Yearbook, 1935, 1957.
Syracuse University Yearbook, 1926.
University of Arizona Yearbook, 1950.
University of California Yearbook, 1948, 1957, 1959, 1960, 1962.
University of Hawai'i Yearbook, 1928, 1932, 1934, 1935, 1936, 1937, 1948, 1949, 1953, 1956, 1958, 1959.
University of Montana vs. Washington State University Football Program, Rogers Field, Pullman, Washington, October 25, 1930.
University of Southern California Yearbook, 1937, 1938, 1957.
University of Washington Yearbook, 1936, 1955, 1956, 1957.
University of Wisconsin Sports News Service.
University of Wisconsin Yearbook, 1932.
U.S. Census Bureau, Manuscript Census Schedules, City and County of Alameda, 1940.

U.S. Census Bureau, Manuscript Census Schedules, City of Berkeley and County of Alameda, 1940.

U.S. Census Bureau, Manuscript Census Schedules, City of Brawley and County of Imperial, 1940.

U.S. Census Bureau, Manuscript Census Schedules, City and County of Fresno, 1940.

U.S. Census Bureau, City of Green River and County of Sweetwater, 1940.

U.S. Census Bureau, Manuscript Census Schedules, City of Hana and Island of Maui, 1940.

U.S. Census Bureau. Manuscript Census Schedules, City and County of Honolulu, 1900, 1910, 1920, 1930, 1940.

U.S. Census Bureau, Manuscript Census Schedules, City of Koloa and Island of Kaua'i, 1940.

U.S. Census Bureau, Manuscript Census Schedules, City of Lahaina and Island of Maui, 1930.

U.S. Census Bureau, Manuscript Census Schedules, City of Laie and County of Honolulu, 1940.

U.S. Census Bureau, Manuscript Census Schedules, City of Laie and Island of Oahu, 1940.

U.S. Census Bureau, Manuscript Census Schedules, City of Lihue and Island of Kaua'i, 1930, 1940.

U.S. Census Bureau, Manuscript Census Schedules, City and County of Los Angeles, 1920, 1930, 1940.

U.S. Census Bureau, Manuscript Census Schedules, City of Makaweli and Island of Kaua'i, 1940.

U.S. Census Bureau, Manuscript Census Schedules, City of Maricopa and County of Pinal, 1940.

U.S. Census Bureau, Census Manuscript Schedules, City of Marysville and County of Yuba, 1930, 1940.

U.S. Census Bureau, Manuscript Census Schedules, Island of Molokai, 1930.

U.S. Census Bureau, Manuscript Census Schedules, Olowalu Village and Island of Maui, 1930.

U.S. Census Bureau, Manuscript Census Schedules, City of Palo Alto and County of Santa Clara, 1930.

U.S. Census Bureau, Manuscript Census Schedules, City of Red Bluff and County of Tehama, 1930.

U.S. Census Bureau, Manuscript Census Schedules, City of San Jose and County of Santa Clara, 1920, 1930, 1940.

U.S. Census Bureau, Manuscript Census Schedules, City and County of San Diego, 1930, 1940.

U.S. Census Bureau, Manuscript Census Schedules, City and County of San Francisco, 1920, 1930, 1940.

U.S. Census Bureau, Manuscript Census Schedules, City of Torrance and County of Los Angeles, 1940.

U.S. Census Bureau, Manuscript Census Schedules, City of Tulare and County of Exeter, 1940.

U.S. Census Bureau, Manuscript Census Schedules, City of Upland and County of San Bernardino, 1940.

U.S. Census Bureau, Manuscript Census Schedules, City of Vallejo and County of Solano, 1930.

U.S. Census Bureau, Manuscript Census Schedules, City of Wailua and Island of Kaua'i, 1930.

U.S. Census Bureau, Manuscript Census Schedules, City of Wailuku and Island of Maui, 1940.

U.S. Census Bureau, Manuscript Census Schedules, City of Waimea and Island of Hawai'i, 1910, 1940.

U.S. Naval Academy Yearbook, 1934, 1957, 1959, 1967.

Waimea High School Yearbook, 1967.

Washington State University vs. Stanford University Football Program, Stanford Stadium, Palo Alto, California, October 20, 1984.

Watsonville High School Yearbook, 1935, 1937, 1938, 1940, 1949.

Weber Normal College Yearbook, 1943.

West High School Yearbook, 1933.

Whittier College Yearbook, 1962, 1963.

Willamette University Yearbook, 1950, 1956, 1961.

Wisconsin Football Facts: Season of 1947 and Athletic Review of 1946–1947 School Year, University of Wisconsin Sports News Service.

INTERNET SOURCES

http://www.12thman.com/ViewArticle.dbml?ATCLID=205236164 (June 12, 2015).

http://www.49ers.com/news/article-2/Paraag-Marathe-Named-Team-President/8f12e082-f0d4–4f40-aeba-911d553f4bec (September 11, 2014).

http://www.100thbattalion.org/history/veterans/officers/katsumi-doc-kometani/ (November 27, 2017).

Abramo, Nick, "Roosevelt Hires Kahooiihala as Football Coach." http://www.hawaiiprepworld.com/football/roosevelt-hires-kahooilihala-as-football-coach/, (June 30, 2016).

Alford, Abbie. "Former NFL Player Involved in Rare Tree Crash at Balboa Park." http://www.cbs8.com/story/26851862/former-nfl-player-involved-in-rare-tree-crash-at-balboa-park (June 21, 2015).

http://www.apiidv.org/resources/census-data-api-identities.php#identities (December 22, 2014).

http://archeologygroup9.blogspot.com/2009/12/jack-yoshihara-osu-football-player.html (February 13, 2015).

http://www.arenafootball.com/sports/a-footbl/aflrtl/mtt/david_wang_991559.html (June 11, 2016).

http://articles.ivpressonline.com/2004–03–06/golden-bulldogs_24190567/2 (November 14, 2014).

Asamen, Tim. "Nisei Greatness on the Imperial Valley Gridiron." http://www.discovernikkei.org/en/journal/2016/3/7/nisei-greatness/ (May 28, 2016).

http://www.asianhalloffame.org/portfolio/manu-tuiasosopo/ (June 17, 2015).

http://www.asian-nation.org/model-minority.shtml (August 13, 2015).

http://asianplayers.com/football (May 25, 2016).

Barnett, C. Robert. "The Portsmouth Spartans." http://profootballresearchers.com/coffin-corner80s/02–10–044.pdf (June 20, 2015).

http://bclions.com/page/staff-joe-paopao (March 2, 2011).

http://www.beasport.com/assets/South_49_89.pdf (July 7, 2016).

http://bengals.enquirer.com/2002/01/05/ben_math_teacher_adding.html (June 10, 2016).

http://biggreenalertblog.blogspot.com/2006/09/former-qbs-son-starring-in-hawaii.html (June 8, 2015).

http://biggreenalertblog.blogspot.com/2008/01/lloyd-lee-moves-up.html (June 9, 2016).

https://bill37mccurdy.wordpress.com/2013/09/16/first-game-at-rice-stadium-september-30–1950/ (May 18, 2015).

http://www.blackpast.org/aaw/ubangi-blackhawks (June 3, 2016).

http://bleacherreport.com/articles/2689429-seahawks-assistant-head-coach-rocky-seto-leaves-team-to-enter-the-ministry, (November 25, 2016).

Bower, Brian. "Where are they Now?" http://russellstreetreport.com/2014/04/18/street-talk/where-are-they-now-edwin-mulitalo/ (April 7, 2016).

http://www.bsubears.com/sports/fball/Records_FB (November 11, 2015).

http://www.bucknellbison.com/sports/hallfame/spec-rel/hall-of-fame-football.html (April 2, 2010).

http://www.buffalobills.com/team/coaches/lal_sanjay/5c6a8125–0a99–46bb-8e26-f0e5da3d8a0b (June 13, 2015).

http://byucougars.com/athlete/m-football/vai-sikahema (June 7, 2016).

http://byucougars.com/staff/m-football/kalani-sitake (April 4, 2016).

http://byucougars.com/athlete/m-football/harvey-unga (May 4, 2016).

"California Birth Directory." www.ancestry.com (June 2, 2010).

http://www.cbsnews.com/news/shahid-khan-from-pakistan-to-pro-football/3/ (May 9, 2015).

https://cdn.americanprogress.org/wp-content/uploads/2014/08/AAPI-IncomePoverty.pdf (July 9, 2016).

http://www.census.gov/population/www/documentation/twps0029/tab02.html (May 16, 2015).

http://cfl-scrapbook.no-ip.org/Paopao.Joe.php (March 2, 2011).

http://www.chaffey.edu/ath-pe/hof.shtml (July 19, 2016).

http://www.chargers.com/team/players/roster/manti-teo (November 10, 2015).

Chong, Cathy. "Golden Time for Football and Friendship." http://www.iolani.org/files/pdfs/coverstory_winter08.pdf (July 20, 2015).

Christi, Cliff. "An Oral History—Gary Knafelc." http://www.packers.com/news-and-events/article-1/An-Oral-History----Gary-Knafelc/ff9ce7a5-bf28–4d0a-a18a-f86643ef5ddc (November 17, 2017).

http://www.cifsf.org/uploads/3/2/0/9/32099267/football-all-stars1922–1999.pdf (March 29, 2016).

http://collinsvillepress.com/files/2014/09/14-CT-Football-Rec-Book.pdf (June 6, 2014).

http://content.cdlib.org/ark:/13030/ft0g5002v1/?brand=calisphere (June 1, 2009).

http://content.lib.utah.edu/utils/getfile/collection/uuath2/id/100/filename/76.pdf (June 9, 2016).

http://content.lib.utah.edu/utils/getfile/collection/uuath2/id/18/filename/115.pdf (June 24, 2016).

Cooper, Amy, "Tongan Americans." http://www.everyculture.com/multi/Sr-Z/Tongan-Americans.html, (May 9, 2016).

http://www.databasefootball.com/players/playerpage.htm?ilkid=FIELDHAR01 (July 28, 2010).

http://www.databasefootball.com/players/playerpage.htm?ilkid=HIPASAM01 (July 28, 2010).

http://www.databasefootball.com/players/playerpage.htm?ilkid=HUGHEHAN01 (July 28, 2010).

http://www.deanza.edu/athletics/football/roster06.html, (August 17, 2015).

http://archive.densho.org/main.aspx (May 8, 2016).

http://www.detroitlions.com/team/history/all-time-roster.html (June 21, 2016).

http://digitallibrary.usc.edu/search/controller/view/examiner-m5845.html?x=1321723638467 (December 7, 2011).

http://www.elliottelevang.com/release/ (May 18, 2015).

http://www.elonphoenix.com/roster.aspx?rp_id=2910 (July 10, 2015).

http://en.montrealalouettes.com/all-time-all-stars/ (August 11, 2016).

http://www.espn.com/espnw/voices/article/17316264/buffalo-bills-co-owner-kim-pegula-talks-women-nfl (August 19, 2016).

http://espn.go.com/blog/dallas/cowboys/post/_/id/4711414/sean-lee-soaks-up-dat-nguyens-wisdom (June 7, 2014).

http://espn.go.com/boston/nfl/story/_/id/12237694/former-new-england-patriots-fan-favorite-mosi-tatupu-suffered-chronic-traumatic-encephalopathy-cte (June 17, 2015).

http://espn.go.com/college-football/player/stats/_/id/158631/scott-phaydavong (September 23, 2015).

http://espn.go.com/college-football/story/_/id/10581659/stanford-cardinal-hires-texas-longhorns-assistant-duane-akina-secondary-coach (July 7, 2015).

http://espn.go.com/espn/hispanicheritage2013/story/_/page/onenationsteelers131008/ hispanic-heritage-month-omar-khan-pittsburgh-steelers-front-office-dreams-big (May 18, 2015).

http:// espn.go.com/espn/otl/story/_/id/8830344/study-junior-seau-brain-shows-chronic-brain-damage-found-other-nfl-football-players (June 17, 2015).

http://espn.go.com/sportsnation/boston/chat/_/id/40436 (May 2, 2015).

http://espn.go.com/video/clip?id=12848278 (June 12, 2015).

http://www.fa-aft6157.org/newsletters/0502_newsletter.pdf (December 26, 2014).

https://factfinder.census.gov/faces/tableservices/jsf/pages/product-view.xhtml?src=bkmk (September 16, 2017).

http://www.fanbase.com/william-tang/ (June 9, 2015).

Feist, Joe Michael. "Japanese Player Relied on Heart." http://hirasaki.net/Family_Stories/Taro_Kishi/A_M.htm (August 10, 2015).

http://www.footballdb.com/players/neo-aoga-aogane01 (September 14, 2010).

http://www.foxsports.com/college-football/john-nguyen-player (January 25, 2017).

Gandhi, Lakshmi. "Former Dallas Cowboy Dat Nguyen to be Inducted into College Football Hall of Fame." http://www.nbcnews.com/news/asian-america/former-dallas-cowboy-dat-nguyen-be-inducted-college-football-hall-n705206 (January 10, 2017).

http://www.gettyimages.com/detail/news-photo/hmong-athletes-j-d-leftwich-high-senior-lineman-bobby-moua-news-photo/136061653 (July 7, 2015).

http://www.glendalehigh.com/big-game-records-glendale-only-legends.pdf (July 13, 2015).

www.gobears.com (February 10, 2003).

http://www.gocreighton.com/ViewArticle.dbml?DB_OEM_ID=1000&ATCLID=208888161 (March 2, 2011).

http://gocrimson.com/sports/fball/2011–12/releases/20111023qgudkg, (June 3, 2016).

http://www.godrakebulldogs.com/ViewArticle.dbml?DB_OEM_ID=15700&ATCLID=209788397/ (March 3, 2015).

http://godrakebulldogs.com/documents/2015/11/25//football_winners.pdf?id=4538 (July 8, 2016).

http://www.goducks.com/ViewArticle.dbml?ATCLID=175546 (June 7, 2013).

Goldman, Tom. "Young Polynesians Make a Life Out of Football." http://www.npr.org/templates/story/story.php?storyId=112970742 (September 22, 2014).

https://www.google.com/search?q=Charlie+Kaaihue+football&biw=1366&bih=667&tbm=isch&im-gil=6JVpjIutMBk7rM%253A%253BaV2RzAxT95ICUM%253Bhttp%25253A%25252F%25252Fwww.tradingcarddb.com%25252FGalleryP.cfm%25252Fpid%25252F10976%25252FCharlie-Kaaihue&source=iu&pf=m&fir=6JVpjIutMBk7rM%253A%252CaV2RzAxT95ICUM%252C_&usg=__1BQfNrqIMmzFzI8bfn9Dub__whQ%3D&ved=0CFYQyjc&ei=ebJzVLXbIo7koAT47oCYCA#facrc=_&imgrc=6JVpjIutMBk7rM%253A%3BaV2RzAxT95ICUM%3Bhttp%253A%252F%252Fwww.tradingcarddb.com%252FImages%252FCards%252FFootball%252F3203%252F3203–104Bk.jpg%3Bhttp%253A%252F%252Fwww.tradingcarddb.com%252FGalleryP.cfm%252Fpid%252F10976%252FCharlie-Kaaihue%3B350%3B247, (June 29, 2015).

http://www.gogriz.com/sports/m-footbl/mtt/john_nguyen_850833 (June 9, 2015).

http://www.gogriz.com/sports/m-footbl/stats/2014–2015/teamcume.html (June 9, 2015).

http://www.gostanford.com/ViewArticle.dbml?DB_OEM_ID=30600&ATCLID=208077543 (June 8, 2015).

http://graphics.fansonly.com/schools/cal/sports/m-footbl/archive/history.pdf (June 17, 2016).

http://grfx.cstv.com/photos/schools/fres/sports/m-footbl/auto_pdf/06-mg-part5.pdf (June 9, 2016).

http://www.gseagles.com/roster.aspx?rp_id=560 (June 11, 2016).

Hawaii Passenger and Crew Lists, 1900–1959. www.ancestry.com (October 20, 2017).

https://www.hawaii.edu/admin/chancellors/westoahu.html (June 11, 2015).

http://hawaiiathletics.com/coaches.aspx?rc=1073 (June 17, 2014).

http: //hawaiiathletics.com/roster.aspx? rp_id=8921 (May 26, 2016).

http://hawaiiathletics.com/roster.aspx?rp_id=11666&path (November 12, 2011).

http://www.hawaiiprepworld.com/football/ilh-football-first-team-all-stars-1920-present/ (June 18, 2016).

http://hawaiisportshalloffame.com/xahyo.htm (June 17, 2015).

http://www.hawaiitourismauthority.org/default/assets/File/13–2%20NFL%20and%20HTA%20to%20Honor%20Inaugural%20Hawaii%20NFL%20Greats%20NR.pdf (June 11, 2015)

http://www.heismancentral.com/ (December 19, 2014).

Hendrics, Martin. "Sanjay Beach Was Catching Ball from Elite QB." http://www.jsonline.com/sports/packers/sanjay-beach-was-catching-balls-from-elite-qbs-b99260168z1–258342141.html (June 11, 2015).

http://www.heraldnet.com/article/20140905/SPORTS01/140909418, (July 15, 2015).

http://www.highbeam.com/doc/1P2–7051776.html (June 3, 2015).

http://www.hinesward.com/hines-ward-biography.php (June 12, 2015).

http://www.historyguy.com/sportshistory/jack_thompson_quarterback.htm (June 16, 2015).

http://www.historylink.org/index.cfm?DisplayPage=output.cfm&file_id=8063 (May 20, 2015).

http://www.hornetsports.com/sports/fball/alltimeroster (February 5, 2014).

http://www.imdb.com/name/nm6485967/?ref_=fn_al_nm_1 (February 21, 2015).

http://interactive.ancestry.com/2469/16081953/1309975328?backurl= http%3a%2f%2fsearch.ancestry.com%2f%2fcgi-bin%2fsse.dll%3findiv%3dtry%26db%3dUSDirectories%26h%3d1309975328&ssrc=&backlabel=ReturnRecord (July 10, 2015).

http://interactive.ancestry.com/7949/cam1764_91–0027/2611309?backurl= http%3a%2f%2fsearch.ancestry.com%2f%2fcgi-bin%2fsse.dll%3findiv%3d1%26db%3dsfpl%26gss%3dangs-d%26new%3d1%26rank%3d1%26msT%3d1%26gsfn%3dConkling%26gsln%3dWai%26MSAV%3d0%26cp%3d0%26catbucket%3drstp%26uidh%3dqc9%26pcat%3d40%26fh%3d0%26h%3d2611309%26recoff%3d7%2b8%26ml_rpos%3d1&ssrc=&backlabel=ReturnRecord (August 12, 2015).

http://www.isr.bucknell.edu/Collections_and_Borrowing/Special_Collections_University_Archives/Yearbooks/pdf/1927/1927_Part_3.pdf (April 2, 2010).

https://issuu.com/ucdavisaggies/docs/2011fbmediaguide/115 (June 21, 2016).

https://issuu.com/sdsuathletics/docs/2014-sdsu-fb-media-guide/171 (August 16, 2016).

http://www.ivyleaguesports.com/sports/fball/2007–08/releases/al-livy_football__2007.htm (September 23, 2015).

Jacobsen, Bob. "A Man for All Seasons." www.asu.edu/alumnivision.com (October 21, 2002).

http://www.jaguars.com/team/management/shad-khan.html (May 9, 2015).

http://www.jsutigers.com/ViewArticle.dbml?DB_OEM_ID=29000&AT-CLID=209390204 (September 14, 2010).

http://www.jt-sw.com/football/pro/stats.nsf/Annual/1928-day (October 26, 2015).

http://www.kcchiefs.com/team/coaches/eugene-chung/697bc44e-1126–4955-a601–9a956f50e1ed (June 11, 2015).

Kelly, Steve. "Doug Baldwin: Pinoy Heart." http://www.seahawks.com/news/articles/article-1/Doug-Baldwin-Pinoy-heart/3ffc0c21–4521–4d24-a19c-035c0f058924, (November 22, 2013).

http://www.kickingworld.com/former-utah-utes-all-american-louie-sakoda-joins-kicking-world-as-kicking-coach, (June 10, 2016).

http://koreanamericanstory.org/the-will-to-win/ November 22, 2017;

Lasquero, Michael. "Wong to Take over Kailua Football Program." http://scoringlive.com/story.php?storyid=11242, (March 7, 2015).

http://library.la84.org/SportsLibrary/HELMS/Football/CIFFOOTBALL1938.pdf (September 6, 2014).

http://library.la84.org/SportsLibrary/HELMS/Football/CIFFOOTBALL1940.pdf (July 18, 2016).

http://library.la84.org/SportsLibrary/HELMS/Football/CIFFOOTBALL1943.pdf (October 17, 2015).

http://library.la84.org/SportsLibrary/HELMS/Football/CIFFOOTBALL1946.pdf (October 17, 2015).

http://library.la84.org/SportsLibrary/HELMS/Football/CIFFOOTBALL1952.pdf (June 7, 2012).

http://library.la84.org/SportsLibrary/HELMS/Football/CIFFOOTBALL1955.pdf (July 21, 2016).

http://library.la84.org/SportsLibrary/HELMS/Football/CIFFOOTBALL1957.pdf (July 21, 2016).

http://www.linfield.edu/sports/hof-member.html?m=105&y=18 (October 28, 2016).

https://www.linkedin.com/in/lloydslee (June 9, 2016).

https://www.linkedin.com/pub/kailee-wong/10/149/5b4 (June 11, 2015).

Loh, Stephanie. "Niumatalolo Makes History," http://www.utsandiego.com/news/2014/dec/21/poinsettia-bowl-navy-ken-niumatalolo-makes-history/ (May 28, 2015).

Lugay, Elton. "Fil-Am NFL Star Doug Baldwin on Lumpia, Football and Beast Mode's Cavities." http://www.gmanetwork.com/news/story/346383/pinoyabroad/news/fil-am-nfl-star-doug-baldwin-on-lumpia-football-and-beast-mode-s-cavities (May 27, 2015)

https://lvironpigs.wordpress.com/2014/08/18/establishing-uclas-all-time-placekicking-records/ (June 8, 2015).

www.mackbrown-Texas-football.com (January 20, 2004).

http://www.marplenewtownfootball.com/wp/2013/08/27/joey-pham-making-strides-millersville/ (August 4, 2014).

http://www.mjc.edu/athletics/football/awards.php (August 8, 2016).

http://www.mysanantonio.com/news/local_news/article/Refugee-football-star-practices-his-faith-4045087.php. (June 12, 2015).

Nakagawa, Martha. "Japanese with Ties to the Valley Take Imperial Tour." http://www.thedesertreview.com/japanese-with-ties-to-the-valley-take-imperial-tour/ (June 6, 2016).

http://www.nasljerseys.com/WFL/Players/H/Holt.Milt.htm (March 8, 2005).

http://www.nfl.com/news/story/09000d5d82a495da/article/johnnie-morton-given-two-years-probation-for-lying-under-oath (June 12, 2015).

http://www.nfl.com/player/blanegaison/2514552/profile (June 11, 2015).

http://www.nfl.com/player/chrisgocong/2495837/profile (June 10, 2016).

www.nfl.com/player/chetmaeda/2519956/profile (April 11, 2016).

http://www.nfl.com/players/edwang/profile?id=WAN272761 (December 24, 2010).

http://www.nfl.com/player/edwinmulitalo/2502235/profile (April 7, 2016).

http://www.nfl.com/player/kevinkaesviharn/2504426/profile (June 10, 2016).

http://www.nfl.com/player/marcusmariota/2552466/profile (January 24, 2017).

http://www.nguoi-viet.com/absolutenm2/templates/viewarticlesNV2.aspx?articleid=175463&zoneid=37 (August 17, 2015).

http://www.nprnews.org/story/2013/06/28/news/for-hmong-american-women-flag-football-breaks-barriers (January 29, 2016).

http://nysharksfootball.com/team/player.cfm?player=183/all=1 (June 7, 2014).

http://www.ohiobobcats.com/sports/m-footbl/mtt/neal_huynh_365746.html (June 11, 2016).

http://onedublin.org/2014/07/23/hamline-university-graduate-erik-wong-on-the-value-of-college-football/ (July 15, 2015).

http: //oregonstate.edu/admissions/blog/2009/05/14/honorary-degree-recepient-jack-yoshihara-passes-away/ (February 15, 2015).

http://www.osubeavers.com/SportSelect.dbml?SPSID=750126&SPID=127145&Q_SEASON=2010 (November 23, 2011).

http://www.osubeavers.com/sports/2011/3/9/208343623.aspx (December 13, 2016).

http://www.oxyathletics.com/sports/fball/awards/1958AllSCIAC (July 13, 2015).

http://www.paloaltoonline.com/news/2014/03/19/palo-alto-names-fung-as-its-new-athletic-director (May 18, 2015).

http://www.pbshawaii.org/ourproductions/longstory_transcripts/LSS%20611%20%20Harrington%20-%20A%20Life%20of%20Gratitude%20-%20Transcript.pdf (March 3, 2010).

https://www.pidf.org/about/board_of_directors/kaulana_park (June 11, 2015).

Powers, Jack. "Art Matsu: Hero amidst Hatred," http://flathatnews.com/2014/10/02/art-matsu/ (July 13, 2015).

http://www.profootballarchives.com/1943pcflric.html (December 13, 2014).

http://www.profootballarchives.com/nich03800.html (June 11, 2015).

http://www.profootballarchives.com/1961uflgr.html (July 7, 2015).

http://www.pro-football-reference.com/players/A/AmanEu20.htm (June 25, 2015).

http://www.pro-football-reference.com/players/A/AnexCh00.htm (August 30, 2014).

http://www.pro-football-reference.com/players/B/BaldDo00.htm (January 31, 2017).

http://www.pro-football-reference.com/players/B/BeacSa00.htm (June 11, 2015).

http://www.pro-football-reference.com/players/B/BrusTe99.htm (May 2, 2015).

http://www.pro-football-reference.com/players/C/ChunEu20.htm (May 13, 2012).

http://www.pro-football-reference.com/players/C/ChunPa99.htm (March 13, 2016).

http://www.pro-football-reference.com/players/C/ClarHe20.htm (August 30, 2014).

http://www.pro-football-reference.com/players/F/FranJo20.htm (October 30, 2015).

http://www.pro-football-reference.com/players/F/FreiRo00.htm (September 12, 2014).

http://www.pro-football-reference.com/players/G/GabrRo00.htm (April 13, 2013).

http://www.pro-football-reference.com/players/G/GoeaLe20.htm (June 11, 2015).

http://www.pro-football-reference.com/players/K/KemoMa20.htm (June 20, 2013).

http://www.pro-football-reference.com/players/M/MorgAr00.htm (June 11, 2015).

http://www.pro-football-reference.com/players/M/MortCh00.htm (June 12, 2015).

http://www.pro-football-reference.com/players/M/MortJo00.htm (June 12, 2015).

http://www.pro-football-reference.com/players/N/NakaHa99.htm (June 15, 2015).

http://www.pro-football-reference.com/players/N/NaumJo20.htm (March 7, 2015).

http://www.pro-football-reference.com/players/N/NogaNi20.htm (August 17, 2010).

http://www.pro-football-reference.com/players/N/NguyDa20.htm (August 7, 2014).

http://www.pro-football-reference.com/players/P/ParkKa20.htm (March 17, 2009).

http://www.pro-football-reference.com/players/P/PolaTr99.htm (April 14, 2015).

http://www.pro-football-reference.com/players/S/SapoJe00.htm (June 4, 2010).

http://www.pro-football-reference.com/players/S/SeauJu00.htm (March 24, 2015).

http://www.pro-football-reference.com/players/S/SimeJo20.htm (July 26, 2016).

http://www.pro-football-reference.com/players/T/TatuLo99.htm (July 18, 2015).

http://www.pro-football-reference.com/players/T/TatuMo00.htm (July 7, 2007).

http://www.pro-football-reference.com/players/T/ThomJa00.htm (June 3, 2007).

http://www.pro-football-reference.com/players/T/TuiaMa00.htm (March 7, 2014).

http://www.pro-football-reference.com/players/T/TuiaMa20.htm (May 14, 2009).

http: //www. pro-football-reference.com/players/W/WangEd20.htm (December 24, 2010).

http://www.pro-football-reference.com/players/W/WardHi00.html (June 7, 2015).

http://www.pro-football-reference.com/players/W/WedeHe20.htm (July 13, 2014).

http://www.pro-football-reference.com/players/W/WongKa20.htm (June 7, 2015).

http://www.pro-football-reference.com/players/Y/YonaWa20.html (October 28, 2015).

http://profootballtalk.nbcsports.com/2014/03/04/broncos-working-out-lofa-tatupu-to-day-after-long-layoff/ (July 18, 2015).

http://profootballtalk.nbcsports.com/2014/05/02/chad-morton-lands-in-seattle-as-assistant-special-teams-coach/, (June 12, 2015).

http://www.punahou.edu/alumni/community-groups/athletic-hall-of-fame/profile/index.aspx?linkid=648&moduleid=101 (February 2, 2016).

http://www.purdueexponent.org/sports/article_2a48d7d4–0eb9–11e0-b766–00127992bc8b.html (May 2, 2015).

http://queenofheaven.tributes.com/our_obituaries/Richard-Manuola-Dagampat--101149226 (June 30, 2015).

http://www.recordnet.com/article/20141119/sports/141119523 (April 1, 2016).

Rice, Grantland. "Who is America's Top Athlete." http://www.wedey.usanethosting.com/rice.htm (November 3, 2005).

Robinson, Greg. "Be a Good Sport About It: Early Nikkei Athletes in Louisiana." http://discovernikkei.org/en/journal/2017/9/5/nikkei-athletes-louisiana/ (November 1, 2017).

Ruck, Rob, "Football's Polynesian Moment: Samoa's Athletic Outliers are Paying a Steep Price for Their Commitment to the Game." http://www.salon.com/2016/02/05/footballs_polynesian_moment_samoas_athletic_outliers_are_paying_a_steep_price_for_their_commitment_to_the_game/ (April 4, 2016).

http://www.scout.com/college/army/story/109026-army-vs-navy-1956 (June 30, 2015).

http://search.ancestry.com/cgi-bin/sse.dll?_phsrc=fSR19&_phstart=successSource&usePUBJs=true&gss=angs-g&new=1&rank=1&msT=1&gsfn=Richard%20&gsfn_x=0&gsln=Ung&gsln_x=0&msypn__ftp=Los%20Angeles,%20Los%20Angeles,%20California,%20USA&msypn=68337&msypn_PInfo=8-%7C0%7C1652393%7C0%7C2%7C0%7C7%7C0%7C1813%7C68337%7C0%7C&MSAV=1&cp=0&catbucket=rstp&uidh=qc9&pcat=ROOT_CATEGORY&h=1977524&recoff=7%209&db=WWIIenlist&indiv=1&ml_rpos=12 (June 4, 2016).

http://www.seattleglobalist.com/2012/07/23/samoans-in-seattle-sue-feds-for-citizen-ship/5580 (July 28, 2015).

http://www.sepiamutiny.com/blog/2006/02/05/desis_in_the_nf/ (June 11, 2015).

http://www.sepiamutiny.com/sepia/archives/001905.html (March 18, 2007).

http://www.sfstategators.com/sports/2008/8/6/HOF.aspx?tab=halloffame (September 7, 2015).

Shanahan, Tom. "Kale Ane Followed His Father's Footsteps Back to Coaching in Hawaii." http://footballmatters.org/kale-ane-followed-his-fathers-footsteps-back-to-coaching-in-hawaii/ (February 2, 2016).

http://slam.canoe.com/Slam/Wrestling/2010/12/05/16435751.html (July 20, 2015).

Smith, Cameron. "Two-Footed Georgia Placekicker Creating Quite a Stir." rivals.yahoo.com/highschool/blog/prep_rally/post/Two-footed-Georgia-placekicker-creating-quite-a-?urn=highschool-278339 (March 2, 2011).

Spalding, John E. "San Francisco vs. East Bay High School All-Star Football, 1932–1938." http://www.weebly.com/uploads/3/0/9/7/30972031/football-aaa-oalall-starhistory1931–38.pdf (December 26, 2014).

http://www.sports-reference.com/cfb/players/doug-baldwin-1.html (June 10, 2015).

http://www.sports-reference.com/cfb/players/sanjay-beach-1.html (June 9, 2015).

http://www.sports-reference.com/cfb/players/john-browne-1.html (November 13, 2014).

http://www.sports-reference.com/cfb/players/dick-dagampat-1.html (June 30, 2015).

http://www.sports-reference.com/cfb/players/joey-getherall-1.html (June 9, 2015).

http://www.sports-reference.com/cfb/players/harold-han-1.html (May 26, 2015).

http://www.sports-reference.com/cfb/players/tauasu-harrington-1.html (September 12, 2013).

http://www.sports-reference.com/cfb/players/pat-hiram-1.html (May 27, 2015).

http://www.sports-reference.com/cfb/players/ryan-kaneshiro-1.html (May 27, 2015).

http://www.sports-reference.com/cfb/players/marcus-mariota-1.html (May 27, 2015).
http://www.sports-reference.com/cfb/players/chad-morton-1.html (June 9, 2015).
http://www.sports-reference.com/cfb/players/johnnie-morton-1.html (June 9, 2015).
http://www.sports-reference.com/cfb/players/mike-nguyen-1.html (June 9, 2015).
http://www.sports-reference.com/cfb/players/al-noga-1.html (August 17, 2010).
http://www.sports-reference.com/cfb/players/curtiss-rooks-1.html (March 24, 2015).
http://www.sports-reference.com/cfb/players/hines-ward-1.html (June 9, 2015).
http://www.sports-reference.com/cfb/players/kale-wedemeyer-2.html (May 27, 2015).
http://www.sports-reference.com/cfb/players/danny-wong-1.html (September 22, 2014).
http://www.sports-reference.com/cfb/schools/dartmouth/1980.html (June 8, 2015).
http://www.sports-reference.com/cfb/schools/hawaii/1971.html (March 29, 2016).
http://www.sports-reference.com/cfb/schools/hawaii/1974.html (March 29, 2016).
http://www.sports-reference.com/cfb/schools/michigan-state/1965.html (March 24, 2015).
http://www.sports-reference.com/cfb/schools/michigan-state/1968.html (March 24, 2015).
http://www.sports-reference.com/cfb/schools/san-jose-state/1957.html (March 29, 2016).
http://www.sports-reference.com/cfb/schools/stanford/1957.html (June 3, 2015).
http://sports.yahoo.com/ncaa/football/players/198906 (July 15, 2015).
Stanmyre, Matt. "Six Years Later, Rutgers Grad Jeremy Ito Is Just a Regular Guy." http://www.nj.com/rutgersfootball/index.ssf/2012/11/six_years_later_rutgers_grad_j.html (June 10, 2016).
Takase, Kalani. "Wong Eager to Assume Reins at Kailua." http://scoringlive.com/story.php?storyid=11249 (June 12, 2015).
Toohey, Terry. "Football: Kim Does It All to Spark Haverford in Winthrop." www.gametimepa.com/ci_26751896/football-kim-does-it-all-spark-haverford-win (August 12, 2015).
http://www.trincoll.edu/pub/news/sports_brochures/football/2010IvyArticle.htm (December 26, 2014).
http://www.uclabruins.com/ViewArticle.dbml?ATCLID=208817184 (July 13, 2015).
http://www.uclabruins.com/ViewArticle.dbml?DB_OEM_ID=30500&ATCLID=208195513, (March 3, 2014).
http://www.und.com/sports/m-footbl/mtt/justin_yoon_976665.html (January 25, 2017).
United States, Draft Registration Cards, www.ancestry.com (November 17, 2009).
United States Veteran's Gravesites, www.ancestry.com (April 24, 2010).
http://www.usctrojans.com/sports/m-footbl/mtt/pola_kennedy00.html (May 24, 2013).
http://www.usctrojans.com/sports/m-footbl/mtt/marques_tuiasosopo_880407.html (October 23, 2015).
Vachon, Duane. "Honor Overcomes Prejudice—Captain Francis Brown Wai, U.S. Army, WW II, Medal of Honor (1917–1944)." http://www.hawaiireporter.com/honor-overcomes-prejudice-captain-francis-brown-wai-u-s-army-ww-ii-medal-of-honor-1917–1944/ (October 17, 2017).
http://www.willamette.edu/athletics/hall_of_fame/members/1996/ (May 22, 2010).
Williams, Ronald. "The People's Champion." http://www.hanahou.com/pages/magazine.asp?MagazineID=&Action=DrawArticle&ArticleID=1124 (July 13, 2015).
http://www.yalebulldogs.com/sports/m-footbl/2014–15/bios/chang_jeho_qqxg (July 7, 2015).
http://www.yoteathletics.com/hof.aspx?hof=13&path=&kiosk= (June 22, 2015).

Index

About the Author

Joel S. Franks teaches Asian American and American Studies at San José State University. He has authored several articles and books on the sporting experiences of Asians and Pacific Islanders in the United States and its empire. He and his wife Cheryl are longtime residents of Silicon Valley. They have raised two wonderful children and are presently proud grandparents.